Sex, American Style

An Illustrated Romp Through the Golden Age of Heterosexuality

by Jack Boulware

FERAL HOUSE

Sex American Style © 1997 Jack Boulware

ISBN: 0-922915-46-6

for free catalog, send SASE to:

Feral House
2532 Lincoln Blvd, Suite 359
Venice, CA 90021
website: www.FeralHouse.com

Designed by Colin Johnston

Cover by Sean Tejaratchi

First edition 1997

10 9 8 7 6 5 4 3 2 1

Table of Contents

Introduction

The genesis for this book came from a tongue-in-cheek column I wrote in 1993 for the *San Francisco Chronicle*, lamenting the good old days when heterosexual people were still making headlines. *Newsweek* had just declared the Year of the Lesbian. Media was dominated by Ru Paul, Jaye Davidson, Sandra Bernhardt, M. Butterfly and afternoon chat shows about a she-male dominatrix stockbroker trapped inside the body of a pre-op transvestite Marine. Straight had become boring.

After doing some research, and struggling to recall faint childhood memories — such as seeing the original trailer for *Deep Throat* at the theater in my hometown in Montana — I was astonished to discover the depth of the sexual revolution. Heteros really did have their day in the sun, and I missed it. Sifting through the remnants of the 1960s and 1970s, it becomes clear that the novelty has worn off. America has long since processed through sex within the "straight community," and curious minds are now debating issues like Ellen DeGeneres, date-rape drugs and harassment in the military.

As the 1990s wind down to the millennium, we see a renewed Puritanical backlash against promiscuity bordering on schizophrenia. The U.S. continues to wallow in a combination tidepool of titillation and censorship, where V-chips and TV network rating systems co-exist in an ever-expanding marketplace of internet porn and Hollywood films about strippers and hookers. Topless clubs are more popular than ever in America, but according to the *New York Times*, Manhattan's Times Square has shrunk from over 150 porn theaters and shops to just 13. Afternoon talk shows alternate guests from slutty teenagers to advocates from Athletes for Abstinance. The publishing industry now provides opposing views for its usual kiss-and-tell memoirs — 26-year-old Tara McCarthy, author of *Been There, Haven't Done That: A Virgin's Memoirs*, signed a no-sex contract with Warner Books which stated, in part: "The author hereby agrees to remain virginal in mind, body and spirit until first publication of the work." Recreational sex has never gone away, but now it's just unfashionable unless juxtaposed with a moral antidote.

In a society that habitually over-farms its own history for entertainment, nostalgia for heterosex revolution also deserves its place on the timeline. In that wide-open sexual frontier, the rules were still being broken, and laws were still being made. The landscape was exciting, titillating, indulgent, self-obsessed and voyeuristic, a time of great truths and greater lies. (Many believe the hetero revolution even helped pave the path for the emerging gay rights movement.) Looking back, one might easily ask the question, "What the hell were we thinking?" For this period of time, dating roughly from the Pill to the plague, we were thinking about our pants.

Like the 1920s, this was another version of America's sustained adolescence, where people remained young far past the previous generation. Free love, save the trees, stop the war all combined into a flashpoint of innocent decadence, where sex was considered on a par with shaking hands. You never needed to know where the party was, because it was happening all around you. If you were a hetero-afflicted youngster in the 1960s and 1970s, your formative years were spent in a racy world of braless and shirtless TV actors, sexy album covers, Dad's magazines and Mom's bell-bottom boyfriend with the Corvette. If your adult years coincided with this sport-sex explosion, you attended political rallies, cruised fern bars and discos or sprang for liquid lunches with people from the office — all for the express purpose of getting laid. You might have found yourself owning a little black book and a waterbed. Perhaps you climbed into hot tubs at wife-swapping parties. You might have found yourself on a date to see a showing of *Oh! Calcutta*. You might have rediscovered yourself as an autonomous, sovereign sexual organism without any hang-ups at all, man.

This era could easily appear naive and corny to the jaundiced eye, but without hip-huggers, mini-skirts and mink-penis jewelry, this country would be even more repressed. The angora bedspread crowd can't be ignored. They were the trailblazers, the pilgrims discovering new islands of the nation's sexual psyche. Many celebrities and media figures emerged from

these expeditions. Theories developed and were eagerly devoured by a hungry public. Institutions flourished, from racy publications to the social settings of swinger's clubs and communes. Entire genres of sex-related products were born. Hundreds of people became millionaires from the promise of great sex, and millions of Americans took the bait.

But there have also been repercussions. After living decades as free-lovin' hedonists, accustomed to a casual sexual lifestyle, many found themselves ill-prepared to live in a world without it. Once you've experienced such freedom and tolerance, everything afterwards would naturally seem like an inferior imitation. And successive generations are maturing into a world where monogamy and latex are facts of life. Why live the swinging single lifestyle these days, when the end result is often personified by that sad old guy in the nightclub, wearing a bad toupee and worse sportcoat?

But for all the missteps of the hetero revolution, it left a definite burn on our cultural cerebellum. The hows and whys have already been discussed. The myths have long been created and perpetrated. All that remains is what you're holding, a bread-crumb trail through a collection of select artifacts and icons from an overlooked slice of America's history. This book will be a familiar look back in time for those who lived it, and a sociology lesson for those who missed it. And perhaps a prescient glimpse into our near future. Once they discover the miracle AIDS protein shot, who knows? It may happen all over again.

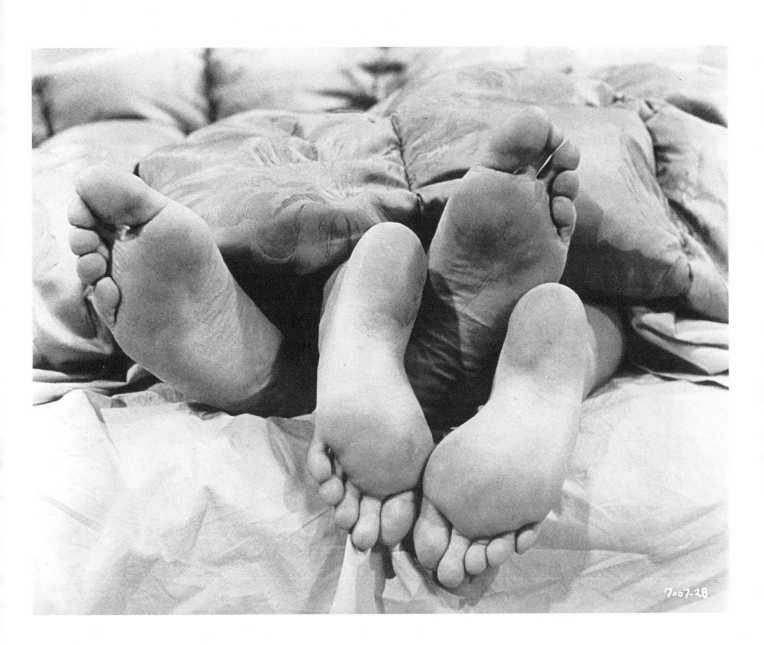

7007-28

She's the GODMOTHER of them all!

They call her "Coffy" and she'll Cream you!

si Samuel Z. Arkoff presents
an American International Picture
"COFFY" starring PAM GRIER · BOOKER BRADSHAW · ROBERT DOQUI · WILLIAM ELLIOTT · ALLAN ARBUS · SID HAIG
Produced by Robert A. Papazian · Written and Directed by Jack Hill · COLOR by Movielab
© 1973 American International Pictures, Inc.

While the trenchcoat crowd flocked to hardcore theaters and drive-ins — soaking up infinite combinations of acid-crazed hippies, biker gangs, chicks-in-prison and sadistic Nazis — a mainstream audience secretly craved the same subjects. And so the legit film biz cranked out pseudo-porn, storylines that stretched across the board, from war movies to westerns and social comedies, as America strained to get a peek at its own sexuality. Bare breasts and butts or several people in bed together were suddenly considered acceptable because of name actors and directors. If the characters and scenarios weren't built around swingers and swappers and prostitutes, sex oozed

Movies are Magic

into the frame in other ways. Characters were seen walking through the pastiche of racy neon signs in flesh districts of major cities. Hundreds of 35mm cameras tilted their Panavision lenses down lengths of bodies, followed hands and lips over bare skin. On-screen couples skipped the bedroom entirely and were seen performing lusty contortions in vehicles, public buildings or underwater.

Top names in the industry capitalized on the trend, shedding clothing and pretenses for top billing on the marquee, often rewarded by critics

THE SAUCY SILVER SCREEN:
(clockwise from top) Promotional lines for Pam Grier's Coffy *promised "she'll cream you!"; Gene Wilder and Zero Mostel ponder the inevitable in* The Producers; *Woody Allen befriends yet another co-star; Jane Fonda's* Barbarella *may have caught Ted Turner's eye*

CUT, BLOW & GO:
Beatty and yet another customer

WARREN BEATTY: You dumb cunt, everybody fucks everybody, grow up, for Christ's sakes. You're an antique, you know that? Look around you — all of 'em, all these chicks, they're all fucking, they're getting their hair done so they can go and *fuck;* that's what it's all about. Come into the shop tomorrow and I'll show you — 'I fucked her, and her and her, and her, and her — I fucked 'em all!'...That's what I do, I fuck. That's why I went to beauty school, to fuck. I can't help that, they're there and I do their hair and sometimes I fuck 'em. I stick it in and I pull it out and that's a fuck; it's not a crime.

GOLDIE HAWN: ...Well, I'm glad you told me.

— from *Shampoo*, 1975

Isabelle Adjani, Brigitte Bardot, Candace Bergen, Jacqueline Bouvier Kennedy Onassis, Judy Carne, Cher, Julie Christie, Joan Collins, Britt Ekland, Jane Fonda, Melanie Griffith, Goldie Hawn, Bianca Jagger, Diane Keaton, Vivien Leigh, Madonna, Michelle Phillips, Diana Ross, Stephanie Seymour, Carly Simon, Barbra Streisand, Liv Ullmann, Mamie Van Doren, Natalie Wood

— partial list of Warren Beatty's real or rumored sexual liaisons over the past four decades, posted on the Internet

and the Academy of Motion Picture Arts and Sciences. Jane Fonda won a best-actress Oscar for playing a call girl in *Klute.* An X-rated film about a male hustler, *Midnight Cowboy,* won best picture. Another X-rated feature about infidelity among university professors, *End of the Road,* starring Stacy Keach and James Earl Jones, earned rave reviews.

Men and women were playing up sexuality to what today seems cartoonlike. Male actors sported tight pants and bare chests. Women insisted on appearing before the cameras in low-cut braless costumes, or completely topless, showing as much skin as legally possible. And America ate it up.

On-screen women radiated sex unlike any period in history. On the high heels of '50s sirens like Monroe and Mansfield, and Europeans like Sophia Loren and Brigitte Bardot, came America's wave of '60s and '70s actresses who became known for saucy roles and lack of wardrobe. These weren't innocent World War II pin-ups — you *knew* these women were getting it on. Appearances that got the blood pumping included Raquel Welch in *100 Rifles, One Million Years B.C., Bedazzled* and *Myra Breckinridge;* Jane Fonda in *Barbarella* and *Klute;* Ann-Margret in *C.C. and Company, Carnal Knowledge* and a memorable tangle with a baked bean-soaked sofa in *Tommy;* Dyan Cannon and Natalie Wood in *Bob & Carol & Ted & Alice;* Valerie Perrine in *Lenny;* Jacqueline Bisset's wet T-shirt diving scene in *The Deep;* Diane Keaton snorting coke and picking up guys in *Looking for Mr. Goodbar;* Pam Grier in *Coffy* and *Foxy Brown;* Julie Christie in *Don't Look Now;* Brooke Shields and Jodie Foster setting the kinderwhore precedent in *Pretty Baby* and *Taxi Driver;* if one squinted real hard, even Barbra Streisand seemed alluring. It was a wonder anyone got anything done at all.

On the male side of the coin, each actor staked out his own area of testosterone magnetism. No woman could ignore the combination of suave sophistication and chesthair forest sported by Sean Connery in the various James Bond adventures. Warren Beatty became the handsome yet hesitant stud; Jack Nicholson was the foul-mouthed lecherous devil; Burt Reynolds was everyone's favorite cracker cocksman; James Caan took his shirt off enough to join the club; Jim Brown wore tight pants and did a lot of heavy lifting; Ryan O'Neal, Paul Newman and Robert Redford had the baby blues working for them; and Peter

Sellers was weird and eccentric enough to always have the best babes on his arm.

A popular genre for macho guys was the role of the studly detective-slash-secret agent, surrounded by young females in a perpetual state of estrus. Both Connery and then Roger Moore benefited from the Bond series, performing on-screen trysts in airplanes, automobiles, life rafts or behind an underwater coral reef. James Coburn conquered his fair share of the fairer sex in the Flint series, as did Dean Martin in the Matt Helm films, Ron O'Neal in *Superfly* and its sequels and Richard Roundtree as private dick John Shaft, who hosted women in the shower without bothering to remove his wristwatch.

A new generation had seduced the wallets of Tinseltown, a raw burst of youthful hip-hugger hormones, shot through a tunnel of instant fame, dope and too much money. Offscreen, stars were often even more lascivious than the roles they played. Were movies reflecting the new sexual freedom, or were people imitating a fantasy lifestyle they portrayed in movies?

It was difficult to distinguish the two, as Hollywood entered the Era of Cock. Actors quickly gained reputations as swingers, driving along the Sunset Strip with the top down, hitting the party circuit in tight jeans and tinted sunglasses. Some posed for women's magazines in the buff, like Burt Reynolds. Others pushed it much further, and legendary stories of sexual debauchery circulated. Omar Sharif and Peter O'Toole chased women and drank until dawn after a long day of shooting *Lawrence of Arabia*. Jimmy Caan cruised co-eds at Hefner's mansion. Jim Brown hosted down-and-dirty pool parties at his home. Jack Nicholson boasted to a *Playboy* reporter that he had fucked four girls in one day. Warren Beatty was said to have been arrested three times by the L.A. vice squad, and off the set he supposedly wore black leather pants and carried a whip.

No mention of stars who figured in the sexual landscape would be complete without Woody Allen, a nebbish freckled comedy writer who blossomed with the sexual revolution (and much later, who would get into that whole thing with his stepdaughter). In the course of expressing and personifying the sexual anxieties that everyone was experiencing at the time, Woody got a lot of action, a reluctant stud. The '60s and '70s comedies he wrote, directed and starred in are still memorable —

I'd like to do a love scene with him. I haven't seen him nude since he was six and I'd sure as hell like to find out what all the shouting is about.
— Shirley MacLaine on her brother Warren Beatty

If I come back in another life, I want to be Warren Beatty's fingertips!
— Woody Allen

Warren could be president if he wanted to be. He could win with the votes of the women he has loved!
— Hollywood columnist Sheilah Graham

Warren is the most divine lover of all. His libido was as lethal as high-octane gas. I had never known such pleasure of passion in my life.
— Britt Ekland

He has the kind of magnetic sensuality you could light torches with.
— Vivien Leigh

He was insatiable. Three, four, five times a day, *every day* was not unusual for him. I had never known anything like it.
— Joan Collins

The best I've ever had!
He can keep going all night!
— anonymous lovers

If I tried to keep up with what was said of me sexually, I would be as Frank Sinatra once said, speaking to you from a jar in the University of Chicago Medical Center.
— Warren Beatty

Why had he never taken any of his relationships as far as marriage? "We move in a time when tranquilizers, polygamy, so many alternatives are offered to working out the difficulties of a marriage. This business of you go with a person, you live with a person, you marry a person, you divorce a person, you marry *another* person — there is no substitute for the particular depth that is provided by time. Why don't you ask about the value of monogamy and genius it requires?" He was showing those wide, Pepsodent molars again.

"Do you feel you don't really know yourself well enough yet to take on the responsibility of marriage?"

"I don't want to say that. I just want to be able to tell the truth."

"What do you mean by the truth?"

"A man tells the truth to a woman. A woman tells the truth to a man." Oh!

— from an interview with Warren Beatty by Rex Reed, 1967, *Esquire*

THE AGE OF CHICK:
The Raquel Welch One Million Years B.C. *poster that rocked one million boys' bedrooms; Ann-Margret in her sweater days; Ursula Andress started the trend of James Bond babes in the classic* Dr. No *(note careful pistol positioning)*

the sexual hijinks of Peter O'Toole and Peter Sellers in *What's New, Pussycat?*; the infamous Orgasmatron of *Sleeper*; or the honeymoon bed scene in *Bananas*, as narrated by Howard Cosell. The film based loosely on the book *Everything You Always Wanted to Know About Sex* featured Gene Wilder as a psychiatrist who falls in love with a sheep, a "What's My Perversion" game show where a rabbi gets whipped by a dominatrix as his wife eats pork in front of him and the still-hilarious scene in which Burt Reynolds and Tony Randall command a Mission Control team inside a man's body, coordinating the erection and ejaculation of sperm.

The 1975 film production of the Thomas McGuane novel *92 in the Shade,* shot in Key West, was fraught with a well-publicized love triangle, detailed in the pages of *People* magazine. While author McGuane was having simultaneous affairs with actresses Margot Kidder and Elizabeth Ashley, who were both appearing in the film, his wife, Becky, was carrying on with Warren Oates, another actor in the film. When it was over and everyone was spent, emotionally as well as physically, McGuane's wife married actor Peter Fonda, the star of the film, and McGuane ended up marrying Margot Kidder.

As it got harder to distinguish fiction from reality, mainstream audiences were treated to the skankiest era of film Hollywood has ever seen.

Russ Meyer's *Vixen*, released in 1968, is generally acknowledged to be America's first softcore film hit. No explicit sex was portrayed, but the main character, Vixen, was an unforgettable female film archetype — sassy-mouthed, aggressive and constantly horny. Meyer pulled out all the stops, depicting frenzied scenes of incest, adultery, couple-swapping, spanking, rape, bondage, cars, motorcycles, lesbians and a memorable moment at a barbecue where Vixen lewdly rubs a fish all over her body. Meyer had been producing T&A features for years, but the crisply edited *Vixen* was one of his most profitable, costing only $72,000 to shoot and grossing over $6 million the next two years. 20th Century Fox signed him up to a multi-picture contract, and his next film, *Beyond the Valley of the Dolls*, written by his friend Roger Ebert, proved even more popular. He then made *The Seven Minutes*, adapted from an Irving Wallace novel about a pornography trial, which tanked, despite an appearance by

Tom Selleck. Meyer went back to doing movies his way, and anyone who has dipped into his Bosomania series realizes it was a smart decision.

The following year, Paul Mazursky took major studio money and directed a feature called *Bob & Carol & Ted & Alice*, starring Elliott Gould, Dyan Cannon, Robert Culp and Natalie Wood. Set in a swinging Los Angeles of hipster reefer parties and go-go nightclubs, the film attempted to put into perspective the then-current curiosity of couple-swapping.

Filmmaker Bob has an extramarital affair while on a location shoot in San Francisco. Since he and his wife Carol once spent a weekend together at a groovy Esalen-type human potential retreat, he tells her about the tryst. She understands completely. Bob then returns home a day early to discover that Carol is having an affair with her tennis instructor. Instead of getting mad, Bob shakes the guy's hand and mixes everyone a round of drinks.

Bob and Carol tell their friends Ted and Alice about their sexual adventures. Their friends are stunned, but agree to accompany them on a road trip to Vegas for the weekend. While hitting the hi-balls, lounging around the hotel suite, the conversation returns to sex. The couples confess their attraction to each other's spouses, and the decision is made to do the old switcheroo. Trying to act nonchalant, Ted shrugs, "First we'll have an orgy, and then we'll go see Tony Bennett." Everybody climbs into bed and starts making out with their new partners, but they discover, after all the anticipation, that nobody can really complete the act.

America salivated at this ode to wife-swapping, reportedly the first major film to show two couples in one bed, but the hard-core porn industry mocked the attempt. Al Goldstein's review in *Screw* sniffed: "Pure hokum combined with marketing research that was based on shoving a straw up the director's ass and getting high on his farts could be the only excuse for making such drivel."

More racy films churned out as the decade closed. The Oscar-winning *Midnight Cowboy* stars Jon Voight as a small-town dishwasher turned Manhattan gigolo. Jane Fonda wanders the galaxy in the sci-fi sex spoof *Barbarella*. The 1968 farce *The Secret Life of an American Wife* features Walter Matthau and Edy Williams in the tale of a neglected wife who poses as a call girl with one of her husband's clients. In *John and Mary*, Dustin Hoffman picks up Mia Farrow in a singles bar and didn't

I worship women! I get any woman I want because I give of myself. And who can refuse such human warmth. If all my affairs have been satisfactory it's because of my total understanding of women. I can satisfy all of their desires. Egyptian men really are very good in bed — I think it's because from boyhood it's the only thing on their minds.

— **Omar Sharif**

I go out with actresses because I'm not very apt to marry one. I also like Hollywood starlets, they are even greater egomaniacs than I am. They talk about themselves the whole time and I don't have to talk myself.

— **Henry Kissinger, dubbed the "Superkraut Playboy," a frequent consort of Jill St. John, Liv Ullmann, Candace Bergan, Claire Bloom, Ursula Andress and Marlo Thomas, among many others**

Women are my drugs and alcohol. I admit I like women a lot. Young. Old. Plain. Pretty. Any women — I don't mind. Though, I'm no good with swingers. I don't like what they do or what they represent.

— **Burt Reynolds**

**EVERYBODY DO
THE HARLOT
SHUFFLE:**
*Jodie Foster as a street
tart in* Taxi Driver *(left);
Barbra Streisand wore
the best hooker outfits, in*
The Owl and the Pussycat
*(below); Jane Fonda
again, as a call girl in*
Klute *(bottom)*

I have very wicked ideas. I'm sure that as
you're sitting at your great desk you have
all kinds of strange things going through
your mind. You should never be ashamed
of things like that. Nothing is wrong. Do
you mind if I take my sweater off? I like to
sort of walk around here with no clothes
on. I think people wear clothes much too
often, don't you? I think in the confines of
one's house one should be free of clothing
and...inhibition. I think the only way that
any of us can ever be happy is to let it all
hang out. You know, do it all...and fuck it.

— **Jane Fonda** from *Klute*, 1971

learn her name until the next morning. (Not to
mention Hoffman's infamous seduction by the
leopard-print older woman in *The Graduate*.)
But America would witness the true depths of
the sexual revolution in 1970, when Barbra
Streisand attempts to capitalize on the trend
by playing a prostitute.

Adapted by Buck Henry from the Broadway hit comedy by Bill Manhoff, *The Owl and
the Pussycat* features George Segal as a stuffy,
frustrated writer, unlucky enough to live in the
same apartment building as Streisand, a chatty
fake-fur hooker with a low-cut nightie and
window-shattering voice. Her character is,
unsurprisingly, shrill and annoying. Her tricks
demand weird things from her: one lies in a
coffin, another wraps himself in cellophane,
another ties her to a chair and rolls hardboiled
eggs at her while she yells, "Bombs away!" She
gradually drives Segal completely nuts, along
with the rest of the audience. Like most of the
films of this era, *Pussycat* doesn't age well over
time, and is marginally noteworthy for an
appearance by future porn star Marilyn
Chambers, and, supposedly, the first utterance
of the word "fuck" in a major Hollywood film
by a female star. Streisand shot a nude scene,
with the condition she could veto it if she
didn't like it, which she didn't. Director
Herbert Ross used the footage anyway, but
fogged the image so the detail couldn't be
seen. Years later, stills from the sequence —
miraculously unfogged — appeared in *High
Society* magazine, and Streisand successfully
sued the publication.

Streisand nude mythology continued into
the 90s, with the discovery of a 15-minute chunk
of hardcore porn footage circulating among
underground collectors that looked suspiciously
like Babs. The grainy black-and-white clip has
no credits or any indication as to its origin. The
hairstyle and poor filmic technique date it to be
roughly around the mid-'60s, approximately the
time Streisand's career took off. Copies vary
widely in quality, and dubbed-in soundtracks
range from generic rock and roll to Streisand
hits like "The Way We Were." Although the
thought is intriguing of such a show business
icon spawning from greasy beginnings, closer
examination of the actress's face reveals none
of Streisand's distinguishing moles and blem-
ishes, and the girl is generally assumed to be
someone else.

The 1970s continued the sexual trend, lay-
ering social commentary on top of the
shenanigans. The 1970 satire *Hi, Mom!* por-

trayed Robert De Niro as a Vietnam vet who alternated his free time between bombing apartment houses and making adult movies. In 1971 it was Jane Fonda's turn to play a prostitute, co-starring with Donald Sutherland in *Klute* — more Manhattan hookers, more kinky clients, rock and roll, junkies and pimps and dealers, and for those interested in such details, the braless pre-implant breasts of Hanoi Jane. *The Harrad Experiment*, a 1973 adaptation of the best-selling novel about a sexually experimental co-ed college, starred Don Johnson, his future ex-wife Melanie Griffith and future ex-mother-in-law Tippi Hedren. Opening credits to the 1975 film *Shampoo*, with Warren Beatty as a motorcycle-riding hairdresser who sleeps with all his clients, included the sounds of people having sex. The 1976 release *Inserts* starred Richard Dreyfuss as a once-famous film director who turns to making porn films. Blake Edwards' 1979 sex comedy *10* introduced both newcomer Bo Derek to white boys and the concept of cornrows to white girls. America gasped as yet another wife of photographer John Derek (joining the ranks of Linda Evans and Ursula Andress) takes off her clothes and exposes a body so skinny it looked as though several ribs had been removed. Three films spun off the series of Xaviera Hollander's *Happy Hooker* books. A sanitized 1975 version starred a brunette Lynn Redgrave as the Manhattan madam, but two years later when *The Happy Hooker Goes to Washington* was released, with Joey Heatherton, George Hamilton and midget Billy Barty, the main character had turned into a blonde. A third spinoff in 1980, *The Happy Hooker Goes Hollywood*, changed the madam's coif back to brunette.

There would be many odd moments during this time — new sexual images America had never before envisioned. For instance, the middle-aged bare ass of Kirk Douglas in the 1970 western *There Was a Crooked Man....* was certainly something different, as was the first full-length X-rated cartoon, 1972's *Fritz the Cat*, based on the underground comics of R. Crumb. And the visual impact was undeniable of two people having sex in sped-up motion, to the theme of the *William Tell Overture*, in 1971's *A Clockwork Orange* with Malcolm McDowell.

Two '70s films caused a stir in particular. Although *Carnal Knowlege* was written by noted playwright/cartoonist Jules Feiffer, and directed by Oscar winner Mike Nichols, it was declared obscene in Georgia upon its release.

In the opening credits scene of *Barbarella*, Jane Fonda performs a weightless striptease of her astronaut's clothing. After this scene was shot on the set in Rome, the assistant make-up artist, who covered her body with foundation make-up, went out drinking one night, and started bragging in the bistro that he had caressed the breasts, buttocks and inner thighs of Jane Fonda. When news reached his wife, she purchased a handgun to seek her revenge, and it took a personal visit from director Roger Vadim to discourage her from killing her husband.

I mean, I love my friends. I still love them. I mean, I love them very much. It's just that they're just — well, that's all that's on their minds is sex, sex, sex, sex and sex. If it's on your mind all the time, it can't be a very good thing, can it? I mean, shouldn't it just happen? It used to just happen.

— **Dyan Cannon (Alice) at a visit to her therapist,** *Bob & Carol & Ted & Alice*

WHO'S NEXT:
The gang's all here for the big wife-swap (above);
After a life's work racking up a list of women in
Carnal Knowledge, *Jack Nicholson settles for*
prostitute Rita Moreno (below)

JACK NICHOLSON: It's not as easy getting laid as it used to be. I don't think I fuck more than a dozen new girls a year now. Maybe I'm too much of a perfectionist. This last one came so close to being what I wanted. Good pair of tits on her — not a great pair. Almost no ass at all, and that bothered me. Sensational legs. I would have settled for the legs if she had just two more inches here, and three more here. Anyhow, that took two years out of my life.

ART GARFUNKEL: You don't want a family?

JACK: I don't want to put it down, but who needs it?

ART: You can't make fucking your life's work.

JACK: Don't tell me what I can and can't do. You're so well off?

— **from** *Carnal Knowledge,* **1971**

The story itself was hardly obscene, following two guys from their college years through middle age, detailing their sexual exploits along the way. Art Garfunkel was the sensitive one, Jack Nicholson was the arrogant prick who runs through dozens of women, and at the end of the film, they both sit and watch a "ball-buster" slide show of Nicholson's conquests throughout his life. What Georgia most likely objected to was the full nudity (rear and side views) of Ann-Margret and Nicholson, images that today pale in comparison to the number of times American audiences have suffered through Madonna's breasts or Mickey Rourke's ass.

Also controversial in its day was the 1973 import *Last Tango in Paris,* directed by an Italian, Bernardo Bertolucci, starring an American, Marlon Brando, with dialogue in both French and English. Originally rated X, the stylish film starred Brando as a 45-year-old widower with "a prostate like an Idaho potato," hoping to rid himself of the memory of his wife's suicide. Brando arrives to inspect a Paris apartment for rent and meets Maria Schneider. Within 15 minutes they are having sex. They agree to have a no-questions-asked sexual relationship, the depiction of which is still fairly explicit by today's standards. They both try to orgasm without touching. Brando supposedly penetrates her anally with butter. He asks her to clip her fingernails and stick her fingers up his ass while he envisions her having sex with a pig. Schneider keeps thinking about her young filmmaker boyfriend, and when she asks to break it off with Brando, he refuses, so she shoots him dead. The film's taboo nature resonated strongly in U.S. culture at the time, but obviously not so for NBC *Today Show* reviewer Gene Shalit, who grumbled, "The only obscene thing about *Last Tango* is the five-dollar admission price."

Also emerging in the early '70s was the new and lucrative genre of blaxploitation. Football stud Jim Brown was Hollywood's first black star, and studios quickly capitalized on his bronze buffed physique. Brown ended up shirtless in film after film, doing love scenes with everyone from Raquel Welch (*100 Rifles*) to a dwarf (*Slaughter's Big Rip-Off*). Fellow jocks Fred "The Hammer" Williamson, Jim Kelly and Ken Norton soon joined the stud club, but it would be a funky Isaac Hayes groove that stirred the glands of female movie-goers into a chocolate-shake delirium.

Set against the twin slums of 1971 Times

Square and Harlem, Richard Roundtree strode across American screens as private dick John Shaft, in turtleneck and beltless slacks. He was one of the first screen detectives to have a girlfriend as well as his own bachelor pad, and certainly the first who keeps his pistols in the freezer. *Shaft* became the most recognizable blaxploitation film in history, and centered around the PI getting hired by a Harlem drug lord to find his kidnapped daughter; it featured heroic fight scenes, racial tension and the exasperated police force who need him more than he needs them. When one cop asks, "Hey, where the hell you goin', Shaft?" he responds, "To get laid...where the hell you goin'?"

But Shaft was popular in part because he was begrudgingly on the side of the cops, which appealed to many white audiences. The black community would get a more realistic hero the following year, when Ron O'Neal starred as Youngblood Priest in the 1972 cult classic *Superfly*, a similar formula of sex, flashy clothes and Harlem, with a hit soundtrack by Curtis Mayfield. Despite being shot on a shoestring budget, the film grossed over 6 million at the box office. Unlike Shaft, Priest worked only for himself, a coke dealer looking for redemption, one last score to retire and get out of the business forever.

In 1973, the sexual pendulum shifted to the other side, as another archetype emerged, the busty black female who, when she was nice, was very nice, but when she was mad, she wasn't about to put up with any shit from the guys. If the mere mention of the name Pam Grier still buckles the knees of many men, imagine her initial appeal in 1973's *Coffy*, when the curvaceous star avenges a cheating boyfriend by shooting him in the crotch with a rifle. That same year saw the debut of the statuesque Tamara Dobson as six-foot-two narcotics agent *Cleopatra Jones*, but Jones never achieved the psycho impact of *Foxy Brown*, another Grier film from 1974, in which she seeks revenge on a female drug pusher by hunting down her man, hacking off his member with a big knife and presenting the drug czarina with a jar o' penis.

Exploitation might be looked down upon by snobs and critics, but there was good money in it. Many popular actors and directors paid the bills by doing softcore films, from Charles Grodin and Adam West to Joan Collins, who tried to jump-start her fame by appearing in *The Stud* and *The Bitch*, two negligible stories written by her sister Jackie. Long before

When it was finally time for our sex scene, the director told me to act as if I was sex-starved. He wanted me to snap mid-scene, rip off Raquel's shirt. In Hollywood they babble a lot about Motivation, I figured this director had one of two: he wanted some bosom on the screen, particularly as it was Raquel's bosom, or he just wanted to piss off some white folks.

We began the scene and I started slowly, with sensitivity, suddenly started pawing at Raquel's clothes. Her bosoms were exposed, I was kissing her and holding her and...she became incredibly sexy to me. She wasn't lying on the bed, being submissive. She was wild, defiant, she kissed with her lips, her teeth, it became a sexual contest of who would conquer who in that bed.

Cut.

During that first take I had noticed that Raquel preferred to have her face to the camera, as most stars do. I didn't care, knew her face was prettier than mine. So when we returned from the break, resumed filming, I put my face on the side of Raquel's, gave her access to the camera. While I was over on the side I kissed Raquel's ear, and her body jumped. Hmmmmm. I stuck my tongue in softly. Raquel started heating up, so did the scene. She was sensitive in the ear.

We took another break, Raquel strode over to me.

She said, "Jim, if you don't mind, please don't stick your tongue in my ear."

"Why?"

"It'll mess up my make-up."

— **Jim Brown describing the making of the 1968 western *100 Rifles*, from his 1989 autobiography *Out of Bounds***

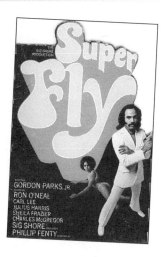

TAKE NO SHIT:
Pam Grier in a pre-castration moment from
Foxy Brown *(left); Ron O'Neal looked for one*
more score in Superfly *(right)*

GREAT WORK IF YOU CAN GET IT:
The wandering eyes of Dean Jones in Disney's
The Love Bug *(top); Michael Crichton's voyeuristic*
predecessor to Jurassic Park *(right); A post-*Batman
Adam West in The Specialist

The Godfather, Francis Ford Coppola directed at least two porn films, an early-'60s stag-party tit show called *Tonight for Sure*, and the other a 1962 grindhouse effort titled *Bellboy and the Playgirls*, originally a German sex film with added 3-D voyeuristic peephole footage shot by Coppola. Predating his *Jurassic Park* blockbusters, Michael Crichton wrote *Extreme Close-Up*, which *Penthouse* breathlessly referred to as "America's first great voyeur movie." Before starring as John Shaft, "the private dick who's the sex machine to all the chicks," Richard Roundtree appeared in *What Do You Say to a Naked Lady?*, a racy feature made by *Candid Camera*'s Allan Funt. The same year *Laverne & Shirley* debuted on network television, a Cindy Williams appeared in *The First Nudie Musical*, the story of a young filmmaker who attempts to save his studio by making a porn musical, including a "Dancing Dildos" production number. The 1977 sex comedy *Can I Do It...Til I Need Glasses?* featured Robin Williams, whose footage was abruptly tacked on to the film after his *Mork and Mindy* fame.

The crossover between mainstream and hardcore continued with the 1970 release of the XXX-rated *A Party at Kitty and Stud's*, starring a pre-action hero Sylvester Stallone as "Stud," humping women on green paisley sheets. The film showed no shots of him erect, and Stallone reportedly received $200 for his efforts. A re-edited video version later appeared, retitled *The Italian Stallion*. *Deep Throat*'s Harry Reems also starred in the R-rated horror film *Demented*. Porn queen Marilyn Chambers began her film career with an uncredited role in *The Owl and the Pussycat*, then returned after a healthy porn stint to appear in the David Cronenberg horror flick *Rabid*. To complete shooting of a party scene full of nude people for the film *10*, Blake Edwards and Julie Andrews invited actual porn actors to appear on-camera, including Serena, Seka, Constance Money and Jamie Gillis (as well as one young girl walking around carrying a knife, wearing a Charlie Manson button). Also making a transition from porn to mainstream was Georgina Spelvin, who played a prostitute in *Police Academy*.

But a downside of the sexual revolution was flushing up to the surface of mainstream cinema. Financed by a doting Manhattan pop art scene, the increasingly wealthy Andy Warhol poured his money into creating an art, film and publishing collective called the

Factory, a warehouse space covered in tinfoil, attracting a peculiar collection of art brats, disaffected heiresses and assorted hangers-on. The communal Factory lifestyle was often as excessive as the films they produced. At parties, Warhol strolled through the crowd asking women the size of their husbands' cocks. Drug orgies went for days at a time, participants losing all sense of time or place. Warhol regulars would visit the libidinous "Dr. Robert" for amphetamine and vitamin shots, whose office waiting room constituted a pick-up scene for rich speed freaks.

Amidst tedious experimental films such as several hours of static footage of a skyscraper, Warhol also produced several R- and X-rated features that remain on video store shelves. Among the best known and still marginally watchable are *Andy Warhol's Bad* and 3-D versions of *Dracula* and *Frankenstein*, wherein the mad doctor sticks his arm inside a dead body and groans, "To know life, you must fuck death!" *Women in Revolt*, a 1972 parody of the sexual revolution, cast drag queens in the roles of women's libbers.

"We really wanted to be the Walt Disney of porn," the ever quotable Warhol told *Playboy* in 1973, "but smut is no longer chic."

A depressing 1972 art-house quasi-documentary called *Ciao! Manhattan* offered another view of the Warhol whirlwind, focusing on the sex-and-drugs decline of 1960s "it girl" Edie Sedgewick. It took only a few years for Sedgewick to slip from *Vogue* cover model and New York talk of the town to having on-camera amphetamine sex in Warhol films, and ending up a drugged-out shell of a person, living in California in an empty swimming pool. As did many who took the fast road in the sexual revolution, she failed to clear the last hurdle, and died in 1971 at 28.

Reaching a larger audience, with a similarly downcast tone, was Richard Brooks' *Looking for Mr. Goodbar*, a seedy 1977 adaptation of the novel by Judith Rossner. Diane Keaton plays a repressed young schoolteacher who hits the singles bars, sleeps with a few guys and finds herself reborn as a much-sought-after disco babe. The nightlife scenes were like looking into a mirror for young American audiences, punctuated by then-current designer-jean fashions and a soundtrack that included Boz Scaggs' "Lowdown" and "Backstabbers" by the O'Jays. Unfortunately, Keaton bumps into sleazebags like Richard Gere and Tom Berenger, and winds up murdered. The drama

Oh, wow, what a scene that place was — that heavenly drug-down-sexual-perversion-get-their-rocks-off health spa. I was already so bombed I don't know how I got there. I got down to the pool, where all the freaks were. I met Paul America at the pool and I told him we were probably in danger if we stayed, but we were so blasted we forgot what was good for us and what wasn't, and the whole placed turned into a giant orgy...every kind of sex freak, from homosexuals to nymphomaniacs...oh, everybody eating each other on the raft, and drinking, guzzling tequila and vodka and Scotch and bourbon and shooting up every other second...losing syringes down the pool drains, the needles of the mainline scene, blocking the water-infiltration system with broken syringes. Oh, it was really some night...just going on an incredible sexual tailspin. Gobble, gobble, gobble. Couldn't get enough of it. It was one of the wildest scenes I've ever been in or every hope to be in. I should be ashamed of myself. I'm not, but I should be.

— **Edie Sedgwick, describing a film shot at Dr. Robert's spa, from tapes for the 1972 film** *Ciao! Manhattan*

ROUGH AROUND THE EDGES:
Warhol's arthouse version of Frankenstein *(top); George C. Scott getting ejected from a porn theater in* Hardcore *(above)*

today seems heavy-handed and lengthy, but at the time constituted a reality check for many, revealing the dark side of the singles scene that other mainstream Hollywood releases hadn't explored.

Two years later, *Hardcore* would forever puncture the image of the sex revolution as a groovy, fun-loving lifestyle, while simultaneously pissing off the porn industry. The 1979 Paul Schrader-directed story details a Calvinist father's search for his teenage daughter, who has run away from her Midwestern upbringing. On his journey into the big-city underworld of porn and prostitution, George C. Scott steps inside an adult theater and sees his little girl on-screen — a sad yet compelling mainstream release that cast a dark shadow over subjects that, only a decade earlier, were depicted as fun and rebellious.

One could argue that mainstream films acted as a visual barometer of the nation's heterosexual tastes, but then again, one could also argue that Hollywood's take on the American way of life was just as trivial as it was in the '30s and '40s. It's certainly true that today, the sexual revolution is in hibernation, and big-studio releases are playing it safe with bombastic action spectacles calculated to appeal to all ages, meant to ensure high return on the investment. In that respect, perhaps, Hollywood is accurately reflecting the sexual mood of the country — making money and protecting the children's best interests now take precedence over the tastes of discriminating adults. If adult audiences are expecting sex in their movies, with the degree of freshness and innovation that emerged in the '60s and '70s, Hollywood is not the place to look.

Going to the theater for an evening of X-rated smut isn't what it used to be, thanks to the VCR. By 1982 there were roughly 3 million VCRs in the country, and 22 million households receiving cable TV, through which 200 adult entertainment stations were available. In other words, America no longer steps out of the house and puts on a dark trenchcoat to enjoy quality erotic entertainment. The industry shoots features on both video and 35mm stock, and immediately transfers the film to VHS for release. Convenience has usurped the magic of an evening on the town, an evening of magic that has now been condensed into the annual

Hooray for Hardcore

Adult Video News awards presentation, the Oscars of porn, held each year in Las Vegas.

On January 7, 1996, adult film star Jenna Jameson stepped up to the microphone at the Aladdin Theater for the Performing Arts and smiled sweetly at the assemblage of tuxedos and evening gowns, real boobs and fake boobs, celebrities and nobodies. The attractive blonde was not only co-hosting the evening, but was also crossing her fingers, having been nominated for best new starlet, best performer of the

POTPOURRI O' PORN:
Vintage films from the era, and a typical theater where they were screened

New York — G series, M series (which included Linda Lovelace)
San Francisco — 200 series, OZ series, Collection series, Diamond Collection
Los Angeles — Pretty Girls and Playmate series, NM series, Erotica Unlimited, Danish International, Watergate Girls

— early explicit loops series

Ass Pumpin
Passion Ruse
L'il Squeeze
Kelly Mint
Misty Winters
Alice Thatch
Ronda More
Veri Knotty
Sally Deer
Veronica Melon

— names of actresses that starred in One Day Wonders, i.e. 8 mm loop films

the hottest 16mm films in new york
100% on the peter meter
"absolutely the best sex show in the city" AL GOLDSTEIN · SCREW
LOOPS
six all new, all color 16mm films
electro love
NEW YORK PREMIERE 16mm COLOR
LIVE BURLESK
11 SHOWS DAILY · 9am till 1am
mini cinema   7th AVE BET   581-48and49 ST   5968

P lot 1. A woman alone at home becomes aroused by reading or handling some phallic-shaped object. Masturbation follows. A man arrives — is invited inside, sexual play begins; Plot 2. A farm girl gets excited watching animals copulate. She runs into a farmhand, or a traveling salesman, and sexual play begins; Plot 3. A doctor begins examining a woman and sexual play begins; Plot 4. A burglar find a girl in bed or rapes her or vice versa; Plot 5. A sunbather or skinny dipper gets caught and seduced.

— five basic stag film plots, from *Contemporary Erotic Cinema* by William Rotsler

year, best couples sex scene (shot on film), best actress and best supporting actress. Flanked by twin nude Statues of Liberty and electronic marquee signs that blazed "Ed Powers in Concert" and "Phantom of the Orgasm," Jameson proudly announced that the industry had collectively released a record 5,500 titles for 1995. "That's a *lot* of product," she breathed huskily.

Thirty years ago there was virtually no product, because there was no porn industry. The little sex on celluloid that could be obtained was found on stag loops — short films that essentially remained unchanged dating back to the silent film era, when raunchy outtakes from *Valentino* circulated among the Hollywood cognoscenti. Up through the 1960s, 8mm loops cost a few dollars to produce, and sold via mail-order for anywhere from $5 to, later on, up to an astonishing $75 apiece. A peep-show booth, screening two minutes of porn, could gross over $10,000 a year. If you were producing loops, you couldn't help but make money. That is, *certain* people made money. The mob already ran the country's publication distribution system; to take over the porn syndicate was a natural and necessary extension of the operation. But for those putting out the product, the status quo was getting to be routine. Porn directors were getting bored. Why not aim for something higher? Why not try to be taken seriously and become the Eisenstein of suck-and-fuck?

Directors started shooting in 16mm, first bumping the footage down to 8mm for resale, then releasing it as 16mm. They added actual sound, and although most of the audio from this period was terrible quality, at least patrons could hear the muffled grunts and squeaks of the sofabed. Music soundtracks were spliced in, often beginning with a high-hat as a blouse was unbuttoned, then kicking into a cheesy soul or R&B groove stolen from a popular record.

The early porn loop aesthetic usually included pimply girls with dirty feet and sweaty guys in sideburns, all sporting robust thatches of pubic hair, going at each other on a dirty-looking white angora bedspread. The "location" was usually someone's apartment, accentuated by garishly patterned curtains, green shag carpet and orange vinyl furniture. Producers and directors often changed names and biographies with each release, targeting them to specific cities or markets. Pinning down anybody's real name or background is next to impossible. Hardcore insertion sequences were spliced in from other films, continuity was lax or nonexistent, plots were written at the time of shooting, and often made little sense. In retrospect, most of this period of porn is about as titillating as a Discovery channel special on rhesus monkeys. Today's various compilations of these '60s sex loops give one the impression maybe they were better off rotting in obscurity, but filmmakers were less concerned with cinematically perfect lighting than getting arrested and thrown in jail.

Although porn was still the domain of the trenchcoat crowd, Hollywood jumped on the bandwagon and began releasing X-rated features, which at the time meant frontal nudity. But Tinseltown would never be able to compete with the hardcore loops that showed penetration — incontrovertible evidence of sex taking place. The "B" exploitation market of the 40s and 50s was evolving towards adult themes, as directors like Russ Meyer consciously closed the gap between films made for teenagers and those that catered to adult tastes (in the case of Meyer, this meant gargantuan breasts jiggling into the lens).

Directors could feel the industry's growing pains, but it would take the Danes and Swedes to actually jump-start America's porn revolution. In 1967, Denmark became the first Western country in the world to abolish all pornography laws, and the following year, Swedish director Vilgot Sjöman's *I Am Curious (Yellow)* came across the Atlantic, a sexually explicit love story in two parts (*I Am Curious [Blue]* was less sexual) with political overtones that was enjoying much acclaim in Denmark and Sweden. The film would gain its prominence because a print was seized at customs, headed for its distributor, Grove Press. *Yellow* was tried in U.S. District Court and found to be obscene. Those Americans who did eventually see a print of the film (the case was later reversed) were left with two impressions — either it was an intelligent, cinematic story of two young people living through a politically volatile period of history who happened to have on-camera sex with each other, or it was a pretentious piece of crap that didn't have enough sex scenes.

The next year, when Denmark hosted an international sex fair called Sex 69, San Francisco filmmaker Alex de Renzy and cinematographer Jack Kerpan flew across the Atlantic to record the proceedings, and interviewed the vendors and participants. The feature-length *Pornography in Denmark* cost $15,000 to produce, and would eventually gross over $2 million. The straight-forward documentary tone attracted larger audiences not usually drawn to the loop films — businessmen, college students, and couples who were genuinely curious about the world's

"SIZZLING SEX...above par production and ...the acting comes across...unusually crisp ...this film (has the) answer." *Tim Beckley/Hustler Magazine*

THE TEENAGE SEXMAIDS

...COME SWIM IN AN OCEAN OF DESIRE...

Starring
JULIA FRANKLIN
Kim Pope   Diane Black
Cynthia Prescot   Darby Lloyd Raines

Produced & Directed by:
Frank Renfro
Music by
Peggy Reed

"...fun, fantasy & everything else...this movie reaches a multitude of climaxes on several levels of riotous imagination..." *Sir Magazine*

Ⓧ IN COLOR: FOR ADULT SAILORS, MERMAIDS AND FISH

NO MORE QUESTIONS: *According to one reviewer from Hustler, this film had the answer*

*C*irca 1970, John William Abbott directed a documentary film called American Sexual Revolution, *hosted by a man in his mid-40s, sporting a greying goatee, brown sportcoat and necktie. In one sequence the host interviews the cast of an 8mm porn loop, which has just finished filming a threesome — Bob and two blonde girls named Sherry and Diane. All in their early 20s, and lounge on a studio set consisting of white shag carpet and yellow beanbag chair. Sherry wears a poncho, smoking a cigarette.*

HOST: Kids, I have one final question, and I'm going to ask you to lay it right on the line with your answer. It's in two parts. Number one, I wanna know, do you enjoy your work? Your work being the making of sexual motion pictures. And the second part is, when you do this — when you do these films — do you ever find yourself getting emotionally involved with your partner? Bob, let's start with you.

BOB: I don't really enjoy my work. As far as getting involved, the only time I get involved is if — for example, Diane. I work with her most of the time. And Diane and I have a great deal of mental energy going for each other, so when I work with her, then I do enjoy my work. But other than that, uh, the majority of people you work with, uh, it's purely a monetary thing with them, you know. It's nothing, man, it's just lust and that's it. None of them turn me on.

HOST: Sherry, how about you?

SHERRY: Well, actually, mostly it's really just an easy job. I don't enjoy it, but I don't dislike it either. You meet some pretty far-out, groovy people, you know. And you meet some really bad people, but anything you do

HOST: Do you ever get involved with any of the people you meet

SHERRY: *[pause]* Not really, no.

HOST: Diane, how has it affected you?

DIANE: Well, I can't say that I exactly enjoy my work, I can't say that I dislike it either. It's an easy way to make money, to be honest with you.

changing sexual morality. Another Danish import was called *I, A Woman,* distributed by Radley Metzger, who later directed under the name Henry Paris. (Lest we think all Scandanavians were exclusively chin-scratching intellectuals, one loop from late-'60s Denmark became known as the notorious "pig-fucking movie.")

Around the same time as de Renzy's Denmark film appeared another documentary by de Renzy and Bill Osco called *History of the Blue Movie,* a collection of vintage porn clips throughout the century. Osco would then turn around in 1970 and direct one of the world's first full-length fictional hardcore features, *Mona, the Virgin Nymph,* about a girl who preserves her virginity by performing fellatio on men, instructed by her father — a film still remembered by many with a tiny sigh. Adult film critic Jim Holliday has matter-of-factly noted that "the film has no wet shots, but does offer penetration in an era known for inserts."

As the industry picked up steam, the sleazy theaters that screened X-rated films grew into entire districts of America's cities. Much like today's Internet, everyone was rushing to get a piece of it, if only to say they were there at the genesis of something new. Hardcore action was soon available at box offices on Times Square in Manhattan, Broadway in San Francisco's North Beach, Baltimore Street in Baltimore, Santa Monica Boulevard in Los Angeles, Wells Street in Chicago, Hennepin Avenue in Minneapolis, and the Greenwood district of Seattle. Down South, in Texas and the Carolinas, drive-in theaters became popular places for exhibiting X-rated films.

Although films were shooting in New York and the Midwest, much of the production in these early years was based in the San Francisco area, where porn producers all owned their own theaters to screen them. A 1971 *Playboy* article on the nation's booming porn industry insisted San Francisco had the most hardcore porn "this side of Denmark" (except maybe for the pig-fucking). And in a boomtown where a feature hardcore could be made for $15,000 to $50,000, the return on a single film could potentially reach into the millions. Obviously, it was time to come up with some ideas that would stick to the ribs.

Russ Meyer stood by his timeless theme of pendulous breasts. Gerard Damiano and Chuck Traynor brainstormed the *Deep Throat* concept of pubic-hair-snuffling fellatio. The Mitchell Brothers staged the notorious sling sequence in *Behind the Green Door.* And someone else came up with the genius idea for a short film called *Confessions of a Stunt Cock*.

Porn-specific genres would emerge. The sex-soaked twists on an old classic such as Chaucer, Voltaire's *Candide*, or *Pygmalion*. The porn versions of vintage Hollywood films like *Double Endemnity* and *Laura*. The anonymous Victorian novel adaptations, the spoofs of mainstream genres such as detective stories and fairy tales, the fantasy themes of pizza deliveries, nurses, cowgirls, stewardesses, Catholic girls, tropical islands, cheerleaders, and wacky scientists. The beauty of going for cheap laughs not only distracted censors and broke the tension of someone attending his first porn film, but the campy vaudeville humor also made you forget how bad the editing was.

The *Emmanuelle* series utilized international travel to various locations. The *Taboo* series focused on incest. The *Inside* and *All About* series slapped together old and new footage of current actresses of the day (occasionally even notifying the star of the project), including *Inside Georgina Spelvin* (1974), *Inside Marilyn Chambers* (1976), *Inside Jennifer Welles* (1977), *Inside Desiree Cousteau* (1979), *All About Gloria Leonard* (1979), *Inside Seka* (1980), *Deep Inside Annie Sprinkle* (1981), *All About Annette* (1982), and all the way up to 1995's industry releases of *Deep Inside Debi Diamond* and *All About Steve*. Repackaging of old loops yielded series like *Diamond Collection* and *Peep Show*, but perhaps the best-known loop title was *Swedish Erotica*, a far-reaching packaging of hardcore loops, magazines and books under the umbrella theme of racy Scandinavia. Many featured John Holmes and Seka, neither of whom appeared remotely Swedish, nor did their furniture.

In 1976 Sony released its first VCR for consumers, and the industry quickly capitalized on the new medium. *Deep Throat* reportedly was the first porn film to go Beta, and sent directors scurrying to their back archives to dupe off everything they'd ever shot. Tapes sold initially for up to $300 apiece, often costing as little as 50 cents to make, and adult videos constituted over half of all pre-recorded industry sales.

By this time, America had become a one-stop shopping shack for smut, according to *Time* magazine. In a 1976 cover story called "The Porno Plague," *Time* saw the industry divided into two categories. The "old porn" consisted of peep shows, sleazy photo magazines and porn paperbacks, mostly produced and distributed by organized crime. "New porn" manifested in theater films, glossy magazines and sex

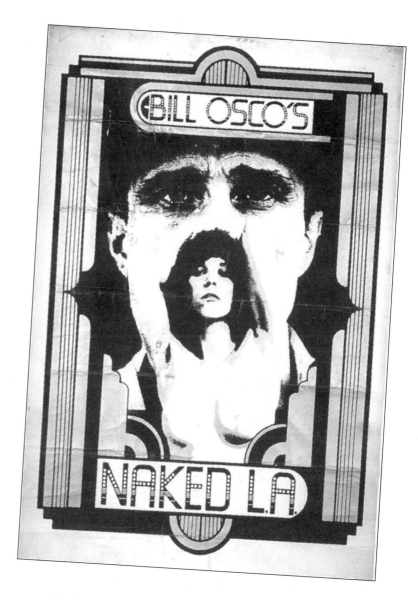

THE BIG GUNS: *Classic features from heavyweight directors Bill Osco and Gerard Damiano*

THE FIRST CAR-CHASE PORN MOVIE!

PASSION PROCESSION
x

introducing
VANELLA
LANI LUCAS

also starring
PAUL SCHARF

Honestly doctor,
I was only giving
him a massage!

Heartbeat slow...
I have just the
remedy for that.

I'm learning
what to do
'til the doctor comes.

I'm improving
my technique in
nurse/patient
relations.

NEW WORLD PICTURES presents

It's what they do off duty
that's really private!

PRIVATE DUTY NURSES

STARRING
KATHY CANNON • JOYCE WILLIAMS • PEGI BOUCHER
PRODUCED, WRITTEN AND DIRECTED BY GEORGE ARMITAGE • A NEW WORLD PICTURES RELEASE   R

W e live in far too permissive a society. Never before has pornography been this rampant. And those films are lit so badly!

— from "My Speech to the Graduates" by Woody Allen

newspapers — independent of the mob, and primarily an outgrowth of 1960s youth culture.

This Pepsi generation of porn baffled film critics. If decent citizens were going to stand in line to see films like *Deep Throat*, the mainstream press was obligated to write it up. The early years were covered diligently by *Variety*, running next to reviews of current releases from Hollywood. Critics had no precedent; there was no Hedda Hopper or James Agee of porn. After the novelty of hardcore features wore off, the mainstream left future smut coverage to underground adult newspapers like the *Berkeley Barb*, *Screw*, and the *L.A. Free Press*, where film criticism developed its own dialect. Terms originated like "peter-meter," "ucky-fucky," "crotch opera," "money shot," "jizz-lobber" or the all-inclusive "suck-n-fuck," and are still practiced with glee within the pages of current industry trades like *Screw*, *The Spectator*, *Adult Video News* and *Adam Film World*.

Unlike today's porn stars, many of whom are discovered lap-dancing for college money, performers from the early era were a few years older, having already gained experience in theater, film or commercials. The first wave of porn actors were earthy and hippie-natural compared to the sleek, silicone and steroid-enhanced models now common to the industry. There was no star system at the outset, but as the media swarmed to this new breed of superstars, it didn't take long for the trappings of success to manifest. By the mid-'70s, porn had created its own Erotic Film Awards, the hard-partying precursor of the *AVN* Awards. To add further comparison, the Los Angeles Pussycat theater chain established a porn Walk of Fame along Santa Monica Boulevard, which included feet and handprints of Marilyn Chambers, Linda Lovelace, Harry Reems and John Holmes. Some of the first wave of superstars would last the long haul and still work in the business today, others had a successful run and retired — most disappeared after a few years.

Raised Herbie Streicher, a self-described "nice Jewish boy from Westchester," Harry Reems was a New York actor who appeared with the National Shakespeare Company, then worked in early porn loops as both star and "stand-in" stunt penis. After Gerard Damiano cast him in *Deep Throat*, his popularity soared. He told reporters his specialty was that he could ejaculate on a 15-second cue and still keep track of where the camera was. The *Village Voice* compared him to Marlon Brando in *Tango*, and applauded "his superb performance of sexual swordplay without sexual swagger." He once was named correspondent in a divorce suit brought by a man whose wife appeared opposite him in a porn flick. After *Deep Throat* and *Devil in Miss Jones,* also directed by Damiano, he gave the non-porn industry a shot, including a low-budget Canadian cop film, as well as the 1980 R-rated horror flick *Demented* (credited under the name Bruce Gilchrist), but returned to porn when Hollywood didn't recognize him. At the height of his fame he lived in a Malibu beach home, developing a gallon-of-vodka-a-day drinking habit. Eventually he found himself digging in a dumpster, asking for handouts. By the early 90s Reems had cleaned himself up, married, and become a church trustee. He currently works as a real estate agent in Park City, Utah.

Seka was a Virginia Army brat who entered the business in 1976 at age 26, naming herself after a Las Vegas blackjack dealer. Her dyed-blonde hair made her known as the "Marilyn Monroe of porn," and combined with a tough on-screen persona, reminded many of a mixture of white trash and royalty. Seka soon became the biggest-selling performer in the business, appearing in the film *Blonde Fire,* and often working with John Holmes in the *Swedish Erotica* series. By 1984 she had appeared before Congress to defend her First Amendment right to act in porn films, and in the early '90s hosted a late-night radio sex program in Chicago.

A New York actor who graduated with honors from Columbia University, Jamie Gillis appeared in plays and drove a cab before answering an ad for nude modeling and discovering a more lucrative industry. He has made hundred of films, from early loops to *The Opening of Misty Beethoven, The Story of Joanna* and many other well-received porn features. By 1980 he had won the Erotica Award for best actor three times. He still works in the industry today. In addition to creating the *Dirty Debutantes* series with Ed Powers, he also has starred in and produced an innovative, unscripted collection called *On the Prowl,* a forerunner of the Buttman verité videos.

Originally from Pittsburgh, Pennsylvania, John Leslie acted in summer theater productions, worked as a magazine illustrator and photographer, and sang in R&B bands before he entered the industry in 1975, to appear in early classics like Alex de Renzy's *Femmes de Sade* and the Mitchell Brothers' *Autobiography of a Flea.* His character actor face allowed him to play a wide variety of roles. Leslie currently lives in Northern California, writing and directing adult features.

Paul Thomas also came to porn from the

Arlene Elster and Lowell Pickett hosted the First International Erotic Film Festival in December 1970, at their theater in San Francisco. Future Hollywood bad boy Don Simpson did publicity, *Rolling Stone*'s Annie Leibovitz shot photos for the ads, and *Saturday Review* film critic Arthur Knight was one of the judges.

legitimate stage, where he appeared on Broadway in *Hair* and *Tommy*, toured with the American Ballet Theatre, and starred in both stage and film versions of *Jesus Christ Superstar*. He also made commercials for Winston cigarettes and Wrigley's gum before his porn career took off. His blonde good looks and gentle demeanor made him in demand for porn features through the '70s and '80s, and he now works directing features.

Annette Haven worked as a model and cabaret dancer before turning to porn in the mid-'70s, directing one of her first films herself, 1975's *Once Upon a Time*, a time-machine trip to the Cro-Magnon era. The attractive, dark-haired ex-Mormon rapidly became one of the industry's most sought-after stars, known for her hard-nosed professionalism and rapid-fire intelligence. She lives in Northern California, an expert gardener whostill appears in the occasional feature.

One New York actress and former cast member of *Damn Yankees* was working behind the camera, helping her friend Harry Reems on adult film sets, when Reems suggested her to Gerard Damiano, who cast her as the star of *The Devil in Miss Jones*. She adopted the popular theater pseudonym of Georgina Spelvin, and started a new adult film career at the age of 36. Her competent acting skills established her as a lead attraction for many years.

Johnny Keyes was a former boxer and legitimate actor before being cast by the Mitchell Brothers in *Behind the Green Door* and developing into the industry's first true black porn superstar. Keyes's trim, athletic figure and body control assured him later starring roles in *The Resurrection of Eve*, *Heavenly Desire*, *Sex World* and others.

One-time Brooklyn high school teacher Ron Jeremy Hyatt tried his hand at stand-up comedy before dropping his surname and following his true passion for sex, one of his first films being the 1979 *Tigresses (And Other Maneaters)*. One of the few adult stars able to service himself orally, Ron Jeremy's substantial girth has made him the Belushi of porn, a gluttonous, unapologetic party animal nicknamed "The Hedgehog." Jeremy still acts and directs today, as well as making cameo appearances in Hollywood films.

Richard Pacheco visited Northern California in 1968 on a humanitarian social outreach project funded by the Ford Foundation, ended up one evening on a commune with a bunch of naked hippies and the next day called the East Coast to quit his job. His first adult film was *The Candy Stripers*, and he would

Bill Osco's 1976 feature *Alice In Wonderland* was released in several versions from R to XXX, and the actress who played Alice, *Playboy* centerfold Kristine DeBell, reportedly performed in all her scenes. She later went on to appear in the soap opera *The Young and the Restless*.

later star in many classics, including *Talk Dirty to Me*, before retiring from the business, and turning to writing and legitimate acting work.

Joey Silvera came to the industry from New York, and found steady work beginning in the early 1970s, his quiet, unattached on-camera presence reminiscent of a little autistic boy who can't believe his luck. Silvera still regularly appears in starring roles, and recently launched his own video series.

After a stint on *The Gong Show*, blonde Carol Connors landed her first adult role as the nurse in *Deep Throat*, and quickly achieved a following for her Candy roles in *The Erotic Adventures of Candy* and *Candy Goes to Hollywood*. She moved into directing, later becoming a body builder, and tussled in a lawsuit with a jazz singer over the use of the name they shared.

Candida Royalle graduated at the top of her high school class and gave the valedictorian speech at her commencement. After working as a commercial artist, she started auditioning for adult films, and starred in a number of them, including *Champagne for Breakfast, All the Senator's Girls* and *Hot and Saucy Pizza Girls*. She still works behind the camera directing features.

Ellen Steinberg worked on films as set decorator, camera assistant and script girl before director Gerard Damiano discovered her selling tickets in a theater in Tucson. She changed her name to Annie Sprinkle, and became well-known for her large breasts, open sensuality and willingness to share her knowledge of liquid excretions and internal plumbing. Along with Seka, she was one of the first porn stars to market her own line of used mail-order panties. She appeared in many films, including *Centerfold Fever* and *Seduction*, before turning to directing, and developing a live stage act that co-stars a speculum.

Other performers of porn's first Golden Age included Candy Samples, Constance Money, Sharon Mitchell, Leslie Bovee, Serena, Desiree Cousteau, and Kay Parker. This era of porn would be nonexistent, however, without the directors, who treated their work as seriously as Truffaut, or as nonchalantly as a junior high school project.

After a New Hampshire prep-school education, Alex de Renzy married and became an instructor in the Air Force's Survival School in Reno. A brief stint as a craps dealer and a zoology student landed him in early-'60s San Francisco as a photographer for Gordon News Service. On the side, de Renzy spent $75 to make a 600-foot film of a girl stripping, and sold it for

HERE KITTY KITTY:
Examples of feline-themed features, many years before the debut of Cats

GERARD DAMIANO'S
THE
STORY
OF
JOANNA
IS THE STORY OF LOVE

Gerard Damiano's critically acclaimed 1975 film *The Story of Joanna*, starring Terri Hall, Jamie Gillis and Zebedy Colt, nearly played an important role in New York state politics. Shot at a rented mansion in Newport, Rhode Island, Damiano hosted nightly dinner parties for cast and crew that bordered on medieval feasts. Unfortunately, a disgruntled gardener alerted media to the fact a porn film was shooting at the mansion, which was owned by Martin Carey, brother of Hugh Carey, the then-governor of New York state. Before reporters could show up, Damiano had found out ahead of time, and immediately shut down the set. As the crew furiously packed up equipment, Damiano sat in a chair, wondering aloud, "Maybe I do belong in a run-down hotel." Shooting eventually wrapped in another similar location, an opulent private girls' school, and the story never leaked to media. Although *Joanna* was praised for its sophisticated tone and intellectual dialogue, heavy S/M themes forced Damiano to trim 20 minutes in order to obtain a visa in England.

$250. He soon quit his day job and opened the Screening Room theater to show his own loops.

After the success of *Pornography in Denmark*, de Renzy established a reputation as one of the early giants in directing. He drove sports cars and motorcycles, lived in a hillside estate in Marin with a succession of women, all of whom lent a hand in his productions. Teenagers who worked in a local photo store eagerly awaited the latest rolls of film dropped off for developing — still shots from de Renzy productions — delivered by a beautiful porn star in a convertible. Critics called him the Jean-Luc Godard of erotica's *nouvelle vague*. *History of the Blue Movie* was the subject of a long, praiseworthy article in the *New York Times*.

De Renzy would follow with several popular features over the years, including *Babyface* (starring former Oakland Raider Otis Sistrunk), *Pretty Peaches*, *Wild Things 1 & 2* and *Two Women*. Still making films today, he saves the credit of "de Renzy" for features, and markets raunchier material under the name "Rex Borsky."

After Bill Osco made *Mona, the Virgin Nymph*, he released *Dark Dreams*, which introduced a pre-*Deep Throat* Harry Reems, and then in 1976 teamed up with Bud Townsend to direct one of the more ambitious adult films ever produced, a porn musical version of *Alice in Wonderland*.

Matt Cimber's primary claim to fame was a marriage to Jayne Mansfield, before he directed early adult features which posed as sex documentaries, with names like *He and She* and *Black African Sexual Power*. Cimber was later responsible for opening Puss 'n' Boots, one of the first porn film nightclubs in Los Angeles. Radley Metzger — aka Henry Paris — distributed the Danish film *I, A Woman*, went on to make his own films, including *Private Afternoons of Pamela Mann*, *Naked Came the Stranger* and his award-winning 1975 opus *The Opening of Misty Beethoven*. Ron Sullivan reportedly made up his pseudonym, Henri Pachard, from the combination of Picard watches and his dog's name Henry, and grew popular for films like *Devil in Miss Jones II*, *Sexcapades*, *Great Sexpectations* and countless other features that frequently had a scene set in the bathroom. He still can be found directing the occasional feature. Anthony Spinelli was one of the hottest directors in the late '70s and early '80s, with top-rated features like *Sex World*, *Vista Valley P.T.A.* and *Talk Dirty to Me*. Mickey Zaffarano, aka Mike Zaffrano, was a Manhattan theater owner and reputed mob figure who produced the legendary *Debbie*

Does Dallas, an extremely popular X-rated film that had very little to do with football, cheer-leading or the city of Dallas. One of the early porn kingpins, Zaffarano dropped dead of a heart attack in 1979, when FBI agents conducted a raid on his New York office.

One of the industry's first female directors, Gail Palmer contributed the classics *Erotic Adventures of Candy* and *Candy Goes to Hollywood* to the lexicon, among others. In the 1980s, her own erotic adventures led her to Hunter Thompson's hot tub in Woody Creek, Colorado, where she claimed he drugged and molested her. The case was dropped.

Al Goldstein and Jim Buckley are best known for creating *Screw* magazine, but man-aged to produce a few films themselves. Their goofy 1973 *It Happened in Hollywood* came off as a porn version of *Laugh-In*. One scene starred the Flying Fucks circus act, where a woman leaps through the air, lands magically on her partner's penis, and then rides a bicycle whose seat has been replaced by a mechanical phallus operated by the pedals. A man orgasms so hard over the phone it sprays out of the receiver. A roomful of people have sex to the song "Hava-Na-Gila." A later film, *S.O.S.* (Screw on Screen) was a 1975 version of their publication, a sex-themed variety show hosted by the two, which featured vintage loops, and interviews with tattoo artist Spider Webb and a woman billed as "the singing cocksucker from Missouri."

Not to be left out of the publisher-turned-director racket, *Penthouse* magazine's Bob Guccione spent $30 million to produce *Caligula*, the story of one of Rome's most decadent emper-ors. The production values are top-notch, but the cast veered wildly from well-known actors like Malcolm McDowell and Peter O'Toole to bimbo *Penthouse* pets. The overall result was an embar-rassing mess, and screenwriter Gore Vidal angrily demanded his name removed from the credits.

There would be no adult section in video stores today without these pioneers, yet a quick visit to your local adult emporium will yield but a fraction of the porn produced in the '60s and '70s. By modern standards, it's too slow-moving. Stories take forever to unfold and get to the sex, and the attention given to dialogue, music and costumes seems ludicrous. (Oddly similar to the hyper-fast action films of today versus the taut, well-acted *noir* stories of the 1950s.) And yet, after flipping through hundreds of video boxes that scream four hours of consecutive facial cum shots, a visit back in time to the true adult feature trailblazers actually seems refreshing.

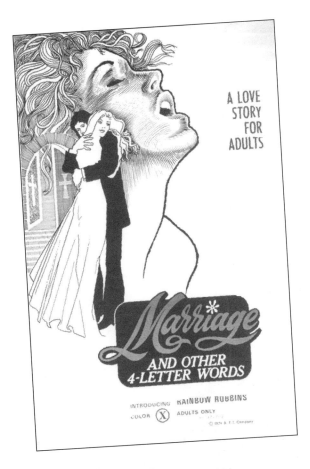

BE SINGLE FOREVER:
The crumbling of an established social order,
or just another way to sell tickets?

Kristine Heller — Cindy Johnson, Karen Kushman, Karen Cusick, Dolores Coubron, Kathy Thomas, Kathy Kane, Kathy Kirk, Kathy Kline, Kathy Collins, Kathy Carlton, Kathy Christian, Kathy Kusick

Herschel Savage — Joel Caine, Jack Black, Jack Blake, Joel Black, Hubert Savage, Vic Falcone, Paul Hues, Bill Berry, Billy Bell, Loel Laiter, Jack Baron, Gerald Greystone

Heather Young — Colleen Anderson, Colleen Davis, Kelly Mint, June Meadows, Lemon Young, Lemmon Yellow

Sharon Kane — Shirley Wood, Shirley Woods, Jennifer Walker, Jennifer Holmes, Sheri Vaughan

Richard Pacheco — Dewey Alexander, Mark Howard

Joey Silvera — Joey Civera, Joey Long, Joey Short, Joey Scott, Joe Arnold, Joe Skeg, Joe Masseria, Joseph Nassi, Eric Marin

Anthony Spinelli — Wes Brown, Arvid Bellar, George Spelvin, Leonard Burke, Sybil Kid, Wendy Lions, Sam Weston (supposedly his real name)

Ken Scudder — Ken Cotton, Ken Struders, Stuart Hempole, Terence Scanlon, Ken Scott, Ken Darwin, Ken Redd, and the San Francisco street intersections of Grant Lombard, Grant Stockton and Turk Lyon

— porn actor/actress pseudonyms

If you've been waiting ...Here's the one!
A movie for the 70's with HARD ACTION & BEAUTIFUL WOMEN!
...SHE ALWAYS COMES OUT ON TOP!
LADY on TOP
in Color X For Ladies and Gentlemen over 21

GERARD DAMIANO'S

DEEP THROAT

HOW FAR DOES A GIRL HAVE TO GO TO UNTANGLE HER TINGLE?

EASTMANCOLOR ⓧ ADULTS ONLY

THE POTEMKIN OF PORN:
Lovelace wasn't credited in the poster, but her presence was felt throughout the film, especially by co-star Harry Reems.

The history of America's most famous porn movie is as sordid as you could imagine.

Chuck Traynor was a high-school dropout who spent three years in the Marines, became a crop-dusting pilot, then flew for a small airline. In his spare time he started taking crotch shots of girls, then moved up to film loops, working out of his topless bar in Florida. He met a sad white-trash girl named

Deep Throat

Linda, the daughter of a Yonkers, New York cop (depending on the source, her last name was either Boreman or Marchiano), and she started working in his bar. He seemed to have money. He was flamboyant, he had a nice car, he flew planes. And he was into sex.

According to Lovelace, she was forced to participate in orgies, work as a prostitute and have on-camera sex with

During the initial 39-week run of **Deep Throat** at Manhattan's World Theater, **Tonight Show** sidekick Ed McMahon arrived one night with six friends and a case of Budweiser. According to the theater manager, McMahon parked his entourage outside the theater after the credits rolled, and chatted up the film with passersby.

HER EXCLUSIVE, INTIMATE STORY!

FOR THE FIRST TIME IN PAPERBACK
CENTERFOLD PHOTO IN FULL COLOR

INSIDE
LINDA LOVELACE

BY LINDA LOVELACE
STAR OF DEEP THROAT

I simply thought everyone was willing to play clit-rubbing games. Chuck wasn't. I automatically pushed him back when his big cock started pushing into me, and I may have tried to sneak out and run away. But I didn't get away with it this time. Actually, I really didn't want to. The fat rocklike muscle tore into me like a battering ram, and I nearly fainted from the shock....I came in seconds and the rockets were all on time.

— from *Inside Linda Lovelace*

REGIS: But what's *next,* Linda? I mean, *surely* it's a limited field. You can't go on like this forever. I mean, really, is the public ready for **Deeper Throat**?

LOVELACE: I don't know. [s*he draws a delicate line with her finger from her throat down between her breasts*] There's a lot of room from here to here...

— *Regis Philbin Show* in Los Angeles, 1973

people in short kinky loops by Traynor and others — golden showers, fisting, and foot insertion. One 1969 loop called *Dogarama*, featured her having sex with what one reviewer termed "a haggard hound."

According to legend, Traynor hypnotized Lovelace to overcome her gag reflex — a sword-swallower's trick he had learned while visiting a Japanese hooker in the military — thereby teaching her the stunt that would bring them both fame. They paired up with Gerard Damiano, a former Queens hairdresser turned film director, who had directed sex pseudo-documentaries like *Marriage Manual* and *Sex U.S.A.* (pairing up unknown actors Harry Reems and Linda Lovelace) and had recently completed *This Film Is All About...*, a straightforward exploration of the New York sex industry. Having seen Lovelace's deep-throat trick, the team planned a big-budget feature centered around this gag reflex gimmick.

Traynor and Damiano found an investor, Lou Perry, whose father, Tony, put up $25,000 for the film. The money people wanted a blonde with big boobs, but Damiano insisted that Traynor's girlfriend do a screen test. She was brought in for one of the strangest acting auditions the fledgling porn industry had seen. Damiano asked her to recite the children's poem "Mary Had a Little Lamb" — first straight, then while laughing hysterically. She got the part, and she was provided an actual script. Her previous loops had no scripts whatsoever, but in *Deep Throat* her speaking parts added up to five whole pages. This was the big time. Damiano came up with the name "Linda Lovelace," explaining that there had been a BB and an MM, and he wanted an LL.

Harry Reems was an actor friend of Damiano's from New York, then working under the name Tim Long, and was hired initially as a crew member, provided that he drove Damiano's car to Miami. When the actor cast as the crazy doctor didn't work out, Reems was promoted to be Lovelace's co-star. She was paid $75 for her presence in the film, Reems got $100, and Traynor received $100 a day as "production manager," which added up to $1,200.

The plot of *Deep Throat* was goofy and full of bad jokes, and created a genre of lame-brained silliness that to this day only porn seems to get away with successfully. But in 1972, it was a novel approach to sex, and made it seem like harmless fun. The freckle-faced Lovelace plays a young girl who drives a deep blue Caddy with a white vinyl top. (The bruises on her legs, she explained years later, were from Traynor beating her in their hotel room.) Lovelace lives with a roommate in a typical Florida one-story condo with orange vinyl furniture. But she doesn't enjoy sex. She has never had an orgasm, and tells her roommate she wants to hear bells, bombs, and "dams bursting." Her roommate says, "Do you want to get off, or do you want to destroy a city?" and suggests a doctor – Harry Reems. (The film was almost titled *The Doctor Makes a House Call.*)

After a perfunctory examination, Reems' professional diagnosis is that Lovelace has her clitoris located in the back of her throat. Lovelace is made to understand that in order to satisfy herself and achieve orgasm, she should simply just give guys head. She tries it on the doc – in a revolutionary, esophagus-expanding, pubic-hair-snuffling technique that still astounds the young and old alike no matter how many times you see it – and her ensuing orgasm is intercut with ringing bells, exploding fireworks and a launching rocket. The plot is set for the rest of the film, a star was born and America never looked at oral sex in quite the same way again.

In an era where most porn filmmakers were stealing existing wah-wah guitar songs and crudely slapping them into the sound mix without rhyme or reason, *Deep Throat* was distinctive for its original music soundtrack. Not only did it have its own dopey theme song, the cheezy fuzz-box guitar and organ-based R&B hippie jams were customized to the scenes, intercut with cornball bubble noises and other sound effects. As a final frisky gesture, audiences walked out of the theater, chatting about the closing credits: "THE END and deep throat to you all."

The film opened in June 1972, and was an immediate sensation. On a $25,000 budget, shot in 18 days, *Deep Throat* made $1,300,000 during a 39-week run at Manhattan's World Theater on West 29th, near Times Square. The film was eventually shut down by New York Judge Joel J. Tyler, who fined the World $100,000, saying "a nadir of decadence...this feast of carrion and squalor." The World retaliated by putting on its marquee in giant red letters: "JUDGE CUTS "THROAT" – WORLD MOURNS." Similar busts occurred in Miami Beach, Dallas, Los Angeles, Chicago, Boston and other cities. A Lansing, Michigan garbage-man refused to remove any trash from a theater chain showing the film. Protestors in

*I*n Deep Throat, **when Lovelace hears the news that her clitoris is located deep in her throat, she breaks into tears. Reems, as the doctor, attempts to console her:**

Reems: Listen, having a clitoris deep down in the bottom of your throat is better than having no clitoris at all.

Lovelace: [**sobbing**] That's easy for you to say. Suppose your balls were in your ear!

Reems: Then I could hear myself coming!

JUNGLE FEVER:
While living in Southern California, Reems and fellow porn star Jamie Gillis dubbed themselves "The Slut Brothers," and had an open invitation to the Playboy mansion.

When Deep Throat *opened in Memphis, Harry Reems was indicted for conspiracy to transport obscene material across a state border. Hollywood celebs Jack Nicholson and Warren Beatty both offered their public support, and the conviction was later reversed. During the trial, Reems went on a college lecture tour, and received letters of praise:*

To be honest, you were not al all what we had been expecting, and we were pleasantly surprised not only at your general articulateness, but especially at your knowledge of the legal issues involved in your case and their ramifications.

— from the president of the Harvard Law School Forum

Considering the speakers we have had this year — Pay Moynihan, Ralph Nader, Margaret Mead, F. Lee Bailey — one would think that whoever followed them would, comparatively, draw only an average ovation. Not so with your lecture. With a good admixture of humor and education, and being not at all condescending, yours was one of the better talks we've had all year.

— from Tufts University

HOW DEEP DOES IT HAVE TO BE:
Jamie Gillis and friends in a dramatic aside
from Deep Throat II.

There's this foot, see? The camera focuses in on this foot. it's asleep, in bed. Then it wakes up, its toes wiggle, it rubs around a little bit. Then it gets up and goes in and takes a shower, and dries itself off and gets dressed in a boot. All the time you don't see anything but the foot. Then the foot goes out, it's walking along the street, and after a while it gets to a door, and the door opens and its talking to another foot, a lady-foot, and then they go inside. The camera goes up to the hands — you see money being exchanged, so you know it's not exactly an ordinary everyday encounter — and then the two feet get undressed and get into bed. Now's the time when the audience thinks that it's finally going to see who belongs to those feet! But no, the girl starts kissing the foot and fondling it, and then the foot goes up to the girl's crotch and starts, you know, fooling around, and pretty soon the toe is screwing her, and then all the toes, and you have to know that although I taught Linda every trick, still, I taught some tricks to some other girls, so this one girl could stretch herself, you know? So that pretty soon the whole foot was inside her, screwing her. You'd think that'd be enough, but then — we'd thought up this other thing. The first foot, the man-foot, had this tube attached to it that ran along the sole of the foot and up along the back of the leg, and we'd mixed up this batch of evaporated milk and egg white. So after a while, the foot comes out of the cunt and up on the girl's stomach, and somebody squeezes the syringe at the end of the tube and the foot 'comes' all over the girl's stomach. So that's **The Foot!**"

— plot of a Traynor early porn loop called *The Foot,* from *Blue Money* by **Carolyn See,** 1974

Milwaukee stormed the box office with their pockets full of pennies. Some theaters received bomb threats.

But all the attention had a reverse effect on the curious public. *Deep Throat* caused such a stir, well-heeled professionals now had a legitimate excuse to go see an adult film. Suburban matrons in mink stoles were waltzing into the show, curious to see the phenomenon all their friends in Westbury and Westchester were talking about.

The *New York Times* did a lengthy feature on Damiano. Johnny Carson told *Deep Throat* jokes. Woodward and Bernstein code-named their Watergate mole "Deep Throat." The phrase entered the lexicon of American language for keeps. Even today, news agencies refer to "Deep Throat" as a synonym for an anonymous source.

Hugh Hefner prepared America to meet its first porn superstar. Lovelace posed for a nude layout in *Playboy* ("Say 'Ah!'"), and it was evident the editors had never before featured such an uninhibited woman who, you know, did all that stuff on camera. Lovelace and Traynor became regulars in the Hefner inner circle, meeting celebrities like Clint Eastwood and Tommy Smothers at mansion parties. Linda did countless magazine covers and press interviews, with Chuck usually dominating the proceedings, interrupting to tell the oft-repeated story about how he learned the secret from a Japanese hooker. In December of 1972 Lovelace traveled to Los Angeles and placed her hands and feet into a permanent cement memorial in front of the "Big Cat," the flagship of the Pussycat Theatre chain on Santa Monica Boulvard.

Sammy Davis, Jr. became their friend (and if you believe Lovelace's books, a slavering, sex-obsessed wife-swapper who actually gave Traynor head while he watched a movie). Shel Silverstein talked of doing a country/western album with her. Buck Henry and Milos Forman toyed with the idea of doing a film. An offer came in for commercial work from Head Shampoo, and Lovelace actually did appear in a spot for an Encino, California shoe store.

They made *Deep Throat, Part II.* Fellow porn actress Andrea True introduced Lovelace and Traynor to a friend at Pinnacle Books, and a book deal was struck for a $40,000 advance, plus a ghostwriter. *Inside Linda Lovelace* was published as an autobiography of her life and how she loves, loves, loves sex and can't get enough of it and people with hang-ups should just lighten up, you know? A foldout color

centerfold featured Linda in blue nail polish and nothing else. The initial print run was 1 million.

By June 1973 *Deep Throat* had grossed nearly $4 million, the most successful and profitable blue movie ever made, and reportedly played for 365 consecutive weeks in Los Angeles. By 1982 the film was said to have earned $100 million, and was the first porn movie ever transferred to videotape (Beta, of course). A production company named Arrow tried to cash in on the craze by releasing *Confessions of Linda Lovelace* in 1974, a rehash of *Deep Throat* footage, spliced together with another film called *Love Witch*, which starred a woman who looked, sort of, like Lovelace.

Realizing the success of *Behind the Green Door*, the opportunistic Traynor soon hitched up with its star, Marilyn Chambers. Lovelace was still recognized by people in hotel lobbies — celebrities like Rex Harrison, for instance — but after Traynor left, her career fizzled. She appeared in a sex farce called *Pajama Tops* in Philadelphia, but it closed after a week. Another book was done about her memories with Traynor, *The Intimate Diary of Linda*

AL GOLDSTEIN: Do you enjoy the taste of sperm?

LOVELACE: Oh, yeah, I do. I love it. It's caviar to me. I can't understand why other chicks get so totally turned off by it. I never spit it out.

GOLDSTEIN: How would you describe the taste?

LOVELACE: I really couldn't describe the taste...you'd have to taste it. Try it.

— *Screw* **magazine**

SECOND COMING:
Nobody's watching, and nobody cares

The book should have been called *Inside Chuck Traynor*. Even the sexual incidents they thought up for me — for example, making love to a mother-daughter combination — were things that had happened to Chuck...I hate the thought that people today can still pick up that piece of trash and think it has anything to do with me or with my life. Which is why I'm so delighted that Chuck Traynor, in a 1976 interview with Leonard Lyons, told the truth: "I wrote the book *Inside Linda Lovelace* with another guy before Linda and I split up. I created all the sex situations in it just as I created Linda Lovelace."

...Sometimes I feel that I'm a real prude — more of a prude than anyone I know. Whenever I hear someone talking about the sexual revolution or the new sexual freedom, I don't look on that as progress. People who are into promiscuity — I'm sorry to say — have a problem. My feeling is this: If people can keep it between themselves and their mates, that's just fine. But love-making should be a two-person proposition. No more, no less. It's just nobody else's business.

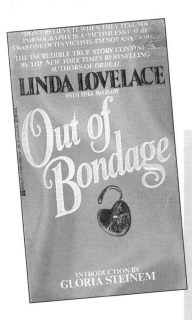

WHAT WAS I THINKING:
The bestselling confessional story that took two books to tell

Some people ask me whether the woman's movement is using me a bit. It's only natural they would use me as an example of what can happen to a woman involved in pornography. This is the way I want to be used, these are the causes I want to be involved in. My relationship with feminism has never been one-sided. They use me to show people what can happen when an innocent person is dragged down into the pornographic sewer. And at the same time they deliver the message I want delivered: There is a way out.

— from *Out of Bondage*

Lovelace, but the publisher rejected it because it wasn't enough like the first book, forcing Lovelace's friends to rewrite it. Another movie was put together, a sex comedy called *Linda Lovelace for President*. According to Lovelace, she says she was promised no sex scenes and no nudity, was fired when she refused to perform a sex scene, and ended up agreeing to appear nude and finish the film. She was slated to star in a film called *Laurie*, by the producers of *Emmanuelle*, but was fired after refusing to have sex with the director. Another sex farce was staged in Vegas, *My Daughter's Rated X*, but was also short-lived.

She was offered other films, including one group who promised a million dollars, deposited in a Swiss bank account before filming began, if she would make one more *Deep Throat*, but she turned them all down. Lovelace eventually married, and for a few years, lived on welfare. In an autobiography titled *Ordeal*, published in 1980, Lovelace recounted her porn career, denying much of *Inside Linda Lovelace* and claiming she did everything in her life under fear of getting beaten by then-boyfriend Traynor. *Ordeal* would make her the darling of anti-porn zealots, who used her as a poster-girl example of the unspeakable horrors indigenous to the porn business. She would write another autobiography, *Out of Bondage*, in 1986, which chronicled her life during the *Ordeal* period.

Gerard Damiano sold his ownership of *Deep Throat* for $25,000, and later explained to reporters that he couldn't really talk about it, saying, "Do you want me to get both my legs broken?" His interest in the documentary form and attention to arty techniques continued in his later films, but he frequently had to tone down the highbrow pretentions and Catholic obsessions for the raincoat crowd, who were the biggest customers and demanded more sex and less art. His next film after *Deep Throat* is also considered a landmark feature, *The Devil in Miss Jones*, a dark, dramatic story in which a virgin spinster, played by Georgina Spelvin, commits suicide and is granted a reprieve by the devil to make up for lost time. Co-starring Harry Reems, Marc Stevens, a snake and some enema equipment, *Miss Jones* won the Critics Prize at the Avoriaz Festival. (A 1983 sequel, *Devil in Miss Jones II*, directed by Henri Pachard, still featured Spelvin but without Reems.) Damiano still directs features today, but none have made such an impact as *Deep Throat*.

THE CROP CIRCLES:
Two versions of porn's first stud, artfully cropped for maximum distribution

As the industry does today, the early era of porn films focused primarily on the female stars. Guys were considered interchangeable, and only those capable of a dependable performance got work the next week. One man emerged to prove the exception to this rule, and became porn's first male superstar.

John C. Holmes was born in Pickaway County, Ohio, and

John Holmes

left home at 16 once he knocked out his stepfather in a fight. After spending three years in the Army, he married and drifted through a variety of jobs. The gangly, somewhat homely young man would drive an ambulance, stir vats of chocolate, sell everything from shoes to furniture and Fuller brushes, and operate a forklift before a chance encounter with a professional photographer in the bathroom of a poker parlor.

In 1968, Sharon Holmes returned to her home in Glendale, California from her job working for a pediatrician. Inside the bathroom she noticed her husband, John Holmes, measuring his penis.

"What are you doing?" she asked.

"What does it look like I'm doing?"

"Is there something wrong? Are you afraid it's withering and dying?" she said, laughing.

"No, I'm just curious," said Holmes.

Sharon went to the bedroom, laid down, read a magazine. Twenty minutes later, Holmes walked into the room. He had a full erection.

"It's incredible," said John.

"What?"

"It goes from five inches all the way to ten. Ten inches long! Four inches around!"

"That's great," said Sharon, turning a page of her magazine. "You want me to call the press?"

— from "The Devil and John Holmes," by Mike Sager, *Rolling Stone*, 1989

A STAR IS BORN:
An exotic metaphor about volcanos shot in Hawaii (right); The Legend of Johnny Wadd (below)

The exact conversation has never been recorded, but it most likely included mention of the size of Holmes' penis, a terrifying appendage that when erect measured variously 12.5 inches to 15 inches.

After posing for photographers and dancing in clubs during the late 1960s, Holmes started doing short loop films. His reputation spread throughout the industry, and anyone who glimpsed his equipment never forgot it. He moved to features, and his name appeared in advertising and publicity on a par with his female co-stars. In 1971, an entire section was devoted to him at the Porno Exhibit in Copenhagen.

His biggest success arrived with a series of films put together by Bob Chinn and Damon Christian that spoofed the hard-boiled Raymond Chandler/Dashiell Hammett detective genre. Holmes starred as private eye Johnny Wadd, porn's Sam Spade, who used his large penis "to reward his allies and conquer his enemies,"and appeared in the pseudo-noir titles *Johnny Wadd, Tell Them Johnny Wadd is Here, Liquid Lips, The Jade Pussycat, China Cat* and *Blonde Fire,* surrounded by the most beautiful porn starlets of the day.

Women and men alike all wanted to sleep with Holmes. People wrote for locks of his pubic hair. Men wanted him to autograph their wives' breasts, and women asked him to deflower their daughters. Holmes told salivating reporters that he had to get as many as 17 erections for each camera set-up, that he used to meet girls in the cemetary after high school and fuck on the pink marble slabs, that he had enjoyed sex in airplanes, helicopters, trains, elevators, kitchens, bathrooms, on rooftops, in caves, storm cellars and European bomb shelters, under a table in a restaurant filled with people, and 50 feet underwater while wearing scuba gear. He bragged he'd been with three governors, two of their wives and one senator, who was "really a freak." A rumor spread that a young Holmes actually was the actor who played the Eddie Haskell character from the TV program *Leave It to Beaver,* but the actor was in reality Ken Osmond, who also spent time denying another rumor that he was supposedly rock star Alice Cooper.

At the height of his fame, Holmes had 27 fan clubs, earned $1,500 a day, and boasted of making $500,000 a year. He once said his penis was "bigger than a pay phone, smaller than a Cadillac." Film critics called him the "Paul Bunyan of the bedroom." A porn dealer was quoted in *Playboy* as saying, "Without John Holmes, California porno wouldn't be what it is today." He drove a brand-new El Camino. His trademark was a large

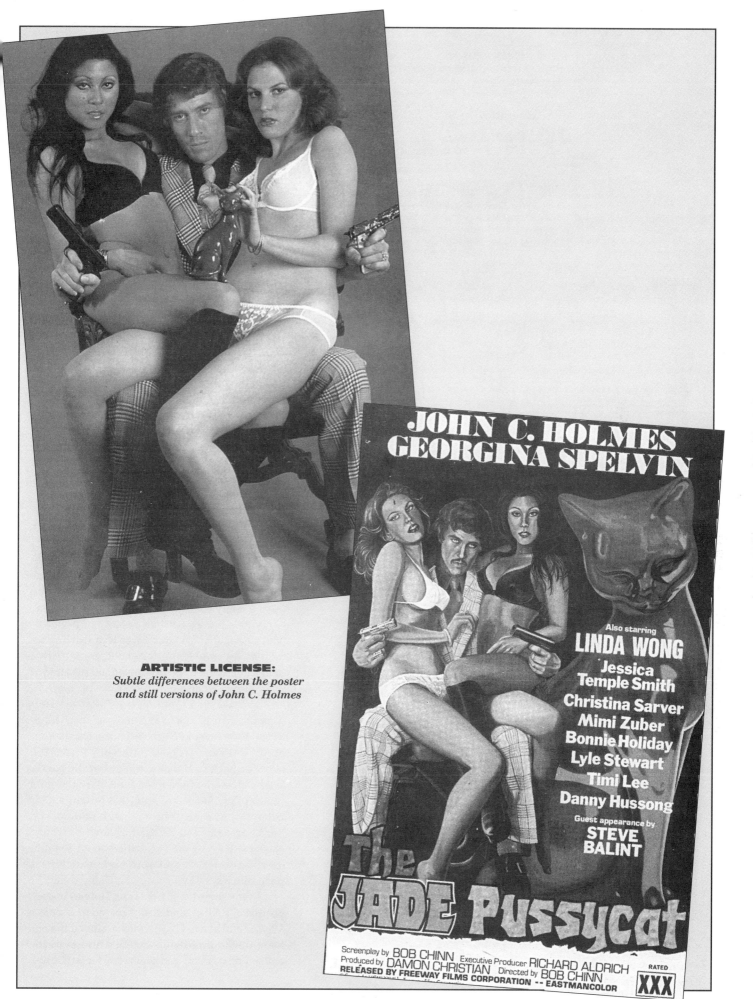

ARTISTIC LICENSE:
Subtle differences between the poster and still versions of John C. Holmes

I've never found a girl who could not take it. It's really in the way you do it, though. I've had some women say they've had guys half my size who couldn't get it in. The problem is that most guys don't know how to read a lady and what she really wants. With some, you have to be gentle and romantic, and with others you just have to get down and dirty. The secret is that you have to get in touch with what they want. Personally, I think it's all great fun. It's something everybody does, and the more you practice, the better you get at it. I can see a girl in a restaurant now and tell you what she likes and how to approach her...

Sometimes you get a girl to work with who is gorgeous and with a fantastic body. That makes it all much easier. But I can concentrate on just one aspect of a girl if she doesn't sexually appeal to me. I can concentrate on the color of her nipple or something like that and it gives me the necessary mental focus.

— from a 1982 interview

diamond solitaire. He also designed a big gold and diamond ring in the shape of a dragonfly, and an 8-inch-wide gold belt buckle that depicted a mother and baby whale swimming in the ocean. Holmes traveled all over the world attending film openings, and turning private tricks. He appeared in everything from big-budget extravaganzas like *Autobiography of a Flea*, to the Batman spoof *Dickman and Throbbin*, the 3-D feature *Hard Candy*, and a series of low-budget 8mm loops with a woman named Seka, released as *Swedish Erotica*. It was said that nobody could ever deep-throat him, but as porn historian Jim Holliday has noted, "cheat techniques have been used to provide the illusion."

In his career spanning over 20 years, John Holmes made nearly 2,500 hardcore shorts and features, including gay films. He was estimated to have had sex with 14,000 women, two generations of leading ladies, from Seka and Marilyn Chambers to Ciccolina. Although he was the first man to receive the X-rated Critics Organization Best Actor Award, he was really just a non-threatening, gum-chewing guy who just happened to sleep with more women than any other man on the planet. He accepted a gig as spokesperson for the "Incredible John Holmes Super Pump" penis extension device. His career was chronicled in a 1981 pseudo-documentary called *Exhausted*.

Holmes also had a dark side. In 1973 he began acting as a police informant for porn and prostitution to LAPD vice detectives. He developed a nasty coke freebase habit, and started carrying a Samsonite suitcase full of freebasing equipment. The 24-hour party was starting to take its toll, and Holmes stole luggage, delivered drugs and helped his mistress turn tricks to keep him in freebase.

The so-called "Four on the Floor" murders took place in 1981, a brutal beating/drug robbery of the Wonderland Gang in Laurel Canyon above Hollywood. Police eventually traced the slayings back to Holmes, who knew the parties involved and had provided the killers the information they needed to enter the building and commit the crime. A jury found him innocent, but he remained in jail on unrelated burglary charges. He eventually testified about the murders, was released and went back to making porn movies.

In the summer of 1985 John Holmes tested positive for AIDS, and died three years later in a VA hospital at age 43. His wife cremated the entire body, fulfilling his dying wish that his notorious penis not be cut off and preserved for posterity.

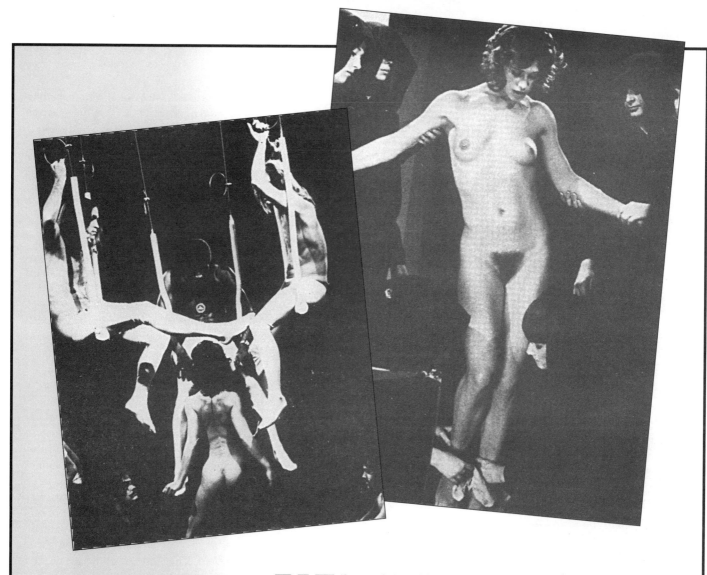

While studying film at San Francisco State University
in the late 60s, brothers Jim and Artie Mitchell realized there was more money to be found in making short sex
loops than trying to join the boring, straight world. Just get a
few hippie girls and guys together, get 'em naked, light up a

Behind the
Green Door

joint, roll film and tell them when to switch positions.
Anything went as far as scenarios, as long as the story got to
the sex pretty quickly. One film, for instance, was centered
solely around its location of a paper bag factory, where one of
their friends worked.

The brothers soon realized the downside of trusting others
to buy and distribute their films, and on July 4, 1969, they

"BEHIND the GREEN DOOR"
starring
MARILYN CHAMBERS
a
mitchell brothers' film group release

Behind the Green Door received exceptional reviews:

"Catnip for young couples" — **Playboy**

"In terms of lighting, photography, technical experimentation and erotic content, it stands pretty much alone" — John Wasserman, **San Francisco Chronicle**

"It's sex as ritual, sex as fantasy, sex as it can only be in the movies" — Arthur Knight, **Saturday Review**

"Miss Chambers is a 20-year-old lovely fresh-faced 'innocent'...who does everything quite realistically" — Jim Harwood, **Variety**

"*Behind the Green Door* is an erotic classic. It is almost more a woman's film than a man's and several women I know who have seen it say 'At last!'" — William Rotsler, *Adam* magazine

"This time they may have gone too far — even for me" — B. Wakefield Boyer [a nonexistent critic, in reality, their scriptwriter]

"She was no farmer's daughter, but she could make things grow"

"Bring a date — Chicks love it!"

"New projection equipment — 100% brighter picture"

— **advertising lines used by the Mitchells to promote their early loops**

opened the O'Farrell Theatre, a few blocks from City Hall, to show their loops. They bought ads in newspapers, and it wasn't long before the place was attracting a crowd. Local obscenity laws assured the Mitchells frequent appearances in San Francisco courtrooms. They established such a first-name basis with vice officers, all it would take was a phone call for everyone to agree on a court time. But all this was small potatoes. Everybody was doing loops. The Mitchells wanted to really make a splash — a big-budget feature film that would put them on the map as filmmakers.

Marilyn Briggs grew up in an upper-middle-class Connecticut household, daughter of a Manhattan advertising executive, a cheerleader and AAU diving champion. From the age of 15 she was working as a model, appearing in TV spots for Pepsi and Clairol, and in the Barbra Streisand film *The Owl and the Pussycat*, playing the blonde girlfriend of Robert Klein. She moved to San Francisco, married a hippie bagpipe player and kept going out on acting auditions, while working in a health food restaurant. One day she answered an ad in the *San Francisco Chronicle* for actresses, met the filmmakers — a couple of brothers in jeans and sneakers — and was hired to be the star of their 337th film, called *Behind the Green Door*. They agreed on a new name for her — Marilyn Chambers.

The storyline of *Behind the Green Door* was based on an anonymous porn semi-classic, a G.I. favorite that had been floating around since World War II. The Mitchells updated certain elements, but kept the central plot intact. A truck driver tells his buddy about a bizarre sex club he had visited, where a young girl was forced to participate in a kinky sex show. The bulk of the film is a flashback to the club — the club with a green door. Chambers arrives at the club, and is ravaged by six women dressed as witches from Hamlet. The Green Door opens and black actor Johnny Keyes enters, dressed as a bizarre voodoo apparition in painted face, bear-claw necklace and white leotard cut away at the crotch. Keyes and Chambers perform a steamy interracial sex scene, after which Chambers is suspended in the infamous sling and has sex with five guys at once, while an audience of fat ladies, midgets and assorted freaks break into an orgy of their own. Seized by a moment of heroic clarity, the truck driver grabs Chambers and rushes her out of the club.

Green Door cost $60,000 to produce, and would go on to gross an estimated $50 to $60

million before going to videocassette. When it
premiered at Cannes, the film ended to complete silence. The brothers were certain they
were finished. Then one man in the audience
started yelling, "Fuck...fuck...fuck..." and
the entire crowd picked up the chant: "FUCK...
FUCK...FUCK...." Uncertain whether this
was a good or a bad thing, the brothers ran out
of the theater, chased by a standing ovation.

   As the film was gearing up for its New
York City premiere at the World Theater, the
Ivory soap company released its new box
design, photographed two years earlier, which
happened to feature a young blonde model
named Marilyn Briggs. Supermarkets across
the nation were stocked with Ivory Snow soap
boxes emblazoned with the image of a porn
actress holding up a happy baby. Excited by
such good fortune, the Mitchells immediately
capitalized on the irony and fired off press
releases around the country, alerting the media
to the Ivory Snow girl's porn debut: "She's 99
and 44/100 percent pure!" *San Francisco
Chronicle* columnist Herb Caen passed on the
tip, but Earl Wilson of the *New York Post* was
the first to mention the soap scoop, and for
weeks the World was packed to the rafters.
People waiting in line would include everyone
from business suits on their lunch hour to
John Lennon and Yoko Ono. The night of the
premiere, a man named Chuck Traynor visited
the Plaza Hotel where the *Green Door*
entourage was staying, and asked to speak
with Marilyn Chambers. She became a household word, the subject of references on
America's ultimate barometer of *Zeitgeist*,
Johnny Carson's *Tonight Show* monologues.
Ivory Snow angrily pulled all its boxes off
the shelves.

   It's arguable that Marilyn Chambers was
the world's first true porn star. Linda Lovelace
was there first, but she relied exclusively on her
deep-throat gimmick, and was considered a one-
trick pony. *Devil in Miss Jones* star Georgina
Spelvin also appeared early on the scene, but
she was older, already in her mid-30s.
Chambers represented youthful American innocence personified — friendly, sweet-faced, with
blonde hair and a nice smile. The camera loved
her.

   Since shipping such material across state
lines was a federal offense, the Mitchells wisely
screened the film in their own theaters up and
down California. They premiered their films in
style — live music, dancers, black-tie waiters
circulating with silver trays of champagne.

STOP THE SOAP:
*The publicity shot that caused
the soap to bubble (above); A
soaking wet still image from the
later years (below)*

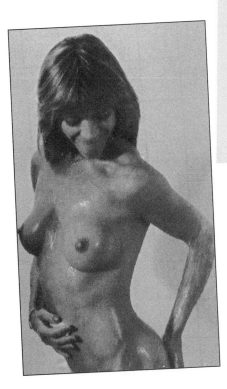

According to **Bottom Feeders** by
John Hubner, on opening night of
Behind the Green Door at the
O'Farrell, co-star George McDonald
and two of his friends tripped on
acid, and were seen in the lobby
scrounging around the carpet, hunting for a joint they had already finished in their limo outside. To further
add to the milieu, projectionist Vince
Stannish accidentally mixed up the
sequence of reels, and played them
in the order 1-3-2. Nobody noticed.

TONGUE-IN-CHIC:
Mitchells reflecting society's trends, from the CB craze (above), to experimental photography (right) and the emerging video revolution (below)

Their theater was frequented by politicians, journalists, musicians and athletes, a clubhouse atmosphere of a revolving party. They gave heavily to local charities, including police and fire departments, and were generous to anybody in the city who was doing something they believed in — political campaigns, publishers, theater producers, musicians. They hired a local artist to transform the outer wall of their theater building into a colorful mural of wildlife. *Time* magazine would dub them "the Potentates of Porn." They were arrested hundreds of times over the years, and eagerly fought each charge in court, setting several precedents that protect others in the porn business even today.

The Mitchells would produce more features that are still considered classics of the genre. *The Resurrection of Eve* followed in 1973, also starring Marilyn Chambers, and was considered by many to be even better than *Behind the Green Door*. But Chambers was antsy to build her career, and left the brothers to hook up with Chuck Traynor, who reportedly dumped Linda Lovelace for her. Chambers would make several more well-received films, including *Insatiable I and II, Up 'N Coming*, and the *Private Fantasies* series, write books and sex advice columns, appear in the David Cronenberg horror film *Rabid*, and even enjoy a belated singing and stage acting career. She currently lives with her family in Southern California.

Perhaps feeling betrayed, the brothers released a documentary called *Inside Marilyn Chambers*, featuring clips and behind-the-scenes interviews with her and her co-stars of *Green Door*. They continued making films. *Autobiography of a Flea* was released in 1976, based on a 17th-century porn story. The lavishly costumed production starred John Holmes, Jean Jennings, Annette Haven, John Leslie, and an invisible talking flea who lives on the body of a young girl, narrating the entire story as it unfolds. *CB Mamas* was released the same year, cashing in on the current fad. Following a court case involving *Green Door*, in which a judge wrote that the film would appeal to the prurient interests "of the citizens of Sodom and Gomorrah," the Mitchells turned around and named their next movie *Sodom and Gomorrah*, co-starring an elaborate spaceship, an anteater and a chimpanzee. Press materials were careful to quote the judge whenever possible. For the New York premiere of the Biblical-themed extravaganza, the Mitchells didn't trust the shifty theater owners, and flew their high school buddies out to Manhattan to monitor the box offices themselves as the film opened simultaneously in 26 theaters. Although the brothers shot their wad to the tune of $500,000, the most ever spent on a porn film at the time, the critics were not kind, and called the epic a disaster.

As the video revolution unfolded, the Mitchells transferred their film library to video, took orders over the phone and shipped their wares around the country, videos selling for a whopping $129.95 apiece, playback machines for a fat-and-sassy $1,100. When their suppliers cut costs of videos, the brothers downsized their chain of 11 theaters and formally reopened the O'Farrell as a live venue in January 1977 with the Ultra Room — a lesbian bondage show viewed by individual booths, behind glass windows. Reviewers raved about their ingenuity, and lines formed down the block to witness the newest, most explicit live sex acts to be seen anywhere in the world. Other acts soon followed — the Kopenhagen Room, the Shower Room, the Green Door Room and a separate theater called the New York Live. The building would be raided regularly by police over the years, the Mitchells either winning cases or getting them overturned on appeal. Chambers even returned to the O'Farrell in the early '80s to shoot a couple of ultra-hardcore B&D films, and appear in a series of live performances that were shut down by local cops — many of whom made sure to ask her for an autograph.

But the increased tension of brothers working so closely together would take its toll in 1991, when Artie's constant partying and erratic behavior reached a level at which his brother Jim was forced to intervene. On the evening of February 27, Jim paid a visit to Artie at his suburban home in Marin, and shot him dead in what friends later referred to as an act of "Okie justice." The ensuing trial generated international "tough love" headlines, and Jim was sentenced to six years in prison. The O'Farrell Theatre today remains one of the country's top adult theater attractions, and recently has expanded to the World Wide Web, but the company still does big business selling videos of past films, in particular *Behind the Green Door.*

CLASSICAL GAS: *Much fun and much money spent on updating the classics, from the anonymous* **Autobiography of a Flea** *(above) to the $500,000 epic* **Sodom and Gomorrah**

I n 1979 the Mitchell brothers proudly presented a run of Honeysuckle Divine at the O'Farrell Theater. Divine was a stripper and hooker from Washington D.C. who eventually found her unique niche as a comedic vaginal freak show. The media was there on opening night:

"I do a clean act," she began happily, removing the mop from her shopping cart and propelling it about the stage by emplying a motive force not generally associated with housework.

"Now," she said brightly, "let's do some sing-alongs." Out came the tin horn, in went the tin horn and out came one of the most moving versions of "Jingle Bells" it's been my pleasure to hear.

"She has a nice personality," observed one of the TV guys.

Next, Honeysuckle blew out some candles ("They love me at birthday parties"), delivered an extended panagyric on the merits of Jergen's lotion ("I'd like to do a commercial for them, but they won't let me") and followed that by unleashing a veritable Niagara of the estimable unguent.

Finally, Honeysuckle Divine lay supine on the floor, dabbed talcum on her publics and effortlessly sent billowing puffs of white powder into the air.

"We have," the TV man cried exultantly, "a Pope!"

— **John Wasserman,** *San Francisco Chronicle*

erformance art, Vegas shows, the modern dance movement — onstage nudity barely rates a mention these days, unless it's to comment on the male's underendowed physique as a metaphor for squandered acting lessons. That exhiliration of live, titillating prurience is now taken for granted in the collective memory. We accept the peep shows, lap-dances, bachelor party girls and gag-gift Strip-O-Grams as part of our nation's vast wealth of contributions to the world. So-called "gentleman's clubs" are standard in every American city, where thick-neck men in suits share the gawking with blue-collar guys wearing pagers. Teenagers stepping inside one of the country's

Live Nude!

2,500 tittie bars will never know the many arrests and court battles that led to the mammary mambos they are witnessing before finishing high school. Oddly enough, given the prevalence of topless clubs in the U.S. today, it was actually the professional theater world that first gave nudity some legitimacy and challenged authority, beginning with Michael McClure's controversial play *The Beard*.

His sexually-charged drama between a man and woman, which wound up with an act of cunnilingus, held its third and fourth performances in 1965 at The Committee nightclub in San Francisco's North Beach. Both shows were surreptitiously tape-recorded by police. The fifth performance was interrupted with whirring

FIDGETING ROOM ONLY:
(clockwise from top) Killing an afternoon in a California topless bar; a typical strip contest that Americans know and love; Method acting out in unidentified theater production

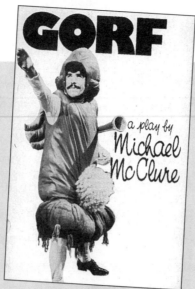

Take a flying cock and balls, a blind motorcycle Lesbian, a pair of dancing TV sets, a hard-hat laborer and his wife, shepherds, motorcycle outlaws, naked tap-dancing stars, a fair girl, and a giant hairy elephant's hindquarters. Accompany them with sounds issuing from a band of cherubs paying a range of styles from Puccini to Spike Jones — and throw them into a plot that echoes everything from *Oedipus at Colonus* to *Who's Afraid of Virginia Woolf?* You still haven't exhausted *Gorf*'s parameters. It is a part in eternity, a bubble.

— from the introduction to Michael McClure's 1974 play *Gorf*, by San Francisco director John Lion

White boys are so sexy
Legs so long and lean
Love those sprayed-on trousers
Love the love machine

My brother calls 'em rubble
They're my kind of trouble
My daddy warns me "no no no"
But I say "White boys go go go"...

...Black boys are nutritious
Black boys fill me up
Black boys are so damn yummy
They satisfy my tummy

I have such a sweet tooth
When it comes to love
Black black black black black
black black black
Black boys

— lyrics from *Hair*, 1967

During a 1968 performance of *Hair*, in one of the all-nude scenes, one of the male actors began to get an erection. The theater was silent. When the boy's penis achieved a full erection, he smiled, and the audience of 1,200 gave him a standing ovation.

cameras and the arrest of the cast members on charges of "obscenity," "conspiracy to commit a felony" and "lewd and dissolute conduct in a public place." The sixth performance, staged in Berkeley and represented by the ACLU, was punctuated by the appearance of over 100 expert witnesses, including several photographers whose duty was to record the police filming and recording of the show. Police and members of the District Attorney's Office arrived early to shut down the show, and were outshouted by the audience, who wildly cheered the actors, author and their attorneys. The police left quietly after the curtain, but the city of Berkeley brought charges of "lewd and dissolute conduct in a public place." Five months later, the ACLU succeeded in getting the case dropped from San Francisco Superior Court. (McClure recovered sufficiently to write another sexually-laced play called *Gorf*, a 1974 mythical satire, which followed the adventures of the main character Gorf, costumed as a giant purple penis and testicles.)

The first all-nude off-Broadway play in New York was *Che*, a late-60s sexually provocative drama about Che Guevara, where men played female parts, and women played the men's roles, including future porn star Marlene Willoughby as Fidel Castro. On opening night, all ten cast members and the theater's janitor were arrested on charges of obscenity, public lewdness and consensual sodomy. For their ability to push the envelope of convention, everyone was sentenced to $500 or 60 days.

The Living Theater company also explored the limits of sex and nudity, occasion-ally upstaged by its own audiences. During one of its shows at the Brooklyn Academy of Music, *Tulane Drama Review* critic Richard Schechner stripped himself naked and ran onto the stage, attempting to fondle members of the cast. Nudity and simulated sex extended even to productions by the Joffrey Ballet, and the repertory company of the Yale School of Drama, whose flower-children version of Euripides' *The Bacchae* led to another off-Broadway staging, renamed *Dionysus in 69*. Of *Dionysus* nudity and staged intercourse, a cautionary *Life* cover story, "Sex in the Lively Arts: How Far Is Far Enough?" grumbled, "Because some playgoers have already grown fairly accustomed to stage nudity, they are beginning to take it for granted."

Nudity wasn't the only taboo being broken off Broadway. In 1967 Tom O'Horgan staged a black comedy called *Futz!*, the story of a farmer persecuted by his moralistic neighbors for his simple desire to sodomize his pig in peace. It proved so popular *Futz!* was later made into a film.

Also that year saw the debut of *Hair*, a "tribal love-rock musical" produced by Joseph Papp, in collaboration with multi-millionaire aviation heir Michael Butler. Hippie culture had hit the big time with a whacked-out melange of rock and roll, marijuana, LSD and sex. The production opened at the Public Theater off-Broadway on October 7, 1967, not long after the Summer of Love. Sold-out shows soon sent it to Broadway. The big dramatic nude scene came with members of the cast shedding their clothing and standing in silence, facing the audience. New York police never intervened, because the law did not prohibit nudity unless the actor moved. By 1972, productions of *Hair* were being staged in Los Angeles, London, Paris, Copenhagen, Stockholm, Munich, Belgrade and Sydney. Children were singing, in all languages, rock lyrics about finding cocks in beds, and chocolate-flavored black boys. A film version would be released years later, directed by Milos Forman, starring Treat Williams and Beverly D'Angelo.

Hair looked like a serious social effort compared to 1969's *Oh! Calcutta!*, a sex revue that became one of New York's longest-running shows in the history of theater. Conceived by British drama critic Kenneth Tynan, literary manager of England's National Theater, *Calcutta!* brazenly trumpeted the world of the hetero, much like *The Boys in the Band* would later do for gays. The title referred to a pun on the French idiom for "what a nice ass!" The $100,000 budget was the highest ever for an off-Broadway play, enough to hire the best names in the business to contribute — from Samuel Beckett, Bruce Jay Friedman and John Lennon to Jules Feiffer, Edna O'Brien, Sam Shepard and Tynan himself. The June 1969 premiere at the Eden Theater, a former burlesque house on the Lower East Side, was choked with people. Cadillacs and Rolls Royces double-parked down the block, jettisoning Ed Sullivan, Joe Namath, Julie Newmar, Shirley MacLaine, Hedy Lamarr and other celebs. The original New York cast featured actor Bill Macy, who later starred as Bea Arthur's husband on the sitcom *Maude*, and the San Francisco production starred Louise Hatch, daughter of Bishop Robert M. Hatch, of the Massachusetts Episcopal Diocese. Critics of the show were generally not kind, but everybody went to see it anyway, and for years productions were supported by busloads of

During the original New York production, cast member Bill Macy attended a bar mitzvah. When someone asked him what he was doing in *Oh! Calcutta!* Macy reportedly took out his penis, laid it on the banquet table and said, "*That's* what I'm doing!"

A BIG DEAL:
Tabloid paparazzi catch celebrities attending premiere of Oh! Calcutta

One night after the closing nude scene, I turned to the audience and said 'Good night.' Immediately, one woman shouted out, 'Go get dressed.' I felt like I was getting kicked in the stomach. And then half of the audience started applauding, while the other half began booing and the two groups tried to drown each other out.

— *Oh! Calcutta!* **cast member Leon Russom, describing the show's previews in** *Newsweek*

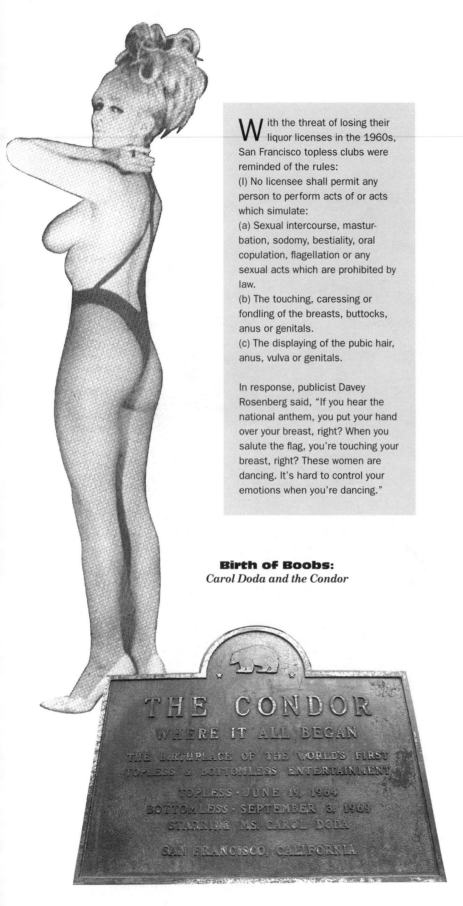

Birth of Boobs:
Carol Doda and the Condor

With the threat of losing their liquor licenses in the 1960s, San Francisco topless clubs were reminded of the rules:

(I) No licensee shall permit any person to perform acts of or acts which simulate:

(a) Sexual intercourse, masturbation, sodomy, bestiality, oral copulation, flagellation or any sexual acts which are prohibited by law.

(b) The touching, caressing or fondling of the breasts, buttocks, anus or genitals.

(c) The displaying of the pubic hair, anus, vulva or genitals.

In response, publicist Davey Rosenberg said, "If you hear the national anthem, you put your hand over your breast, right? When you salute the flag, you're touching your breast, right? These women are dancing. It's hard to control your emotions when you're dancing."

curious Manhattan tourists. A two-hour film version was released in 1971, and begins with the audience entering the theater, while the actors prepare backstage.

It wasn't long before such explicitness dribbled out the doors of the theaters and into bars and nightclubs. New York's first topless waitresses reportedly started working in November 1966, at the Crystal Room on E. 54th Street. This was noteworthy for New York, but out in California, topless was already old news.

On the morning of June 19, 1964, 450-pound nightclub press agent Davey Rosenberg opened the *San Francisco Chronicle* and noticed the sudden popularity of the topless bathing suit by Los Angeles designer Rudi Gernreich. That afternoon, he bought two suits at I. Magnin for $25, and dropped them off at the go-go jazz club he was representing, called the Condor. That evening, Condor owner Gino Del Prete handed one of the suits to waitress Carol Doda and asked her to model it for the patrons. The Condor immediately had a line out the door, and other North Beach clubs immediately followed with their own topless girls — Yvonne D'Angers, Tosha and Gay Spiegelman, billed as the "Topless Mother of Eight."

Based on the advice of a doctor in the audience, Doda began weeks of silicone injection treatments, growing from a 34-inch bust to a hefty 44, explaining to reporters, "I expand with the heat." Newspapers went nuts trying to write stories about the new craze, without actually showing photos of breasts. Police raids on the clubs ended with not guilty court verdicts, and the shows continued.

For 23 years, Doda personified San Francisco's topless scene to the rest of the world. Traffic backed up Broadway for blocks, from tourists and sailors to celebrities like Sinatra, Bardot and Berle, all to watch her lower down from the ceiling each night on a white baby grand piano. She placed her breasts in wet cement on the Broadway strip, and had them cast in dental plaster as a benefit for the Women's Board of the San Francisco Museum of Modern Art. A single appearance on the UC Berkeley campus attracted 20,000 students, including one kid who fell out of an oak tree. Her breasts were insured with Lloyd's of London for $1.5 million. She received a Business Person of the Year Award from Harvard University. She starred in a theatrical revue called *The Rise and Fall of the World (As Seen From a Sexual Position)*, which featured the Bolshoi Ballet, and a production number where Doda seduced King Kong atop the Empire State Building. The silicone for Carol Doda's treatments was manufactured by General Electric, and soon became the industry's standard method of pneumatic dancer enhancements. (When someone alerted GE to the fact that its product was being used by strippers, however, the company abruptly stopped manuacturing it, and Dow Chemical picked up the fake-boob baton.)

In its heyday, San Francisco's Broadway strip boasted 28 topless clubs, many of which featured freezing girls, dancing in go-go cages mounted on poles outside the front doors. Neighborhood billboards advertised a bare-breasted Doda in a joke campaign for milk. The familiar photograph of racy blinking signs was ingrained as a neon landscape of sexual freedom, a frequent backdrop to films and TV shows, from *The Streets of San Francisco* and *The Graduate* to *Dirty Harry* and Russ Meyer's *Mondo Topless*. All types of gimmicks emerged to chat the tourists inside the door, from he-she love acts to a topless shoeshine parlor, topless ice cream stand and topless all-girl jazz band.

Doda and the Condor were quickly challenged for the coveted title of first topless in the U.S. by Los Angeles club owner Walt Robson, who claimed his Phone Booth preceded the Condor by two months. Sticklers pointed out that Robson's club was topless, but his girls didn't dance, and therefore the crown of topless dancing belonged to the Condor. This must have been a bitter pill for Robson, who went out of his way to form the Preservation of Topless Association, spending $350,000 in legal fees to fight Southern California courts for the privilege of topless entertainment. Before Robson faded from the scene, his Phone Booth club made the front page of the *L.A. Times* in 1969, with the arrest of dancer Jean Chanel (40-18-36). Reporters gleefully quoted Chanel's justification: "Dancing is as legitimate an art as acting or singing — and it's better than some other occupations open to women."

On the opposite end of the country, topless manifested in clubs, but increasingly the peep show venue, perfected by Times Square, seemed most appropriate to the harried men of crowded cities — a quick peek for not much money, and then it's home on the train. The Wurlitzer Building offered naked girlie shows before getting its first bust in 1970. The Mini-Cine offered studio tours, where people could peek through windows and watch the actual filming of a sex loop. There was no admission

In 1968, Vicky Drake, candidate for student body president of Stanford, was asked what her campaign platform was: "38-22-36," the 21-year-old blonde language student replied. Outside classes, she worked as a topless dancer in the San Francisco club scene. Her campaign consisted of posters of herself nude with the slogan "Vicky for Pres."

To accurately judge a 1960s topless dancing obscenity case in Sacramento, California, Judge Earl Warren Jr., moved his entire courtroom into the Pink Pussy Kat club. Dancers Suzanne Haines (pictured) and Sheila Brendenson did their routines for the jury, and for their efforts received a not guilty verdict.

FOLLOW YOUR NOSE:
*Typical Los Angeles
strip bar ad of the late 1960s,
with an unforgettable slogan*

Two Ground Rules for Times Square Sex Perverts

1) Never sit directly next to another patron. If you do, he'll think you're queer and might get nasty. Always space yourselves at least one seat apart, more if possible.

2) Use the toilet for jerking off only. If you have to piss during the show, go to an unoccupied seat in the back row — and do it on the rug. The sound of urine splashing on a cement floor can be distracting.

— from *Screw*, 1967

charge, but at the bookstore a book and studio tour together cost $5. An early review in *Screw* describes a rather unerotic tableau — the male star couldn't get an erection, so the man and woman just posed on a bed, while crew members took light readings.

New York may not have given the country topless dancing, but it did conjure up something nobody else had thought of — wet T-shirt contests. It was just like topless, except it was completely legal! As soaked mammaries entertained bar drunks in a great swath across the Continental 48, the concept of topless quickly caught fire in the opposite direction from San Francisco. A logical collision occured in the Midwest, where a young man in Ohio named Larry Flynt was one of the first to franchise the idea of a go-go dance club. His Hustler Club in Dayton featured framed pictures of mobsters over the bar, labeled "Hustler Club Board of Directors." By the mid-70s, everyone was familiar with wet T-shirts and topless strippers. Obviously it was time for some rules. States began legislating to protect citizens from themselves, arguing over fine points like minimum stage height in a topless bar. When was it appropriate to serve alcohol in topless joints? Bottomless joints? Attorneys made lots of money defining legal terms like "table-dancing," "lap-dancing," "couch-dancing."

Soon the business became a free-for-all. "Texas-style" couch dancing was dreamed up by a club owner in Seattle. Mary's Club in Portland, Oregon hung up a sign saying "Where Seamen Meet." Urgent neon messages like "Live Nude Girls!" became part of the architecture in seedier urban areas — as if dead nude girls were also an option. Above the runway of the Pussycat Theater at Broadway and 46th Street in New York, a big sign was mounted that announced, "GIRL POWER!"

Simulated intercourse shows, i.e., "love acts," carved out their own special brand of appeal. One 25-year-old man who did four shows a day at the Bottoms Up in Los Angeles was asked how he kept up the pace. He explained he slept between shows, and ate only raw hamburger — five pounds every day.

Other oddities included professional female mud wrestling, reportedly begun by promoter Bruce Rosenbaum in Catawiffa, Pennsylvania in the early 1970s. His team was called the Milwaukee Hustlers. For variety, Rosenbaum kept rotating the act's primary battlefield ingredient, from mud to mashed sweet potatoes, creamed corn, chocolate pudding, oatmeal, creamed spinach, spaghetti with marinara sauce, peanut butter, vanilla ice cream and Jell-O.

Another entrepreneur also saw an obvious niche and wasted no time. In 1979 Steve Banerjee opened a Hollywood nightclub called Chippendales, starring a troupe of slick-chested male exotic dancers and a female-only admission policy at the door. The idea quickly expanded to branch clubs in New York, Dallas and Denver, as well as a line of calendars, videos, greeting cards and other products. An interesting sociological phenomenon emerged from the Chippendales' success — while men historically had watched female dancers in stoic, anonymous quietude, women who attended male strip shows screamed their voices hoarse, and pawed at the guys' jockstraps like starving refugees. In some cases, they probably were.

Nudity and sex in theater today offer no sense of surprise or shock whatsoever. *Oh! Calcutta*, for instance, ended its once-invincible run by closing to empty houses. It is as if audiences have now intellectually processed the concept of naked actors on a stage, and have moved onto other titillations, such as a bunch of cute singing cats. Conversely, the business of stripping is bigger than ever, the number of clubs roughly doubling between 1987 and 1992. The modern topless bar has found itself a new label — the gentleman's club, a polished-brass sanctuary of cocktails, cigars and expense accounts on credit cards. Strip club owners from around the country congregate each year at the Gentlemen's Club Owners Expo in Reno, for panel discussions, trade shows and the Exotic Dancer of the Year Contest. National franchises run clubs from coast to coast, standardizing everything from floor plans and matching drink cups to the pattern of the carpet.

WET T-SHIRT PROMOTER TO CONTESTANTS: Don't show anything from the waist down. I didn't say you couldn't flash. But if you show anything from the waist down you get disqualified....Anybody else have anything they want to put in the office right now, to have it guarded?

APPREHENSIVE GIRL: Me. Take me in the office and guard me.

— **from documentary filmed at Mother's Bar in Chicago, 1976**

All strippers are self-conscious. You have to be, totally naked in front of a bunch of strange men. All you can think of is how you look to them. The strangest things pass through your mind, like, "I never should have eaten that doughnut for lunch." You become convinced it landed on your hips. You worry about the monthly water-weight crisis. Water weight feels worse than it looks. You feel spongy and fat, but your breasts look great...

What do dancers do when they get their period? This is one of the most common questions asked about strippers. Some girls book off, but most continue to dance. Often they use a diaphragm and a tampax and either hide the string or cut it off. They change frequently. I must admit, though, I've seen more than one string fall down into sight...

Some people thrive on dancers' self-consciousness. A plastic surgeon used to come around to watch the shows. When the show was over, he'd say to the dancers, "You would look so much prettier with a nose job," or, "Your breasts are so flabby," or, "You need a little nip and tuck in the tummy," or "A face-lift would take years off you." After he'd totally reduce you to a mass of jelly, he'd hand you his card and be gone. He got a lot of business that way. I always thought he was insensitive and totally unprofessional. Some girls found it impossible to perform after talking to him.

— *Queen of Burlesque*, an autobiography by Yvette Paris

Previous generations of American song have always been sexy to some degree, but nothing could prepare the country for this onslaught of hormone-mad beasts. Even Sinatra in his prime couldn't compete with a sweaty, long-haired rock god swinging a Les Paul guitar, singing about wanting to be your "backdoor man," hip-hugger pants full to bursting with a teenage girl's worst nightmare. Billie Holiday might have had a sultry voice, but how could she compare to a primal scream emitting from a braless Tina Turner or Janis Joplin, shimmying in a multi-orgasm trance?

This period of music's overt sexuality was unprecedented in history, and manifested not only

Turn It Up

in lyrics and album art, but live performance and crowd behavior at clubs and concerts. Sex was inescapable, spanning across all genres, from pop to soul, country, rock, blues and jazz. You couldn't turn on the radio without hearing someone singing about "making sweet love," or "once, twice, three times a lady." Admittedly, much of it seems sexist in retro-spect, but the women were steadily gaining on the men, learning to own their sexual allure, striking nasty poses for their album covers and *Rolling Stone* photo spreads. It wouldn't be long before girl groups made a comeback, and when they did, we were con-fronted with the apparition of the slutty Runaways.

Pretty faces have been used for years to sell records, and the 1950s saw a slew of young

SOMETHING'S BURNING: *(clockwise from top) Crooner Tom Jones and an uncharacteristically covered-up chest; Trademark hip shakes and fingernails from Tina Turner; The Ohio Players developed a sweet tooth*

A 1973 issue of *Oui* magazine proclaimed that Johnny Mathis had gotten more women pregnant than any man who ever lived. Simultaneously, rumors circulated that he was gay. Man or woman, who could resist that smile?

The 1968 album *Two Virgins* by John Lennon and Yoko Ono sold one million copies in advance, but the record had to be distributed with a brown paper overleaf hiding everything but their faces.

well-coiffed women gracing the covers of bossa nova, lounge and easy listening records, but by the '60s it exploded into all-out raunch. Among the best examples of this exploitation were the Ohio Players, whose entire oeuvre of album photography — naked women covered in dripping honey or wrapped in fire hoses, with the band peeking out from around a thigh — was one bush shot away from porn. Dolly Parton barely kept the basketballs covered, photo assistants helped Tanya Tucker yank on the skin-tight pants — even Carly Simon, Cher and Linda Rondstadt were flashing their nipples, to the delight of young boys who lingered in music stores, flicking through the albums. Taking the idea to the extreme, John and Yoko's full-frontal nude *Two Virgins* album cover left nothing to the imagination, but it had to be shipped to stores in a plain brown wrapper. One controversial promotional image for the Rolling Stones' 1975 album *Black and Blue* featured a young girl straddling the record, bound and bruised. Model Anita Russell was thought to be too beautiful to portray the down and dirty S/M image the Stones wanted, but once she emerged from make-up and wardrobe, she appeared so convincing, so the story went, that Mick Jagger graciously helped tie her up for the shoot.

People materialized out of the ether to specialize in this burgeoning area of interest. A 1963 album called *Erotica*, a recording of two people fucking, was aired on avant-garde FM radio stations. Topless girl bands appeared in nightclubs. Country troubadour Kinky Friedman adopted the persona of Chinga Chavin, who played a guitar made from a toilet seat, and released an album of X-rated songs. John and Yoko spent their honeymoon in an Amsterdam bed, surrounded by the international media. The 1970s band 10cc chose its name to refer to a measurement of human sperm — since a 9cc emission of ejaculate was considered normal or standard, obviously, 10cc was superhuman. Ex-pharmacist Barry Kerr staged a multi-media event titled "An Evening With The Flasher" at Manhattan's Beacon Theater, billing the show as "the first X-rated concert." The evening featured footage of Kerr's own porn film, *Forbidden Under Censorship of the King*, a rock band called Pool-Pah, go-go girls and strippers. Reviews were tepid, and Kerr later admitted to a reporter, "To tell the truth, this was the first time we had actually run through the entire show." Also in New York, the classical music community saw the concert debut of Charlotte Moorman, the world's only topless cellist. Despite earning a Master's of Music at the University of Texas, studying at Juilliard and playing with the American Symphony Orchestra, Moorman gained her notoriety by performing bare-breasted, and getting arrested for indecent exposure.

But such shenanigans would not be restricted to classical music. Frantic girls stripped off their panties and bras and threw them at hairy-chested crooners like Tom Jones and Englebert Humperdinck. Iggy Pop and Jim Morrison popped their noodles to audiences. Grace Slick once sucked a lollipop and hoisted her bare breasts to approaching storm clouds, hoping to stop the impending rain (it didn't work). The Tubes' concerts featured porn movies playing above the band, topless back-up singers and a free admission policy to anyone who arrived naked. While the rest of the Stones jammed behind him, Mick Jagger hopped aboard a giant phallus and rode it out over the audience, until confetti blew out of the tip and shot all over the crowd. An X-rated act called Blowfly featured hot chick dancers and a repertoire of songs like "All Aboard the Fuck Train."

With all this taking place onstage, one would think offstage would be just as promiscuous. It was. Fueled by the music, as well as a variety of liquids, chemicals and powders, people were foresaking the show in favor of nightclub bathroom trysts all over the country, from San Francisco's Fillmore and the Whisky-Au-Go-Go on Sunset Strip, through the Heartland terrain on over to the Fillmore East and CBGB's, where snot-nosed street punks peered through holes in the walls to watch. Monster live shows like Woodstock, the infamous Day on the Green concerts and the nationally televised California Jam '74 were famous for chicks stripping off their tank tops while sitting on guys' shoulders, and why stop there? Couples were soon sneaking off to scrump in the bushes like hogs in heat, oblivious to the show they had crashed to see.

One stopping-off place for rock bands in Los Angeles was called the Castle, a crumbling old mansion in the Hollywood Hills with high ceilings, grand pianos, and a tower room. Amidst the overgrown grounds and dirty swimming pool, bands like the Jefferson Airplane and the Velvet Underground hosted the sort of degenerate drug orgies that one would expect from such company. Other groups like the Allman Brothers gained reputations for their all-night hotel orgies, with hairy hippies rolling around on the floor of the Holiday Inn, everyone

In designing the cover of the Rolling Stones' 1971 album *Sticky Fingers*, Andy Warhol's original idea of photographing actual severed human fingers was abruptly shelved. The next best idea was to use an image of a well-endowed guy's crotch. Although rumored to be Mick Jagger's crotch, the image was one of three crotch shots of three different models. Warhol used one shot for the outer Levi's crotch, and one for the inside sleeve Jockey shorts crotch, and never told the models which one he used.

There was always a big sex scene with us. The White Panthers were the party of dope, rock and roll, and fucking in the streets — but mostly fucking in the streets! That was our crusade — *the act*. The act was more important than the person you did it with 'cause it represented freedom. Our van was like a rolling fucking mattress. And of course we used "free love" as a pickup line. It was like if you wouldn't do anything you were being counter-revolutionary! Fucking was like playing music. In fact, I still look at music like a sex act.

— interview with MC5 bassist **Michael Davis** in *Motorbooty*, **1990**

ALL THE SEX THAT FITS:
Rolling Stone *kept tabs on who's hot, from David to Donna*

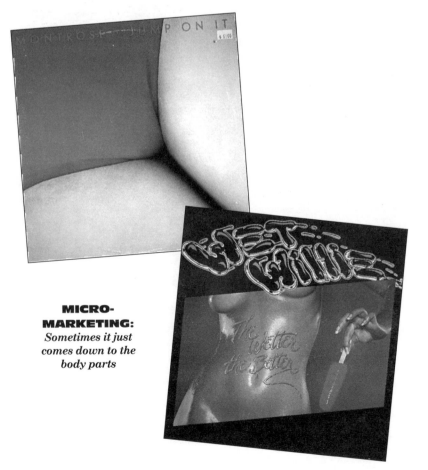

MICRO-MARKETING:
Sometimes it just comes down to the body parts

tweaked out of their minds on speed. Cocaine was so much a part of the Manhattan music sex scene that it became known as "Brill Building Aspirin."

Although many have pointed to disco as an urban gay phenomenon, heteros also hit the dance floor throughout the '70s, gamely learning silly moves like "The Hustle," if they didn't, they weren't going to get laid. Even in the Midwest, thousands of miles from Studio 54, discos were opening up near campuses and shopping districts, complete with shag carpet up the walls and dance floors with blinking colored lights. It didn't make much sense to listen to disco by yourself — you had to seek out the scene. Guys were primping themselves with leisure suits and platforms, and girls were squeezing into spandex unitards and roller-skating shorts, all to shake shake shake their booties on a 10-square foot floor of red and blue tiles, accompanied by one-shot hits like "Funkytown," "The Hustle," or an absurdly remixed disco version of "1812 Overture." Coke spoons glinting between the lapels added to a guy's appeal to women, and the females' ultra-tight dresses slit way up the side guaranteed them a male companion for the rest of the night.

Urban myths circulated. After one of his concerts, a gallon of sperm was supposedly found in Elton John's stomach. Or was it Rod Stewart's stomach? Or was it Rod Stewart's sperm, in Elton John's stomach? One of the better stories concerned a 1967 drug raid on a party at Keith Richard's England estate. Nineteen police supposedly came upon a raunchy orgy in progress, with Mick Jagger to be found eating a Mars bar out of Marianne Faithfull's vagina. While it was true that Richard, Jagger, Faithfull and six other male guests were lounging about watching TV and listening to music, with Faithfull clad only in an orange fur bedspread, there was no orgy, and therefore no chocolate cunnilingus. Faithfull later admitted that she had given the cops a brief flash of her nude body, a detail immediately seized upon by the newspapers, but confirmed that was the extent of the orgy. She wrote in her own autobiography: "Mick retrieving a Mars Bar from my vagina, indeed! It was far too jaded for any of us even to have conceived of. It's a dirty old man's fantasy — some old fart who goes to a domina-trix every Thursday afternoon to get spanked. A cop's idea of what people do on acid!"

The porn business provided interesting gigs for some musicians, some of whom actually allowed their real names to be credited.

Elephant's Memory, who recorded with John Lennon, provided music for many film soundtracks, including "You Want to Love Me and I Want to Love You" from *The Opening of Misty Beethoven*, and the title theme from *Take Off*. Wall of Voodoo's version of "Ring of Fire" was used in the cowgirl sequence of *Nightdreams*, The Plugz's "Electrify Me" graced the soundtrack of *New Wave Hookers*. The Andrea True Connection — responsible for the hit disco single "More More More" — was fronted by former porn star Andrea True. Marilyn Chambers sung the title tune from her own film *Insatiable*, called "Shame on You." Forgotten until recently, this material is now repackaged in stores for your convenience.

But even if you never attended a single concert or went to a nightclub, America was still taunted with sexually suggestive music, via the radio. This was the emergence of the first generations of youth who could boast not only of premarital sex, but of the songs that conjured up that initial magic moment. If you were female, the first time a boy put his hand down your pants might well have been accompanied with "Baby Hold On" by Eddie Money, and if you were a guy, the first time your girlfriend let you put it inside her may have been serenaded by Labelle's "Goochie goochie ya ya ya" or the sax solo from Gerry Rafferty's "Baker Street."

While adults nodded to the songs in frisky agreement, children were tapping their toes, completely unaware that the Atlanta Rhythm Section's hit single "Imaginary Lover" was actually a ditty about jerking off. Charlie Rich sang about getting behind closed doors, when the girl makes the guy "glad that I'm a man." Ray Stevens recorded a novelty song about the nation's obsession with streaking. The Isley Brothers begged the girl to "take me to the next phase." The Starland Vocal Band nudged and winked to listeners about afternoon delights. Ian and Silvia's "Pillow Talk" got down to basics, as did Joe Tex's "I Gotcha," or Donna Summer's "Love to Love You, Baby." Whether AM or FM, lyrics poured out of the speakers at such alarming levels of lewdness that in 1971 Vice President Spiro Agnew launched an effort to clean up rock music, sending out a warning that radio stations might lose their licenses. Nobody listened, and Agnew resigned under corruption charges. It would take the formation of Tipper Gore's Parents' Music Resource Center in 1985 to pave the way for those "explicit content" warning labels, and we all know how effective those have been.

UNDERWEAR IS FOR PRUDES:
Arresting album art by Linda Ronstadt, Tanya Tucker and Carly Simon

Why don't we do it in the road? / No one will be watching us
— **The Beatles**

Here I am, baby, come and take me
— **Al Green**

She's a lady / and the lady is mine
— **Tom Jones**

And when she gets behind closed doors / Then she lets her hair hang down / And she makes me glad that I'm a man / Cause no one knows what goes on behind closed doors
— **Charlie Rich**

You know that I need a man / You know that I need a man / When I ask you to, you just tell me, maybe you can
— **Janis Joplin**

Brown sugar, how come you taste so good? / Brown sugar, just like a black girl should
— **Rolling Stones**

He gave the ladies a lick and a promise
— **Aerosmith**

Sitting here jacking off reading Playboy / you've got me in a ball trap
— **Rod Stewart**

Five bob job / She gets bubble gum on her knees
— **Nick Gilder**

Stoop down baby, and let your daddy see / You got somethin' down there baby, worryin' the hell out of me
— **Chick Willis**

Do I have to put my handcuffs on you, mama? / Do I have to keep you under lock and key?
— **Parliament**

Torn between two lovers, feelin' like a fool
— **Mary McGregor**

We can share the women, we can share the wine
— **Grateful Dead**

That's why they call him The Streak / Fastest thing on two feet
— **Ray Stevens**

Lay lady lay / Lay across my big brass bed
— **Bob Dylan**

I got a rocket in my pocket / The way for you to stop it — rock it
— **Little Feat**

Put your hand in my pocket / grab onto my rocket
— **Kiss**

I'm lying peaceful and my knees are open to the sun / I desire him
— **Patti Smith**

I got something that'll sho 'nuff set your stuff on fire
— **Rufus, featuring Chaka Khan**

Way down inside, honey, you need it / I'm gonna give you my love
— **Led Zeppelin**

She reached over and she squeezed on my rocks / I lost it all in the popcorn box
— **Starz**

I got my cock in my pocket and I'm shovin' it through your pants / I just want to fuck you and I don't want no romance
— **Iggy Pop**

Don't pull your love out on me baby / If you do, then I think that I'll maybe just lay me down and cry for a hundred years
— **Hamilton, Joe Frank & Reynolds**

Yummy yummy yummy I got love in my tummy
— **Ohio Express**

Jam up and jelly tight / You look a little naughty but you're so polite
— **Tommy Roe**

Makin' love in my Chevy van and that's alright by me
— **Sammy Johns**

Do it, do it, do it 'til you're satisfied
— **BT Express**

Ooh, I need a dirty woman / Ooh, I need a dirty girl
— **Pink Floyd**

Pretend your face is a Maserati and it's looking for her garage
— **Ted Nugent**

Take me baby for your little boy / You're gettin' 300 pounds of heavenly joy
— **Howlin' Wolf**

Just let your love flow like a mountain stream / And let your love grow with the smallest of dreams
— **Bellamy Brothers**

Gimme some lovin' every day
— **Spencer Davis Group**

Don't you struggle, don't you fight / Don't you worry 'cause it's your turn tonight / Let me put my love into you, babe
— **AC/DC**

Kiss my aura, Dora. Mmm, it's real angora. Would you all like some more-a? Right here on the floor-a?
— **Frank Zappa**

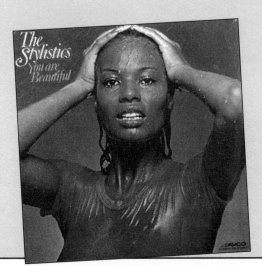

Though it's cold and lonely in the deep dark night / I can see paradise by the dashboard light
— **Meat Loaf**

I must have been through about a million girls / I love 'em, then I leave 'em alone
— **Elvin Bishop**

Wham bam thank you ma'am
— **David Bowie**

They can't compete with that pillow talk of mine
— **Ian and Sylvia**

Benihana, like a flower / What a turn-on
— **Marilyn Chambers**

It's Friday night, I need a fight / If she don't spread I'm gonna bust her head
— **The Sweet**

Me and Mrs. Jones, we got a thing goin' on / We both know that it's wrong, but it's much too strong to let it go
— **Billy Paul**

Here come the dancers, one two three / It's all part of my fantasy
— **Bad Company**

What a difference a lay makes
— **Blowfly**

Mississippi queen, she taught me everything
— **Mountain**

Where the little girl in the Hollywood bungalow? / Are you a lucky little lady in the City of Lights?
— **The Doors**

If you can't be with the one you love, love the one you're with
— **Stephen Stills**

I'll have to keep you pleased in every way I can / Gonna give you all of me as much as you can stand
— **Barry White**

Do a little dance / Make a little love / Get down tonight
— **KC & the Sunshine Band**

More, more, more / How do you like it, how do you like it?
— **Andrea True Connection**

You and I don't pretend we make love / I can't feel any more than I'm singing / I'm in you....
— **Peter Frampton**

She said, "You don't look like my type, but I guess you'll do" / Third-rate romance, low-rent rendezvous / He said, "I'll even tell you that I love you, if you want me to"
— **Amazing Rhythm Aces**

Imaginary lover never goes away / it's my private pleasure
— **Atlanta Rhythm Section**

Wang dang doodle, all night long
— **Koko Taylor**

My ding-aling / I wanna play with my ding-aling
— **Chuck Berry**

Just let me know, if you wanna go, to that home out on the range / They got a lotta nice girls
— **ZZ Top**

Gotta get on up, like a sex machine
— **James Brown**

If you want a do-right, all-day woman, you gotta be a do right, all night man
— **Aretha Franklin**

I say coke, she say yes / Dim the lights, you can guess the rest
— **Roxy Music**

Show her she's your favorite gal / stick your tongue in her birth canal
— **the Gizmos**

You know what I'm talkin' about / Come on baby, let your love come out / If you believe in love, let's get it on
— **Marvin Gaye**

Bang a gong, get it on, get it on
— **T. Rex**

Well, all night long you star with me in a soapbox fantasy / Making cum stains on the pillow where your sweet head used to be
— **Chinga Chavin aka Kinky Friedman**

She's a very kinky girl / One you won't take home to Mother
— **Rick James**

LIFE BEFORE TIPPER GORE:
(clockwise from top left) Blind Faith's nod to pedophilia; Frampton comes apart; Charlie Rich makes an offer; The Cars bring back Vargas; Iggy Pop with his pants on; Funkadelic on the art of the dance; The Stylistics get wet; Al Green wants YOU

They were young, independent and adventurous, and their job took them around the world to exotic lands. Their friends were their co-workers. Most had attended college, but this was a different kind of education altogether. These new breed of stewardesses were there to represent the airline with a friendly smile, and help a traveling businessman (at that time primarily male) make his trip worthwhile and memorable. They smiled, mixed drinks, adjusted pillows and sashayed down the narrow aisles in the airline-required uniform of tight mini-skirt and knee-high boots.

Come Fly Me

Obviously, they were complete nymphomaniacs. Or at least that's how it seemed. As the travel industry blossomed in the 1960s, and more Americans were flying for business reasons, the airlines experienced a shortage of stewardesses. To boost recruitment, ads appeared in women's magazines and campus newspapers, begging young women to join up and see the world. American Airlines boasted that its stews could swim in the Pacific, ride horses in Arizona and ski in New England, all in one week. Pan Am was looking for "well-proportioned, attractive" young women. Eastern spoke of its Miami instruction center as the "finest school for

WE'LL SHAKE OUR TAIL FOR YOU: *(clockwise from top) Three-dimensional porn, tours of swinging London, and cross-state commuting, Texas-style*

To inaugurate a jet-passenger service, an airline invited a number of VIP's to take the first flight. After the trip was under way, the pilot's voice came over the intercom, making the usual "our flight time will be..." announcements to the passengers, and after a moment he said, "I could really go for a coffee and a blowjob right now." An embarrassed stewardess, realizing he had inadvertantly left on his microphone intercom, raced up the aisle to inform the pilot. Just as she was about to enter the cabin, one of the VIP's called after her, "You forgot the coffee, honey!"

— urban legend in circulation during the 1970s

**SEEK AND
YE SHALL FIND:**
*Sometimes all you have
to do is ask*

Want to be
An Airline
Flight Attendant?

OUR MONTHLY NEWSLETTER AND
INFORMATION PACKET CAN HELP YOU!

For FREE INFO clip & mail to:
SKYLINE
E. TROPICANA, SUITE 727C
S VEGAS, NEVADA 89109

State _____ Zip _____

LL FREE 1·800·634·6167

Instant Gratification!

Introducing QuickieTicket! Southwest Airlines' new instant ticket machines that let you ticket yourself in under 30 seconds! It's as easy as 1) pass your credit card through the slot; 2) select your destination; 3) choose either Executive or Pleasure Class; 4) push whether you want one way or round trip. Then just take your ticket and head for the gate! So if you don't have time for a warm smile or a friendly "How do you do!", just stop by Quickie. And get your ticket in an instant!

That's love, Southwest style!

IQ of at least 105
Height between 62 and 69 inches tall
Slim, well-proportioned figure.
— **United Airlines requirements for stewardesses, 1965**

brides in the country." United Airlines instituted a crash program to immediately hire 1,600 stews. According to a United personnel manager, quoted in a 1965 *Newsweek* article entitled "Girls, Girls, Girls," their stewardesses had to be nothing short of miracle workers, able to dazzle even the crankiest commuter: "It is she who has to supply the magic quality that makes him come away smiling, even when his steak was cold or he had his martini served in a paper cup."

A United recruiter stressed to a reporter that "We are not looking for the Jayne Mansfield type," but one eager young applicant admitted, "Let's face it, becoming an air stewardess is still one heck of a good way for most girls to get a husband."

The founding of Southwest Airlines in 1971 signalled a bold new direction for airlines in general, and stewardesses in particular. To promote their revolutionary every-seat-the-same pricing policy, President Lamar Muse devised a bold public relations campaign for the fledgling Dallas, Texas airline that took advantage of the state's natural resource of beautiful young women. As the Dallas Cowboys football team would do a year later with its squad of half-naked cheerleaders, Southwest was unabashed about using the image of an attractive stewardess to turn heads and take advantage of the current fashion trends of hot pants and mini-skirts. Billboards and advertisements emphasized comely Texas beauties in go-go boots, running their hands along the back of a chair, offering the camera a cocktail with a sweet come-hither smile. Muse even wrote an open letter to sex symbol Raquel Welch, asking if she wouldn't mind putting her acting career on hold to come work for the company. This obvious sexual tease complemented perfectly the fact its home base was located at Love Field in Dallas, and begat the self-titled nickname, "Love Airline." Southwest's rapid growth was unprecedented for a young airline, and a U.S. Department of Transportation study would later describe the company as, "the principal driving force behind dramatic fundamental changes" in the industry.

Other airlines followed suit. Pan Am ran advertising campaigns with soft-focus photos of beautiful young servile women. While Continental adopted the suggestive catchphrase "We'll shake our tail for you!" PSA announced "Come Fly Me!" and promoted its flights with images of stewardesses shaking pom-poms. Many air carriers' regulation uniforms specified high heels, visible cleavage and mini-skirts that ended six inches above the knees.

With such a bounty of young beauties soaring the friendly skies and taunting motorists from magazine ads and the nation's highways, an image soon circulated that stews were ravenous man-hungry sluts ripe for the plucking, surfing an insatiable, never-ending quest for male companionship, whether it be marriage or just a quick tryst during an aptly named "layover." She became aviation's equivalent of the French maid, waltzing up and down the aisle dressed in skimpy attire, doting on men, attending to their every whim. America beheld its newest fetishistic icon. She saw herself on television as the butt of racy jokes by Johnny Carson and Woody Allen, and as a willing accomplice in the "Mile High Club." Publishers and film producers wasted no time in capitalizing upon the phenomenon, and stewardesses became the focus of numerous books and movies.

One of the earliest of these efforts was the 1963 film *Come Fly With Me*, a Hollywood comedy about three stewardesses trying to catch husbands, starring Hugh O'Brien, Karl Malden and a bevy of young actresses. Other mid-'60s movies and TV shows utilized flight attendant characters, but it would take a best-selling book to burn the myth into America's brain.

Coffee Tea or Me? (The Uninhibited Memoirs of Two Airline Stewardesses) appeared in 1967, chronicling the ribald adventures of two horny stewardesses named Trudy Baker and Rachel Jones. While the prose read suspiciously as if ghostwritten, the book resonated with a public who either had witnessed such behavior, or were willing to believe wild stories that perpetuated the myth. Trudy and Rachel gleefully recounted their favorite U.S. cities, and provided an eyelash-batting "stew's-eye view" of each town. Atlanta was noted for the Kitten's Korner bar, which ran free tabs for stews. Montreal featured plenty of mounties who took them on dates in canoes, the structural design of which "provides relative protection from too vigorous advances." Detroit was mentioned for its "ample male population who know where the action is and who are willing to spend money to make it happen." Chicago's hometown girls were too jealous of the layover stews, and kept their prized males out of reach, and Texas was, well, Texas: "In Dallas, the stewardess sport is to cruise the streets in search of young oil tycoons. Once you've exhausted that possibility, you go after old oil tycoons."

A 1973 made-for-TV comedy based on the book, also titled *Coffee Tea or Me?*, starred John Davidson, Louise Lasser and Karen Valentine as the busy stewardess who juggled two husbands

Engineers
Gravely lacking any background, academic or practical, in the arts or humanities, engineers will try to make chit-chat about the aircraft's performance characteristics or outer space or why the ball always comes down after it goes up. It's best to feign ignorance if you're interested; engineers hate anyone to know anything about their sphere of knowledge.

Actors
Actors usually try very hard to appear humble. They expect this unexpected humility to completely sweep a girl off her feet, or at least result in an autograph request or a quickie in the jump seat...Every stewardess accepts a date with an actor at least once in her flying career.

Doctors
The stewardess consensus is that doctors usually make their pitch via a note placed on their tray after dinner. Usually, it will contain something terribly clever like, "I am a doctor. I'm staying at the Mark Hopkins. My room number is 2030. Nine o'clock."

Politicians
If you do become

entwined with a politician, you can count on a secret, over-the-shoulder romance that must be carried on between votes on poverty programs and fund-raising appearances with his wife. It's better in the long run to stay away from politicians unless you figure they're going to lose in their next election and return to private life. When that happens, they're likely to divorce their wives for losing the election or them, and might even consider taking you on as a permanent addition to their new household and career.

Newspaper Men
Obviously, newspapermen are spoiled by your public relations department. In fact, they're spoiled and drunk enough to think you come with booze, food, limousine and free ticket. Their approach is often direct, clumsy, distasteful, arrogant, lewd and highly annoying.

Advertising Men
Advertising men are insecure. Their need to conform to every little whim of fashion indicates this. And because they're insecure, they approach us as they would a potential account, anxious to get

all they can now because tomorrow we might sign up with another agency.

Teachers
If you've been around at all you know that female teachers rank among the world's greatest swingers. Put a knowledgeable guy in a bar loaded with women of different backgrounds and he'll head for the teacher. He knows. The same goes for the masculine version...both sexes are weary of being looked at constantly by their boards of education for any violation of the highest code of personal conduct. Put them on an airplane where there isn't likely to be that scrutiny and you've got a man or woman on the prowl.

— from *Coffee Tea or Me?* by Trudy Baker and Rachel Jones, 1967

on different continents.

Naturally this concept was too rich to waste on television and bookstands, and adult film producers chimed in with a series of X-rated stewardess romps. Ads for one late-'60s effort titled *The Stewardess* boasted, "Now at last on the wide-screen — the most talked about girls in America — the one, the only...*The Stewardess*. The unpublishable novel is now America's most controversial film!" A 1969 film by Sherpix, Inc., *The Stewardesses*, was originally a softcore exploitation story of a group of acid-tripping stewardesses who utilize an 18-hour layover in Honolulu to embark on an extended orgy with the crew and passengers, one stew fantasizing about having sex with a table lamp in the form of a Greek marble bust. The result apparently was so popular that the adult production company Caballero re-edited the film with hardcore porn sequences spliced into the story, and released it under the same title in 1981.

Among many other porn versions, *The Swinging Stewardesses* was released in 1972, portraying four stewardesses on a transatlantic flight to Zurich, each taking up with a different guy. In Radley Metzger's 1976 *The Opening of Misty Beethoven*, starring Jamie Gillis and Constance Money, the updated *My Fair Lady* storyline featured transatlantic airline flights that offered passengers First Class with Sex, or First Class Non-Sex. *Love Airlines* from 1978 starred X-rated household name Georgina Spelvin as the president of Sex Airlines, where porn movies were screened continuously throughout all flights, and the stewardesses serviced male passengers. *Rockin' With Seka* appeared in 1980, featuring Seka as a lollipop-sucking stewardess named Sweet Alice, and a 1983 hardcore remake of *Coffee Tea or Me?* featured Tara Aire, Erica Boyer, Jamie Gillis and Paul Thomas.

Stewardesses today are old news. "Flight attendants" is the preferred term, and instead of nubile college co-eds, men and women of all ages are serving airline passengers their sodas and peanuts. Airlines have expanded their reach to embrace the growing family travel market, and stews as a porn film genre have gone the way of candy-stripers and cheerleaders.

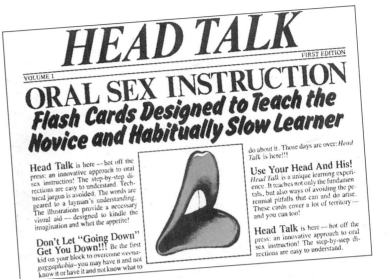

WORDS OF WISDOM:
Humorous advice books on how to properly administer oral sex, written by a stewardess for a major airline

Thank you for finally recognizing the fact that women, when given the opportunity, enjoy nude pictures of the male body. We think it's a great beginning but we have a suggestion for improving your future editions:

Show more! You're covering the best part!

We feel that women should have the opportunity to see pictures of the male body without turning to smut literature. Bravo to you for your first efforts in this direction.

747 Cabin Crew enroute to Honolulu — Lin, Carol, Karen, Linda, Lile, Ellen, Marlene, Sue, Jan, Alice, Goldie, Maureen, Mary Kay, Lynn, Celeste, Kathy, Beverly

— letter to the editor of *Playgirl*, September 1973

From the most expensively produced men's magazine, on down to a ratty massage parlor ad tabloid in a puddle on the bus station floor, America received more and more sex journalism as the era wore on. Presses across the nation were churning out nudity — cheery co-eds playing peek-a-boo with a tree, bronze-chested firemen lounging on a redwood deck, hairy hippie couples playing hide-the-kielbasa — feeding the country's growing hunger for looking at photos of itself without clothes. Sandwiched between the flesh were articles, cartoons and other filler, but let's face it, most of this stuff was purchased to whack off. And occasionally,

ad All About It

some of it even got read.

For many men (and little boys, poking around their fathers' personal effects to find a copy), *Playboy* personified the pinnacle of the male pornographic experience. From its launch in 1955, to a peak circulation in 1972 of 7 million copies, the magazine remained approximately the same — nude young women with skinny waists and big breasts, lifestyle advice on how to be a cultured guy and articles on sports, religion, Nazis or the mob to remind you it wasn't all just about looking at titties. Hefner's magazine also actively donated money to sex-related causes, providing financial support through the Playboy Foundation for things like

ASK FOR IT BY NAME:
A sampling of mainstream newsstand spice

Si Non Oscillas, Noli
Tintinnare
(if you don't swing,
don't ring)

— **Latin inscription
in carved-wood door-
way of Hugh Hefner's
private chambers,
Playboy mansion,
1340 North State
Parkway, Chicago**

SPOILS OF VICTORY:
*Hugh Hefner's twin
accoutrements of girls
and casinos*

Staff at the Mansion were able to keep track of the master's
amorous activities by his Homeric consumption of Johnson's
Baby Oil. At one point, [Hefner personal assistant] Bobbie
Arnstein complained to [executive assistant Dick] Rosenzweig
that ordering the stuff was becoming an embarrassment —
crates containing fifty economy-size bottles were regularly
humped into his quarters by the housemen, manfully trying not
to smirk.

— **from *Bunny: The Real Story of Playboy* by Russell Miller, 1984**

legalized abortion campaigns and sex education
in schools. More so than any other men's
magazine, *Playboy* achieved some sense of
literary worth on the shelf — today, people deal
in vintage *Playboy*s across the world, poring
over lists of available issues like accountants,
noting condition, price and any distinguishing
photo spreads.

With such success came the much-discussed
eccentricities of its founder. Hefner's fondness
for Pepsi, round beds and baby oil became legendary, as was his increasing agoraphobia and
relentless pursuit of an idea. One of his memos
to the staff ran 39,000 words, another meeting
lasted for 26 hours straight. His empire grew to
include books, casinos (where Playmates could
frequently be seen shaking it on the disco floor
or cheering on a craps table), a DC-9 jet called
the Big Bunny and a 1968 television show called
Playboy After Dark, hosted by Hef himself.

A feminist backlash to the *Playboy* party
came early on, when Gloria Steinem put on the
bunny tail and went undercover to write an
exposé in a 1963 issue of *Show* magazine. Debbie
Harry, later the singer for Blondie, said the
most arduous requirement to be a bunny was to
"keep smiling while infuriated wives stubbed out
cigarettes on your thighs." The casinos and
hotels closed up, as did the book club and TV
show, and two expensive feature films, Roman
Polanski's *Macbeth* and an adaptation of the
book *The Naked Ape*, both lost money. Who
cared, the thing was still making millions.
Obviously the magazine idea was a winning formula, and should be imitated.

In the mid-'60s, an artist from Brooklyn
named Robert Charles Edward Sabatini
Guccione was selling mail-order pin-up pictures
in London, living off checks from his father. He
was an avid reader of *Playboy*, and decided to
start his own magazine based on its format. He
took the first photo session himself, in 45 minutes. The premiere issue of *Penthouse* ran
120,000 copies, selling out in five days, and gave
the world another classic twist on nude photos.
Because women were portrayed as being in a
constant state of self-examination, *Newsweek*
claimed they were caressing themselves as if
"they were looking for lumps." In October 1971
Guccione started a smaller-sized companion
magazine with less images and more stories
called *Forum*, designed to appeal to women. By
1985 *Forum* was printing over half a million
copies, its fictional letters about fraternity
orgies and horny housewives penned by out-of-
work writers. As with *Playboy*, the *Penthouse*

book clubs, casinos and films like *Caligula* would drain the coffers, eventually forcing the magazine to close down most projects and shift to videos and the internet.

In February 1970, *Penthouse* gave *Playboy* its first serious run for its money when they published the mainstream media world's first shot of pubic hair. Two months later, Guccione did it again, the issue selling out of 500,000 copies, and in August 1971 he followed it up with a full-frontal centerfold. *Playboy* realized it had to retaliate quickly in order to remain on top, and to save face ran a full-frontal nude foldout in January 1972. The great Pubic Wars began. Who could show more? The stage was set for someone to plumb the true depths of raunch.

"Anybody can be a playboy and have a penthouse," read the publisher's statement of *Hustler*'s 1974 premiere issue, "but it takes a man to be a hustler." White-trash topless bar owner Larry Flynt had cast his bid for pornographic immortality. Publishing from his hometown of Columbus, Ohio, and appealing to truckers and other working-class men, Flynt's magazine immediately distinguished itself with gnarly cartoons about bodily functions, nude Polaroids from readers and photo layouts of women with their vagina lips spread so wide, the reader felt like an amateur gynecologist. But Flynt still wasn't playing ball with the big boys yet.

In the spring of 1975, the young publisher was approached with a package of photos taken four years earlier. An Italian photographer had spent days baking in the sun in a small boat off the island of Skorpios, stalking the private estate of Jackie and Ari Onassis with a telephoto lens. One day Jackie O walked out of the house nude, looking younger and more attractive than her 41 years. The sweaty photographer quietly clicked off 48 shots, and since that time he had been attempting to sell them. A few ran in an Italian magazine named *Playmen*, and a few more in underground sex rags in New York, but America's newsstands had not yet seen them, and *Playboy* and *Penthouse* had both declined the offer. Flynt bought the shots of the former First Lady for $18,000, ran five of them full-page in his August 1975 issue, and within days had sold a million copies. The photo spread made international headlines, and with that one issue he claims he became a millionaire. Retailers reported that 60 percent of the sales were to women. Flynt further milked the idea by issuing a poster of one of the photos, and minting a silver-dollar-sized coin with her naked image on one side,

Hefner sits on the edge of the bed. Nice platinum-hazy light shines down from recessed rheostat dim-dim lovelies in the ceiling. His bathrobe collapses in nice highlife folds.

"How many times have I been out of this house in the last two years?" he says. He leans over and puts his head down practically between his knees. A wiry guy! "About nine times," he says, answering himself.

Then —

——heeeewack——

— he snaps upright, he pulls that great angular smile into his face, his high cheekbones move out.

"But I don't need to leave here. Why should I? I've got more right here now inside this house than most people ever find in a lifetime!"

— his eyes turn on — old shining Ampex moon — "I've got everything I want right here. This place is run like a hotel. I mean, I'll take you down and show — No, it isn't! Hotels shut off about two o'clock in the morning, you want to get something — This place is run like a hotel ought to be run. It goes 24 hours a day. There's a full kitchen staff 24 hours a day, a chef, anytime I wake up, I can get anything I want. I've got a staff of 25 people here on a 24-hour schedule. I've got an Ampex engineer on the staff! That's right! There's so much equipment in here, I had to have a — this must be the only house in the country with an Ampex engineer on the staff! I sent him to the Ampex school in San Francisco. He's on 24-hour call.

— from "King of the Status Dropouts" in *The Pumphouse Gang* **by Tom Wolfe, 1968**

OUT OF THE CHUTE:
Initial ad campaign propaganda for the fledgling Penthouse, *from Bob Guccione*

Pornographer Palaces

In 1978, Larry Flynt moved from his 24-room mansion in Columbus, Ohio, opposite a private school for girls, to a Beverly Hills home he leased from Jacqueline Bisset. He then purchased a Mediterranean mansion whose previous owners included Errol Flynn, Robert Stack and Sonny and Cher, and stuffed the place with antiques, including a collection of Tiffany stained-glass lamps. The basement would contain a life-size replica of the Kentucky cabin where he grew up, inside of which was a sauna. His Israeli-built Westwind jet was painted "labia-pink."

Bob Guccione contracted to have his two Upper East Side Manhattan townhouses combined into one, featuring Carrara marble floors, an indoor pool with blue tiles laced with pure silver grout, a 24-k gold mosaic whirlpool, a toilet carved from a solid block of marble, bronze sconces in the shapes of females touching their own breasts, millions of dollars of paintings, and a private hair salon.

Hugh Hefner's original Chicago mansion sported a round motorized bed, a king-sized water bed covered with Tasmanian opposum fur, and an extensive art collection. Upon moving to his 30-room mock Victorian-Gothic mansion in Los Angeles, he had the five-acre property remodeled to include a fish pond, swimming pool, lagoon, fake waterfalls and underwater grotto. His private DC-9 jet was painted black and furnished with a dance floor, disco, conference room, lounge and bar, gourmet kitchen, built-in video screens, sunken Roman bath and a 6 x 8 bed furnished in Himalayan goatskin with a spread of Tasmanian opposum pelts.

PRINCE OF PUBIC HAIR:
The emerging kingdom of Gooch

They were still fighting the sexual revolution. Our starting point was that the revolution had already been won.

— **Bob Guccione on** *Playboy*

and Ari Onassis and John F. Kennedy on the reverse.

To ensure his tastelessness, *Hustler* ran centerfolds of a 50-year-old woman, another who was eight months pregnant, and another who weighed 300 pounds. His pointed views would earn him a bullet from an intended assassin who has never been found, limiting him to a wheelchair the rest of his life. Like his predecessors, Flynt would cultivate many celeb friends, including Dennis Hopper, Frank Zappa and Timothy Leary. With the help of another woman connected to the White House, Ruth Carter Stapleton, he briefly became a born-again Christian, appointing Yippie satirist Paul Krassner to run *Hustler* in his absence.

America had three distinct men's porn rags, each innovative and much-imitated. Beginning with the noisy launches of both *Penthouse* and *Hustler*, each of which bad-mouthed the competition, no love would ever be lost between the gentlemen pornographers. In 1976, Flynt printed two cartoons in *Hustler*, one suggesting that *Penthouse* publisher Bob Guccione engaged in homosexual activity, and the other suggesting that Guccione's girlfriend, Kathy Keeton contracted VD from Guccione. Both sued Flynt for libel. Guccione won a $39.6 million judgement against *Hustler*, which was later overturned on appeal, but Keeton pushed her case all the way to the Supreme Court. Flynt demanded to defend himself to the court, and lost his temper, yelling, "You're nothing but eight assholes and a cunt!" He was removed and arrested for disrupting the courtroom. Charges were eventually dismissed, and Keeton's case was sent back to state court.

In 1972, Hefner heard that Daniel Filipacchi was planning to launch an American version of the French men's magazine *Lui*. Hefner stepped in and cut him out of the deal, and started up *Oui*. The first issue sold 750,000 copies in two weeks, but would later prove to be too costly to continue.

Yet another beef simmered between Hefner and Flynt, who apparently had in his possession a clandestine photograph of Hefner fucking his girlfriend. Flynt planned to publish the shot in *Hustler*. Hefner was made aware of this, and asked politely for the evidence. Flynt refused to give it up. Hefner took the high road, and invited Flynt to dinner at his Mansion. After a luxurious meal, Hefner introduced Flynt to his friends, and gave him a grand tour of the estate. At the end of the evening, which obviously made some impression, Flynt reached into his pocket

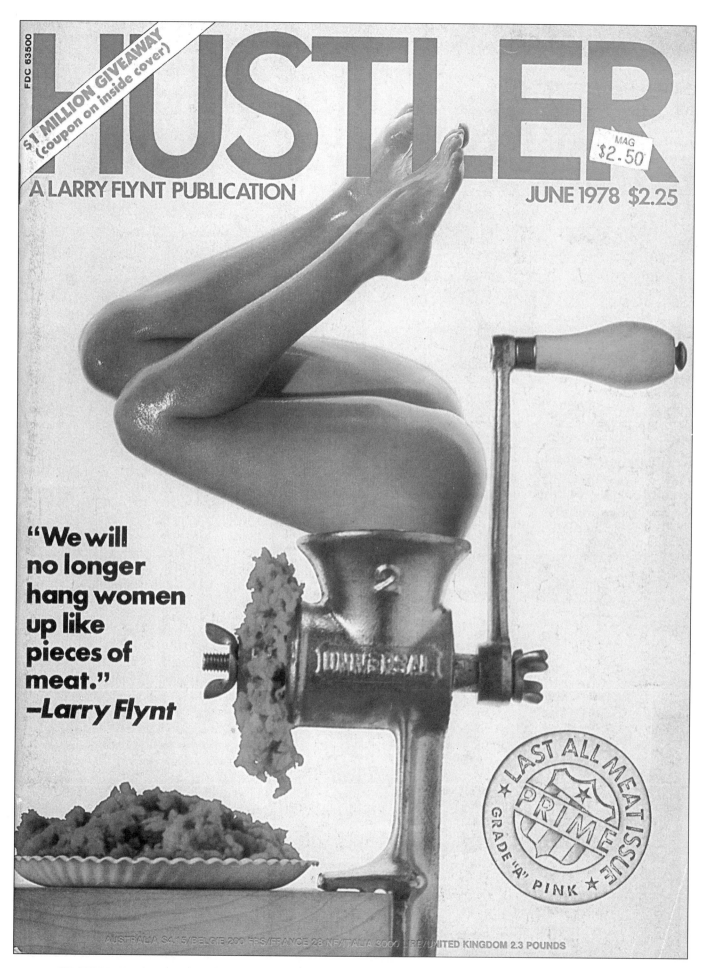

IF YOU CAN'T FIND 'EM GRIND 'EM: *The infamous cover used as a poster image by anti-porn feminists*

JACKIE O KING-SIZE POSTER

Decorate your den, shop, dorm-itory, office, or library with the ex-First Lady in the buff. Be a hit with your friends by having the most controversial conversation piece of the decade.

No. 3901 $4.95

JACKIE O

WHATEVER IT TAKES:
The Jackie O images that made Larry Flynt a millionaire

We at *Playboy* wish you a quick recovery. We stand firmly behind you and your Constitutional right of free speech, no matter whether it is attacked by appointed officials or self-appointed vigilantes [sic]. May you return to Columbus and to your presses soon.
— Hugh M. Hefner

We share your pain and hope for your quick recovery.
— Tom Hayden and Jane Fonda

All my prayers go with you.
— Garrett Morris

— letters to *Hustler* after Larry Flynt's 1978 shooting

and gave back the photo, assuring Hefner no copies were in existence.

But the controversy didn't end with the guys. After Douglas Lamber launched *Playgirl* in 1974, *Playboy* immediately filed suit because of the name. Despite such distractions, *Playgirl* tapped into a loyal audience for the time, selling 1 million copies by its third issue. Obviously there was room for nude male centerfolds on America's newsracks — including the chest shag of Lyle Waggoner and Fabian — and *Playgirl* can still be found on the magazine rack today.

Another magazine specifically for women (and whose back issues can now be found in gay sections of porn shops) was *Viva*, a short-lived concept started by Guccione in 1973 and turned over to his girlfriend/wife, Kathy Keeton. *Viva* boasted itself as being "edited by men who really love women for women who really love men," and Guccione staged its launch party at the Ambassador West Hotel in Chicago, just two doors down from the Playboy Mansion. It folded a very expensive six years later.
Cosmopolitan had been publishing for years, but its popularity soared under the direction of editor Helen Gurley Brown, author of the 1962 book *Sex and the Single Girl*. Their editorial message stressed that not only was it fun to be a frisky girl on the town, women should go out and snag the man they want. In April 1973 they published the first-ever nude centerfold, a grinning Burt Reynolds helping to sell 1,900,000 copies the first day he hit newsstands. Attempting to capitalize on the phenomenon, teen idol David Cassidy soon posed naked for *Rolling Stone*.

But with all this increase in magazines, there still weren't enough to go around. The market was wide open for more, including dueling swinger attorneys. *Gallery* debuted in October 1972, patterned after *Playboy* right down to the identical typeface, layouts and departments. Financier and computer entre-peneur Ronald Fenton established offices in Chicago across the street from *Playboy*'s, and opened up the Gallery Mansion, one block from the Playboy Mansion. The masthead boasted its publisher as being flamboyant attorney F. Lee Bailey, sporting enormous sideburns, who wrote the very first editorial. In that first issue, contributing a book review was Bailey's arch-rival, fellow flamboyant attorney Melvin Belli. Just over a year later, in January 1974, *Coq* magazine debuted, ostensibly put together by photographer George Santo Pietro, who also had his own mansion in downtown Chicago. Belli was listed on the premiere issue's masthead as legal counsel, and inside followed a long, glowing interview with the attorney.

Other men's magazines quickly followed. *Genesis* was edited by the former associate publisher of *Gallery*, and bankrolled by Japanese restaurant owner Rocki Aoki. The Melrose area of Los Angeles became a hub of publishing, producing several magazines including *Adam* and *Adam Film World*, which began in the 1960s as *Adam Film Quarterly*. In the early 1970s a young hippie named Marv Lincoln published 12 quarterly adult film magazines out of the same neighborhood, including *Wildest Films*, *Daring Films*, *Torrid Films*, *Fiery Films*, and *Cinema Close-Up*.

Other magazines took advantage of the country's fascination with sex. Andy Warhol's *Interview* — originally titled *inter/VIEW* — appeared in November 1969, and was careful to feature plenty of nudity from the beginning. The literary magazine *Evergreen*, started by Grove Press, never failed to include sexual material, and always placed a pretty young woman on its cover. After getting in legal problems with his erotica publication *Eros*, Ralph Ginzburg started up *Avant-Garde*, a magazine of the arts which showcased erotica in each issue. (Their motto would be "Down with bluenoses, blue laws and blue pencils.")

But for many Americans, slick glossy magazines were too uppity. Some citizens would never rise to such heights, never purchase such cool products or meet such beautiful women. It was clear there should be rags for the rest of the unwashed masses, and underground newspapers started up around the country — the *Chicago Seed*, the *East Village Other*, the *San Diego Door*. While all of them covered the emerging sexual revolution to some extent, either with articles, ads or comics, a few stuck out as true torch-bearers.

Launched in 1964 by Art Kunkin, the *L.A. Free Press* boasted it was the first underground newspaper which would print any word, any picture, any cartoon and any story. Known on the street as the "Freep," the publication was started with $15 and by the late 1960s had achieved 100,000 circulation. Contributors ranged from Frank Zappa, who edited a special music section, to Ed Sanders, who covered the Manson trial, and Harlan Ellison, who wrote a television column called "The Glass Teat." Articles on sex shared space with reviews of adult films, ads for Topanga Canyon nudist retreats, and of course, personals ads. In 1969

From the French "coq" meaning rooster. You have been told to pronounce it "coke," but that is not entirely correct. In French, "Coq" is an explosive voiceless velar followed by a closed voiceless velar vowel followed by yet another explosive voiceless velar. For those not up on their phonemics all this means is that the sounds are made further back in the mouth then [sic] the word "coke" is pronounced in English. Some of you rusty phonemical fanatics might proclaim that the consonant "c" is in reality an affricative voiceless velar. But you are dead wrong, for if that were the case **COQ** would come out sounding like "choke," which would really tax the already burdened taxemics of this beautiful word.

— **editors of *COQ*,** separating the wheat from the chaff, in their premiere issue, 1974

BAD-BOY BARRISTERS:
Twin tit mags from Melvin Belli and F. Lee Bailey

With this, its first issue, GALLERY Magazine is finally airborne. As with the design, construction and FAA certification of a new airplane, therre has been much agonizing and delay in getting her off the ground — but at last she is flying....

...So that potential contributors will know, I personally think good writing is very valuable, and I will constantly come to blows with the rest of management, stumping for higher rates until we can truthfully say that we pay "top dollar." If I am chronically outvoted on this issue, I have certain clients who can literally steal from our own coffers enough gelt to flesh out the budget...

...The weather along the route is forecast to be good, we fly above it most of the time anyway, and if we have to bore through some heavy stuff, we've got a sturdy ship that's well equipped for fog, snow, sleet, ice and turbulence. Ours is a fast bird with supersonic cruise and inflight entertainment of a high order. So try our airline for a while. It's going to be a blast.

Oh. One other thing. You'll be comfortable. All our seats are first class.

— **from "Publishers Statement"** by attorney F. Lee Bailey, premiere issue of *Gallery,* 1972

GIRLS DO IT:
*The dawn of female
erotica*

Kunkin printed the names, addresses and phone numbers of known California narcotics agents, which proved ultimately to be his downfall. Quality and size soon declined to a thin collection of raunchy personal ads and Kunkin eventually was forced to sell it to porn kingpin Marvin Miller, who fired him and folded the paper. In recent years Kunkin has resurrected the title as a Web-only publication.

The East Coast counterpart to the Freep was the arrival of a dirty little newspaper named *Screw*. One day in 1968, Jim Buckley, a typesetter at *New York Free Press*, came across a story by writer Al Goldstein about being an industrial spy for the Bendix Corporation. The two young men realized they shared a common frustration with not only their current roles in life, but the editorial policy of the *Free Press*, which continually played down the topic of sex. Each put up $165, and on November 4, 1968 they produced the first issue of *Screw*. Goldstein later said they named it *Screw* because he didn't want to call it *Hump* or *Love*, and they knew they couldn't sell it on the street if it was named *Fuck*. Circulation immediately rose, Goldstein claiming their heaviest sales came from Wall Street. Still published by Goldstein (Buckley left the picture some years ago), *Screw* delivers the best local coverage of the New York sexual scene, including club and massage parlor listings, "Peter-Meter" coverage of adult films, all laced with its trademark raunchy humor. The *Screw* empire has at various times included feature films, the late-night cable *Midnight Blue* series, a short-lived magazine about cigars and several homes which editor Goldstein claims he has been shanghaied out of by his ex-wives.

The *Berkeley Barb* was launched in 1965 by Max Scherr, a former law student and stringer reporter for UPI in Mexico. After opening a beatnik bar in Berkeley called the Steppenwolf, a focal point for local poetry readings and art displays, Scherr's increasing interests in politics and the emerging civil rights movement led him to encapsulate the goings-on at his bar into a newspaper. The first issue was "a rag of a sheet," according to his daughter Racquel, but by 1969 the *Barb*'s weekly circulation was up to 99,000. People were buying it on the streetcorners of Paris, its anti-institution slant mirroring the political unrest of the time. In its characteristic witty, sensational style, the *Barb* was the first media source to report on the Black Panthers, the feminist and folk music movements, the San Francisco Be-Ins, even printing letters from women in prison. It was also the first newspaper in the country to run personal ads, and since it was published from Northern California's Hippie Central, the tone gradually grew more sexual. While extremely profitable, the sex ads began scaring away other advertisers, Scherr found himself accused of sexism, and the *Barb* turned into a soap opera. After all, this was Berkeley, and nobody should have the right to oppress anyone else, even if you were publishing a hippie rag. Scherr's staff struck against him, and started up their own paper, the *Berkeley Tribe*. Amidst growing accusations of anti-Semitism, anti-women, anti-whatever, Scherr was bought out by investors, and stayed on as editorial consultant until the mid-'70s. The sex material was consolidated into a separate pull-out section called *The Spectator*, which still continues today. The *Barb* finally folded for good in July of 1980, and its founder died the following year.

Additional exploration into the sexual underground came courtesy of *The Realist*, a political satire magazine started by Paul Krassner in the 1950s that achieved its greatest relevance in the hippie era. In addition to first-hand coverage of political sexual events and interview with major players, *The Realist* found unprecedented notoriety for its poster of a graphic orgy involving the beloved Disney animation characters. Supposedly rendered by former *MAD* artist Wally Wood, among others, the Heironymous Bosch tableau portrayed an unbelievably raunchy vision of cartoon hell — Minnie Mouse sucking the penis of Donald Duck, Mickey sodomizing Pluto, Snow White treating the Seven Dwarves to a circle jerk, among other heinous activities. The poster became a staple of 1960s college dorm rooms, and was — along with LBJ secretly fucking the neck wound of JFK's corpse aboard Air Force One's flight out of Dallas — one of *The Realist*'s finer contributions to American journalism. After four decades, Krassner plans to soon cease publication for the second and perhaps final time.

A common syndrome among publishers is to consolidate several titles to share production and other expenses. This was also true of the hippie underground sex rags. In Chicago, Joseph Reece's umbrella company Compact Publications published several tabloid sex rags including the *National Informer* and *National Insider*, with swingers' personals, articles on adultery and oral sex, columnists Criswell and Church of Satan's Anton LaVey, and regular writers named "Jack Kopf" or "Ivan Urge."

THE NEXT WAVE: *Another crop of men's mags, with some of the models even still wearing clothing*

I went to distributors, the Mafia — they thought the paper was too dirty. They couldn't believe it. I'm attacking the church. I called J. Edgar Hoover a faggot. *Screw* made it by luck.

— Al Goldstein on his success, 1988

**SOMETHING'S
BEGINNING TO STINK:**
The unabashed turn to raunch

America, the land of the Puritan legacy, could now open the pages of a major magazine and find beautiful and sultry women in all their captivating desirability, nipples wrinkled, pubic hair bristling, vaginal lips parted, and eyes brimming with unfettered sensuality. The photographs, delightful in themselves, represented an attitude that was truly revolutionary: **the idea that eroticism needs no rationalization.**

...We believe that it is good for a man to have an erection and that it good for a women to feel her cunt throb with pleasure. It is good for people to embrace, to touch, to kiss, to fondle, to stroke, to lick, to suck, and even to spank or bite if they wish. We believe it is wonderful to fuck, however, wherever, whenever, and with whomever one wishes. So long as there is consent, as long as there is no damage.

— from introduction to collection of *Penthouse* articles

California's Jaundice Press, owned by Larry Rosenstein, aka "Baron of Beavers," was responsible for publishing *San Francisco Ball, Gaytimes* and *Fetish Times*, as well as a line of swinger mags including *National Swing*. A Los Angeles hippie consortium calling itself the Star Family published a quartet of raunchy newsprint sex rags called *Love, God, Hate* and *Finger,* and carved their unique niche by printing all drawings, photographs and writing submitted by their readers — typos and bad grammar intact. Stories ranged from outrageous incest relationships to bestiality, anal sex and genital shaving. *Finger* grew to 40,000 circulation before expiring in the late 1970s, and *Love* continued until 1981, its final issue co-edited by Annie Sprinkle, who wrote one article called "How to Fuck and Type at the Same Time," while pretty much fucking and typing at the same time.

Most amazing of all the sex rags were the weird one-offs, obscure magazines that would suddenly pop into existence, then just as suddenly disappear back down into the bowels of the underground. *Fuck You/A Magazine of the Arts* was one of the many 1960s magazines devoted to poetry. In this case it was exclusively erotic poetry, edited by Ed Sanders, later the author of *The Family.* Published from New Jersey, *Ups & Downs* called itself "the magazine that's blown the Establishment's collective minds!" and featured photos of wife-swapping couples, and everyday people having sex. After moving from their family farm in South Dakota to Hermosa Beach, California, the Dunker brothers — Robert M. and Thomas W. — decided to start their own sex magazine. In 1965 *Horseshit* magazine debuted, a production of "Scum Publishing Company," its articles and illustrations dwelling exclusively on sex and politics, infused with a heavy anti-government stance popular at the time. *Horseshit* published one issue a year for three or four years. The Dunker brothers might easily have summarized an entire era of publishing when they ran an ad in their magazine that read simply: "We're looking for people who like to fuck."

To BALL is to live...everything else is just waiting

— slogan of the *San Francisco Ball* **underground sex newspaper**

pee-pee and do-do go legitimate

SEX IN THE TOILET

ADULTS ONLY   (177)   SPECIAL CALIFORNIA EDITION • SALE OUTSIDE THE STATE FORBIDDEN $1.50

san francisco's explicit edition

BALL

FETISH TIMES PARTY
Event of the century covered in nauseating detail

TEEN BEACH NUDIES
Fried foxes flash on the sand

LOWEST COMMON MASTURBATOR:
The ultimate in underground press

Berkeley Barb

15¢ BAY AREA   20¢ ELSEWHERE

VOL. 6 No. 14 ISSUE 137 (PUB. FRIDAYS) MARCH 29–APRIL 4
2886 TELEGRAPH AVE., BERKELEY, CALIF. 94705 841-9470

FUZZ NO MATCH FOR SPRING SPIRIT

by Terry A. Reim

In Limekiln Creek last weekend, nearly 5,000 people gathered to joyfully celebrate the return of life to the earth, and to honor a man who was the living embodiment of the life force, Neal Cassady.

Many at the Limekiln fest had never heard of him. Neal was portrayed as Dean Moriarty, the lusty and loving hero of Jack Kerouac's "On the Road," the book that came to be called the Bible of the Beat Generation.

The celebration of the beginning of spring is one of the oldest religious experiences known to man. The ancient rite has been practiced for thousands of years to welcome the return of the life and fertility spirits for the reborn seasons.

And that was the mood at Limekiln. The picnic managed to engineer only a few bringdowns.

Consistent with the recent oppressive actions and death trend pervading the establishment, spokesmen of the Vernal Equinox celebration were busted Monday for "operating a camp-ground without a permit."

Vern Gates and Harold Tresey, of the Omega Point Foundation, which sponsored the festival, were

morning on $620 bail.

But the festival itself was an incredible success—success in the sense that as many people came, got close to one another, and got close to Mother Earth again.

The festival was a 3-day experience which began last Friday. Although most of the people arrived early Saturday morning, many of the OPF members and serious campers were present for the Friday festivities.

By mid-afternoon Saturday, close to 5,000 people had arrived; cars were parked along Route 1 for three or more miles above the festival area.

Where Limekiln Creek flows from the forest to the sea, hundreds of people were gathered on the beach, clothed in brightly colored garments or not at all.

Bottles of wine and joints were passed back and forth among the nature worshippers. Others sat on the beach simply smiling and staring out to sea or at the dozen bodies cavorting on spots above the fire.

IN SPRING A YOUNG CHICK'S FANCY...

CAMERA EYE (above) swung on Limekiln scenes from bridge piling, sighting Monterey Sheriff ready to bust two nude bathers (story) more pix, p.3). Meanwhile, at San Gregorio nude-in (below), 200 were nude but there were no busts

no.10 $1.50

FINGER

WITH CASSETTE $5.00

Copyright 1975 © Finger Magazine Diversified Publications, Inc.

taste the forbidden fruit

OH   GOD!

You Don't Mind About My Period, Do You?
Introduced to a Beautiful Life of Slavery by My Sister
Since the Age of Nine I Have Had a Foot Fetish
Curse of the Gigantic Tits

— examples of stories from the reader-written *Finger* **magazine, which was distributed inside a separate envelope**

GOOD GRIEF! ME A MOVIE!

CANDY

The sensational sex-spoofing bestseller*
by TERRY SOUTHERN & MASON HOFFENBERG
now a major motion picture

*Over 2,500,000 copies sold!

P2734

SIGNET

A SIGNET BOOK
COMPLETE AND UNABRIDGED

IAN FLEMING

A JAMES BOND THRILLER

THUNDERBALL

NOW A THRILLING MOTION PICTURE
Starring Sean Connery

007

In the grand pantheon of popular culture, sex in books seems to predate its peer material in film and stage, perhaps because the questionable materials were less expensive to produce, and certainly easier to conceal. As the 1960s unfolded, sex began sneaking into bookstores across the board, beginning first with highbrow European imports and by the 1970s rolled around, hack authors like Jacqueline Susann — even Catholic priests — were cashing checks along with the publishers of those cheap paperbacks sold in Times Square and corner liquor stores. Obviously, America liked a good story, particularly if there was plenty of sex thrown in. So much erotica hit bookstores, it drove Robert G.

Bedside Smut

Reisner to write *Show Me the Good Parts: The Reader's Guide to Sex in Literature* in 1964, listing exact page numbers and reviews of dirty scenes from every porn book ever written.

One reason erotica wasn't published much in America prior to the 1960s was because we were a young nation consumed with solving problems, says Michael Perkins in *The Secret Record*: "An optimistic, successful, and materialist culture is usually not a reflective one. But out of the sixties came a small but significant shift in the national consciousness, which created a receptivity to the demands of our secret selves. People began talking to each other about the quality of their lives. It was a period of inward exploration, when people sought

DOG-EARED DECLARATIONS:
(clockwise from top) Highbrow sex satire of Candy; *Greasy liquor-store literature written under pseudonym; Cover artwork that often suggested more than the contents*

They made her kneel down...with her bust on an ottoman, her hands still tied behind her, with her hips higher than her torso. Then one of the men, holding her with both his hands on her hips, plunged into her belly. He yielded to a second. The third wanted to force his way into the narrower passage and, driving hard, made her scream. When he let her go, sobbing and befouled by tears beneath her blindfold, she slipped to the floor, only to feel someone's knees against her face, and she realized that her mouth was not to be spared.

— from *The Story of O*, Pauline Reagé, 1954, reissued in 1965

As a mistress Sophy was perfection perfected and the long lines and slight curves of her lovely body came to have a special attraction for me as the very highest of the pleasure-giving type...She had learned life from the streets, from the animal side first, but it was astonishing how quickly she grew in understanding: love is the only magical teacher! In a fortnight her speech was better than Lily's; in a month she talked as well as any of the American girls I had had; her desire of knowledge and her sponge-like ease of acquirement were always surprising me. She had a lovelier figure than even Rose and ten times the seduction even of Lily: she never hesitated to take my sex in her hand and caress it; she was a child of nature, bold with an animal's boldness and had besides a thousand endearing familiarities. I had only to hint a wish for her to gratify it. Sophy was the pearl of all the girls I met in this first stage of my development and I only wish I could convey to the reader a suggestion of her quaint, enthralling caresses. My admiration of Sophy cleansed me of

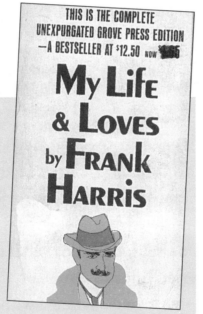

any possible disdain I might otherwise have had of the Negro people, and I am glad of it; for else I might have closed my heart against the Hindu and so missed the best part of my life's experiences.

I have had a great artist make the sketch of her back which I reproduce at the end of this chapter; it conveys something of the strange vigor and nerve-force of her lovely firm body.

— interracial passage from *My Life & Loves* by Frank Harris, 1925, reissued in 1963

spiritual, political, and emotional alternatives. Sexuality was virtually unexplored territory."

And explore it we did, especially once the Supreme Court upheld the right to publish erotic literature in 1966. Assembly-line porn flooded the bookshelves and America's nightstands would never be the same again.

Our Puritan morality notwithstanding, erotica has held the identical appeal since the Gutenberg press. If history can tell us anything, it is that when someone is reading a book, and it becomes apparent the book will have descriptions of sex, the reader often skips ahead to the next sex scene, whether it be *Fanny Hill* or Jackie Collins. Two publishing houses recognized this early, and helped launch the first wave of America's lit porn.

A former Army photographer and son of a wealthy Chicago banking family, Barney Rossett bought the struggling Grove Press in 1951, and soon started the literary magazine *Evergreen Review*, which featured sexually explicit articles and artwork. Grove gained attention in 1959 with D.H. Lawrence's *Lady Chatterly's Lover*, which was labeled obscene and impounded by the Post Office. After the ban was lifted, the following year Grove published Henry Miller's banned *Tropic of Cancer*, and the company was arrested hundreds of times across the U.S., eventually winning in the U.S. Supreme Court. Grove went on to release many titles, from avant-garde dramatists Samuel Beckett and Eugene Ionesco to William Burroughs and reprints of Victorian pornography. In the mid-'80s Rossett sold the Grove name, which continues on as Grove Atlantic. He currently runs the Blue Moon imprint, publishing a combination of emerging fiction and vintage erotica.

Two years after Grove was purchased by Rossett, Maurice Girodias founded Olympia Press in Paris. The business was in his blood, his father being the first to publish Henry Miller's *Tropic of Cancer* back in 1934. After buying and publishing works by Miller, Beckett and French wild men like Apollinaire and Bataille, the young Girodias discovered another way to keep the company afloat. He printed a list of raunchy titles like *White Thighs*, *The Chariot of Flesh* and *The Sexual Life of Robinson Crusoe*, sent it to his regular customers and gathered up a staff of American expatriate writers to create the porn. Olympia's regulars would send in their orders and money, and the staff set about pseudonymously cranking out the books, which would more or less fit the descriptions printed on the list.

And as he began to strike her across the back of her legs, she sobbed, "Oh, why, darling, why?" her long round limbs twisting, as she turned and writhed, her arms back beside her head as before, moving too except at the wrist where they were as stiff as though clamped there with steel, and she was saying: "Yes! *Hurt* me! Yes, yes! Hurt me as *they* have hurt you!" and now her ankles as well seemed secured, shackled to the spot, as she lay, spread-eagled, sobbing piteously, straining against her invisible bonds, her lithe round body arching upward, hips circling slowly, mouth wet, nipples taut, her teeny piping clitoris distended and throbbing, and her eyes glistening like fire, as she devoured all the penitence for each injustice ever done to hunchbacks of the world; and as it continued she slowly opened her eyes, that all the world might see the tears there — but instead she herself saw, through the rise and fall of the wire lash — the hunchback's white gleaming hump! The *hump*, the white, unsunned forever, radish-root white of hump, and it struck her, more sharply than the wire whip, as something she had seen before — the naked, jutting buttocks, upraised in a sexual thrust, not a thrust of taking, but of *giving*, for it had been an image in a hospital room mirror, of her own precious buttocks, naked and upraised, gleaming white, and thrusting downwards, as she had been made to do in giving herself to her Uncle Jack!

With a wild impulsive cry, she shrieked: *"Give me your hump!"*

The hunchback was startled for a moment, not comprehending.

"Your *hump,* your *hump!"* cried the girl. "GIVE ME YOUR HUMP!"

The hunchback hesitated, and then lunged headlong toward her, burying his hump between Candy's legs as she hunched wildly, pulling open her little labias in an absurd effort to get it in her.

"Your hump! Your hump!" she kept crying, scratching and clawing at it now.

"Fuck! Shit! Piss!" she screamed. "Cunt! Cock! Crap! Prick! Kike! Nigger! Wop! *Hump!* HUMP!" and she teetered on the blazing peak of pure madness for an instant...and then dropped down, slowly, through gray and grayer clouds into a deep, soft, black night.

— **from *Candy* by Terry Southern and Mason Hoffenberg, 1958**

Maxwell Kenton is the pen name of an American nuclear physicist, formerly prominent in atomic research and development who, in February 1957, resigned his post, 'because I found the work becoming more and more philosophically untenable,' and has since devoted himself fully to creative writing....The author has chosen to use a pen name because, in his own words again, 'I'm afraid my literary inclinations may prove a bit too romantic, at least in their present form, to the tastes of many of my old friends and colleagues.'

This present novel, *Candy* — which, aside from technical treatises, is Mr. Kenton's first published work — was seen by several English and American publishers, among whom it received wide private admiration, but ultimate rejection due to its highly 'Rabelaisian' wit and flavor. It is undoubtedly a work of very real merit — strikingly individualist and most engagingly humorous. Perhaps it may be said that Mr. Kenton has brought to bear on his new vocation the same creative talent and originality which so distinguished him in the field he deserted. And surely here is an instance where Science's loss is Art's gain.

— **fictitious author's biography for *Candy* (written by Terry Southern), Olympia Press catalogue, 1958**

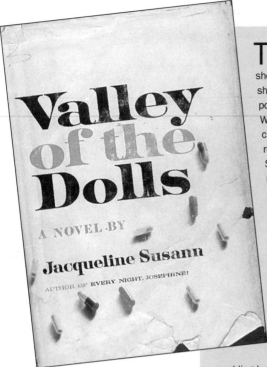

The servants were asleep. The lights were out in the living room. While she was groping for the light switch, she heard a splash in the swimming pool. She walked to the patio doors. Who in hell was in the pool? The cabana lights were on, and their reflection hit the pool. It was Ted! She laughed with relief. Geez, what a nut — swimming nude at this hour. She fumbled at the buttons of her pajamas. She'd jump in and surprise him. No, that would wake her completely, and she had an early call. She was just about to shout to him when she saw the girl coming out of the cabana, hesitating shyly, clutching the towel she had draped around her.

"Come on, drop the towel. The water's heated," Ted called.

The girl looked up at the dark, rambling house. "Suppose she wakes up?"

"Are you kidding? With what she takes an earthquake couldn't wake her. Come on, Carmen, or I'll drag you in!"

The girl dropped the towel demurely. Even in the semi-darkness Neely could see she had a wonderful body. Neely squinted her eyes. She had seen this girl somewhere....Sure! Carmen Carver. She had won some beauty contest, and the studio was testing her.

Ted swam to meet the girl. Neely heard a squeal. "Oh, Ted! Not in the water....Don't!"

"Why not? We've done it every other way." Neely felt her stomach quiver. Oh, God! No — not this! A boy occasionally she had accepted. It was a sickness of Ted's — that's what the psychiatrist had told her. It had nothing to do with unfaithfulness to her. But this!

She grabbed the bottle of Scotch and stumbed up the stairs. She poured a stiff drink and took another pill, then climbed into bed. To hell with Ted and his whore!...

...She shot out of bed. She was dizzy and her head was heavy, but she had to throw that girl out of *her* pool. She held onto the banister as she fumbled her way down the stairs. She groped her way to the light switch and triumphantly flooded the pool with light.

Ted and the girl were scrambling out of the pool as she staggered out, holding a bottle of Scotch.

"Having a good time, kiddies?" she shrieked. "Fucking in *my* pool? Be sure you drain it out. Remember, Ted — *your* children go wading in it every morning."

The girl dodged frantically behind Ted. Neely carefully emptied the bottle into the pool.

"Maybe this'll disinfect it," she sneered.

— *Valley of the Dolls* **by Jacqueline Susann, 1966**

CRITIC JOHN SIMON: I'm asking you what you think you were doing when you wrote that book.

AUTHOR JACQUELINE SUSANN: All right, little man, I was telling a story.

SIMON: You were telling a story?

SUSANN: Why are you so uptight?

SIMON: I'm not uptight. I'll smile charmingly through my false teeth like you.

SUSANN: Let me see you smile.

SIMON: Now look....I'm asking you what kind of story you're telling.

SUSANN: A too-sophisticated story for you to understand because it's dirty....

SIMON: The trouble is, it's not dirty, Miss Susann. If it were honest-to-goodness pornography, it would be a thousand times better than what you have written. At least it would serve the purpose of turning people on.

SUSANN: What's your name? Simple Simon. Mr. Simon, what are you after?

SIMON: I hope you realize that by calling me insulting names, you're making yourself ridiculous! Do you think you're writing art or do you think you're writing trash?

SUSANN: But I've answered you. I told you I'm writing a story.

[Critic Rex Reed interjects to report that Simon admitted before the program he had read only 30 pages of Susann's novel that was under discussion, *The Love Machine.*]

SUSANN: You've only read thirty pages and you're putting me through this inquisition?

SIMON: I've read forty pages actually, after which I couldn't stomach any more. I mean, how many swallows of a rotten stew do I have to swallow before I puke and know that this is inedible? [burst of audience applause]

SUSANN: ...What are your credentials?

SIMON: Not that it matters, but I have a Ph.D. in comparative literature from Harvard.

— **from the *David Frost Show*, July 23, 1969**

In addition to the porn factory, Girodias published manuscripts for J.P. Dunleavy's *The Ginger Man*, and Nabokov's *Lolita*, the story of a widower's love for his step-daughter, which was banned by the French government. American publishers turned down *Lolita*, but couldn't make up their minds exactly why it wouldn't work. Some thought it too sexual, others not sexual enough, one even suggesting the author turn the conflict of man and step-daughter into a farmer/son sexual encounter in a barn. Putnam eventually published an American version in 1958, and it was on its way to becoming one of the most-often-burned books in American history. One of Olympia's later discoveries was a 1968 novel called *Barbara*, by poet Sam Abrams, writing under the name Frank Newman. Set in the 1960s hippie scene of Provincetown, Massachusetts, the story followed a 12-year-old girl who approaches a guru named Max to be sexually introduced into the world, with the ensuing drugs and orgies.

In addition to Olympia and Grove, the third publishing house that dared to print pornography with some shred of literary quality was Essex House, a division of Parliament News publishing. Over time, Essex House published dozens of erotic novels, including those of poets David Meltzer and Charles Bukowski.

One of the unique contributions to the emerging erotica field was the frequent use of pseudonyms, occasionally one culminating in a scandal or publishing hoax. Upon its publication in 1954, *The Story of O* by Pauline Reagé was immediately the talk of Paris. A young French fashion photographer is introduced by her lover into a world inside a chateau, of whippings, sexual assualts, prolonged bondage, humiliation and submission, the branding of her buttocks, genital piercings, lesbian activities, until she is left a willing sexual object, wearing an owl mask, available to any man or woman. After publication, the French literary establishment heavily speculated who could have written the book. Some thought it was written by committee. Olympia published an English translation, which was seized by the French Brigade Mondaine. Undaunted, Girodias renamed it *The Wisdom of the Lash* and reprinted the book, this time missing the preface due to drunken typesetters.

After Grove published a 1965 U.S. version of *The Story of O*, translated by Sabine d'Estrée (widely believed to be Grove managing editor Richard Seaver), America devoured the sadistic descriptions and bondage themes. "An ironic fable of unfreedom, a mystic document that

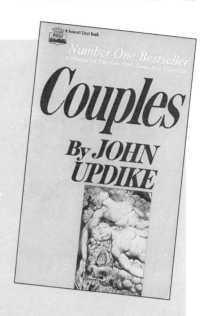

" I think I've discovered that Freddy is seeing Janet. I found a letter in the pocket of a suit I ws taking to the cleaner's."

"How careless of him. Maybe he wanted you to find it. What did it say?"

"Nothing very much. It said, 'Let's break it off, no more phone calls,' et cetera, which might mean anything. It could mean she's putting on pressure for him to divorce me."

"Why would she want to marry Freddy?" He realized this was tactless and tried to disguise it with another question. "You're sure it's her?"

"Quite. She signed it J and anyway her handwriting is unmistakable, big and fat and spilly. You've seen it on her Christmas cards."

"Well. But sweet, it's been in the air for some time, Freddy and Janet. Does it really shock you?"

"I suppose," Georgene said, "there's something called female pride. But more than that. I'm shocked by the idea of divorce. If it comes to that I don't want him to have anything to throw back at me, for the children to read about in the paper. It wouldn't bother Freddy but it would me."

"So what does this do to us?"

"I suppose nothing, except that we must be very careful."

"How careful is careful?"

"Piet. I'm not going to tell you how much you mean to me. I've said that in ways a woman can't fake. I just don't think I could enjoy you

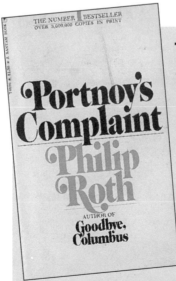

The bus, the bus, what intervened on the bus to prevent me from coming all over the sleeping *shikse*'s arm — *I* don't know. Common sense, you think? Common decency? My right mind, as they say, coming to the fore? Well, where is this right mind on that afternoon I came home from school to find my mother out of the house, and our refrigerator stocked with a big purplish piece of raw liver? I believe that I have already confessed to the piece of liver that I bought in a butcher shop and banged behind a billboard on the way to a bar mitzvah lesson. Well, I wish to make a clean breast of it, Your Holiness. That — she — it — wasn't my first piece. My first piece I had in the privacy of my own home, rolled round my cock in the bathroom at three-thirty — and then had again on the end of a fork at five-thirty, along with the other members of that poor innocent family of mine.

So. Now you know the worst thing I have ever done. I fucked my own family's dinner.

— **from *Portnoy's Complaint* by Philip Roth, 1969**

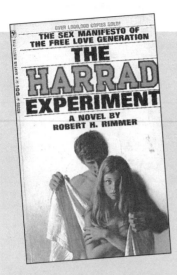

I'm in love...not just with Beth Hillyer who is utterly, completely wonderfully feminine, but I'm in love with Sheila Grove and Dorothy Stapleton...in fact, I'm in love with fifty girls. "Bless them all, the long and the short and the tall..." That's a World War II song my father used to sing...and there's another. "Thank

Heaven for little girls. Only these aren't little girls...they are fully developed women with breasts and swaying behinds and soft round stomachs.

Every day when I go to Physical Education, there they are...girls... naked, swimming in the pool, playing volleyball, doing calisthenics...yelling, screaming, soprano-joyous. If I stand by the pool, one of them is likely to shove me in. When I come up spluttering in the middle of other girls, they splash me, or challenge me to a race, or toss a beach ball at me... and the hour goes by so fast that I can't really believe it is over...and then back to the room and I yell for Beth, only she hasn't come backfrom her classes...so I lie down on my bed and think awhile before dinner. Mostly, I think I am a very lucky Beast.

— from *The Harrad Experiment* by **Robert H. Rimmer, 1966**

Turnbull looked at her for a moment. She was kneeling opposite him on the bed. He unhooked her brassiere, and this time Gillian offered no resistance. He removed it and bit softly at her breasts. They waved at him, pennants in the wind of lust, and he bit deeply into the acid of her dugs. Then he pulled off the black net panties — there was a cellophane sound as they were peeled past her thighs. They stuck at her knees. What he had hoped (and prayed, even) would be a smooth operation was spoiled as he had to fumble about her knees and she arched to let him finish slipping them off. Turnbull rose from the bed and then, clad only in his beard, rejoined her. He watched with the patience of the sages as Gillian removed the earrings and the bracelet. Turnbull delayed it, made it last, stared at the naked woman waiting on the sheets for him. Then, as if making an elaborate bow, he took hold of her and pressed hard against her slightly parted legs. He sewed her body with a thread of bites and kisses, dwelling on the tight high pack of her working hips and patching them with little pink squares.

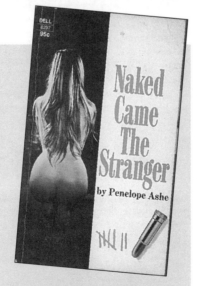

Finally he rose up over her, shadowed her with the majesty of his manhood, noticed that her legs were still closed.

"Not yet, Joshua," she said. "Not yet. Kiss my knees first."

"Your knees?"

"My knees."

"Would you prefer the caps or the hollows?"

"Just kiss them, Joshua."

— from *Naked Came the Stranger* by **Penelope Ashe, 1969**

transcends the pornographic and even the erotic," proclaimed *Newsweek*. "A more dangerous writer than the Marquis de Sade," said the *Times Book Review*. *O* went on to become translated into two dozen languages, a feature film treatment and sales of millions of copies, some of which were publicly burned by outraged feminists. Years later, in 1994, the world's best-kept literary secret was broken by *The New Yorker*. The author's identity was revealed — respected French journalist and woman of letters Dominique Aury, who wrote the book as a private gift for her lover, critic Jean Paulhan. "Pauline" was derived from two well-known European women, and the surname "Reagé" was picked at random from a real-estate registry in the French countryside. (John Heidenry's 1997 book *What Wild Ecstasy* suggests that Dominique Aury itself was a pseudonym for Anne Desclos.)

Another pseudonym hoax began in 1956 when writer Mason Hoffenberg introduced Girodias to his impoverished friend Terry Southern, then living in Switzerland. The two had written a proposal for a satirical book, based on Voltaire's *Candide*, about the sexual adventures of a young girl named Candy, set in the bizarre Manhattan underground. Girodias agreed to do it, but Southern requested his real name not be used, as he was working on a children's book, and didn't wish to be linked with a book of "questionable taste." The three agreed on the stylish pen name of Maxwell Kenton.

Candy was published in Europe in 1958, immediately banned by the Paris authorities, and was withdrawn from circulation, only to resurface with a new cover and the title *Lollipop*. Girodias knew the French police would list the banned titles in alphabetical order, and to an officer running a finger down a list of English-language book titles, an innocuous word like "Lollipop" was less likely to arouse suspicion. The book gathered steady readership in the literary underground on both sides of the Atlantic, and its famous line, "Give me your hump!" was a greeting often heard in the cafes. In 1964 Putnam published American hardcover and paperback versions, with the authors' actual names. It became a national best-seller, a darling of the critics, and a gold mine for pirate publishers — million-copy paperback editions of *Candy* were quickly issued by Greenleaf Publications, Lancer Publications and Brandon House. When Putnam attempted to sue them, each publisher claimed it had merely reprinted the original Olympia Paris edition, which it contended was not legitimately copyrighted, and in turn threatened Putnam with a suit for damages. By the time *Candy* was adapted by Buck Henry into a 1968 film starring Richard Burton, Marlon Brando and James Coburn, it had been reprinted at least 21 times by Putnam, and countless other illegal versions had appeared.

Yet another famous hoax appeared in 1969. The best-selling novel *Naked Came the Stranger* by Penelope Ashe tickled the prurient interests of the country, chronicling the adventures of a female radio talk-show host who insisted on having sex with a variety of men outside her marriage, all of whom were either turning up dead, or with problems that would cause their lives immeasurable grief. Only later was it revealed that "Penelope Ashe" was actually a tongue-in-cheek exercise in erotica by 25 men and one woman from the staff of *New York Newsday*, each trading off writing duties, spinning the great yarn to entertain each other. The *Long Island Press*, in a stroke of insider cleverness (or blind ignorance) proclaimed: "Penelope Ashe's scorching novel makes *Portnoy's Complaint* and *Valley of the Dolls* read like *Rebecca of Sunnybrook Farm*." (A 1975 porn film version directed by Henry Paris would win *Adam Film World*'s award for Best Screenplay.)

Several of America's sweat-stained tomes were reprinted gems from an earlier era. *My Life & Loves* by Frank Harris was originally published in 1925, and enjoyed a renaissance courtesy of a 1963 Grove edition. Harris was an American working as a magazine editor in London, a short little mustachioed man whom H.L. Mencken once termed "happily free from modesty." Others described him as insensitive, extremely pompous, and an inveterate name-dropper, but all agreed he was intelligent and well-read. After helming magazines and writing a few literary biographies, Harris vowed to complete the impossible, to chronicle the adventures of the most fascinating, sexually prolific man in history — himself. Contained to a reasonable five volumes, its self-absorbed sexual frankness was noted for being several decades ahead of its time, as well as a bonanza of free research for psychiatrists. Harris insisted that no biography was honest if it did not deal with sex, and although the lengthy indulgent descriptions of his conquests were the primary reason people read the book, the passages were soundly criticized for their lack of individuality. "The persons involved in them are sticks, not figures," wrote John F. Gallagher in an introduction to the Grove edition. "Anyone

We had pulled into the station parking lot when the bitch fell to pieces. Her eyes were misty when she yelped, "Daddy, are you really going to let me split? Daddy, I love you!"

I started the prat action to cinch her when I said, "Bitch, I don't want a whore with rabbit in her. I want a bitch who wants me for life. You have got to go after that bullshit earlier this morning, you are not that bitch."

That prat butchered her and she collapsed into my lap crying and begging to stay. I had a theory about splitting whores. I think they seldom split without a bankroll.

So, I cracked on her, "Give me that scratch you held out and maybe I will give you another chance."

Sure enough she reached into her bosom and drew out close to five bills and handed it to me. No pimp with a brain in his head cuts loose a youg beautiful whore with lots of mileage left in her. I let her come back.

When at long last I was driving toward my hotel I remembered what "Baby" Jones, the master pimp who turned me out, had said about whores like Kim.

"Slim," he had said, "A pretty Nigger bitch and a white whore are just alike. They both will get in a stable to wreck it and leave the pimp on his ass with no whore. You gotta make 'em hump hard and fast to stick 'em for long scratch quick. Slim, pimping ain't no game of love, so prat 'em and keep your swipe outta 'em. Any sucker who believe a whore loves him shouldn't a fell outta his mammy's ass."

— *Pimp* by Iceberg Slim, 1969

In our society, everything is a lie. You walk down the street and look at the jiggling breasts and tight-skirted asses and in five minutes there are a dozen women you want to fuck and who would like nothing better than to be fucked. But you are not allowed to do it. Moreover, you are not even allowed to think it. You censor yourself. Everyone is afraid. Everyone lies.

— *Mind Blower*, Marco Vassi's first novel, 1970

The Provocative <u>New York Times</u> Bestseller

DELTA OF VENUS
EROTICA BY
ANAÏS NIN

3.50

"One of contemporary literature's
most important writers."
—Newsweek

POCKET

Now followed the performance for which she was famed all through South America, when the boxes in the theatre, deep, dark and half-curtained, filled with society men from all over the world. Women were not brought to this high-class burlesque.

She had dressed herself all over again in the full-petticoated costume she wore onstage for her Brazilian songs, but she wore no shawl. Her dress was strapless, and her rich, abundant breasts, compressed by the tight-waisted costume, bulged upwards, offering themselves almost in their entirety to the eye.

In this costume, while the rest of the show continued, she made her round of the boxes. There, on request, she knelt before a man, unbuttoned his pants, took his penis in her jeweled hands, and with a neatness of touch, an expertness, a subtlety few women had ever developed, sucked at it until he was satisfied. Her two hands were as active as her mouth.

The titillation almost deprived each man of his senses. The elasticity of her hands; the variety of rhythms; the change from a hand grip of the entire penis to the lightest touch of the tip of it, from firm kneading of all the parts to the lightest teasing of the hair around it — all this by an exceptionally beautiful and voluptuous woman while the attention of the public was turned towards the stage. Seeing the penis go into her magnificent mouth between her flashing teeth, while her breasts heaved, gave men a pleasure for which they paid generously.

Her presence on the stage prepared them for her appearance in the boxes. She provoked them with her mouth, her eyes, her breasts. And to have their satisfaction, along with music and lights and singing in a dark, half-curtained box above the audience, was an exceptionally piquant form of amusement.

— **from *Delta of Venus* by Anais Nin, 1977**

could have had such experiences. Yet the use of the pronoun 'I' and the succession of intimate details provide the illusion that they are revelatory about Harris alone." The controversy grew so outrageous that in 1929 two siblings of Byron Caldwell Smith, a man mentioned in the book, were forced to write *Lies and Libels of Frank Harris*, attempting to redeem their brother's name. Harris died in 1931, his sexcapades languishing for years in Paris as titillation for tourists, until a U.S. version reintroduced the memoirs to a public that, apparently, was willing to indulge such literature.

Another reprint worthy of America's salacious reading appetite was Anais Nin's *Delta of Venus*, a collection of 1940s erotica that was reprinted years later, becoming a national bestseller in 1977. While living in Paris, Nin chanced upon a writing gig courtesy of her friend Henry Miller. Similar to the Olympia Press structure a decade later, as well as many current porn publishing enterprises, starving writers could finance their true art by spinning sexual yarns on the side. In Nin's and Miller's case, their fiction was customized for a single anonymous patron, who paid a dollar a page. The writers were given little instruction, other than to "leave out the poetry...concentrate on sex." Faced with mounting bills, Nin and her writer peers studied old literature and medical books, talked to friends, eavesdropped on conversations, anything to spark an idea that satisfied the strict requests slowly driving all of them nuts. Nin finally wrote the mystery benefactor a letter which began: "Dear Collector: We hate you. Sex loses all its power and magic when it becomes explicit, mechanical, overdone, when it becomes a mechanistic obsession. It becomes a bore....We have sat around for hours and wondered how you look. If you have closed your senses upon silk, light, color, odor, character, temperament, you must be by now completely shriveled up." The patron's identity was never discovered. Although frustrated at her predicament and motivated more by a paycheck than the creative muse, Nin managed to write some of the most engaging erotica in the English language, her feminine point of view appealing to women as well as men.

Major publishing houses soon realized the sales potential of sex-charged literature, especially once it was protected by law, and offered up saucy novels from Philip Roth, John Updike — even unabashed hacks like Sidney Sheldon were falling prey to the required cocaine/orgy scene. Robert Rimmer's novel *The Harrad*

Experiment described a groovy alternative school where boys and girls partnered up and had sex with each other for the summer, and spawned an actual Harrad House commune in Berkeley. (A film treatment of the book is worth renting just for watching a tiny-mustached Don Johnson attempt to seduce his future mother-in-law, Tippi Hedren.) Few people had heard of poet Erica Jong until her satirical novel *Fear of Flying*, about a young woman traveling through Europe on a liberating sexual romp, searching for fulfillment of all kinds. Never expecting to even see it published, she instead watched it sell over 3,500,000 copies in the next two years. The anonymous "zipless fuck" — a quickie with a stranger without even having to unzip — entered America's vocabulary, and kept Jong in book contracts for years to come. Another mainstream erotica example from the '70s was *Forever...* by children's author Judy Blume. Page 38 lingers in the memories of thousands of young girls as the ultimate passage to read aloud with friends or under the covers by flashlight — a classic seduction of a virgin teen by an older boy who introduces his penis to her by its nickname.

One of the more flamboyant smut typists was Manhattan socialite Jacqueline Susann. After her 1963 autobiography *Every Night, Josephine*, written from the perspective of her overweight French poodle, she validated her leopard-print lifestyle in 1966 with her first novel, *Valley of the Dolls*, a racy tale of four young girls fighting to make it in show biz. The book shot to the top of the bestseller lists, but reviews were not kind, one writer for *Time* sneering, "It would seem that author Susann has spent most of her time watching people swallow Seconal, slurp Scotch, and commit sodomy. Somebody does one or the other on almost every page, and a large crowd has gathered to watch the exhibition."

Despite the critics, *Valley* entered the *Guinness Book of World Records* as America's bestselling novel of all time — 17 million copies — and spawned a 1967 film that quickly bombed, despite the potent thespian combination of Patty Duke, Martin Milner, Joey Bishop and Sharon Tate. (The 1970 Russ Meyer film *Beyond the Valley of the Dolls*, written by Roger Ebert, was a sequel in name only.) Susann's 1969 follow-up effort, *The Love Machine*, continued the same formula of trashy sex that never grew explicit, and became required thumbing for the beach, selling 14 million copies and spawning a movie deal. She never let a PR moment lapse,

I slipped my nightgown over my head and dropped it to the floor. Then there were just my bikini pants and Michael's pajama bottoms between us. We kissed again. Feeling him against me that way made me so excited I couldn't lie still. He rolled over on top of me and we moved together again and again and it felt so good I didn't ever want to stop — until I came.

After a minute I reached for Michael's hand. "Show me what to do," I said.

"Do whatever you want."

"Help me, Michael...I feel so stupid."

"Don't" he said, wiggling out of his pajama bottoms. He led my hand to his penis. "Katherine...I'd like you to meet Ralph...Ralph, this is Katherine. She's a very good friend of mine."

"Does every penis have a name?"

"I can only speak for my own."

— from the teen novel *Forever...* by Judy Blume, 1975

And it's happening everywhere
  all the time
Any two people you see
  might be practicing this magic
It's hard to believe
  such forces can be loose in the universe
Storms of energy
  everywhere every minute
What a glorious mystery

How can all this coming be happening
  without tearing the universe apart?

I guess we tear it apart
  and rebuild it together
    every day.

When we're fucking, we're at the center of the universe.
Anyone who's been there knows it's true.

— *Coming*, a poetry book by Paul Williams, 1977

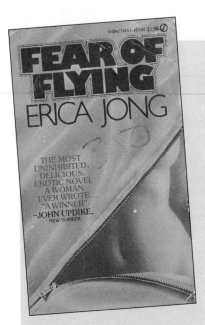

For the true, ultimate zipless A-1 fuck, it was necessary that you never get to know the man very well. I had noticed, for example, how all my infatuations dissolved as soon as I really became friends with a man, became sympathetic to his problems, listened to him *kvetch* about his wife, or ex-wives, his mother, his children. After that I would like him, perhaps even love him — but without passion. And it was passion that I wanted. I had also learned that a sure way to exorcise an infatuation was to write about someone, to observe his tics and twitches, to anatomize his personality in type. After that he was an insect on a pin, a newspaper clipping laminated in plastic. I might enjoy his company, even admire him at moments, but he no longer had the power to make me wake up trembling in the middle of the night. I no longer dreamed about him. He had a face.

So another condition for the zipless fuck was brevity. And anonymity made it even better.

— from *Fear of Flying* by Erica Jong, 1973

The zipless fuck was more than a fuck. It was a platonic ideal. Zipess because when you came together zippers fell away like rose petals, underwear blew off in one breath like dandelion fluff. Tongues intertwined and turned liquid. Your whole soul flowed out through your tongue and into the mouth of your lover.

When you read a lot of the novels of adultery that have been written by women, you see that pattern...very often the woman finds a lover who's not nearly as good in bed as her husband. Certainly, in *Fear of Flying* that's the case; the woman finds an impotent lover. He can't even get it up most of the time. So what's the need that's being fulfilled by this man? It's the need for rebellion, for saying "Look, I'll show you." And I've talked to many, many women who have had affairs — sometimes persistent, constant affairs throughout their marriages — and they tell you overwhelmingly: "My husband is really a much better lover. He satisfies me more often; I reach orgasm more often with my husband; we're more attuned to each other." And so you ask, "Well, why the lover?" And they say, "Ah, I feel great. I feel alive. I feel reborn." What is going on that makes her feel that way? It's being appreciated again, not being taken for granted, being rediscovered as an individual, being validated in the eyes of a new man.

— Erica Jong in *Playboy*, 1975

becoming one of the first novelists to shill her own books on late-night TV. In 1971 she accepted an invitation from 20th Century Fox to fly on a ten-city tour in a jet with "The Love Machine" painted on both sides to promote the film version, starring John Philip Law and Dyan Cannon, which also bombed and disappeared. Her last book before she died of cancer, *Once Is Not Enough*, was a 1973 best-seller, and a 1975 film version continued the grand Susann tradition of tanking at the box office, ignoring the possibly electric work of cast members George Hamilton and Brenda Vaccaro.

Some authors lived the life they wrote about. In the estimation of many, Marco Vassi was the sexual revolution personified — personal, original and shocking. As David Steinberg euologized in *The Spectator*: "For Marco sex was a lens on life itself, a magnifying glass through which the dynamics and foibles of being human become intensified, and so his pursuit of sexual knowledge and experience took on the color of a philosophical quest." In the course of his personal research, Vassi crisscrossed the globe, having sex with hundreds of people — women, men, groups and everything else available — diving into the sexual landscape as vigorously as anyone ever has. After writing 13 sex novels, hundreds of short stories, and editing anthologies, he contracted AIDS, and died in 1989.

Robert Beck, aka Iceberg Slim, was a former Chicago pimp who gave up the street hustle and turned to writing, cranking out 1960s novels like *Pimp, Trick Baby* and *Air Tight Willie & Me* that collectively added up to a bible of coolness for black teenagers. *Pimp* even had its own glossary — getting "Georgiaed" meant you were taken advantage of sexually without receiving money, a "flat-backer" was a whore who got paid for straight intercourse. The reader learned drug slang like "smack," "speedballs," and "coming down." Slim's streetsmart pimp technique of "pratting," pretending to reject women to make them desire you more, had a huge impact on young inner-city kids, and when they grew up to create the hip-hop music scene, they didn't forget him. Ice-T freely admits he took his name from Beck's *nom de plume*. Even today, some used bookstores refuse to stock Iceberg Slim books because "they bring in a bad element."

Then there were the hardcore publishers, early sleazebags like Matt Cimber and Marvin Miller, who made a fortune after JFK was shot by printing a million copies of an assassination photo book. Miller's company Collectors' Publications quickly jumped on the porn band-

wagon, slapping together reprints
of copyright-free books like *Autobiography of a
Flea* and *She Devils*. Many companies merely
pirated books from other houses like Olympia,
while hardcore fiction factories like Holloway
House pumped the paperback porn into the
nation's liquor stores and sex shops, creating
a bastard literary genre with a look and
language that evoked trenchcoats, cheap cigars
and horse racing.

In comparison to the wonderful cover art of
pulp books from the '40s and '50s, these newer
hardcore sex pulps featured quickie covers — a
lopsided line drawing or snapshot hastily
slapped onto the presses at the last minute.
Typical of this literature was the characters
screaming their orgasms in all caps, or the
insanely overwrought language, where a
"vein-bumped cudgel" might force its way into
a "cuntal channel" until it blasted "white-hot
seed." Obviously included for legal purposes,
the introductions to these books are the definition of understatement, the print equivalent of a
doctor in stethoscope introducing an 8mm porn
loop. Such a preface usually went along the lines
of, "[Wafer-Thin Plot Device] is a common phenomenon which only now is receiving attention
among members of the professional psychiatric
community. In their quest to accurately reflect
our society, literary minds have expanded upon
this concept and treated it in a fictional setting,
While it is not our position to judge such moral
grounds, we feel it is important that the following work be seen and distributed..." etc. etc.,
and on the following page would immediately
begin a protracted seduction of a teacher, cabin
boy or border collie.

Hardcore books listed several company
names to sound exotic and European, as well as
to preserve their anonymity. For example, one
'70s novel based in the San Francisco area was
labeled a Liverpool Book, part of the Finlandia
Book Series, with a copyright from Trans-Nordic
Publications in Denmark, followed by a publishing credit from Tiburon Publishing House in
Sausalito, California, and a catalog mailing
address of the Belvedere Book Club (also in
Sausalito). But who are we to scoff? Perhaps
these works are products of the new Anais Nins
or Henry Millers, toiling to make rent while
honing their own poetry or novels. Someday the
highbrow literary world may fawn all over the
recently rediscovered erotic novel *The Kennel
Club* from the mysterious "Gretchen Wilcox."
And we'll all feel a little smarter.

It is not often that we get a chance to see ourselves as others
see us. Author Bill Crosby, who has created numerous words
of undeniable pertinence and validity, had brought to life the full
meaning of this maxim in the two characters of Carl and Amy
Kern...who eventually have this dubious privilege fostered upon
them by their in-laws.

Young Amy Kern is particularly susceptible to the changes
that take place in her handsome architect husband. Being a naturally shy and withdrawn person who has difficulty letting herself
go, she is forced into an increasingly difficult relationship with
her husband. Carl's own stresses are aggravated beyond measure by the antics of his wife's wealthy brother.

The foibles of the very rich had already been superbly dealt
with by F. Scott Fitzgerald in *The Great Gatsby*, and although Tod
Patton does not begin to approach Jay Gatsby's extravagance, he
nonetheless represents a similar kind of challenge to Carl Kern.

It is ironic that Carl discovers that this jaded man who just
happens to be his brother-in-law is also a man of taste who can
offer him the job of a lifetime. Mr. Crosby's book is a moving
and often memorable account of the agonies that this young
couple must go through before they finally find a solution to their
problems. Whether or not this solution is a fortunate one is left
for the reader to decide. We think you will enjoy reading this
book and will find it of highly informative value.

The Publishers

**— foreward to porn novel *The Ravished Couple* by "Bill
Crosby," 1974**

"OOOOHHHHHHH!!" Amy chanted on
and on in time to her husband's and
brother's crushing thrusts against
her cunt and rear passage. Wilder
and wilder they became, plowing into
her between them as if she were
nothing but a rag doll made expressly
for them to use in this cruel punish-
ing way. All three of their coarse
groans intermingled in a symphony of
mad sexual abandonment.

"YES...YES...LIKE THAT...LIKE
THAT...I'MMMMM CUMMING...CUM-
MING...YES FUCK ME HARDER
HARDER HARDER...I'M CUMMING
CUUUUMMMIIINGGG! AAAHHHHH!!!!!

...Both men, sensing their total
conquest of her body and mind,
plunged forward at the same time,
imbedding their suddenly wild ejaculating cocks deep into her pussy and
asshole, pumping their hot male
sperm far, far up into her warmly
welcoming belly as they felt her wom-
anly juices squeezing round their
penises and out around their madly
driving loins.

"HOT BITCH...HOT LITTLE
BITCH!!!" Carl cried out, feeling his
young wife's secretions flooding
around his driving piston.

'GIVE ME YOUR CUM, BABY...
GIVE ME YOUR CUM!!!!!"

**— author Bill Crosby's words of
undeniable pertinence and validity,
The Ravished Couple, 1974**

SNATCH COMICS

WHAT DO THOSE HIPPY CHICKS DO WHEN THEY DO THEIR THING??

©1968 by R. CUM

Since the first monkey scratched a replica of genitalia on a cave wall, the artistic impulse has always included erotic imagery. Sex is one of the most natural and universal processes in the animal kingdom, not to mention a outlet for recreation among those of us with more complex brains. To express and articulate such urges in a creative way is a gift that should be shared. And if you're a scrappy, hungry artist putting together a new painting or sculpture, it might as well be something that will sell. During the mid-60s, sex sold very well.

We take it for granted now, but there was a time when erotica was novel and extremely fashionable in the art world, from modern contemporary pieces

his Is Not Porn

to work from cultures thousands of years old. New York's Sidney Janis Gallery featured Larry Rivers and many other well-known artists in its Erotic Art '66 exhibit. Galleries across the country were slipping more sexually oriented work into their shows, which drove more artists to create more sexually explicit material. At the other end of the spectrum, underground comics were introducing their readers to sexual imagery so radical some printers refused to touch it.

An early exhibit which captured the world's attention was the "First International Exhibition of Erotic Art," a display of 800 works which opened in 1968 in Lund, Sweden. Curated by U.S. sexologists Phyllis and Eberhard Kronhausen, the show

SEALED BIDS:
Genitalia Sumo wrestling from the late 19th century (clockwise from left); Turn-of-the-century French postcard used to illustrate a book of sauce recipes; Issue #1 of the notorious 1960s Snatch *comics*

THE MASTER'S TOUCH
Rembrandt's 17th-century etching, "The Monk in the Cornfield" (above), from the Kronhausens' book **Erotic Art**

The Drs. Kronhausen present

THE FIRST INTERNATIONAL EXHIBITION OF

EROTIC ART

LUND'S KONSTHALL
MUSEUM OF ART
LUND · SWEDEN

3 MAY–31 JULY 1968 · OPEN: 12–5 P.M.

We just collected the films from the past, and then talked to the filmmakers, and the people who were in them, who collected films and books and library materials, and tried to study the industry as well as the professions. And gradually put together all of the things. If you believe that people's sexuality is somehow sacred, then you have an attitude of it which you would refer to it as 'sacred history,' and to be accurate about it. And we found that probably more than even politics, people lie about sex histories. They all want to hide those things, but they're very important. The sexual expressions and artifacts of this century are of tremendous import....

The [San Francisco] city fathers didn't like it, because nobody involved them in it. It was so-so as a museum. It had some good pieces and some bad pieces. The city wasn't helpful, I'll tell you that. Nor was any of the art establishment. You have to understand, the art establishment in the United States is not pro-sex. And are still very much into censorship all across the country. They talk a big game, but they rely on grants from little old ladies who don't want anything too risque....

When the Museum closed, it didn't close because of pressure from the city. It closed for other reasons. It was quite successful. But all the art I still own, and all the rights to it, that was legitimate. The other stuff went back to the Kronhausens. They were putting on a thing, they sent it to Hamburg. And there was an accident at sea, and it was lost, so they could get the insurance for this stuff. But fortunately, in the Atlantic Ocean, there are many aficionados of erotic art in the dolphins, so somehow that art managed to get into private collectors' hands....

— interview with Rev. Ted McIlvenna, curator of San Francisco's International Museum of Erotic Art, 1997

included works from ancient India and Asia to Rembrandt, Picasso and lesser-known contemporary artists. The preview night began with a large coffin covered with black fur, being wheeled out onto the museum floor. Out from its pink interior stepped the 39-year-old Phyllis Kronhausen, wearing only a see-through minidress. The Kronhausens lovingly documented the event in their book *Erotic Art*, running numerous photos of old men and children peering at the explicit paintings and sculptures, as if to show its relative harmlessness on people of all ages.

The Kronhausens' collection was eventually included in the International Museum of Erotic Art in downtown San Francisco, which opened later that same year amidst the tourists and conventioneers of Union Square. The opening night party attracted everyone from columnist Herb Caen and Shirley MacLaine to hipsters and bluebloods. People sipped champagne and marveled at ivory dildos displayed under glass.

The Kronhausens continued researching erotica, publishing other books about the sex industry, before retiring to Costa Rica. According to Rev. Ted McIlvenna, who put together the museum in San Francisco, the Kronhausens claimed to have lost most of their erotic art collection to a ship accident while crossing the Atlantic, but items from the collection mysteriously began popping up for sale around the globe. Today, the world's largest erotic art collection is held at McIlvenna's Institute for the Advanced Study of Human Sexuality, with smaller permanent collections located in Amsterdam, Hamburg, and Leipzig.

Many American artists would achieve prominence for their work that reflected the sexual impulse. Frustrated with her married life, illustrator Betty Dodson began drawing her sexual fantasies as a form of personal therapy. In 1968 her nude artwork was featured in a one-woman show at Wickersham Gallery on Madison Avenue, next to the Whitney, and in two weeks attracted over 8,000 visitors. One mother walked into the show with her ten-year-old daughter before realizing the contents of the exhibit — six-foot renderings of acts of autoeroticism, gay fellatio, lesbianism, and masturbation. She stopped their progress and told her daughter, "We don't want to look at these pictures." The girl replied, "Why not, Mother? It's just a bunch of people wrestling."

Dodson continued her pursuit of sexual independence, conducting seminars in her apartment where women used mirrors to scrutinize their genitals and observe the variations among each other. She went on to write books and offer masturbation workshops, and in 1973 she started the EOA (Equal Orgasms Amendment).

Artwork that focused on body parts made big news in those days. In 1969, video artist Nam June Paik debuted his "TV Brassiere for Living Sculpture" at the Howard Wise Gallery on 57th St. in New York. The TV bra was two picture screens, which could show any two local TV stations, two inches in diameter, fastened with plastic sheets and adhesive tape, to the bare breasts of cellist Charlotte Moorman (who gained some notoriety herself for performing in the nude). Moorman's instrument was connected to her bra, and whenever she created a sound with the bow and strings of the cello, random patterned waves, lines and dots jumped and jerked across the screens.

Many artists favored the penis in their work. New Yorker Anita Steckel fashioned penis-shaped dollar bills, and rendered giant blue penises that were perched on the top of Manhattan skyscrapers. She defended her penis fixation to a reporter from *Viva* magazine: "The erect penis as a part of life should no longer be prevented from being part of art. If the erect penis is not wholesome enough to go into museums, it should not be considered wholesome enough to go into women. And if the erect penis is wholesome enough to go into women, then it is more than wholesome enough to go into the greatest art museums." Others opted for the vagina. One of the hottest female artists of the 1970s, Judy Chicago, was known for her place settings loaded up with labia imagery. Her piece entitled "The Dinner Party" featured 39 ceramic plates with designs of vaginas.

Although females were making headlines with their art, some feminists were appalled at their efforts. To advertise one of her 1974 shows, Lynda Benglis posed for a pinup shot — a photo of herself naked except for a pair of sunglasses, a huge double-dong dildo, and an arrogant, angry expression. Already infuriated over a previous nude cheesecake ad for herself, feminists were not pleased to see this sequel. The ad was scheduled to run in *Artforum*, but their printers refused to print it, and only through a court order was the issue produced. Five of the six associate editors of *Artforum* threatened to resign, and the one who didn't, a Californian, called Benglis "a shameless hussy showing everything from here to Bakersfield." An exhibit of her sculpture work in

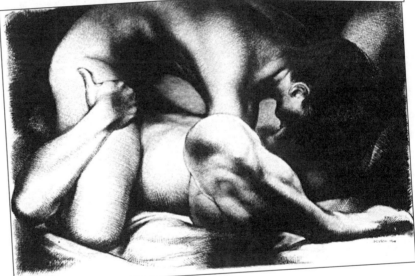

BUNCH OF WRESTLERS:
*Betty Dodson illustrations from her
1968 show in New York*

Over the next few years, there was so much tension and so little communication in our marriage that I stopped wanting sex with my husband altogether. Instead, I began creating monumental masterpieces of art. But in the sixth year, no matter how much I tried to sublimate my desire, hot sexual memories crept back into my consciousness. Once my husband went on a business trip and my horniness spilled over into a private one-week orgy of drawing my sexual fantasies, getting turned on, and masturbating way beyond the point of going blind. I drew all the exciting sexual perversions I could think of, which were actually very few — oral sex, fucking doggie style, and a threesome. Overwhelmed with guilt at my hedonistic debauchery, I destroyed the drawings. I actually tore them up into tiny bits and flushed them down the toilet, afraid someone might find the scraps in the garbage and put the pieces together.

— Betty Dodson explaining her erotic art beginnings, from *Sex For One: The Joy of Selfloving*

Woman masturbating as part of a 1970 performance at The Gallery of Erotic Art, a private gallery on Manhattan's Upper West Side. As the artist stands fifth from right, his wife performs an "erotic dance" on a bed lit from within by colored lights. Use of a flash disguises the fact the room was entirely dark. From photographer Charles Gatewood's book *Sidetripping*.

There's an art you can show to the public and there is an art that is supposed to be something you don't show to the general public. So then that gets to have a name. But every year now there are more erotic shows, and you begin to wonder what the heck "erotic art" means. The word can be interpreted many ways...We use the word "erotic" in the sense of something that will get some sex response, or in the sense that the subject matter is sexy. Perhaps a guy could find a dozen eggs sexy....I think that one can make a case of the fact that if the individual is aroused by something, it's erotic. Or, let's say, some guy in an erotic show presents a tin can or some sliced peaches. Now, there could be something there that he wants you to think about. It may be another way of approaching the subject — just as it could be a convenient sort of cop-out.

— **artist Larry Rivers, 1968**

Philadelphia was mutilated by an angry man, carrying a copy of the offended *Artforum*.

Photographers were also finding fresh material inside America's sexual landscape. Bored with mainstream assignments from *Rolling Stone* and other magazines, Charles Gatewood turned to the seamy underground for inspiration. His 1975 book *Sidetripping*, with text by William Burroughs, took an anthropological trip up the river of decadence to visit sex clubs, strip bars and Mardi Gras debauchery. Joan Semmel took photographs of models engaged in sex, then painted large-format versions of them. Rick Herold utilized a similar technique, photographing orgies and then transposing the images onto canvases of acrylic paint and Plexiglass. At a Herold opening at the Molly Barnes Gallery on La Cienega Boulevard in L.A., 200 attendees witnessed a female admirer remove her dress, and act as a nude human projection screen for one of the artist's orgy-related films.

And then there was the art for arts' sake, that never necessarily saw a gallery. A member of the Warhol entourage named Brigid Berlin was known for her series of "trip books," art collage books which included impressions of outlines of penises. The daughter of a high-ranking Hearst Publications executive, Berlin also made audiotape recordings of people having sex — from herself with a partner, to other couples and complete orgies — and played them over the phone for friends. The tapes were carefully filed and catalogued, as if in preparation for a museum.

No less valid than the highbrow Manhattan gallery scene were the emerging underground comics industry. Starving hippies scurried around New York's Lower East Side, drawing low-paying strips for the *East Village Other* and *Screw* (whose publisher Al Goldstein used many cartoonists, and at one point even hired Seymour Chwast, a design partner of Milton Glaser, to give *Screw* a facelift). Many of these cartoonists were graduates and dropouts of art schools like SUNY, Pratt, and SVA: now-familiar names like R. Crumb, Bill Griffith, Spain Rodriguez, Kim Deitch, Jay Kinney, and Art Spiegelman. In between peddling her comics, Trina Robbins ran a hippie clothing boutique named Broccoli.

It soon dawned on the artists that while they were in New York, center of the universe, the major underground comics publishers were all out in San Francisco — Rip-Off Press, who did the *Furry Freak Brothers*, Print Mint, who did *Zap*, and Last Gasp, who did their line of political-ecological comics. The migration began, and according to Robbins, it was somewhat lemming-like: "If we hadn't hit the Pacific Ocean, we might have kept going."

R. Crumb was one of the first to land in the Bay Area. At that time, comics were distributed primarily in head shops, along with rolling papers and records. The legend apparently is true — in 1968 he sold copies of his comics from a baby carriage on Haight Street. Crumb soon met other artists, like S. Clay Wilson, Rory Hayes and Robert Williams, among others. Their collaborations were accused of being so sexist and dirty, that the group vowed to produce the most shocking, sexually explicit stories possible. Their purpose was both to attempt to top each other, and also to prove to all the critics that if you thought our previous

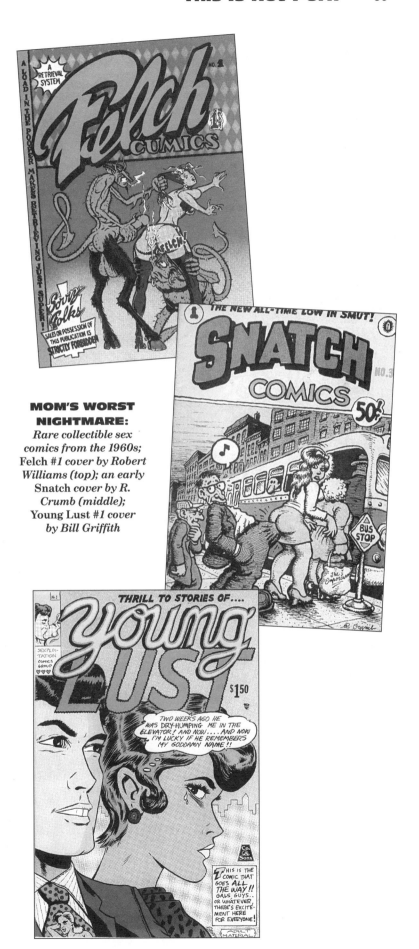

MOM'S WORST NIGHTMARE:
Rare collectible sex comics from the 1960s; Felch #1 cover by Robert Williams (top); an early Snatch cover by R. Crumb (middle); Young Lust #1 cover by Bill Griffith

work was disgusting, check out these.

Half-size comics emerged with wild titles like *Snatch, Cunt* and *Felch*, the insane artwork splashing across the pages, depictions of outrageous jizz-lobbing orgies, wholesome tableaus of family incest, and pirates who chopped off penises with cleavers. The subject matter was so vulgar, the artists signed their work with pseudonyms, and encouraged readers to reproduce the material as much as they wanted. One *Felch* cover by Williams announced that even being in possession of the very comic they were holding was "expressly forbidden." *Snatch* was busted after a few issues, as the Supreme Court began applying local standards to obscenity, and everybody moved on to other projects.

New Yorkers Bill Griffith and Jay Kinney became seized with the idea to do a parody of 1950s romance comics. Griffith suggested they do a whole comic title — the genre hadn't yet been satirized. They agreed to put together a love comic called *Young Lust*, that would portray

"the way people really were," and appeal to both men and women. Griffith peddled the stories around San Francisco, but all the publishers turned it down. The stories — one was about a kinky rock star who kept all the plants in his apartment in bondage — were too weird and extreme. Fortunately a new comics company called Company and Sons agreed to publish it. *Young Lust* #1 appeared in the fall of 1970, immediately went into reprints, and became the third most popular selling underground comic, eventually selling 200,000 copies.

A few years after this intial spate of sex comics, the women were tired of the boys' club, and also wanted to jump into the pool. Last Gasp published *Wimmen's Comix* beginning in 1972, holding the banner of feminism. Beating them to the newsstand by two weeks was *Tits & Clits*, a raunchier title published by two healthy blondes from Los Angeles named Lyn Chevli and Joyce Farmer. In 1976 Trina Robbins was approached by Denis Kitchen of

NO MORE BOYS' CLUB:
*Examples of early 1970s all-
female sex comics*

Kitchen Sink Press to put together an anthology of female comics, and do something interesting other than feminism. Robbins invited women artists to contribute stories that depicted women's erotic fantasies, and came up with the title *Wet Satin*. The resulting first issue was too obscene and refused by a Midwest printer — the same printer who had no problem with printing issues of an all-guys comic called *Bizarre Sex*. *Wet Satin* played the censorship card, claiming discrimination because of gender, and the controversy was written up in *Screw* and *Mother Jones*. *Wet Satin* #1 was eventually printed in San Francisco, and appeared with panels of women seducing men of their choice, or masturbating themselves; one female experienced mind-blowing, electric orgasms courtesy of a mythical, winged man-satyr. The title would last one more issue, after which everyone was too fatigued to continue.

Other lines of comics would capitalize on the country's fascination with sex. Fantasy artwork from Frank Frazetta and *Heavy Metal* became required wall decor in America's dorm rooms, images of well-muscled women keeping watch over the bong. Former *Mad* artist Wally Wood found a second career illustrating risque parodies of classics such as *Alice in Wonderland*. The comics of *National Lampoon* pushed taste to the limits, as did a sexual parody of the old Archies comics titled *Cherry Pop-Tart*.

The novelty of sexual themes in art has long since worn off. It still sells, as it always will, but now that the gates of self-expression are propped open that much wider, there is more room for more sex. America's youth can easily visit comic stores and thumb through explicit titles, and art students routinely plumb the depths of sexual depravity to fulfill project assignments. If Anita Steckel hadn't created giant blue penises atop skyscrapers in the 1970s, somebody else would have done them by now.

FANTASY ART FREAK-OUT:
Typical dorm room poster by Frank Frazetta (left); one of many imitators of Heavy Metal *(right)*

W

Americans of the '60s and '70s depended on TV and radio for their entertainment more than any previous generations, especially teenagers. Underage kids found themselves either driving around in a car or stuck at home with the family, watching the tube. Hidden within these free methods of boredom-fighting was a barrage of sexually charged messages for young people, who were already busy sorting out all the other sexual messages from music, magazines, books and movies. Kids sat in bedrooms across the country, glued to Panasonic ball-on-a-chain transistors, absorbing late-night radio talk shows that dispensed sexual advice. Dens and living rooms flickered with suggestive TV

nton Airwaves

programming, delivered free of charge to imprint upon youngsters and work them into a lather. The electronic babysitter had become the electronic titillator, its inviting pacifier turning into a full-on human nipple. Young boys ogled the braless "jiggle TV" images of *Charlie's Angels* and *Three's Company*; girls chose their favorites from a never-ending supply of TV beefcake — Lyle Waggoner, Erik Estrada or Randy Mantooth. For those too young to act on their impulses, this was their first glimpse into an adult world that seemed to represent sexual freedom. And it was available seven days a week.

Although TV was finally playing a major role in the country's obsession with the act of reproduction, radio was not to be overlooked. Chicago-area

EVOLUTION OF THE BLONDE:
(clockwise from top) The 1960s model, portrayed by a mostly covered-up Barbara Eden; The revamped '70s version, a braless Farrah Fawcett poster that sold in the millions; The '60s guy version, a dishwater Shatner

CHEERLEADER: Bachelor Number Two, what nationality are you?

BACHELOR: Well, my father is Welsh, and my mother is Hungarian, so I guess I'm Well-Hung!

— exchange from *The Dating Game* that was never aired, late 1960s

THE SIXTIES LEG-ACY:
Ellie Mae dipping a toe into Beverly Hills (top); More hillbilly gams from the girls of Petticoat Junction *(middle); Stranded on* Gilligan's Island *in hot pants (bottom)*

listeners in 1968 tuned into the WCFL graveyard shift of Stan the Record Man, who would talk to his listeners in between songs, discussing their relationship problems live on the air. Stan Dale had already enjoyed a long broadcasting career as narrator of the radio shows *The Lone Ranger, Sergeant Preston of the Yukon* and *The Shadow.* On the side, he and his wife, Helen, started teaching sex workshops called the Stan Dale Love-In, where couples and singles attended weekend courses in rented hotel ballrooms to learn exercises in intimacy and tantric sex. Dale's rap included wisdom like, "You are who you think you are. But who you think you are isn't really who you are. You're much more magnificent than that."

Thousands passed through the workshops, and millions watched Stan and Helen appear on *Geraldo*, defending their triadic marriage to Janet, a young woman half their age. Although the audience attacked them, yelling that Stan was Satan and that the women were whores and prostitutes, the Dales insisted they were simply trying to spread a message of love and peace. The Dale workshops, lectures and newsletters continue today under an umbrella organization in San Mateo, California called the Human Awareness Institute.

Progressive new radio formats allowed for the ultimate in experimental audio broadcasting. DJs eagerly pursued any opportunity to play records with dirty words, from Frank Zappa and the Mothers' *Live at the Fillmore East*, to the Rolling Stones' line from *Some Girls* about "Black girls just want to get fucked all night," to comedy albums by George Carlin and Cheech & Chong. Prostitutes, rock stars and groupies dropped by stations for live interviews. Sex and drug advice shows appeared. Disc jockeys would claim to receive head live on the air, or announce entire shifts with a woman sitting in their lap. College radio stations were even taken away from students because of repeated obscenity violations.

While radio pushed the limits of overt sexual content, television attempted its share of similar programming, as network executives began spicing up their shows with bare midriffs, double entendres and storylines dealing with pornography, prostitution and girlie magazines. Although TV was the last medium to reflect the sexual revolution — after books, print and film — it could be argued it had the largest impact of all, reaching a national audience in the millions.

Television audiences of the 1960s began noticing an inordinate amount of female flesh parading across their screens, from *Laugh-In* bikini dancers like Goldie Hawn to the *Gilligan's Island* babes, the girls of *Petticoat Junction* (set in the town of Hooterville), and a buxom blonde genie who called her man "Master." A principal engineer of the sexual lifestyle, *Playboy* publisher Hugh Hefner hosted *Playboy After Dark*, a second version of the magazine brought to life in a swinging bachelor pad living room. Aging hipsters in turtlenecks yukked it up with young co-eds and comedians of the day, while musical entertainment was provided by current rock bands like Deep Purple or the Grateful Dead.

Concurrent with this groovy programming was an influence coming from across the Atlantic, and audiences got their first glimpses of Anglo friskiness. The spy drama *The Avengers* might have gained viewers from its exciting espionage plotlines; then again it might have been the skin-tight costumes of Emma Peel. A strange new half-hour comedy show popped up on PBS, hosted by a lecherous round man named Benny Hill, who ogled busty models in bikinis. Even the comedy sketches of Monty Python occasionally pushed America's sexual button such as a woman in racy lingerie posing on a bed, her words dubbed by a deep-voiced man.

Faced with increasing competition from imported content, U.S. programming executives poured on the coals. In 1969 producers Jim Parker and Arnold Margolin announced their new episodic prime-time ABC comedy program would be "the greatest freedom show of its kind ever produced for TV." Premiering on September 9, 1969, the pilot episode of *Love, American Style* featured a scenario, "Love and the Pill," in which a set of parents worry over their daughter's plans to take her boyfriend on a swinger's tour of Europe. The format was simple — take current sexual subjects of society, place them into an innocent comedic structure, push the patriotic graphics and add some exploding fireworks for the opening. Viewers tuned in each Friday night, eager to see what this week's topic would be: couple-swapping, massage parlors, waterbeds, groupies or perhaps comedian Arte Johnson wrestling with a blow-up doll. In 1972 a "Lovemate of the Week" centerfold appeared, rotating a new girl every show.

The next logical step was "jiggle TV."

Another creation of the mind-numbing Aaron Spelling production company, *Charlie's Angels* was most likely based on a cheesy 1973 film by Ted V. Mikels called *The Doll Squad*,

Love And The Living Doll	Love And The Little Black Book
Love And The Coed Dorm	Love And The Old Swingers
Love And The Groupie	Love And The Cheaters
Love And The Pick-Up	Love And The Swing Philosophy
Love And The Neglected Wife	Love And The Sexpert
Love And The Naked Stranger	Love And The Love Nest
Love And The Married Bachelor	Love And The Suspicious Husband
Love And The Sex Survey	
Love And The Bachelor Party	**— episode titles from ABC's**
Love And The Conjugal Visit	**prime-time** *Love, American Style*,
Love And The Topless Policy	**1969-1974**
Love And The Water Bed	

LOCKED AND LOADED:
Strategically placed rifles from
The Wild Wild West

On October 30, 1968, in Palm Springs, California, KPLM-TV ran the station's usual Midnight Prayer and signed off the air. The typical Sunday evening routine was suddenly followed by 15 minutes of hardcore pornography. Nobody called police until it was over, and even then nobody was angry. According to police sergeant Jim Wall, "People just wanted to tell and confirm what they had seen on the screen."

While doing research for her *Happy Hooker* book in the early '70s, New York City madam Xaviera Hollander hired a shady electronics whiz to help her tape telephone conversations and detect wiretaps. In reality, the surveillance man was getting paid by authorities to record her every move, including a miniature television camera mounted in her bedroom, which secretly beamed images back to a nearby vice squad office. One day the video signal was accidentally picked up by a Spanish-language UHF station, and Manhattan's Spanish TV viewers were treated to 45 minutes of hardcore orgy action from the Happy Hooker's boudoir.

about three beautiful women on a mission to stop an ex-CIA agent out to rule the world. Spelling called his girls "angels," everyday cops turned exciting undercover detectives, thanks to an unseen Charlie, who announced smugly at the beginning of every episode: "I took them away from all that. Now they work for me." Skin-tight clothing was the rule, the braless nipples driving young boys crazy. One controversial episode took place in a prison, and prime-time America watched the Angels open their towels in the shower to be sprayed down for lice. Farrah Fawcett was little-known when the series began, but rapidly became the show's main attraction after release of her swimsuit posters, and walked out on the series after the first year. It would take three actresses to replace the powerful role of Jill Monroe, from Cheryl Ladd to Shelley Hack and then Tanya Roberts — but contractual obligations brought Farrah back for a limited number of guest appearances. Such a premise for a show was apparently too good to waste, so in 1977 Joel Scott directed a porn feature film version called *A Coming of Angels*, where the young women worked for a boss named Andy.

Suzanne Somers was reportedly discovered by ABC executive Fred Silverman in a *Tonight Show* sketch, playing a blonde bimbo in a bikini. Although a bit older and with a son, her skills were evident, and she was hired to be a blonde bimbo in *Three's Company*. Adapted from a British series, the show's storylines were packed with cheap sex jokes, and Somers' braless T-shirts drew objections from religious leaders and critics, but it didn't stop her from becoming TV's hot new sex symbol. A slavering public eagerly opened up their wallets for Suzanne Somers posters and T-shirts, as well as for those pesky nude photos showing up in *Playboy*. She appeared on the cover of *Newsweek*, her clothes falling off her shoulder. At the height of her popularity, she supposedly told reporters, "If you've got it, bump it with a trumpet."

Other hormone queens of the small screen would soon follow, from Lynda Carter to Loni Anderson and the *Hee Haw* girls — even the icy Morgan Fairchild seemed sexy from a distance. Female viewers settled for their pin-up equivalents like Randy Mantooth, Lyle Waggoner from *The Carol Burnett Show* or Robert Conrad from *The Wild Wild West*, who invariably ended up stripped to the waist and tied to torture devices, struggling for his life.

The softcore trend continued with the teen dance shows *American Bandstand* and *Soul*

MORE BLONDES THAT ARE TALLER:
Suzanne Somers forgot her underwear again (above); Loni Anderson, the smartest bimbo in radio

Train, where resourceful cameramen intention-ally zoomed their lenses into America's latest examples of gyrating, bouncing nubile flesh. Executives pitted their sexiest talent against each other for an insipid pseudo-sports competition called *Battle of the Network Stars* that was quickly parodied by *Saturday Night Live* as "Battle of the Network T&A's." Even the venerable Academy Awards telecast was not immune to excessive nudity. The 1974 Oscars was interrupted by a streaker who dashed across the stage behind actor David Niven. Niven's ad-lib, congratulating the streaker for "showing off his shortcomings," was later rumored to be set-up, as was the streaker him-self. The CBS jingle "Turn us on, we'll turn you on" seemed to sum up the approach to pro-gramming, and those in the industry referred to 1977-78 as the "season of sex."

But after the kiddies were put to bed, things got even raunchier. Late-night television was ruled by *The Tonight Show*, where Johnny Carson's monologues provided the truest barometer of the nation's increasing sexual appetite. Amidst the jokes about swingers, stewardesses and Linda Lovelace, Carson kept the show moving with a list of randy guests. One frequent addition was Spanish sexpot entertainer Charo (aka Maria Rosario Pilar Martinez Molina Bazza), whose "coochie coochie" was invariably accompanied by a complete body shimmy, as Ed and Johnny exchanged leering smirks. Although an excellent flamenco guitarist, audiences waited for her sug-gestive, convoluted use of the English language, such as "When I hear whistles, I get bumps all over my goose!" In 1968, author Jacqueline Susann appeared on the program to plug her newest book, *The Love Machine*. Carson asked what she thought of Philip Roth's novel *Portnoy's Complaint*, wherein the main character jerks off into a pound of fresh liver, destined for the family dinner table. "It's a great book," said Susann, "but I wouldn't want to shake hands with the author."

Also contributing to the late-night peep show was Tom Snyder's *Tomorrow Show*. On one early '70s broadcast, porn stars Marilyn Chambers and Jamie Gillis exchanged winks and flirted so much during the segment that the studio crew was heard laughing nervously off-camera. Gillis remembers Snyder being very knowledgable about Linda Lovelace and *Deep Throat* off-camera, but when the red light blinked on, he turned into the consummate broadcasting pro and asked, "There's this

STILL MORE BLONDES: *"Coochie coochie" Charo, without that distracting guitar (above); Angie Dickinson busts another john*

Óne recent Sunday evening, the wife of a New York City lawyer heard gig-gles coming from the TV room of her Upper East Side duplex. Her curiosity aroused, she peeked into the room and saw her 11-year-old daughter huddled in front of the set. The screen showed a man massaging a naked girl with globs of spaghetti. Aghast, the woman flicked her gaze to the TV dial long enough to note that it was set to one of the city's cable channels. By now the scene had shifted to two partially clad couples frolicking on a large bed. The camera quickly panned over a pair of bare buttocks. There was a glimpse of a penis. A string of four-letter words filled the room. "I've got to call Kathy," squealed the daughter, but her mother had already commandeered the phone and was dialing the cable company. "Look" she shouted at the person who finally answered. "I'm a very liberal woman. My husband is a very liberal man. *But exactly what the hell is going on here?*"

— Newsweek, April 1973

KEEP IT IN THE FAMILY:
*Tight pants and short shorts from
the* Dukes of Hazzard *cousins*

JANE CURTIN: The drive against pornography districts in major cities continued to gain momentum this week, as more demonstrations were held in New York. Bill Murray was on the scene at one of them in Manhattan, and has an eyewitness report. Bill?

BILL MURRAY: Thank you, Jane. The Citizens' Committee to clean up New York's porn-infested areas continued its series of rallies today, as a huge, throbbing, pulsating crowd sprang erect from nowhere and forced its way into the steaming nether region surrounding the glistening, sweaty intersection of Eighth Avenue and Forty-Second Street. Thrusting, driving, pushing its way into the usually receptive neighborhood, the excited throng, now grown to five times its original size, rammed itself again and again and again into the quivering, perspiring, musty dankness, fluctuating between eager anticipation and trembling revulsion. Now, suddenly, the tumescent crowd and the irresistible area were one heaving, alternately melting and thawing turgid entity, ascending to heights heretofore unexperienced. Then, with a gigantic, soul-searching, heart-stopping series of eruptions, it was over. Afterwards, the crowd had a cigarette and went home. Jane?

— **from "Weekend Update" news segment,** *Saturday Night Live,* **mid-'70s**

woman in the industry, Linda...what's her name?"

Beginning in 1975, *Saturday Night Live* also pushed it to the limit with sex-related material. Chevy Chase delivered phony news segment jokes about "Fidel Castro announced his pulling out of Angola..A frustrated Angola could not be reached for comment." Sketches were censored so often that writers purposely turned in excessively violent and sexist material never meant to be aired, just so NBC watchdogs would have something to do.

As technology became available to home consumers, people realized they didn't have to wait for racy programming. They could do it themselves. In 1972, as new FCC rules led to community access channels, Sony introduced its Port-a-Pak portable video recorder. By 1975, Sony's Betamax and JVC's VHS formats were battling for public acceptance.

Some eagerly turned the cameras on themselves, and set up tripods in the bedroom for those Kodak "magic moments." The student-operated cable system at Syracuse University screened *Deep Throat* across the campus. Adult cable in Manhattan was available initially only on the Upper East and West sides, but the city's two cable operators, TelePrompter and Sterling-Manhattan, rapidly expanded throughout the city. One Sunday-night series was offered by Anton Perich, whose experimental video troupe performed skits and bizarre sexual acts, such as a man inserting a light bulb into his butt. The *Midnight Blue* series, begun by *Screw* publisher Al Goldstein and radio DJ Alex Bennett, still continues its brand of raunchy comedy and interviews with porn personalities. By the early '80s, a New York swinger with some family money named Robin Byrd jumped on the cable access bandwagon, singing X-rated songs like "Baby let me bang your box!" while dancing nude in front of the camera.

Television and radio today offer an endless parade of sexual programming, from Howard Stern and other shock jocks to hardcore cable channels that are beamed around the planet via satellite. Images of people having sex can now be summoned into the home merely by the touch of a button. The percentage of video porn rentals increases every year. Sex has completely saturated the audio and video airwaves, and the number of people busily e-mailing and downloading porn off the internet contrasts dramatically to the panic once instigated by Barbara Eden's navel.

**HOG-TIED FOR
HIGH RATINGS:**
*Networks try a little light bondage
(clockwise from top), as Robert
Conrad struggles against certain
death; Lynda Carter in captive
reflection; The Angels frantically
search for a blowdryer*

Examples of sexually suggestive primetime programming:

Beverly Hillbillies
1962-71 — America suffered through this sitcom about bohunks in the big city, just to catch a peek of daughter Ellie May, squeezed into pants so tight the zipper required its own team of wardrobe people. Pinup girl and future Manson Family murder victim Sharon Tate appeared in a small role for two seasons, as Mr. Drysdale's secretary.

Blansky's Beauties
1977 — Nancy Walker acted as apartment complex den mother to beautiful Las Vegas showgirls.

Bob & Carol & Ted & Alice
1973 — Based on the film. Storylines about nude swimming, premarital sex and cohabitation outside marriage. Daughter played by Jodie Foster.

Carol Burnett Show
1967-79 — Comedy sketch/variety show which featured young buck Lyle Waggoner, the sole reason many female viewers tuned in.

Charlie's Angels
1976-1981 — Three beautiful female detectives go undercover as models, stewardesses, call girls and centerfolds, taking orders from a speakerphone. Introduced a nation of viewers to braless jumpsuits, reckless hair and gutless Ford automobiles.

Cher
1975-76 — Short-lived variety show after splitting up with Sonny Bono. Bonus for U.S. viewers: no bra.

Chico and the Man
1974-78 — The last two seasons featured busty Spanish entertainer Charo in the role of Aunt Charo, a busty Spanish entertainer.

CHiPs
1977-83 — Just to get

this over with...Erik Estrada, Larry Wilcox, disco theme.

Dating Game
1966-70 — Typical Chuck Barris program wherein young, good-looking people asked each other titillating questions provided by the staff.

Dukes of Hazzard
1979-85 — Good ol' boy comedy about two redneck cousins in tight jeans (Tom Wopat and John Schneider) with a hot car ("General Lee") and an even hotter cousin (Catherine Bach).

Emergency
1972-77 — Randy Mantooth and Kevin Tighe saving lives in tight-fitting paramedic uniforms.

Keep On Truckin'
1975 — Comedy variety show featuring Charles Fleischer, Wayland Flowers and Fred Travalena. Worth watching for racy bumper shots that led to commercials, such as a close-up shot of a braless woman in tight T-shirt patterned with the show's logo. Despite the allure, the program lasted only four weeks.

Get Christie Love
1974-75— Black, sexy female cop, forever on undercover assignment as a prostitute, an obvious ripoff of Pam Grier movies. "You under arrest, sugar."

Gilligan's Island
1974-67— Reruns forever, featuring all-American girl Dawn Wells and pin-up queen Tina Louise, in the role originally created for Jayne Mansfield, who turned it down. Prompted two generations of locker-room philosophical dialogues like, "So, which would you do, Ginger or Mary Ann?"

Happy Days
1974-84 — Long-running nostalgia sitcom based on an episode of *Love, American Style*. Girls watched to check out the Fonz, and guys waited for the rerun of Fonzie's hot biker-babe girlfriend, Pinky Tuscadero.

Hee Haw
1969-71, syndicated until 1993 — Cornball one-liners against a tableau of busty girls in Li'l Abner hillbilly hotpants, including Hefner playtoy Barbi Benton and nude model/actress Misty Rowe. A spinoff program, *Hee Haw Honeys*, 1978-79, featured Misty Rowe and Kathie Lee Johnson, nee Kathie Lee Gifford.

Hot L Baltimore
1975 — Based on award-winning off-Broadway play, and adapted for television by Norman Lear. Featured prostitutes, gay male couples, and much sexual innuendo.

I Dream of Jeannie
1965-70 — The sight of Barbara Eden's ample cleavage made staying home from school something to look forward to. After much debate, her midriff was finally allowed to be shown without a scarf covering it.

Joey & Dad
1975 — Variety show starring Joey Heatherton and her father. Joey was already well-known for a *Happy Hooker* film and a series of sexy mattress commercials.

Love, American Style
1969-74 — Prime-time comedy sketches about the pitfalls and pratfalls of love, incorporating the raciest possible elements of society, from birth control and swingers to blow-up dolls, couple-swapping and massage parlors.

Match Game
1962-69, 1973-79 — Game show that depended on double entendre questions from host Gene Rayburn, as in, "When I get married, I want a man with a big *blank*." Celebrity panelists included wisecracking Richard Dawson and Charles Nelson Reilly.

Maude
1972-78 — Bea Arthur played an independent woman whose daughter, Adrienne Barbeau, kept viewers returning for her enormous cleavage. Estranged husband was Bill Macy, star of the

original stage version of *Oh! Calcutta!* In the first season, Maude stunned America by getting a prime-time abortion.

My Living Doll
1965-65 — Julie Newmar starred as AF 709, the ultimate technological advance in sexism: a beautiful, curvy female

robot, programmed to do anything she was told.

Newlywed Game
1967-71 — Another strange Chuck Barris production, a variation of which is still on the air. The classic urban legend, an exchange between host Bob Ewbanks and a young bridegroom that apparently has basis in fact, goes something like this: "Where's the weirdest place you and your wife have ever made love?" "I'd have to say up the butt, Bob."

One Day at a Time
1975-84 — Divorced mom and her two beautiful daughters. Bonnie Franklin amused America by rarely wearing a bra.

Petticoat Junction
1963-70 — Three leggy daughters help their mother run a hotel in a town called Hooterville. Opening credits featured the girls washing their underwear.

Playboy After Dark
1968-69 — Noteworthy today for uncomfortable-looking rock musician guests. Hefner and Barbara Klein, aka Barbi Benton, first met on the set. Ratings were good, despite *Time* magazine's assessment: "As an actor, Hefner makes a pretty good magazine publisher."

Playboy's Penthouse
1959-60 — Hefner's TV debut, staged as an impromptu party broadcast from his bachelor pad, with hired babes, guest jazz hepcats and the first appearance of the proverbial pipe. Syndicated only.

Police Woman
1974-78 — Blonde cop Sgt. Pepper Anderson (JFK mistress Angie Dickinson) went undercover each week in slutty costumes to catch pimps and johns.

Rowan & Martin's Laugh-In
1968-73 — Fast-paced comedy featuring plenty of racy jokes and visual innuendos. As the show cut to a commercial, viewers read one-liner gags that were written on the stomach of a bikini-clad Goldie Hawn.

Saturday Night Live
1975 — Late-night comedy/variety show that pushed the boundaries of taste. First few seasons were rife with sex-related gags, including random cutaways to audience members, with a credit underneath their face reading "Spells Kunta Kinte with a C." One sketch written by Al Franken and Tom Davis called "Planet of the Enormous Hooters" featured guest star Raquel Welch as a hideously deformed woman on a planet of super-endowed women, who was mocked because her breasts were simply normal sized. NBC censors killed the idea.

Soap
1977-81 — This satire of soap operas offended on many levels, shoving America's face in its own adultery, homophobia, racism, and overwhelming preoccupation with having sex. Before it even hit the airwaves, ABC received over 30,000 letters condeming the show. Longtime TV critic Rev. Everett Parker called the program "a deliberate effort to break down any resistance to whatever the industry wants to put into prime time...."

Sugar Time!
1977-78 — Sitcom about three beautiful young girls who wanted to be rock singers, eagerly rehearsing their group, named Sugar. Starred *Playboy* bunny and Hefner girlfriend Barbi Benton.

Ted Knight Show
1978 — Empty-headed newscaster from *Mary Tyler Moore* got his own empty-headed sitcom as manager of a high-class escort service. Canceled after five weeks.

Three's Company
1977-84 — Sitcom based almost entirely on sexual references and shots of a braless Suzanne Somers, and later her body-double replacements, Jenilee Harrison and Priscilla Barnes. Despite all the cheap sex jokes, nobody ever got any.

Tomorrow Show
1973-82 — Host Tom Snyder, former news anchorman for KNBC in L.A., frequently interviewed members of the sexual revolution, from porn stars to the owner of Plato's Retreat, and a remote broadcast from a California nudist colony. Added two co-hosts, gossip columnist Rona Barrett and human relationships expert Nancy Friday, author of *My Secret Garden.*

Tonight Show (Johnny Carson version)
1962-92 — Regular sexpot guests included Dolly Parton, Charo, Joan Embrey from the San Diego Zoo, matinee lady Carol Wayne, Raquel Welch and other movie and TV stars of the day, prompting wolf whistles from the studio audience. Female viewers gushed over frequent guest host Burt Reynolds. Carson thanked one audience by saying, "I'd blow you a kiss but I heard about an entertainer who did that and fell in love with his hand."

Turn On
1969 — ABC comedy/variety show patterned after *Laugh-In*, with same executive producer George Schlatter. Pilot episode contained so many rampant sexual double-entendres, the sponsor and many network affiliates dropped it immediately. Guest star on the first and only telecast was Tim Conway.

Wild Wild West
1965-70 — James Bond-style espionage set in the Old West, starring the handsome Robert Conrad, who always seemed to be abducted and tied up in a spread-eagled position. There were some good-looking women on the perimeter as well.

WKRP in Cincinnati
1978-82 — Sitcom launched well-endowed blonde Loni Anderson as a marketable sex symbol, seen on posters across the nation.

Wonder Woman
1976-78 — Adventure series based on busty comic book heroine, starred a former Miss World U.S.A., the statuesque Lynda Carter, squeezed into a tight costume, cape and go-go boots. And Lyle Waggoner again.

NETWORK NAUGHTIES: *Erik Estrada discos into history (left); Julie Newmar as primetime's first female robot (this page)*

Prostitution may be the oldest gig in town, but it certainly grew in the public's consciousness during the Golden Age. The loosening of morals in the '60s and '70s gave way to an above-ground status prostitution had never before seen. Plainly, if sex were to be trotted out before the public in advertising, films, books and theater shows, it seemed obvious that it should be more available for someone wishing to pay for sexual services. And the manner in which prostitution gained its status mirrored the country's morality, reflected in the various geographical areas.

In cosmopolitan New York, as wealthy businessmen from all over the world were telephoning their

Wanna Party?

appointments at exclusive brothel mansions in between meetings, blue-collar men were parting the bead curtains of Times Square massage parlors for a low-budget encounter. In California a similar structure was developing with brothels and parlors, but in the Golden State, the prostitutes themselves were organizing — demanding to be treated with respect, and fighting to rewrite archaic laws that failed to reflect the reality of the streets. And in Nevada, where Wild West values had long tolerated prostitution, the casinos of Las Vegas were experiencing what locals would call "the great whore invasions of 73-74," with showgirls asking for — and getting — several hundred dollars per trick. The notorious Chicken Farm (later immortalized in the Dolly

Categories of Johns

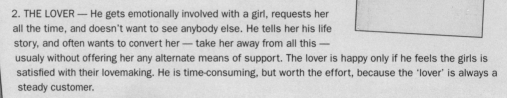

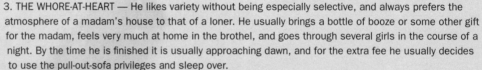

1. THE EASY CHOOSER — He comes in horny and in a rush and hardly has the time for a drink. He just wants to get a quick blow-job, and absolutely no more involvement. No kissing, no holding, no need for faking it on the girl's part. He is in and out in fifteen minutes.

There is a variation on the type of "john" who wants only a blow-job. This one rationalizes that if he does not put his penis inside a vagina he is not being unfaithful to his wife. Strangely enough, this is usually the kind of man who was one of the biggest and wildest swingers before he was married.

2. THE LOVER — He gets emotionally involved with a girl, requests her all the time, and doesn't want to see anybody else. He tells her his life story, and often wants to convert her — take her away from all this — usualy without offering her any alternate means of support. The lover is happy only if he feels the girls is satisfied with their lovemaking. He is time-consuming, but worth the effort, because the 'lover' is always a steady customer.

3. THE WHORE-AT-HEART — He likes variety without being especially selective, and always prefers the atmosphere of a madam's house to that of a loner. He usually brings a bottle of booze or some other gift for the madam, feels very much at home in the brothel, and goes through several girls in the course of a night. By the time he is finished it is usually approaching dawn, and for the extra fee he usually decides to use the pull-out-sofa privileges and sleep over.

4. THE DON JUAN — He comes carrying tales of all the gorgeous airline stewardesses, secretaries, and models he has slept with and who are all after his fantastic body. This type is always young, not necessarily good-looking, and almost never good in bed either. You often wonder where he gets the strength to spend money at your house, because, from the stories he tells, it sounds like he has a pretty good business going for himself!

5. THE INTROVERT HIGH ROLLER — This man, usually more of an intellectual than the usual john, wants to see a girl only once in his lifetime and never again. He uses the madams because he knows they have connections with girls all over the city and can give him access to the variety he craves. He is either a hard-working bachelor concentrating too hard on his career to hang around parties and pick up girls, or if he is married, he usually turns up in the summer when his wife is on vacation. He will call any time of the day or night, whenever the urge strikes him.

6. THE HAGGLER — He sits down and hangs aroud for half an hour smoking as many of your cigarettes and drinking as much of your liquor as he can get his hands on, while making up his mind whether he will go at all. He puts you out of your way to get a special type of girl, even if there are several already sitting around, and when he finally decides to give it a try and you are about to straighten out prices, he gives you a hassle and tries to chisel down your prices. He usually throws in how much it cost him to park his car.

7-A. THE TEMPORARY IMPOTENT — He is impotent on account of too much to drink, fatigue, a fall in the stock market, or pressure at the office. But whatever the cause, it is generally short-lived, and when he comes back in another week he will probably be a good, strong lover again. This man is usually the slightly nervous, sensitive type, and with him we always have patience and try to give him a second chance.

7-B. THE PERMANENT IMPOTENT FREAK — He likes lots of girls in group scenes, or likes to watch lesbian scenes and doesn't care whether the girls are black, white, or green. His permanent debility is caused either by age or some massive complex, and his preferences include fingering the girls until they climax (or fake it), just eating them, masturbating while the girl looks on, and some even like anal intercourse with a dildo or even go as far as carrots, sticks, beads on a string, ice cubes, or any other miscellany that will go up there.

— The Happy Hooker by Xaviera Hollander, 1972

Parton film *Best Little Whorehouse in Texas*) had been open for business since at least the 1890s, but was shut down in the early '70s. Nevada authorities quietly practiced a permissive quota system, until two counties actually pushed legislation through to become the only areas in the United States where prostitution is now completely legal.

Not only were men visiting hookers in droves, the prostitutes themselves were becoming media celebrities. In New York's hoity Upper East Side, a young European woman named Xaviera Hollander achieved notoriety as the nation's most famous madam. Fueled by high-publicity busts for prostitution, her auto-biographical books, beginning with *The Happy Hooker*, became an instant sensation. Not only did she become a household name, her best-seller offered America an education in the inner workings of the prostitution business.

Hollander's success story began fairly sedately as a young married woman, living in Manhattan in the late '60s. After discovering her husband was cheating on her, she went on a nympho bender, then moved in with a guy. One morning he gave her $100. She met another guy, who said he only dated call girls. They spent the night, he gave her $150, and introduced her to his Greenwich Village madam. According to her books, she started work that night, soon out-grew the little operation, and was recommended to Manhattan's two top madams, Madeleine and Daphne.

Daphne's operation worked out of a Lexington Avenue brownstone, and featured a swimming pool and milk baths. Madeleine ran a five-bedroom brownstone in Murray Hill, listing her customers in a black book by their booze preference: Red Label, Mr. Cutty, Mr. Sark (some even made up their own aliases, like Marco Polo, Plato, and Aristotle). Xaviera was hired, still keeping a day job as an office secre-tary, but was eventually rejected by Madeleine, and continued turning tricks for other madams before getting busted in 1970. Asked for her occupation, she replied, "Nymphomaniac," much to the amusement of the rest of the girls in the jail cell. She flew to Puerto Rico and turned tricks in the casinos, then returned and decided to start her own brothel.

She found a space in the East 50s and began recruiting girls — stewardesses, bored house-wives, secretaries and salesgirls — four to seven girls on hand at all times, with 400 available on call of every ethnic group and body type. Her expenses were high. Police payoffs were in cash,

Honolulu Madam
by Iolana Mitsuko / Autobiography of a girl who sold her body to the highest bidder!

I reached behind me and put my fin-gers to the hooks and eyes of my bra, provocatively arching out my breasts, and I saw his eyes glitter and narrow with desire. "It's going to cost you to take me to bed tonight, Bob," I softly told him. "Do you think I'm worth twenty-five dollars for about an hour of good, hot loving?"

"Iolana!" he gasped, his eyes widening with alarmed surprise.

"I'm not a three- or five-dollar crib girl, Bob. The surfing season is about over, so I've got to get the best price I can to save a little money and keep alive until things start booming again. So if you want to sleep with me, you'll have to pay me twenty-five dollars. It's as simple as that."

His jaw dropped. "You...you mean...?"

I nodded. "That's right, Bob. I've decided to do it for pay now. Promises of marriage don't really count for much, and they don't pay a girl's rent or buy her groceries. I'm making you a special offer because you're pretty good in bed and I get a charge out of it. I almost like you enough to give you a last piece before you go back home, but I'm afraid I need the money rather more than the senti-mental gesture. Well, are you still interested?"

His face twisted and I heard a groan. Then he was fumbling in his trousers, bringing out his wallet, counting out two tens and a five, thrusting them at me. "All right!" his voice was hoarse and trembling. "Sure, you're worth that. Now get it all off and let's go to bed."

I smiled and nodded, fighting my tears...

— a hardboiled yet tender moment from Honolulu Madam by Iolana Mitsuko, 1969

BALLS TO THE WALL:
*A choice wire news photo from the 1977
Hookers' Ball of Margo St. James, San
Francisco police chief Frank Gaines, and
the "Wonder Whore" (above); The renewed
version of the Ball, relaunched in 1995*

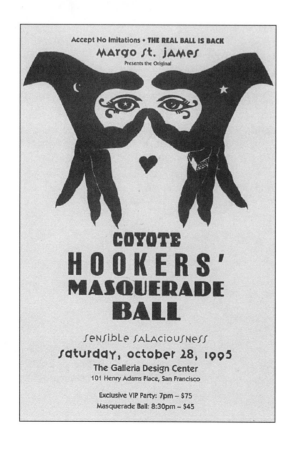

averaging over $1,000/month, but much of the other costs were settled in barter. Food from the Chinese restaurant downstairs, liquor distributors, florists, jewelers, shoemakers, furniture manufacturers, building managers, druggists, telephone installers, were all "serviced" on the exchange program.

Her customers were high-class in both income and demands: 50 percent were stockbrokers, another 10 were bankers, most were married and either bored or visiting the city on business. After straight sex, their most popular request was, in order: a blow job, then anal sex, followed by analingus. Hollander kept a Greek-style anal-sex "specialist" girl on call, as well as a house gynecologist.) It was a very successful operation, and she couldn't keep it a secret any longer.

Hollander's book *The Happy Hooker* appeared on stands in 1972, written at the tender age of 28. Dell coughed up $100,000, the highest fee ever paid for a paperback original at the time. America eagerly devoured every sleazy chapter, and by October it had approached 4 million copies in print. Readers got a behind-the-scenes view of the prostitution reality, including a handy guide to john types, categorized by ethnicity. The subject matter was too racy for Hollander to go on the talk shows of the day, but she would be hounded by journalists throughout the next year. She basked in all the attention, and quickly spawned the sequels *Xaviera!*, *Letters to the Happy Hooker*, *My Life With Xaviera* (by boyfriend Larry), and a photo-illustrated guide to good sex. Soon after the first book, she landed a monthly advice column in *Penthouse*. The film *The Life and Times of Xaviera Hollander* was released, with Xaviera herself appearing as voiceover and fully clothed guest star. Today, Xaviera Hollander still writes a regular column for *Penthouse*.

On the opposite side of the economic spectrum, New York's massage parlor business flourished during this same time, a scene that quickly was monitored by *Screw* magazine, whose offices happened to be located above one such establishment.

One of the first parlors to openly flourish in New York was the Pink Orchid, 200 E. 14th off Third, started by two City College students, one a musician and carpenter, the other an attorney's son. During the summer of 1970, they averaged 40 customers a day, each masseuse averaging $300 to $500 a week, and were forced to expand their empire. Ceasar's Retreat, 219 E. 46th St., was unique for offering its customers complimentary champagne and heated herbal-oil massages. The facility featured mock-Roman decor, masseuses in togas, circular baths and a plaster-cast Romanesque statuary and fountain. A massage was $20, but for $100 a customer could get a champagne bath with three women.

The idea of prostitution disguised as massage quickly spread across the country. Also picking up the Roman hedonist idea was the Circus Maximum in Los Angeles, run out of a three-story townhouse off Sunset on La Cienega. The parking lot held 80 cars, and the 30 masseuses were required to wear mini-togas. Their slogan said it all: "Men haven't had it so good since the days of Pompeii." And in Chicago, after headline writers kept referring to massage parlor proprietor Harold Rubin as Weird Harold, he shrugged and made it the name of his parlor.

Northern California produced an entirely new type of prostitute – independent, organized, and on even terms with major political players. The grand madam of San Francisco high society, Sally Stanford, made headlines for marrying the heir to the Gump fortune, providing girls for drunken bashes at the Hall of Justice and buying a prized steer and naming it after a police sergeant. Her heyday capitalized on an earlier era of lonely post-war men, who circulated around the Bay Area port, but she left a glamorous legacy of prostitution in her wake for those to come. Stanford eventually retired from the business in the 1950s to open a restaurant across the bay in Sausalito, and dabble in local politics.

In the early 1960s a young girl from Bellingham, Washington moved to San Francisco, fell in with some North Beach hipsters, renamed herself Margo St. James and started turning a few tricks. After getting arrested, she saw firsthand that hookers were treated unfairly, and they – she – deserved better. In 1973 St. James formed Call Off Your Old Tired Ethics (COYOTE) – a loose organization with a tight budget – at the time the only prostitutes' rights organization in the country, and certainly the only to ever have its name chosen by author Tom Robbins. In 1974 COYOTE stopped the common quarantine of hookers in the county jail, and ended mandatory penicillin injections for all women locked up for solicitation. From 1974 to 1976 the group convened three national hooker's conventions – two in San Francisco at the Glide Memorial Church and Hyatt Regency Hotel, and one in Washington D.C. to coincide with the bicentennial.

New York massage parlors grew very familiar with a particular client named Bernard Gottlieb beginning in 1972. The distinguished-looking man frequented the parlors, always arriving in a very well-tailored suit, carrying a black satchel full of sex toys. His specific requests for bondage sex, including posing for photos that he would take himself, earned him the nicknames "Bondage Bernie," or simply, the "rich weirdo." Gottlieb always paid in crisp $100 bills, and periodically appeared very tan, from skiing in Aspen. Someone once asked him about his peculiar tastes. Gottlieb stared out the window and said solemnly, "We are who we are."

Many Times Square massage parlors were secretly owned by some of the city's wealthiest landlords, according to a 1972 article by Gail Sheehy. The Hodas's Harem parlor was owned by Sol Goldman, of the billion-dollar Goldman-DiLorenzo real estate firm. One thousand tricks a day were reportedly turned in the Raymona Hotel on Eighth Street, owned by Madison Avenue socialite builder Ian Woodner. Several prostitute hotels and parlors, including the Eros I gay theater, were owned by prominent heart surgeon Dr. Alvin Bakst. A strip along West 42nd, which included Peepalive, Roman Massage Parlor, Rector Books, and Bob's Bargain Books, was owned by a corporation whose principal officer and attorney was Edward R. Finch II, the son of a New York State Appellate Court judge, and the uncle of President Nixon's son-in-law, Edward Finch Cox. Other prostitution/pornography landowners included members of the Association for a Better New York, Park Avenue banks, and members of Mayor Lindsay's own Times Square Development Council.

An Atlanta man showed up at the 1973 arraignment of several women charged with prostitution, and testified that not only had he gone to their apartment for sex, he also filed a complaint with the Federal Wage and Price Control Board, protesting the fact they had raised their fee by ten dollars.

In April 1972, a very shy man named Arthur Bremer, in suit and vest, walked into New York City's Victorian Studio massage parlor on 46th and Lexington, but was so tense during his massage he couldn't achieve orgasm. One month later, at a Maryland political rally, Bremer pulled a gun and shot the governor of Alabama, George Wallace.

Manhattan hookers frequented Eighth Ave. between 34th and 35th streets, which became known in 1972 as the Minnesota Strip, because whenever anyone asked the hometown of a prostitute, she often answered "Minneapolis."

St. James wanted to take the concept further, and organized the first World Whores Conference in Amsterdam, uniting prostitutes from all over the globe. Perhaps more than any other person, she helped to rewrite archaic prostitution laws, and pushed for legal reform that more accurately reflected the times and changing social attitudes towards hookers.

But like the classic hooker opening line "You want to party?" St. James also liked to cut loose, and from 1974 to 1979 she produced and hosted San Francisco's annual Halloween masquerade Hooker's Balls, bizarre bacchanalias staged in full cooperation with local police and fire departments, all proceeds going to fund COYOTE. Famous faces who attended throughout the years included George Carlin, Huey Lewis, Chevy Chase, Francis Ford Coppola and a presumably less angry O.J. Simpson. A famous wire photo appeared of SFPD Chief Frank Gaines partying with St. James, causing one local newspaper editor to nearly lose his job for making copies and distributing it to beat cops. Her final Ball in San Francisco attracted a sold-out crowd of 20,000, punctuated by its founder's grand entrance astride a live elephant.

After a self-imposed exile of several years in France, St. James returned to San Francisco in 1995, started up the annual Hooker's Ball again and continued fighting for prostitution reform. In 1996 she ran for city supervisor, with news organizations from CNN to the *L.A. Times* falling over themselves to get interviews with the hooker-turned-politican.

Nevada prostitution has always operated independently from the rest of the country, and most of it in the past 30 years is due to Mustang Ranch founder Joe Conforte. Born to Sicilian immigrants, Conforte ran away at 15 and drifted across the U.S. throughout the 1950s, serving two short stints in the Army, running fruit stands, stealing cars, getting married, having a child, getting divorced. He opened his first brothel in a hotel in Oakland, across the street from City Hall. Despite regular payoffs, he was forced to move, and set up shop in San Francisco, catering to Oriental men. After the place was busted, he paid a fine and in 1955 moved to Nevada because it seemed like a state where anything goes. Gambling was legal, taxes were low and Nevada was earning the money of states with twice the population. But in the two big cities, Reno and Vegas, they wanted no brothels, because it would bring more heat on their casinos, which were already held in keen interest by Washington, D.C.

Conforte secured a patch of alfalfa pasture eight miles east of Reno, at the intersection of three counties, and opened the Triangle River Ranch. Joe claimed he was the first to use the word "ranch" in a whorehouse name. Reno taxis would offer a flat $15 round-trip rate, but many waited so long in the parking lot they would go in themselves, and often a passenger would have to wait for his driver. Rumors spread that in nearby Wadsworth, newspaper guys got half-rates and judges were served free.

Conforte met his future wife, Sally, and together they opened another house. The first was named the "White House," the second the "Green House." Regular customers included city, county and state officials. Joe got cocky, arriving in Reno casinos with babes on his arm, tooling down the streets in a convertible packed with beautiful women, mocking the authority that still dared to keep prostitution illegal. He opened two more houses, one on the ridge where Highway 6 crossed into California. He named it "The Pass," which did booming business during deer hunting season. Another, the Desert Inn, opened near Carson, next to a competitor's Starlight. Among those uncomfortable with the expansion was the local District Attorney.

In 1959, Conforte tried to set up the D.A. in a carefully crafted scenario that would trap the attorney into buying drinks for a minor, and ease up the heat on his whores. The D.A. ended up having sex with the young girl; Conforte called him on it, and tried to extort him. Their conversation was recorded on tape, creating what was then the second longest piece of recorded evidence in the history of Nevada's justice system. Conforte was arrested for extortion twice, and posted bail. He had to sell one of the brothels to make the payments. In February 1960 a jury found him guilty of vagrancy, and Conforte would eventually carry the case all the way to the U.S. Supreme Court. He closed the Green House and moved the girls to the White House in neighboring Lyon County. In March 1960 two D.A.s, sheriffs and deputies arrived at the Green House, poured gasoline over everything and burned the place to the ground.

A microphone was discovered in each bedroom, ostensibly to protect the girls in case a john got rough, she could scream and help would come. The authorities wondered if all the tricks were secretly recorded on tape, and how many were prominent men.

We did some wild things. Sometimes we stuck pins into his joint. Other times we would see what we could get up his ass without Vaseline. Lots of times, though, we concentrated on rattling his head.

Sherry once went outside and scooped up a goldfish from the pond. She brought it back, squirming and flopping, and dropped it on his chest as he lay tied down. She told Rex she was going to let it flap around on his stomach and then she would execute it while he watched. He was such a worthless, selfish, bullshit creep that he was going to be responsible for the poor innocent fish's death simply to satisfy his weird needs.

I don't know who he imagined the fish was, but he was shattered as it met an unseemly death, with its head chopped off, on his belly.

Another time at my place I was trying to think up something strange. I suddenly remembered that our chihuahua had given birth to several puppies which died. Carl had put them in the freezer to keep until he could bury them in the backyard. So I lashed Rex to the bed and brought him the puppies on a plate. I told him he would have to eat them. Rex turned green and purple, but he didn't flinch a muscle. I'm sure he would have done it if I had made him.

But my imagination wasn't up to Rex. And that wasn't my scene, despite the enormous amounts of money he paid. The last I heard, he had nails hammered all over the walls of his den, with stirrups at the bottom, like a medieval rack. One girl tried to hang him by the balls.

With Rex, the minute he came, he snapped right back to normal. Even if he was covered with blood and minus half of his short hairs, he was immediately transformed into a soft-spoken, thoughtful, intelligent, nice guy.

He wrote children's books.

— The Joy of Hooking by Virginia Graham, 1974

8468-0001*$1.75

a who's who of the stars' sex lives!

The Joy of Hooking
by Virginia Graham

Hollywood's favorite play-for-pay girl and the star witness who broke the Manson case!

Undaunted, Conforte switched to a 60-foot trailer, which could easily be moved around the river bottom, traveling among three counties, after a warning phone call from a friendly informant. At the trial for extortion, Conforte was sentenced to three to five years, and would be free on bail for almost two years, never once thinking of quitting the business. Taxi drivers and tourists had to inquire in saloons which location he was keeping the girls. Conforte hired spies to stake out the sheriff's office, following patrol cars and warning by telephone. He went to prison for extortion, and was later charged for tax evasion.

Some months later *San Francisco Chronicle* columnist Herb Caen wrote about the microphones, wondering how many people were sweating out who owned the tapes. Jokes circulated. Conforte denied any customers had ever

been taped, and filed suit from jail against Caen and the *Chronicle*. The court awarded $1 for damage to his reputation, and $10,000 as punitive damages against Caen. Released from jail in the early '60s, Conforte plotted his comeback.

A competitor had opened up a house while Conforte was in the joint, closer to Reno in Storey County — with four trailers and 12 girls. He named it "Mustang." After his release, Conforte met with the owner of the Mustang, and claimed he was the pioneer, he had exclusivity. They agreed on a price, paid over five years. Conforte bought land west of Mustang, stocked it with trailers and added tenants who paid low rent and were registered voters. He then proposed legal prostitution to the authorities, "Ordinance No. 38," which was unheard of. No state, city or county in the entire United States had ever legalized prostitution. Conforte sweetened his

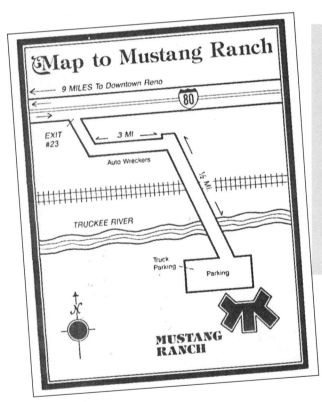

1. The "house-girl," the girls in resident in the Mustangs, Mabel'ses, and Sheri'ses of today.
2. The "showgirl-swinger." Swinger, incidentally, is the qualifier which, attached to any woman, accuses her of occasional whoring.
3. The cocktail waitress swinger.
4. The occasional adolescent, sometimes called the "Utah Lolita."
5. The "call girl," who is called by hotel bellmen or pitmen, but who has no pimp.
6. The "call girl," reachable only through her pimp.
7. The "California secretary," that great, blanketing catch-all name for every woman who gets the idea to try it and find out what it is like.
8. The "streetwalker," the girl who is at least temporarily unconnected and who strolls around in Europe, in New York, in Las Vegas.

— the eight types of prostitutes, according to Nevada attorney Tom Pursel

BROWN: Joe, damn it. You don't do things this way! You simply must come to the office. You can't do things by phone.
JOE: Oh hell, this is simple. A guy claims he got the clap here and..."
BROWN: There's other reasons, Joe.
JOE: Like what?
BROWN: Well, for one, your line is tapped.
JOE: Balls! How do you know?

BROWN: An Assistant Department of Justice Attorney told me so.
JOE: You mean we're tapped right now? You mean they're running a tape on us right this very fucking minute?
BROWN: Every word!
JOE: Jesus. I better stop swearing.

— from a conversation between Joe Conforte and his attorney, Stanley Brown

proposal by suggesting an official license fee of $18,000 a year. The county ordinance passed in 1971, thanks to his tenant constituency, and the payments began. When the county realized it was still broke, Conforte graciously increased his payments to $25,000.

The Mustang Ranch grew into the most famous cathouse in the world. Customers came from all over the globe, from visiting dignitaries to U.S. congressmen, state governors and celebrities. Conforte raked in tons of money, spending it on lavish items like ankle-length mink coats, and charmed the community by giving away dozens of turkeys every holiday season. Conforte loved giving interviews, and bought local politicians billboard advertising when they couldn't afford it. Conforte was eventually forced into bankruptcy after owing the IRS $13 million, and spent 18 months in prison.

Most of his assets were sold off, including the Mustang Ranch, but in the lobby still hang elegant framed portraits of Joe and his wife, Sally.

During this time, it was impossible to pick up a newspaper or magazine and not see a headline about prostitution. Clearly the country was headed in a direction far different than the Eisenhower years. Discussion about hookers was more frank and honest than ever before. Prostitution was no longer just about that "certain house" down the street. The sexual pay-to-play was demystified and out on the table for all to see. Some of this new information was shocking, some of it ridiculous, some of it sad. But America was definitely curious about our "ladies of the evening." Now all we had to do was attempt to make sense of it.

Bob Maheu was right hand man to Howard Hughes during the 1960s and 1970s. The enthusiastic Maheu was intent on running a clean operation, and gave the order to all the Vegas hotels: 'no girl-running.' Business at the Desert Inn and the Sands dropped off immediately, so he was forced to reconsider and open his doors to the girls. One of his PR men realized he needed some briefing on the subject, and slipped him a memo:

"Bob, if you get into the hotel business you back into the whore business. It's the innkeeper's lot. It was that way when Dickens stopped at those English inns where half topless wenches would pour his ale and ask if there would be anything more upstairs. Every man who enters the business must decide how he feels about pandering or, at least, supplying the furniture of love.

I think that we can accept, after what has happened in recent years, that man is sex-obsessed. The books, the movies, the ads, the pornography, should make it clear that nature and not hotels made man erotic. Now in most businesses an owner can decide whether to have any part of the sex business, but not the hotel owner. He has what men need for intercourse, rooms and beds.

We know that men are polygamous as hell, that most men have the secret goal of knocking off dozens of lassies without the wife knowing. It's hard to pull off in your home town, whereas it's easy when you leave town on business. But even in another town you need a hotel. Which is why in every hotel the man away from home puts it to the bellboy. The girls, knowing this, use the hotel as a base. It would be hard to find a veteran hotel man who hasn't spotted a gal at a table, gone up to her, bought her a drink, and asked, 'Honey, how does it work?' This, in his first year. After talking to a hundred, he knows. Your employees educate you. If you have been a hotel man for twenty years, you have had more feed-in than the sex scientists. You get it from chambermaids (and brother, that can be detailed), from waiters on room service, from cocktail waitresses.

You talk to the boys on the vice squad. You get it from the maitres and the showgirls. Every Las Vegas hotel has a sex authority, the wardrobe mistress. Every hotel has a Kinsey, he's the choreographer. So, when the original Vegas men got into the hotel business, they no more pioneered sex in hotels than Nixon pioneered Washington taxicabs. When they opened, there was such a run of whores to Las Vegas, such a nationwide assumption that this was the Mecca, that the owners actually tried to keep the numbers down."

— from The Girls of Nevada, Gabriel R. Vogliotti, 1975

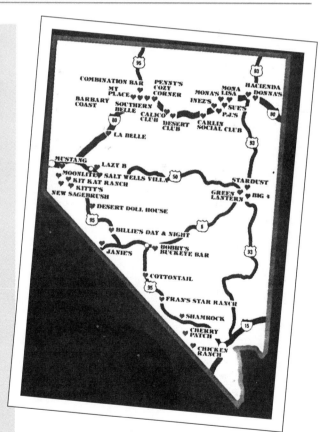

ROAD TRIP ANYONE?:
One of many maps published in the 1970s of Nevada brothels

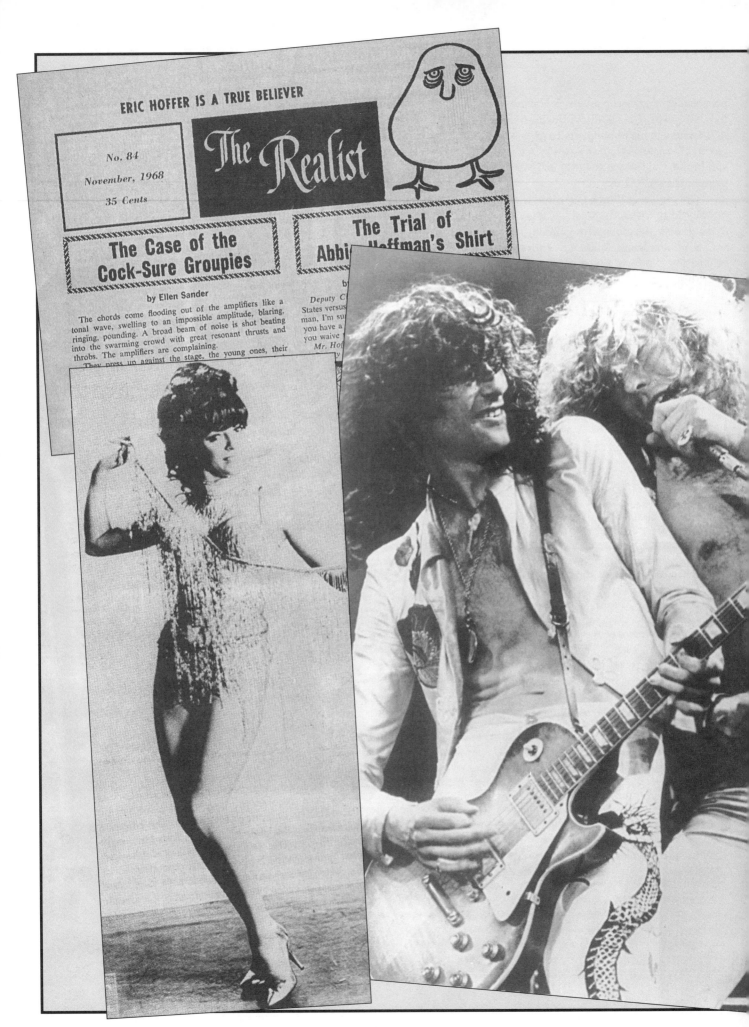

ERIC HOFFER IS A TRUE BELIEVER

The Realist

No. 84

November, 1968

35 Cents

The Case of the Cock-Sure Groupies

by Ellen Sander

The chords come flooding out of the amplifiers like a tonal wave, swelling to an impossible amplitude, blaring, ringing, pounding. A broad beam of noise is shot beating into the swarming crowd with great resonant thrusts and throbs. The amplifiers are complaining.

They press up against the stage, the young ones, their

The Trial of Abbie Hoffman's Shirt

by

Deputy C
States versus
man, I'm su
you have a
you waive

Mr. Hoff

Some women have been attracted to powerful men despite their better judgment. In the '60s and '70s, a heightened, increasingly lurid interest in sex readily manifested in the media's coverage of American musicians, sports figures and politicians. They were not simply professionals going about their business, but sex symbols, ripe for the attention of women who wished to kick up their heels and get in touch with their own sexuality. Men responded to such amorous advances with vigor, and stud personalities like Mick Jagger, Wilt Chamberlain and even the liver-spotted congressman Wilbur Mills emerged. Women showered these cultural figures with endless

Backstage Pass

amounts of sex for the taking, with two primary results. The concept of a richer sex life through male career achievement became part of the country's unabashed libidinal landscape, but on a sadder note, it was responsible for millions of young, untalented men picking up a guitar, football, or political platform — for the express purpose of getting laid.

Musicians have always harbored sex appeal, and if Elvis and Jerry Lee were the first wave of sex-soaked rock and rollers, the second generation

It molded superbly, we applied some baby-oil to his hair and he only got stuck for five minutes. I had been counting aloud before we thrust Noel into the mold, and when I announced the crucial moment, he became panicky and began to get soft, thus instead of diving mightily straight in, we had to shove it and pound it in, and it twisted like a worm.

— **excerpt from Cynthia Plaster Caster's diary about Jimi Hendrix Experience member Noel Redding (as reported in** *I'm With the Band***)**

SEE ME, FEEL ME:
*A Polaroid self-documentation from
the Plaster Casters, Dianne (left), and
Cynthia (right)*

of panty-soaking studs kicked in with British imports like the Beatles and the Stones (Ed Sullivan's one Beatles broadcast attracted *73 million* viewers). What young female could walk past a newsstand and not notice the teen magazine headlines, screaming "25 HOT NEW PIN-UPS!" What girl could witness a shirtless, sweaty 115-pound rock star in hip-hugger leather pants — who rides a 100-foot artificial penis that rises off the stage, swings over the crowd and spews confetti all over the first 30 rows of the concert — and not wake up the next morning, realizing she's just molested the stuffing out of her teddy bear?

Rock groupies were so prevalent in the '60s they were attracting attention all by themselves, apart from the bands. By the end of the decade they weren't just screaming teeny-boppers, they were ravenous, leering young women, consummating their passion for musicians in hotel rooms, stairwells and on ratty backstage sofas. If mainstream media were discussing this new phenomenon of sex-crazed fans in rapt wonderment, the attitude prevailed that there was nothing wrong with it. Much like the bands they adored, groupies' attitudes reflected their geographical roots.

The Los Angeles groupie scene seemed the best-documented, perhaps because the music industry was based there, and Southern California attracted females who desired closer proximity to their favorite musicians. Many groupies started as editors, writers and photographers for teen magazines like *16, Tiger Beat, Flip, Teen Screen*, and later, *Circus* and *Creem*. Others were the daughters of Eisenhower-era San Fernando valley executives, and rebellion was only a bass player's hotel room away. A central groupie scene developed around the Landmark Motor Hotel, where visiting rock bands would stay while on tour. In 1965, two secretaries charted a helicopter to fly over the Benedict Canyon mansion where the Beatles were staying, then landed the chopper and actually made it past security inside the house. Another enterprising woman gained access to rock stars' hotel rooms by dressing up like a maid; yet another had herself delivered in a packing crate via UPS.

Frank Zappa became a tireless chronicler of groupie culture in southern California. He formed a band of groupie girls he called the GTO's, or Girls Together Outrageously, and produced their album on his Bizarre label, called *Permanent Damage*. One of the most well-known GTO's member, Pamela Des Barres, was a live-in nanny to Zappa's family. Her bestselling book *I'm With the Band* depicted a debauched life spent in late-'60s Los Angeles, sleeping with rock stars like Jimmy Page, Mick Jagger and Keith Moon. The GTO's later lived communally in the old Tom Mix home in Laurel Canyon, and they first appeared in public at Shrine Expositionan L.A. rock dance hall. Their costume: white T-shirt (no bra), and a diaper, with "G.T.O." written on the behind.

Groupies in New York were known for their aggressiveness, coming on strong to musicians — too strong for some guys who weren't accustomed to the Manhattan hustle. They ranged from Bronx teenyboppers to professional girls working for record companies, magazines, PR firms and booking agencies. Women spent hours hanging out at Max's Kansas City, hoping to catch the eye of a sleazy guitarist in mascara and skin-tight velvet pants.

But while L.A. and New York groupies were more star-struck, known for trying to see how many rock stars they could sleep with, those in San Francisco were pegged as being hippie girls who also befriended the bands, often living in their homes or finding administrative work behind the scenes. In the Midwest, Chicago gained a reputation for being hometown to the notorious Plaster Casters. In 1968, a Windy City IBM key-punch operator named Cynthia Albritton achieved renown for making casts of male rock stars' penises — Wayne Kramer, Aynsley Dunbar, the Jimi Hendrix Experience and actor Anthony Newley, among others. She stalked rock groups over the years, black suitcase of equipment in tow, shopping for potential models. When rock-star demand outstripped supply, the Casters settled for roadies. After years of fighting over the collection with Herbert Cohen, an ex-partner of Frank Zappa, Cynthia filed suit in 1991 to regain possession of her beloved statuettes, and the collection is now back home with its founder.

The media swarm didn't end with mainstream magazines and Zappa's underground cult following. In 1969, record producer Alan Lorber realized an increase in groupie activity and saw an opportunity. He found six girls, flew them to New York, put them in a recording studio for 12 hours and let them talk — two at a time, in separate booths (facing each other but eight feet apart for that "lifelike stereo effect"). Lorber spent 100 hours editing the tapes, and the album *The Groupies* appeared later that year on Earth Records, the inner label running the disclaimer, "The girls heard on this LP report

TOWERS OF POWER:
(left to right) Jimi Hendrix (#00004, 2/25/68); a friend from school; a fellow student; Hendrix bandmate Noel Redding (#00005, 3/30/68); Hendrix road manager Don Ogilure (5/5/68)

Plaster Caster casting recipe:

Materials: 1. Plaster, 2. Alginates, 3. Alginates and water measuring scoops, 4. Baggies, 5. Vaseline, 6. Knife (spatula), 7. Container (vase), 8. Container (pastic cup), 9. Container (coffee can) 1/4-1/3 filled with water, 10. Water thermometer (unless you trust your hand).

Procedure: Probably Sandi should begin plating the rig right off. Cynthia then shakes the can of alginates powder well and opens it. She greases the interior of vase with vaseline, while Sandi should, at some time, lubricate the rig with Vaseline for protection. Cynthia meaures 15 scoops of powdered alginates into the vase; she taps the scoop each time against the can to distribute it evenly, and levels the top off with the knife. It MUST be an ACCURATE measure! Then she measures 15 VERY PRECISE water units 70°F. into the plastic cup. She pours the water into the alginates powder in the vase. Immediately she beats it with the knife, using a vigorous sweep of the arm, for a little less than 45 seconds. The result should be a creamy compound.

At the very time the alginates is ready, the rig should also be at its hardest (or, at its BEST whatever). If this has been readily achieved, either Cynthia or Sandi must have the rig thrust straight into the alginates, without hesitating, guiding it down toward the bottom, until the balls are just submerged. If possible, the rig should be kept in this position for about one minute.

As soon as the rig withdraws back into its normal size so that it slips neatly out of the mold without affecting the impression, Cynthia removes the mold from the vase, prying it out with the knife if necessary, while Sandi, if at liberty to abandon her rig, should commence adding powdered plaster to the coffee can containing water, and mix it with her fingers, sifting out the lumps in the same manner. If the noble rig still requires Sandi's services, it must be Cynthia's job to mix the plaster. When it feels relatively thick and creamy, immediately pour it into the mold.

The mold should be supported in someone's hands through this all. It should be poured to the top so that the surface will serve as a sturdy base for the model.

When the plaster has hardened (it will feel cold to the touch), she carefully removes it from the mold (it might be necessary to slice the side with the knife). It is dusted off and any extraneous particles are filed off. The plaster cast is now ready for display, etc.

To keep the mold properly moist and acceptable to make another cast, the mold should be wrapped in a Baggie. As the molding and casting proceeds, all containers used must be cleaned and scraped immediately before the residue hardens. Do not pour alginates or dry plaster down the drain or into the toilet. And, of course, take care not to neglect the all-important rig.

GTO's: Girls Together Outrageously, Occasionally, Only, Openly, Overtly
GS: Get Smart
MZ, FZ/GZ: Mr. Zappa, Frank Zappa/Gail Zappa
Chickweblis: Us, the chicks: a name we call one another
Chickwebli: All of us
Cones: Colored hang-ups
Klondikes: 40's gun molls
Bailies (Jack, Bill or Beatle): titties
JHE: Jimi Hendrix Experience
Rob: Bob Dylan
BCP's: Birth Control Pills

Moche: Anything revolting
T.T.: Tiny Tim
Blackback: Whitefront Discount Store
TCB: Take Care of Business
Bozo-ing: Daydreaming
Melancolony: Melancholy
Heidi: a snot-nosed kid
O.T, O.F.: Obvious toupee, obvious fall
Goddess: Greased-up guy with fluttery eye-ashes and come-hither look

— groupie glossary of Pamela Des Barres, from *I'm With the Band*

Top Ten Groupie Hangouts (Los Angeles)
1. Landmark Motor Hotel, not far from major record studios. Most groups stayed here.
2. Backstage, Rose Palace, Pasadena, noted for groupies who "groove on guitarists."
3. Backstage, Whisky Au Go Go on the Strip
4. Tropicana Motor Inn, near Elektra Records and a bunch of topless joints
5. Canyon Country Store, a Laurel Canyon grocery near homes of music industry people
6. Music City, largest record store in L.A., where rock stars bought their records

7. Wally Heider's Studio 3, popular for its perfection, used by CSN, the Stones
8. Chateau Marmont hotel on the Strip, the pool out back was secluded enough that nobody could see groupies come and go
9. The Troubadour, folk club where groupies alternated between the upstairs backstage and the front-room bar
10. The Sunset Strip, 3 miles of road from the Aquarius Theater to beyond the Whisky

— from *Groupies and Other Girls*

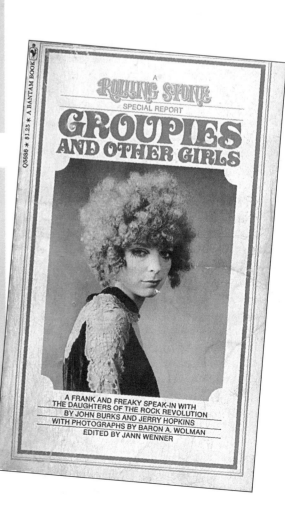

A ROLLING STONE SPECIAL REPORT

GROUPIES AND OTHER GIRLS

Q5686 * $1.25 * A BANTAM BOOK

A FRANK AND FREAKY SPEAK-IN WITH THE DAUGHTERS OF THE ROCK REVOLUTION
BY JOHN BURKS AND JERRY HOPKINS
WITH PHOTOGRAPHS BY BARON A. WOLMAN
EDITED BY JANN WENNER

their actual life experiences, feelings and opinions within the pop music scene."

Many musicians paid back their sexual favors by writing songs about girls. Frank Zappa's *Chunga's Revenge* featured the song "Road Ladies," Kiss penned an ode to Cynthia in Chicago with "Plaster Caster" on their album *Love Gun*. Even the Monkees got into the swing of things with "Star Collector," a thinly disguised ditty about the girls of the road. And in perhaps the best-known tribute to groupies, Grand Funk's "American Band" immortalized the legendary "sweet, sweet Connie," a young woman familiar to rock bands touring through Arkansas. Groupies would achieve their ultimate place in history in 1995, when the ballot of Arkansas state congress offered a candidate who sounded very familiar to middle-aged musicians. But "Sweet" Connie Hamzy would fail to capture the office, despite having claimed a poolside tryst with then-governor Bill Clinton.

Sports groupies had existed for years. One legendary story had it that slugger Babe Ruth was once asked how many times he performed sex with a particular girl in his hotel room. Ruth supposedly pointed to the nightstand ashtray and replied, "Count the cigars!" But as salaries and media exposure increased, athletes were more visible — and available — than ever before. Girls who favored sports heroes rapidly became known by many names: "Annies," "Shirleys," "Starfuckers" or the ubiquituous term "Bimbos."

Many were stewardesses who introduced themselves to jocks flying en route to a game. Others were desk clerks at hotels, staffers in the offices of sports teams or 9-to-5ers in the business world who followed their favorite teams on tour. They met the athletes at their hotels, nightclubs or the field, passing the guys notes or asking for autographs. Girls would often set up their girlfriends with athletes, and sports bars across the country filled up with young, slinky women, hoping to catch the eye of the latest *Sports Illustrated* cover boy.

Girls would discover the basic difference between athletes. The golfers were described as gentle, football players were intelligent, most of them having been to college, as opposed to baseball players, who came across as boisterous, and hockey players, who were known as crude. Single guys were harder to deal with than married guys, who were more sensitive to women, and would graciously remove their wedding rings while on the road.

The sexual side of sports was soon no secret to the rest of the country. Wilt Chamberlain's

Out on the road for forty days
Last night in Little Rock put me in a haze
Sweet, sweet Connie is doin' her act
She had the whole show and that's a natural fact
Up all night, with Freddie King
I got to tell ya, poker's his thing
Booze and ladies keep me right
As long as we can make it to the show tonight
We're an American band...

Four young chiquitas in Omaha
Wuz waitin' for the band to return from the show
Feelin' good, feelin' right, it's a Saturday night
The hotel detective he was outta sight
Now these fine ladies, they had a plan
They wuz out to meet the boys in the band
They said, "Come on dudes, let's get it on!"
And we proceeded to tear that hotel down
We're an American band....

— Grand Funk's "American Band"

When I come back here next year,
I wanna see you again
What's your name, little girl,
what's your name?
— Lynyrd Skynyrd

Plaster Caster, grab ahold of me faster
She calls me by the name of Master
She's a collector
She wants me all the time to inject her
— Kiss

If you don't go down on me,
someone else will
— The Sweet

Stand in the front just a-shakin'
your ass
I'll take you backstage, you can
drink of my glass
— Aerosmith

— more lyrics about groupies

I tend to be very fickle. I get tired of a girl fairly quickly, and when I do, I "fire" her. Who knows — I may already have fired one or two girls who would have made ideal wives for me if I'd kept them around long enough to really get to know them.

— from *Wilt* by Wilt Chamberlain, 1973

WILT

Just like any other 7-foot black millionaire who lives next door

79-621 WARNER PAPERBACK LIBRARY

16 PAGES OF PHOTOGRAPHS

An autobiography by Wilt Chamberlain and David Shaw

Usually, we'd go straight from the ball park to a bar and then to his room or some other player's room. And the couples would start coming in. There was one night when the Infielder had a bunch of really good movies.

One shows an orgy with four or five couples, all hooked up together. Then the next movie just had a man and his woman in different positions. One had a cat and a woman, then another a dog and a cat. He had so many of them, I forget what they were all about. But I do remember that most of them were pretty good....

He told me not to look. But it was hard not to. One couple had got up off the floor and was balling in a chair. I really didn't know what to look at first — the movies or the people. My eyes just kept going around and around the room. (Laughs) It all seemed to be so funny that I nearly laughed out loud, but the Infielder kept telling me, "Ssshh. Now you be quiet."

— **baseball groupie "Sue Ann," divorced cosmetologist mom from Oklahoma**

million-dollar bachelor pad was the subject of a feature photo spread in *Life* magazine. Books by baseball players Joe Pepitone and Jim Bouton included rollicking locker-room stories of sexual conquests, Joe Namath was frequently photographed with a succession of beautiful young women, often at his Manhattan bar Bachelors III, and NFL wide receiver Lance Rentzel made headlines by getting himself arrested for exposing himself to a 12-year-old girl.

Oddly enough, golfers received their fair share of female attention. One married golf groupie named "Pauline" described the final putt of a long pro tournament, after which her girlfriend exclaimed, "Oh, I'm so glad this thing is over. I've had so many pricks stuck in me the last four days, I feel like a pincushion."

Political groupies also were nothing new, from Thomas Jefferson to Grover Cleveland, Warren Harding, FDR and Eisenhower, but since these men were elected officials in an age of respectful news decorum, little was ever disclosed of their overt friskiness. All that would change in the '60s and '70s, as Capitol Hill bunks were bouncing with everyone from Marilyn Monroe to secretaries and office staffers. The Kennedy brothers and LBJ lit the pilot light with their well-documented shenanigans, but there were other, seedier liaisons, two of which created international scandals.

Senator Wayne Hays of Ohio, the married, 65-year-old chairman of the House Administration Committee, was known throughout the Beltway as a petty tyrant, bullying everyone from House barbers to elevator operators. The blonde 33-year-old Elizabeth Ray was a would-be actress and model with a history of depression and psychiatrist sessions, who wandered from job to job before getting hired as a secretary for Illinois congressman Kenneth Gray, a party animal who kept a yacht full of women. Hays took Ray to dinner and in April 1974 hired her to be his clerk/mistress, she later told reporters. She was not asked to do any Congress-related work, but entertained Hays at her office and apartment. Her code name for him was "Ha," his for her was "Agent 55," the last two digits of her private office phone.

"Supposedly, I'm on the Oversight Committee," she would later say, "but I call it the out-of-sight committee. I can't type, I can't file, I can't even answer my phone."

Unable to keep the secret, Ray would call media people like columnist Jack Anderson and *Penthouse* publisher Bob Guccione, threatening to tell stories about her affairs with Hays and others; she even offered to trap Henry Kissinger in a sex scandal. She had a ghostwriter pen a novel based on her adventures, *The Washington Fringe Benefit*. She held off on going public about the affair until the publisher Dell was ready to cash in on the publicity. She eventually let *Washington Post* reporters listen to tapes of their phone conversations, with Hays assuring her their sex/job arrangement would continue despite his new marriage. Essentially, he was finished.

Hays initially denied all the charges, but then admitted the affair to 300 colleagues in the House of Representatives, and resigned as chairman of the House Administration Committee. Ray parlayed her new-found fame into bit parts in Hollywood movies like *Scorpio*, and photo spreads for *Playboy* and *Hustler*.

Also in 1974, the seedy saga of congressman Wilbur Mills unfolded with the help of a friendly Washington policeman. On October 7, police pulled over a sleek blue Continental limo that was speeding with its headlights off toward the Jefferson Memorial. Inside were two men and three women, drunk from an evening of partying at a Caribbean nightclub. One of the men, an elderly gentleman, had a nosebleed and scratches on his face, and one of the women, a hysterical blonde, sported two black eyes. The blonde suddenly bolted from the car and jumped into the Tidal Basin, the murky backwaters of the Potomac, before getting fished out by one of the officers. A local television crew heard the call on their police-band scanner and sped to the Memorial, thinking a kidnapping was in progress, and their cameraman caught a policeman leading the elderly man away, saying "Come on, Mr. Congressman, you don't need this bad publicity."

The elderly man was married, 65-year-old representative Wilbur Mills, a 36-year congressman, 17 years of which was spent as chairman of the Ways and Means Committee. The blonde was Mrs. Annabella Battistella, a busty 38-year-old divorcee and mother of four, who often appeared onstage at the Silver Slipper strip joint in D.C., under the name "Fanne Foxe, the Argentine Firecracker."

The "bad publicity" immediately took off. Mills's reputation as a square, boring married guy disintegrated as reports rolled in of his secret life as a champagne-drinking regular at strip joints in Washington and Los Angeles. Many speculated that his sudden party-animal behavior was from a 1973 operation for a ruptured spinal disc, others said it stemmed from a

When asked the secret to his success, 1970s Olympic swimming gold medalist Mark Spitz answered that for motivation, he imagined a different girl at the end of every lap in the pool.

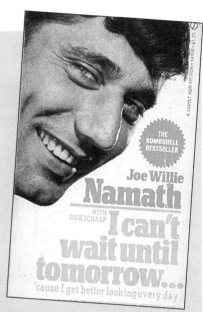

The World According to Broadway Joe

If a doctor told me I had to give up drinking, I'm sure I could give it up tomorrow. If a doctor told me I had to give up women, I'm sure I'd give up doctors.

I like women. I prefer tall blondes but, shoot, I really like them all, tall, short, experienced, innocent, amateurs, pros, blondes, brunettes, just about everything there is, except redheads... I guess I just haven't met the right redheads yet.

I've got respect for women, all kinds of women. There are some girls I meet who I know are not going to be easy. I mean, sometimes I'm a genuine eighteen-point underdog. They like me and they like my company, but they don't want a guided tour of my apartment. I can understand that. Well, no, I can't really understand it. I can't imagine anyone who doesn't enjoy sex, who doesn't want sex all the time. It's the best thing ever invented.

I don't date much — I mean, I don't take girls to dinner or to the theater or to the movies very often — but I like to go out at night and just see what I bump into. I'm lucky, I suppose. I bump into a lot of good things. Maybe it's the kind of life I lead. I fly a lot, and I'm kind of nervous in planes, so I like to talk to the stewardesses. If they make me feel good in the air, I like to do the same for them on the ground...When I'm in New York, I've got a field of about four million females to choose from, and most of the best ones seem to live in my neighborhood, the swinging East Side. I believe in being a good neighbor.

— from *I Can't Wait Until Tomorrow...'Cause I Get Better Looking Every Day*, by Joe Namath with Dick Schaap, 1969 scrapped plan to campaign for president.

Mills initially denied they were anything more than friends, and even held a press conference in Battistella's dressing room after one of her burlesque performances, where he referred to her as "my little ole' Argentine hillbilly." But gossip spread quickly. People around him made jokes at his expense, and considered him a sad old fool. The once-distinguished Mills resigned his chairmanship and enrolled in treatment for alcoholism, quietly returning to Congress some months later.

By contrast, Foxe's career seemed to take off. She starred in the film *Posse From Heaven*, where she played a stripper who dies and goes to heaven. With the help of a ghostwriter, she wrote *Fanne Foxe – The Real Story Behind the Headlines*, in which she claimed she had an abortion of Mills's baby.

Other political peccadillos smacked less of groupie behavior than paid mistresses. A divorced young mother, Colleen Gardner, former aide to Texas representative John Young, came forth with tape-recordings that proved she was

I've looked on a lot of women with lust. I've committed adultery in my heart many times. This is something God recognizes I will do and God forgives me for it.

— **President Jimmy Carter 'fessing up in *Playboy*, mid-'70s**

Nobody else could sleep with Dick. He wakes up during the night, switches on the lights, speaks into his tape records, or takes notes — it's impossible.

— **Pat Nixon on then-president Richard Nixon**

Just after Thanksgiving, 1974, stripper Fanne Foxe performed for two nights at the Pilgrim Theater in Boston. Claiming to be just a friend, 65-year-old Representative Wilbur Mills chartered a Lear Jet for $800 to catch the show, and during the performance he drunkenly wandered down to the front row of the theater. Having stripped down to nothing except a feathery pink dressing gown, Foxe called out from the stage, "Mr. Mills, Mr. Mills, where are you?" Mills suddenly popped up from the front row, walked onstage, took her hand and gave her a hug, stopping the show in its tracks. Photographers were presented a clear shot of the chairman of the House Ways and Means Committee — one of the most powerful married members of Congress — clutching a busty exotic dancer, a photo which appeared in newspapers throughout the country.

hired at $26,000 a year to work in Young's office and have sex with him. More congressmen were implicated in sexual shenanigans throughout the mid-'70s, including Alaska senator Mike Gravel, Virginia senator Harry Byrd, Louisiana Representative Joe Waggonner, and Utah Representative Allan Howe. The *Washington Post* revealed that California Representative Robert L. Leggett had been keeping a second family for years, a mistress and two children, who received about $20,000 of his $50,000 yearly salary. Leggett was caught red-handed.

"I was always under the impression that what you did in your personal life — albeit I've stretched the point a bit — as long as it didn't affect the way you handled the people's business, was really not the people's concern," said Leggett at the time.

It's debatable exactly how much of the sexual lives of women and powerful men is any of our concern, but if we have learned anything from history — at least where incumbent presidents, sports jocks and rock stars are concerned — the groupie phenomenon is far from over.

In 1974, after their first date — which ended up with sex at her apartment — Ohio senator Wayne Hays, the married 65-year-old chairman of the House Administration Committee, supposedly told the blonde 33-year-old Elizabeth Ray, "Show up tomorrow, keep your mouth shut, make yourself available to me, and I'll pay you $11,000. If it turns out you can do any work, I'll pay you $12,000."

Many young women on Capitol Hill were hired as clerks and secretaries during the swinging seventies, often solely as payment for providing sexual pleasure to men working in the Sam Rayburn building, a place one veteran hill woman described as "a river of semen."

"Life at the top" for women on The Hill tends to involve something like sucking the Speaker of the House off — even if you only have to do it to the old guy once a month!

— anonymous Washington woman, quoted in *Adam* magazine

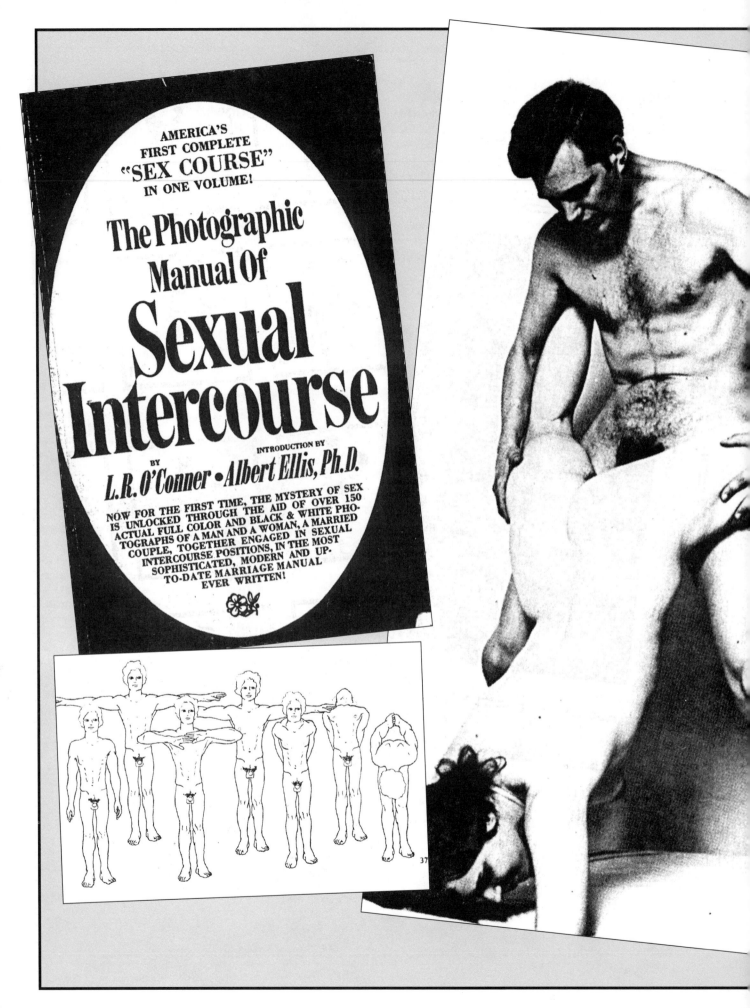

AMERICA'S
FIRST COMPLETE
"SEX COURSE"
IN ONE VOLUME!

The Photographic
Manual Of
Sexual
Intercourse

BY
L.R. O'Conner

INTRODUCTION BY
Albert Ellis, Ph.D.

NOW FOR THE FIRST TIME, THE MYSTERY OF SEX IS UNLOCKED THROUGH THE AID OF OVER 150 ACTUAL FULL COLOR AND BLACK & WHITE PHOTOGRAPHS OF A MAN AND A WOMAN, A MARRIED COUPLE, TOGETHER ENGAGED IN SEXUAL INTERCOURSE POSITIONS, IN THE MOST SOPHISTICATED, MODERN AND UP-TO-DATE MARRIAGE MANUAL EVER WRITTEN!

37

The 1960s and 1970s were marked by America's relentless pursuit of the orgasm — extended, mutual or just plain multiple, it had to be achieved. If we could send a man to the moon, we could figure out how everyone could experience a mind-blowing orgasm that made us black out right there on the sofabed. From university intellectuals to bored suburban housewives, the goal was set — we'd better be arching our backs like jungle cats in bed, right now. Hell, look at the neighbors, will ya? Why shouldn't we? Questions raced through everyone's minds. What's a clitoris supposed to look like? Is it okay to masturbate? Is the woman-on-top position any better than the one that looks like a wheelbarrow?

Do It Right

Fortunately, this is America, the land of capitalism, where as soon as a market is realized, it becomes oversaturated with products for sale. Sexual advisors of every stripe immediately started pumping out information to the starving sexual illiterati, trumpeting repetitive, often erroneous wisdom for the sake of a quick buck. There was talk of today's world "exploding socially from the impact of a swinging new sexual concept." It's a "new generation guided by a new beat" — the "old world is dying or is already dead," man. After the Pill became available, sex was thought of as recreational, a spirited game of tennis without clothes or rackets. And just look at what it does for your complexion! After decades of repression, we weren't simply talking

EVERYTHING YOU NEED TO KNOW:
(clockwise from top) One of the top-selling sex manuals, with emphasis on the word "marriage"; Another manual's "Position forty-four," aka "The Wheelbarrow"; Breathing exercises from the National Sex Forum

THE NATIONAL BESTSELLER AT $12.95 NOW $4.95

The Joy of Sex
A Gourmet Guide to Love Making

COMPLETE AND
UNABRIDGED
ILLUSTRATED EDITION

EDITED BY ALEX COMFORT, M.B., Ph.D.

BIBLE OF THE NIGHTSTAND:
Alex Comfort's illustrated classic informed adults and titillated youngsters

Little-known sexual phrases

FEUILLE DE ROSE — Tongue stimulation of the anus and perineum in either sex.

COITUE *A LA FLORENTINE* — intercourse with the woman holding the man's penile skin forcibly back with finger and thumb at the root of the penis and keeping it stretched all the time.

SKIN GLOVES AND SKIN THIMBLES — They consist either of a whole glove, or better a series of finger-cots the size of a thimble, each covered with a bristly cloth ranging in texture from soft fur to hard nylon pile with a tuft of bristles where the nail would be on a finger.

GAMAHUCHE — French for extended pussy-kissing.

GOLDFISH — Two naked people tied and put on a mattress together to make love fish-fashion, i.e. no hands.

GROPE SUIT — Consists of a very tight rubber g-string with a thick phallic plug which fits in the vagina and a roughened knob over the clitoris. The bra has small toothed recesses in the ups which grip the nipples and is covered all over inside with soft rubber points. Can be worn under day clothes, if you can stand it.

KAREZZA — going on and on and on while avoiding male orgasm.

PATTES D'ARAIGNÉE — (literally, "spider's legs"), tickling erotic massage, using the pulps of the fingers, with the *lightest possible* touch, aiming to stimulate not so much the skin as the almost invisible skin-hairs.

POSTILLIONAGE — putting a finger in or on your partner's anus just before orgasm.

SAXONUS — pressing firmly on the male urethra near the root of the penis to prevent ejaculation and (hopefully) conception.

VIENNESE OYSTER — lady who can cross her feet behind her head, lying on her back, of course.

BUTTERED BUN — woman who has recently had relations with another man: unexpected turn-on for some males.

A LA NÉGRESSE — from behind.

MOUTH MUSIC — genital kisses.

FLANQUETTE — the half-facing group of sexual postures.

CUISSADE — the half-rear entry positions.

CROUPADE — any position in which he takes her squarely from behind.

CASSOLETTE — the natural perfume of a clean woman.

BIRDSONG AT MORNING — what your partner says in orgasm.

— from *The Joy of Sex: A Cordon Bleu Guide to Lovemaking* by Alex Comfort, 1972 frankly about sex, we were babbling about it like fools.

Magazines kept up a steady stream of advice articles — even the wholesome *Reader's Digest* ran 1970s articles aimed at youth called "I Am Joe's Man Gland" and "I Am Jane's Breast" — but it would be the more tangible, solid medium of books where the boom was really located. Pop sex advice manuals cluttered the nightstands of America —from encyclopedias and massage handbooks to so-called "pillow books" and reprints of the *Kama Sutra* and *Perfumed Garden*, as citizens frantically searched for the big Sexual Secret that would put their minds at ease, get the orgasms flowing and keep everyone up with his hip friends. Unlike the weighty Masters and Johnson's *Human Sexual Response* and other academic studies, these pop books were the literary equivalent of network television programming — accessible to the masses, with a minimum of statistics and charts. They flooded bookstores by the millions.

Among the most popular of these guidebooks was *The Joy of Sex*, by Alex Comfort, an obstetrician, nudist and family man who took the Epicurean tone of the popular *Joy of Cooking* cookbook and applied the concept to preparing a smorgasbord meal of complete, satisfying sex. The 1973 volume was soon accompanied by a sequel, *More Joy of Sex*, both profusely illustrated with sketches of an earthy couple having sex, oddly reminiscent of Charles Manson and Squeaky Fromme without the knives. This long-haired hippie man with sideburns and his long-haired woman with armpit hair were quickly picked up as universal images of sensuality, and imitated by other sex manuals.

Also a runaway best-seller was *Everything You Always Wanted to Know About Sex — But Were Afraid to Ask*, by San Diego psychiatrist David Reuben. Touting its author as "the new apostle of sanity in sex," the 1970 book palavered on about such topics as premature ejaculation, sex toys, aphrodisiacs, abortion, frigidity and prostitution, structured as a series of questions (from the title "Afraid to Ask," get it?). Example "queries" included "What is pornography really like?" or "What is the angle of the penis during erection?"

In retrospect, the publisher's claim of "sanity in sex" seems downright ludicrous, when you consider that millions of curious Americans were reading that, next to water, a warm bottle of Coca-Cola was the best douche liquid available. Reuben's advice comes off as particularly dated in the areas of transvestism, fetishes and

H old up the garter belt like a veil and peep over it. Now get tough, drop one side of the belt, swing it first slowly...and then let fly!

— from *Striptease*, a how-to guidebook for undressing in front of your husband, by Libby Jones, 1968

WHAT'S YOUR SIGN?: *Secrets of the Zodiac unlocked at last*

E very woman in this world has more sexual potential packed into her pelvis than a corral full of wild stallions. Females are designed, equipped and destined to have as many as 40 orgasms an hour, three times a night, seven nights a week, 52 weeks a year. Fortunately for the men of America, even though they have it, most ladies don't flaunt it. And that's part of the problem.

— from *How to Get More Out of Sex* by David Reuben

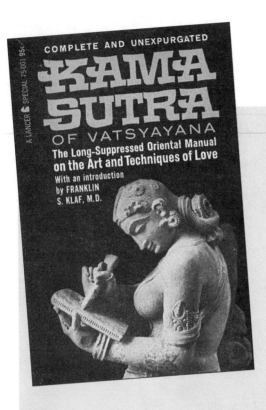

When a man and woman meet with the sole object of entering into the reciprocal pleasures of love, they generally embrace in one of the following ways:

5) When a woman clasps her lover as closely as a serpent twines around a tree, and pulls his head towards her waiting lips, if she then kisses him making a light hissing sound "soutt soutt" and looks at him long and tenderly — her pupils dilated with desire — this posture is known as the *Clasp of the Serpent*.

6) When a woman places one foot on the foot of her lover, and the other around his thigh, when she puts one arm around his neck and the other around his loins, and softly croons her desire, as if she wished to climb the firm stem of his body and capture a kiss — it is known as the *Tree Climber*.

But these two attitudes of passion are only a prelude to the actual union.

7) When a man and a woman, lying on a bed, embrace each other so closely that their arms and thighs are entwined in a gentle friction, it is called the *Union of the Sesame Seed with the Grain of Rice*.

8) When a man and a woman take each other violently and without fear of pain or harm, as if one wished to penetrate the body of the other, even if the woman is sitting astride his knees or standing against him or lying beneath him, her abandonment is known as the *Union of Milk and Water*.

— from *Kama Sutra of Vatsyayana: The Long-Suppressed Oriental Manual on the Art and Techniques of Love*, Lancer Books, 1964

Do not drink rain-water directly after copulation, because this beverage weakens the kidneys.

If you want to repeat the coition, perfume yourself with sweet scents, then close with the woman, and you will arrive at a happy result.

Do not let the woman perform the action of coition mounted upon you, for fear that in that position some drops of her seminal fluid might enter the canal of your verge and cause a sharp ureteritis.

Do not work hard directly after coition; this might affect your health badly but go to rest for some time.

Do not wash your verge directly after having withdrawn it from the vagina of the woman; until the irritation has gone down somewhat; then wash it and its opening carefully. Otherwise, do not wash your member frequently. Do not leave the vulva directly after the emission, as this may cause canker.

The coition, if performed standing, affects the knee-joints and brings about nervous shiverings; and if performed sideways will predispose your system for gout and sciatica, which resides chiefly in the hip-joint.

Do not mount upon a woman fasting or immediately before making a meal, or else you will have pains in your back, you will lose your vigour, and your eyesight will get weaker.

It is pretended that to look into the cavity of the vagina is injurious to the eyes. This is a question for a physician, and not for a mere adviser.

After ejaculation do not remain close to the woman, as the disposition for recommencing will suffer by doing so.

It is also not well constantly to wear vestments made of silk as they impair all the energy for copulation. Silken cloths worn by women also affect injuriously the capacity for the erection of the virile member.

Fasting, if prolonged, calms the sexual desires; but in the beginning it excites them.

The abuse of coition is followed by the loss of the taste for its pleasures; and to remedy this loss the sufferer must anoint his member with a mixture of the blood of a he-goat with honey.

Women are more favoured than men in indulging their passion for coition. It is in fact their specialty; and for them it is all pleasure; while men run many risks in abandoning themselves without reserve to the pleasure of love.

— from *The Perfumed Garden*, 1886, reprinted 1963

The Perfumed Garden   12/6   Translated by Sir Richard Burton of KAMA SUTRA fame

FULLY ILLUSTRATED
The most daring book ever written on
THE ARABIAN ART OF MAKING LOVE

cross-dressing — subjects which 20 years later are pretty much accepted behavior, from rock stars and models to top NBA basketball players. Reuben's underlying tone of homophobia also seems charmingly narrow-minded today. Homosexuals are not born that way, wrote Reuben, and if they just found the right psychiatrist (such as himself), they stood "every chance of becoming a happy, well-adjusted, heterosexual." Woody Allen's hit 1972 comedy had little in common with the book, other than the title and typeface, but it was perhaps the first film to take its audience inside the male genitalia for an action-filled sperm launch sequence.

Other sex manuals appeared and disappeared, giving little advice other than endless photos of a couple having sex in every position imaginable. Their appeal seemed to weigh very little on the advice side, and more on the lurid nature of the photographs. Some of the earlier manuals were too shy to portray actual humans engaged in sex, and instead substituted wooden anatomy dolls, giving sex an unusually faceless quality.

Few magazines in America refused mail-order advertising from the publishers of *How to Pick Up Girls!* by Eric Weber. This low-budget, 1970 classic was the ultimate handbook on becoming a wolf (and in retrospect sounds suspiciously like the lines used by Ted Bundy on his victims). Those who sent in their money were treated to Weber's tongue-in-cheek advice on scoring as many chicks as you could possibly want — as told through interviews with 25 young single women whom Weber dubbed "The Fabulous 25." Flush with success, Weber self-published a 1974 companion volume, *The Complete Guide to America's Best Pick Up Spots!*, and in 1978, Hollywood would slap together a kooky made-for-TV treatment of *How to Pick Up Girls!*, starring Desi Arnaz, Jr., Richard Dawson and Abe Vigoda. Unlike most books mentioned here, *Pick Up Girls!* is still in print and selling strong today.

In the early 1960s, Helen Gurley Brown was just another young married woman toiling at an ad agency. Frustrated by a lack of responsibility, she wrote a book about what it's like to be a single, man-hungry neurotic woman in today's world. *Sex and the Single Girl* rose to the top of the 1962 best-seller lists, coaching young females on where to find and ensnare a guy, and how to transform their apartments into "a sure man-magnet." After dashing off a 1964 sequel, *Sex and the Office*, Brown was hired as editor of *Cosmopolitan* magazine, which has spun endless variations on the theme ever since.

WHICH WAY TO TURN:
*More advice than any
nation deserves*

7

7. FACE-TO-FACE POSITION (Woman-Supine Position)
The woman's legs are raised high so as to rest on the man's shoulders. As her hip is raised, the insertion is very deep. Her hip is subject to violent motions during the sex movements, so that this position gives her psychologically comfortable feeling, too. She should not spread her thighs too wide.

15. FACE-TO-FACE POSITION (Man-Supine Position)
Movement is less free than in Position 13, but since her breasts are placed directly over his eyes, this position will serve to increase not only the man's sexual feeling but also her own. This position, too, gives the female more satisfaction than to the male.

15

25. FACE-TO-FACE POSITION (Man-sitting Position)
This is the position in which the woman sits with her legs crossed in front and holds the man's hip in her arms. The insertion is deep and the local stimulation is adequate. Closely-pressed grinding motion is possible in this position.

25

30. FACE-TO-FACE POSITION (Side Position)
The woman bends her right leg with the right thigh pulled close to her body and the other leg stretched out freely. Only the lower part of her body should be twisted to the right. Although the woman is extremely limited in her sex movements, she can have a special stimulation effect.

35. REAR-ENTRY POSITION (Woman-Prone Position)
This is the position in which a stool as high as a tea table is used. This position is most acceptable by women of all rear-entry positions, since she can hide her face. Sex movements are also easy.

— typical deck of how-to cards from the 1970s; this one is called _Forty-Eight Authentic Art Ways_, printed in Japan and translated into broken English, yet retaining the cultural bias of the era

30

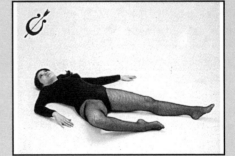

35

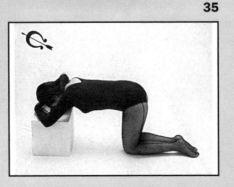

But while young secretaries could find solace in Brown's downtown, Capri-pants sassiness, orgasmless women were still adrift out in the suburbs, hunting for their clitorises. Fortunately, *The Sensuous Woman*, by "J", appeared in stores in 1970, and held housewives's hands through the thorny thickets of sensuality exercises, masturbation, body painting and harem costumes, ostensibly transforming the harried mom into a supercharged, self-confident tigress. Written by Joan Terry Garrity, a Manhattan book promoter who used a pseudonym for fear of her mother's reaction to the book, *The Sensuous Woman* offered advice both sound and inane, such as how to fake an orgasm for your husband: "Throw in a few extra wriggles and a yelp or two along the way to match his passion — but be careful not to ham it up too much." The book sold millions, as did sequels *The Sensuous Man* and *The Sensuous Couple*, and paved the way for feminist psychiatrist Lonnie Barbach's *For Yourself* in the mid-'70s, which assigned women orgasm-related "homework" in order to teach them how to satisfy themselves.

And yet there were women who not only couldn't fathom advice from the business female, they certainly didn't want to hear about sex from a man, even if he was supposed to be the new "apostle of sex." In 1969 a Boston women's conference group began collecting papers and notes from their discussions and selling mimeographed copies to other interested women. A bound version of their research appeared in 1971, called *Our Bodies, Ourselves,* and bylined by the Boston Women's Health Book Collective. Subtitled "A Book By and For Women," *Our Bodies* was immediately required reading for independent women, and dispensed thorough information on subjects like childbearing, rape, menopause, abortion, lesbians, VD and health care, as well as a detailed look at the female internal plumbing. Men appeared sparingly throughout the pages, as either rapists or bearers of sperm. The book is still in stores today.

By the mid-'70s the Gold Rush was over. America now had hundreds of sources from which to receive sexual advice, most of which is humorously outdated, and which linger in the $2 sections of used bookstores. But the juggernaut steams ahead, and anybody can be a sex advisor these days, as long as he or she has a Web site and a shelf of reference books.

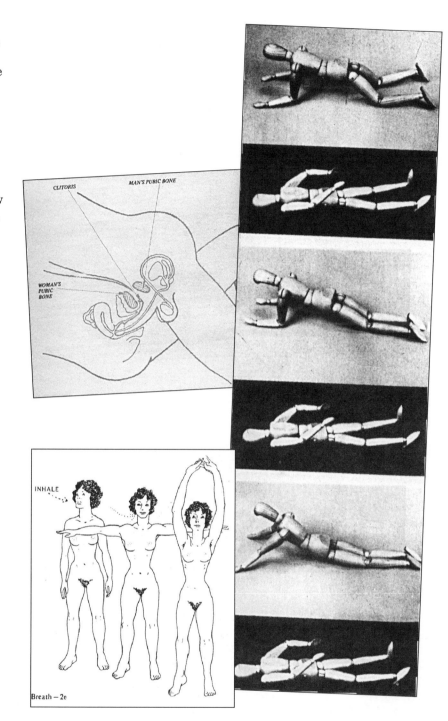

WHEN WORDS WON'T HELP:
Visual aids for the language-impaired

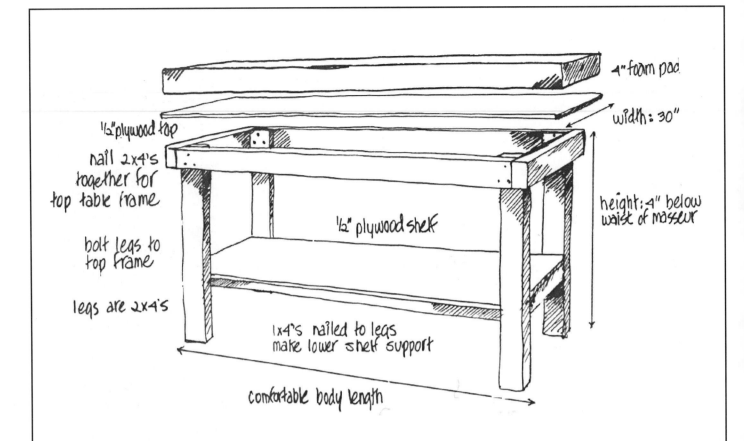

4" foam pad

width: 30"

½" plywood top

nail 2x4's together for top table frame

bolt legs to top frame

legs are 2x4's

½" plywood shelf

height: 4" below waist of masseur

1x4's nailed to legs make lower shelf support

comfortable body length

the art of sensual
MASSAGE

by Gordon Inkeles & Murray Todris
with photographs by Robert Foothorap

Work on a room until it *feels* mellow. The room's design is largely a question of individual taste. Most people enjoy fixtures for candles, incense and oil lamps. Hang them from the ceiing if you like. A sound source with earphones is a fine touch. Thick rugs and pillows. Soft diffused light during the day. Colored glass in the windows. Plants and flowers. Everything in a massage room should delight the senses...

   Hang three infra-red lamps from a rack over your table. Adjust the height of your lamps so that the three circles of light they produce cover the entire table evenly. Usually a height of two and a half to three feet is about right. With a little extra effort you can make the lamp rack adjustable so it can be raised above your head while you're working and lowered when you want to warm your partner....

   Include an electrical outlet for a vibrator in the center of your lamp rack or very near the table. Be sure to arrange the outlet so that the vibrator cord doesn't drag over your partner. A small waist high table near the massage table is a handy extra platform for oils, incense, and alcohol. The room should be near a sink and a bath or shower. Keep it warm and quiet and far, far away from the distractions of this world.

—from *The Sensual Art of Massage* **by Gordon Inkeles & Murray Todris, 1972**

Great Opening Lines

Please feel free to use them whenever you want. A lot of guys have already used them with a lot of success. And I'm sure you will, too.

• Do you have an aspirin? (spoken in a pained voice)
• How long do you cook a leg of lamb? (to pretty girl in grocery store)
• Is my tie straight? I'm going to an important meeting and I want to look just right. (on the elevator, or office building lobby)
• What color are your eyes? They're beautiful.
• I love you. (used half in jest at parties and singles bars)
• You're Miss Ohio, aren't you. I saw your picture in the paper yesterday.
• Are you a ballet dancer?
• Is there a post office near here?
• Do you like this blouse? (in a department store)
• Are you French?
• Did you drop this handkerchief? (you've just pulled it out of your pocket)
• What kind of dog is that? He's great-looking.
• Wow! What a beautiful day!
• You look sad.
• Come in out of the rain. (when you have an umbrella)
• What do you think of the play? (intermission at the theatre)

• You look sensational in that!
• Are you a model?
• If I had a million dollars, I'd buy that for you. (in front of painting at museum)
• Didn't I meet you in Istanbul?
• Who's your dentist?
• Don't ever cut your hair.
• Don't tell me a beautiful girl like you doesn't have a date tonight.
• If we were in a restaurant, I'd have the waiter send you a drink. (at dentist's waiting room)
• When I see someone like you I thank my lucky stars I'm not married.
• Now I understand why you have such a fantastic figure! (to jogging girl)
• Catch! (after throwing her a frisbee or ball)
• The onion soup is really good. (at the lunch counter)
• Are you Natasha, my contact? (pull hat down low, and pretend to be a spy)
• What do bean sprouts taste like? (in health food store)
• How many miles per gallon do you get on that? (to woman on bicycle)
• Could you recommend a good book for a friend in the hospital? (in bookstore)

— from *How to Pick Up Girls* by **Eric Weber, 1970**

THE complete guide to
AMERICA'S BEST PICK UP SPOTS!
by Eric Weber
M. Rob Frazier

910 Fantastic Places to Pick Up Girls!

If you're going to be in one place for a while, take a class. That's right, sign up for some adult education course. In social dancing. In bridge. In photography. In basic sociology. In macrame. In psychology. Which reminds me...Join a sensitivity training group. There are some that are on-going, and others that are just for one evening. It's a great place to meet women. It's one place where you not only *can*, but are supposed to be absolutely "honest." Say that you're lonely and that you were really turned on by Barbara when she walked into the room, and you'd really like to get together with her. Say that you find her really attractive and you'd love to sleep with her. It's the perfect place to do that. If she says that she doesn't know you well enough, be understanding, but drop in a couple of hints about inhibitions, and let the rest of the group pick up on it.

— from *The Complete Guide to America's Best Pick Up Spots*! by **Eric Weber and M. Rob Frazier, 1974**

ERIC WEBER'S WORLD-FAMOUS $5.95
HOW TO PICK UP GIRLS!
NEARLY ONE MILLION COPIES SOLD!
NEW ENLARGED EDITION!
You saw the smash-hit ABC movie! Now read the book that inspired it!

You must be relatively suspicious of any pseudo-type characters, as this is where the T-f type ["Mr. Two-Faced"] is usually found. He is numbered among some of the arrogants, phony intellectuals, surf and ski bums, and many others with obviously put-on personalities. He is always a man of weak character, which is why he enjoys feeling that he has "conquered" a girl and disgraced her by making love with her. This fellow is the dark dog who resembles the young snob in the story who, when asked to marry the girl he has made pregnant, says, "I wouldn't marry her; she's not worthy of me. She got herself knocked up without being married!" It's no joke. It's incredible, but true! There are many facets to every man, and the more you are exposed to them, the less likely you are to make a major mistake when the time finally comes to bed down for a life of fun and family. In the meantime, having recognized women's right to enjoy premarital sex — as men have for years — play the game of life and love...and enjoy it to the hilt!"

— from *Swingers Guide for the Single Girl: Key to the New Morality* by Marie & Hector Roget, 1968

A list of the positive aspects of getting involved with a married man:

1. He can be your devoted slave and remain "faithful" to you for years.
2. He will love you more passionately than the woman he married, and prefer your company to hers.
3. He will spoon-feed you the praise and appreciation you rarely get from the single fellow who thinks telling you that you have pretty eyes might be construed as a proposal of marriage.
4. He is often generous with gifts and money. If he isn't, you can explain the economic facts of life.
5. Any visiting married man on an expense account is the greatest date since Diamond Jim Brady. He will take you to the best restaurants, the best night clubs, order the best champagne.
6. He will give you sound advice about your job, insurance investments and even about getting along with your family and other men.
7. He is frequently marvelous in bed and careful not to get you pregnant.

— from *Sex and the New Single Girl* by Helen Gurley Brown, 1970

The Sensual Nude: Erotic Ideas

- thin gold chain dangling over your bare, browned skin
- painted toenails — vermilion, gold, silver?
- pretend tattoo (painted on) — small, temporary, on one breast or buttock
- waist-long hair
- beauty mark — anywhere unexpected
- perfumed powder on your fanny
- jewel in your navel (use spirit gum)
- feather fan to wave over your breasts, over his genitals
- ribbons hanging from your hair
- shoulder-length filigree earrings
- satin pillow — beside your hips
- thick brass slave bracelet on one bare upper arm
- antique watch on a chain — ticking between your breasts
- musky perfume near your secret hollows
- bizarre peacock eye makeup
- long ivory cigarette holder between your lips
- elbow-length kid gloves
- african amulet around your neck
- body painting on your stomach
- velvet choker

— from *Cosmopolitan's Love Book: A Guide to Ecstasy in Bed* by the editors of *Cosmopolitan*, 1972

The Whipped Cream Wriggle

If you have a sweet tooth, this is the one for you. Take some freshly whipped cream, to which you have added a dash of vanilla and a couple of teaspoons of powdered sugar and spread the concoction evenly on the penis so that the whole area is covered with a quarter-inch layer of cream. As a finishing touch, sprinkle on a little shredded coconut and/or chocolate. Then lap it all up with your tongue. He'll wriggle with delight and you'll have the fun of an extra dessert. If you have a weight problem, use one of the many artificial whipped creams now on the market (available in boxes, plastic containers and aerosol cans) and forego the coconut and chocolate.

— from *The Sensuous Woman* by "J," 1970

The Feathery Flick

Raise her right through the roof with this one. Locate that fascinating clitoris — the most sensitive little sex organ in her body — with your tongue. Flick the tip of your tongue back and forth along the top of the shaft, in much the same way you would stroke a banjo but, of course, with a much ligher touch. Now flick up into the mons area, back down again along the clitoral shaft, and *finally*, when she is very excited, move your tongue down to the tip of the clitoris and continue with a feathery flick until she comes.

—from *The Sensuous Man* by "M," 1971

Masculinity Exercise Number 1

This one is to make you more aware of your tactile sense. Gather a number of household items with different textures, like a moist sponge, a pair of pliers, bread soaked in cream soda, a razor blade, coffee grounds, two or three cockroaches, phlegm, and so forth. Dim the lights. Sit on a comfortable chair, blindfold yourself, and *slowly and gently* run your hands over the objects. Let the special texture of each imprint itself on your fingertips.

Now sit back and re-create in your mind the way each object felt. Recall the cold, chitinous backs of the roaches and their tiny, flailing legs. Remember the cool slime of the phlegm, the unexpected slice of the razor. You'll be surprised at your tactile memory.

Touch everything one more time and go drink a glass of seltzer. Rest.

— from "The Way to Become the Masculine He-Man" by Chris Miller, *National Lampoon*

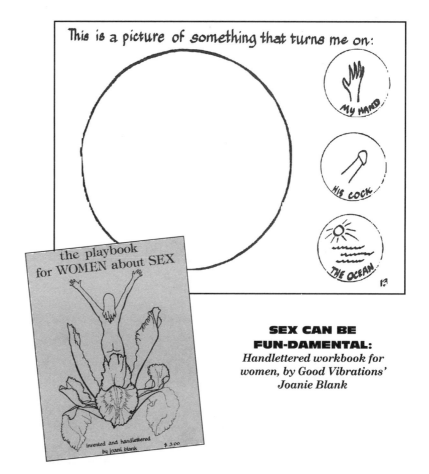

SEX CAN BE FUN-DAMENTAL:
Handlettered workbook for women, by Good Vibrations' Joanie Blank

COMPLETE
AND UNABRIDGED.
FIRST TIME
IN PAPERBACK.

MASTERS' AND JOHNSON'S
BREAKTHROUGH BESTSELLER

HUMAN SEXUAL INADEQUACY

BY WILLIAM H. MASTERS, M.D.
AND VIRGINIA E. JOHNSON

A BANTAM BOOK

13739-5 ★ $4.95 ★

Wilhelm Reich

THE SEXUAL REVOLUTION

Toward a Self-Regulating Character Structure

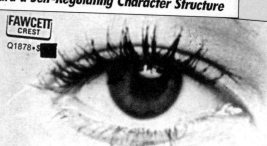

FAWCETT
CREST

Q1878 • $

the new
sexual role of
women

Free and Female

Barbara Seaman

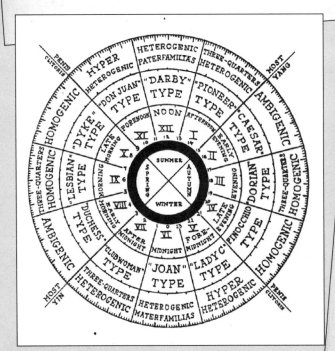

13

he Golden Age of Hetero was noted for the reams of sexual research generated during its time. The spectrum of theory ranged from the long-term work of Kinsey and Masters and Johnson to the independent feminist projects of Betty Friedan and Shere Hite, studies of subliminal body language and sexual power of tarot cards, and the orgone energy philosophies of Wilhelm Reich. Even a total crackpot like Gavin Arthur, grandson of president Chester Arthur, could stake his claim in the game, toiling in a run-down hotel room, plotting the many intricacies of human sexuality on a circular wheel.

What Does It All Mean?

Not only did Americans read about these theories in their family newspaper, they could buy them in a local bookstore. Absorbing such information made you feel intelligent and curious. You could learn about sex without feeling lecherous. And if anyone saw it on the night-stand, it looked to be not just cheap titillation, but the fruits of a heightened intellectual pursuit.

Diagrams and charts were rendered, columns of data were compiled. Millions of dollars were spent examining humans as if they were guinea

ANSWERS ON DEMAND:
Various theories for all your sexual needs, from reliable and logical to loopy and schizophrenic

The medium was introduced as a potential enhancement of the touch exercises by direction given at the end of the roundtable session. If a particular fragrance proved objectionable or occasioned any distress to either partner, the unscented material was substituted during the particular time period. A different fragrance category was chosen at random and introduced daily. After each of the individual categories of fragrance had been experienced once and personal reactions reported, subsequent choice was marked by marital-unit preference.

In addition to the unperfumed lotion there were nine fragrance categories represented in the moisturizer-lotion medium introduced concomitantly with direction for the sensate-focus exercises. Four were popularly conceptualized as being of "feminine" orientation, all of them bouquets: floral; a mossy green; a floral, woody blend; and oriental. The remaining 5 fragrance categories were considered "masculine": lavender bouquet; modern ambery, sweet bouquet; citrus bouquet; fresh citrus plus woody, floral bouquet; and a sharp fragrance with balsamic notes.

Based upon available data, individual preferences for particular fragrance categories have correlated only with personal experiential material elicited during history-taking. Within the concept of this form of psychotherapy, however, any expressed fragrance preference would be maintained, altered, or extended subject to further adaptive or learning opportunities. In certain instances the material reflects the preference as an integral component of an established sexual value system. However, information obtained within the investigative design is considered only as a basis for conjecture, to be used in planning future research direction.

— portion of a scientific study conducted with perfumed moisturizing lotion, *Human Sexual Inadequacy* by Masters and Johnson, 1970

pigs. Measurements were taken of erection angles and vaginal secretion levels. Calipers and electrodes were applied to vaginas and penile shafts. College students were shown slide shows of pornography, and asked to fill out questionnaires. Scientists monitored the brain's copulation-reward areas in laboratory rats. Such findings were not without an understated sense of humor. One late-'60s report stated: "An amusing by-product of these laboratory studies concerns the effectiveness of a fresh stimulus. A male rat utterly exhausted following a series of copulative encounters with one female will rouse himself, copulate again, and ejaculate again if a new female is introduced."

Prominent were two well-funded studies that set the standard for sexual research. After years working as a zoologist and expert entomologist, Alfred Kinsey donated his gall wasp collection to a museum and established the Institute for Sexual Research at Indiana University in the 1940s. He began conducting sex surveys, publishing his Kinsey Reports of sexual behavior in men and women in the late '40s and early '50s. After studying case histories of 10,000 white males and females, the reports concluded that 1) most humans masturbate, 2) the clitoris is important in orgasm, 3) females can experience multiple orgasms and 4) a peculiar result in which an 11-month-old baby achieved 14 orgasms in 38 minutes.

Interview-based technique changed the course of sexual research. Paying close attention to Kinsey's work were Dr. William H. Masters and Virginia E. Johnson. Masters became interested in sex while attending the University of Rochester School of Medicine and Dentistry, where he researched the estrus cycle of the rabbit. After working as a gynecologist, he established the Reproductive Biology Research Foundation in St. Louis in 1964, working initially with prostitutes. Masters placed an ad for someone to help interview and screen volunteers, and met Mrs. Johnson, who was separated from her husband and looking for work. Over the next eleven years, the two studied 694 men and women, and realized 1) all women are naturally multi-orgasmic, 2) the vagina involuntarily expands to a size sufficient for containment of the penis, and 3) men and women can maintain effective sexual function into their 80s.

Their book *Human Sexual Response* was released in 1966 in a plain brown wrapper, with no advertising. The authors were attacked for encouraging pornography, promoting venereal disease and ignoring common moral decency and traditional human values. The book nevertheless sold over 250,000 copies and was translated into nine languages.

The Masters & Johnson Institute in St. Louis offered two-week treatment programs for patients with sexual difficulties, occasionally using surrogate partners as part of the therapy. The practice backfired in 1969, when clinic participant Edwin Calvert sued the two for $2.5 million. He claimed Masters and Johnson had used his wife, Barbara, as a surrogate sex partner, which caused her to pursue and have sex with a series of anonymous men. By the time the case was settled out of court in 1972, Masters and Johnson's practice of surrogates had stopped. The legal risk was too great.

Human Sexual Inadequacy, published in 1970, studied premature ejaculation, orgasmic dysfunction and the delicately-worded "erective failure." Among their discoveries: "There is no uninvolved partner when sex is a problem," and "The outcome of clinical care improves immeasurably when a couple works together to help overcome problems in their relationship." Success rates in Masters and Johnson's studies were, reportedly, 97.8% for premature ejaculation, 80.7% for female frigidity and 73.8% for male impotence. The report concluded that the greatest cause of dysfunction is fear, and once the fear is taken away, nature will take its course. *Inadequacy* became a standard text for sex therapists, and the Masters and Johnson Institute was so popular that by 1977 it was estimated there were over 6,000 sex centers across the U.S., and the American Association of Sex Educators and Counselors listed over 600 members. In 1992 Masters and Johnson divorced after 21 years of marriage. Two years later — due to Masters' Parkinson's disease and a more complex landscape of sexual problems — the Institute closed for good.

Another report was published in 1974 by the Research Guild, Inc., a survey of sexual behaviors in 24 U.S. cities and suburbs, commissioned by the Playboy Foundation. *Sexual Behavior in the 1970s* found that premarital sex was acceptable and increasingly trendy — between 50% and 80% of women had sex before getting married. Not only were people engaging in more oral and anal sex, they were doing it more frequently. Married couples 25 or younger were having sex 154 times a year, compared with 130 a generation ago, and 50% to 90% of men and woman admitted to becoming sexually aroused by erotica. Contrary to media hype, only 2% of married males (and less for females) had

1. The organs fill with fluid: erection with *mechanical tension.*
2. This leads to an intense excitation, which I assumed to be of an electrical nature: *electrical charge.*
3. In the orgasm, the electrical charge of sexual excitation is discharged in muscular contractions: *electrical discharge.*
4. This is followed by a relaxation of the genitals through a flowing back of the body fluids: *mechanical relaxation.*

— **Orgasm Formula, from *The Function of the Orgasm* by Wilhelm Reich, 1947**

The changes I underwent in my three and a half years in orgonomy were profound. As I grew more and more "natural" I began to see things around me quite differently. The meaning of sex and love became clearer to me and I came to understand that the people who claim that they represent two different drives in man are influenced to see things this way by their armoring.

Sexually, I found myself able to tolerate more and more pleasure, without clamping down in anxiety, and I found that the sexual pleasure I experienced was increasingly intertwined with my soft, tender feelings. I felt infinitely freer sexually than ever before, but it had nothing to do with the so-called sexual revolution which has produced a phenomenon Reich called "freedom peddlers."

"Freedom peddlers" go around tantalizing and titillating people with sugarplum visions of the new world they claim we are about to enter. They advocate immediate sexual freedom without ever taking into consideration the fact that the people in this world are sex-starved and have been for centuries. It's ignorant and irresponsible to offer a starving man a full-course dinner; he has to start out with broth. The human race will have to rise up out of its sexual abyss slowly and carefully like a deep-sea diver trying to avoid the bends.

— **from *Me and the Orgone* by actor and frequent *Tonight Show* guest Orson Bean, 1971**

Because of his vertical posture it is impossible for a naked ape to approach another member of his species without performing a genital display. Other primates, advancing on all fours, do not have this problem. If they wish to display their genitals they have to assume a special posture. We are faced with it, hour in and hour out, whatever we are doing. It follows that the covering of the genital region with some simple kind of garment must have been an early cultural development....

...There may be a copious sweating by both male and female immediately following sexual climax and this may occur regardless of how much or how little physical effort has been put into the preceding sexual activities. However, although it is not related to total physical expenditure, it does bear a relationship to the intensity of the orgasm itself. The film of sweat develops on the back, the thighs and the upper chest. Sweat may run from the armpits. In intense cases, the whole of the trunk, from shoulders to thighs, may be involved. The palms of the hands and soles of the feet also perspire and, where the face has become mottled with the sexual flush, there may be sweating on the forehead and upper lip....

...The typical mating posture of all other primates involves the rear approach of the male to the female. She lifts her rear end and directs it towards the male. Her genital region is visually presented backwards to him. He sees it, moves towards her, and mounts her from behind. There is no frontal body contact during copulation, the male's genital region being pressed on to the female's rump region. In our own species the situation is very different. Not only is there prolonged face-to-face pre-copulatory activity, but also copulation itself is primarily a frontal performance.

— from *The Naked Ape* by Desmond Morris, 1967

participated in mate-swapping, but extra-marital sex had contributed to over half of separations and divorces.

This last statistic probably didn't amuse Albert Ellis, a psychotherapist and author of several sexuality books during the '50s and '60s, including *The Encyclopedia of Sexual Behavior*. A newspaper columnist and devoted advocate of sex without guilt, Ellis gained particular notoriety for a speech before the American Psychological Association, where he reportedly declared that marriages can sometimes be helped by "healthy adultery."

For those Americans who preferred the single-theory model of sexual philosophy, many others besides Ellis were also popular during this time. Even though many had been dead for years, reprinted versions of their works were rescued from obscurity and began appearing once again on bookshelves and coffee tables. British physician Henry Havelock Ellis (no relation to Al) gained fame around the turn of the century for being one of the first to address and discuss sexual deviance. His seven-volume *Studies in the Psychology of Sex* was supposedly responsible for coining the terms "auto eroticism" and "narcissism." Nineteenth-century German forensic psychiatrist Richard von Krafft-Ebing drew attention for his comprehensive case studies of sexual aberration, including sadism and masochism, compiled in the book *Psychopathis Sexualis*. In 1950 German gynecologist Dr. Ernst Grafenberg published a medical article about a specific and highly sensitive area of the vagina called the G spot, which could experience its own orgasms separate from the rest of the female plumbing. When this paper flushed to the surface in the late '70s, a book called *The G Spot* was immediately published of an informal survey, claiming that many women ejaculated a fluid through their urethras, and that in order to experience such an orgasm, you had to have sex in the rear-entry position. Americans grew even more confused when the book told them all that foreplay the other books were advocating was not advisable, because clitoral stimulation would distract women from locating their true G spots.

Perhaps the most infamous rediscovery of the 1960s was the work of Austrian psychiatrist Wilhelm Reich. A former protégé of Freud, Reich's theories on sex were so revolutionary that he was ultimately rejected by the psychiatric profession, and after his death in prison in 1957, many of his papers were burned. Obviously, he was a special person.

Reich's ideology centered around the belief that an inadequate orgasm in humans left surplus energy in the body — which he termed orgone — that might encourage unhealthy urges. Only a total orgasm could release these negative energies. In fact, releasing sexual suppression in everyone, children and adolescents included, would overthrow traditionally stifling social institutions. If everyone had the best sex they could possibly have, the world would become a better place. New words like "genital frustration," "sex-economy" and "orgastic potency" entered the vocabulary courtesy of Reich. Orgone was also the force behind the planets, helped explain flying saucers and was synonymous with God. Reich built boxes called "orgone accumulators" to collect life-giving rays and beam them to the person who sat inside the box. The contraptions were sold as sexual stimulation devices and cures for cancer.

Reich was considered chic in many circles, often heard quoted at Hollywood parties and around the campfire at communes. Celebrity fans ranged from Jack Nicholson to Orson Bean, who wrote *Me and the Orgone: One Man's Sexual Revolution*. Reich's life and work also provided the basis for Dusan Makavejev's 1971 film *W.R. — Mysteries of the Organism*, where the main character hollers from her apartment window: "Politics is for those whose orgasm is incomplete!" Years later, people still read his books, as much for entertainment as advice. Porn star Nina Hartley has told the story of being a six-year-old in the attic of her parents' house, curling up under an old orgone blanket, not knowing its purpose, but somehow sensing its properties.

Orgasm also played a prominent role in the resurgence of tantra, popularized by the 1974 book *Tantric Sex* by Robert Moffett. This timely repackaging of ancient Hindu tantra and Tibetan/Buddhist tantra beliefs stressed the technique of *karezza* — the means of indefinitely delaying orgasm — to sublimate the animal tendencies into spiritual ecstasies. Such mutual reinforcement sex would destroy inhibitions while simultaneously reducing the drive for self-gratification. Man and woman would ride the wave together for hours, aroused but just below the threshold of involuntary orgasm. Apparently this was, and is, reputed to be pretty nifty, if one has the time.

Some areas of research remained within a specific subject. Three separate studies explored the growing phenomenon of swinger culture. A survey of 280 swingers in the suburban Chicago area, published by Illinois anthropologist

While a man on the make cannot touch the woman if he is to play the game fairly, it is perfectly permissible for a woman on the make, at this stage of the game, to touch the man. This touch can exaggerate the uneasiness of the man into whose territory she has cut.

A touch on the arm can be a disarming blow. "Do you have a match?" Steadying the hand that holds it to her cigarette can allow a moment of flesh-to-flesh contact that may be effectively troubling.

The contact of a woman's thigh, or her hand carelessly brushed against a man's thigh can be devastating if it is applied at just the right moment.

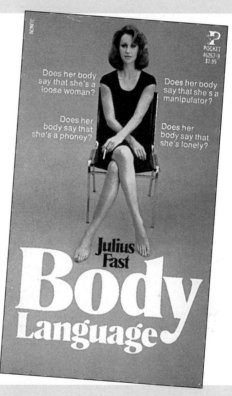

He has dozen of little gestures, perhaps unconscious ones, that send out elaborations of his sexual message. When Mike leans up against a mantel in a room to look around at the women, his hips are thrust forward slightly, as if they were cantilevered, and his legs are usually apart. There is something in this stance that spells sex.

Watch Mike when he stands like this. He will lock his thumbs in his belt right above the pockets, and his fingers will point down toward his genitals. You have surely seen the same stance a hundred times in Western movies, usually not taken by the hero, but by the sexy bad guy as he lounges against a corral fence, the picture of threatening sexuality, the villain the men hate and the women — well, what they feel is a lot more complex than hate or desire or fear, and yet it's a mixture of all these things. With his blatant body language, his leather chaps, his cantilevered groin and pointing fingers he is sending out a crude, obvious but effective signal. "I am a sexual threat. I am a dangerous man for a woman to be alone with. I am all man and I want you!"

On a minor scale, less blatant, Mike sends out the same message.

— from *Body Language* by Julius Fast, 1970

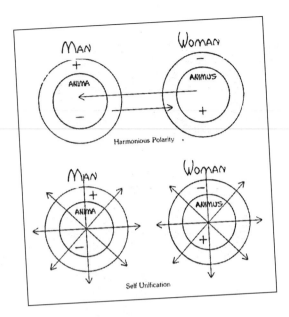

Harmonious Polarity

Self Unification

MAN/WOMAN, WOMAN/MAN:
Mysterious diagram from The Mystery of
Sex *by Laurel Elizabeth Keyes, 1975*

Yellow Pagers

They get their pleasure from fucking people in *categories*, the way they might be listed in the *Yellow Pages*. One example is "groupies," who go for Rock Groups. There are also Writer-Fuckers, Singer-Fuckers, Doctor-Fuckers, Athlete-Fuckers, Gangster-Fuckers. There are Tycoon-Fuckers, who fuck with the jet set from Ibiza to Puerto Vallarta. There are even Charity-Fuckers, to whom no ecstasy would be greater than jumping into bed with the *New York Times*' "100 Neediest Cases."

Deflowerers

There are men who get their only kicks from leading virgins down the primrose path, and women who won't be satisfied until they compromise the pope.

Daredevils

Some men can't be happy unless they're fucking a police sergeant's wife on the steps of the precinct station.

Statisticians

Some people enjoy measurements; their pleasure comes from the arithmetic of fucking: the size of a partner's sex organs, the precise timing, the angle of entry. I know an attractive young woman who is a member of Mensa, an organization restricted to people in the top two percent of intelligence. One night she ran in all excited and said, "Last night I laid a man who made 302 strokes!" Another Mensa looked at her and said, "You weren't fucking, darling. You were counting."

Miscellaneous

There are Geographuckers, whose pleasure comes from fucking in strange new places; Gadgeteers, who dig electric toothbrushes, vibrators and other small appliances. There are Totalizators — people who go in for quantity...There are Conversationalists, who fuck only because it gives them something to talk about the next day; Professors, who enjoy passing on sexual knowledge; and Students, who expect every fuck to teach them something. There are an infinite number of Specialists; probably the most numerous are Loveseekers. Their pleasure comes from believing with all their hearts that *this* fuck is True Love.

— from The Rape of the A*P*E* by Allen Sherman, 1973

Gilbert Bartell, compared contemporary suburbia to a similar plight of urban cities described by historian Arnold Toynbee: "Anonymity, Alienation and Anomie...They sit in silence and look at television. The woman, who feels restricted to the household environment, believes she should be out doing things....The man wants to be in on the 'scene,' to know 'where it's really at' and so his fantasies lead to swinging." Bartell's conclusion was that although swinging couples seemed outrageous in their swapping preferences, most possessed a common characteristic of inherent normality — average, commonplace and uncomplicated. So-called "sick" people, in the Freudian sense of the term, stayed away from the swinger scene.

Another study, by sociologist and practicing nudist Carolyn Symonds, focused on swingers in Southern California. Symond determined that California swingers fell into two categories. Utopian swingers were concerned with building a better world, and establishing small communes where they could practice sexual freedom in peace and happiness. Recreational swingers were men and women, often married couples, who believed that sex was a viable alternative to playing bridge or golf.

A third survey, conducted by UC Berkeley graduate students James R. and Lynn G. Smith, who were actual members of the swinger community, centered in the San Francisco Bay Area. The Smiths' data suggested that swinging with multiple sex partners had, at least in some cases, a high ability to repair damaged self-images and damaged self-esteem. Not only did people feel better about themselves, in many cases swinging actually strengthened a marriage or relationship. Jealousy was not as present if a married couple swung with another couple, rather than with an unattached single person. But in a form of envy the Smiths called "dyadic jealousy," a husband and wife might experience the green-eyed monster when a couple with whom they had been swinging, started swinging with a third couple.

Also gaining popularity were surveys and reports produced by what could best be described as Pop Culture theorists — scientists, sociologists and journalists who, although not necessarily experts specializing in the topic of sex, were able to sufficiently capitalize on the trend.

Such nightstand chic included several studies that approached human sexuality from the perspective that we were merely another animal in the kingdom. *The Naked Ape*, a pop anthropology summary of man's sex habits written by zoologist Desmond Morris, sold millions of copies throughout the late '60s, holding that the biological nature of man has formed the social structure of our civilization, not the other way around. Morris listed several facts that clearly were included to titillate as well as inform. Among them, humans were supposed to possess the largest penis of any of the 192 other species of apes. Human female breasts were unique among primates because they protruded in a characteristic shape, an example of what Morris termed "sexual signaling." Most species were said to have specific breeding seasons, but man has none. (Unless you account for cold winters, or perhaps Spring Break.) Morris' book was eventually made into a tongue-in-cheek 1973 film with Victoria Principal, produced by Hugh Hefner.

California biochemist Dr. Robert S. de Ropp also checked in with *Sex Energy*, a survey of such an energy and its role throughout the animal kingdom, from one-celled organisms up to humans, including a spectacular tribute to the penis of the flea, purportedly the largest and most complex sexual organ on the planet.

Julius Fast's *Body Language* addressed the new science of kinesics, interpreting those physical signals that humans unconsciously send to each other. This 1970 guide promised to tell readers "how to make advances without taking chances!"

Others jumped into the game, having little qualifications other than a willingness to learn, a big cash advance and a hefty sexual appetite. Children's song author Allan Sherman, best known for his early '60s novelty song "Hello Mudda, Hello Fadda," published in 1973 a witty overview called *The Rape of the A*P*E* – The Official History of the Sex Revolution* (A*P*E* being an acronym for American Puritan Ethic). Sherman's chronology was thorough, covering the years 1945 to 1973, but the official status of the book was no doubt influenced by its publisher, *Playboy*, which allowed Sherman access to its overflowing archives.

New York journalist Gay Talese began work on a book in 1971, conducting research and interviews into the psyche of America's sexual revolution. A draft was to be completed in 1974, but Talese kept delaying the final version, and continued racking up the bills, selling off further publishing rights to finance his quest. He moved to the Sandstone commune in Los Angeles, and participated in group orgies. He hung out at the *Playboy* Mansion, frequented brothels and even took a job at a massage parlor. Some accounts say he flaunted his new-found sexual prowess, boasting of conquests. After nine years, the

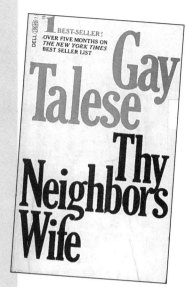

"Can we have sex?" he asked. She shook her head.

"I don't do that," she said. "I don't French either. I only give locals."

"*Locals?*"

"Hand jobs," she explained.

"Okay," he said, "I'll have a local."

"That will be extra."

"How *much* extra?"

"Fifteen dollars."

Too much, he thought. But in his aroused condition he was in no mood for bargaining, and so he nodded and watched with curiosity and anticipation as she sprinkled his groin with puffs of powder and adroitly proceeded to stroke his orgasm — expertly sensing, not a second too soon, the moment to whish a Kleenex from the nearby box.

— participatory journalism from *Thy Neighbor's Wife* by Gay Talese, 1980

I nstead of fulfilling the promise of infinite orgastic bliss, sex in the America of the feminine mystique is becoming a strangely joyless national compulsion, if not a contemptuous mockery. The sex-glutted novels become increasingly explicit and increasingly dull; the sex kick of the women's magazines has a sickly sadness; the endless flow of manuals describing new sex techniques hint at an endless lack of excitement. This sexual boredom is betrayed by the ever-growing size of the Hollywood starlet's breasts, by the sudden emergence of the male phallus as an advertising "gimmick." Sex has become depersonalized, seen in terms of these exaggerated symbols. But of all the strange sexual phenomena that have appeared in the era of the feminine mystique, the most ironic are these — the frustrated sexual hunger of American women has increased, and their conflicts over femininity have intensified, as they have reverted from independent activity to search for their sole fulfillment through their sexual role in the home. And as American women have turned their attention to the exclusive, explicit, and aggressive pursuit of sexual fulfillment, or the acting-out of sexual fantasy, the sexual disinterest of American men, and their hostility toward women, have also increased.

— from *The Feminine Mystique* by Betty Friedan, 1963

In my mind, as in our fucking, I am at the crucial point:...We are at this Baltimore Colt-Minnesota Viking football game, and it is very cold. Four or five of us are huddled under a big glen plaid blanket. Suddenly we jump up to watch Johnny Unitas running toward the goal. As he races down the field, we all turn as a body, wrapped in our blanket, screaming with excitement. Somehow, one of the men — I don't know who, and in my excitement I can't look — has gotten himself more closely behind me. I keep cheering, my voice an echo of his, hot on my neck. I can feel his erection through his pants as he signals me with a touch to turn my hips more directly toward him. Unitas is blocked, but all the action, thank God, is still going toward that goal and all of us keep turned to watch. Everyone is going mad. He's got his cock out now and somehow it's between my legs; he's torn a hole in my tights under my short skirt and I yell louder as the touchdown gets nearer now. We are all jumping up and down and I have to lift my leg higher, to the next step on the bleachers, to steady myself; now the man behind me can slip it in more easily. We are all leaping about, thumping one another on the back, and he puts his arm around my shoulders to keep us in rhythm. He's inside me now, shot straight up through me like a ramrod; my God, it's like he's in my throat! "All the way, Johnny! Go, go, run, run!" we scream together, louder than anyone, making them all cheer louder, the two of us leading the excitement like cheerleaders, while inside me I can feel whoever he is growing harder and harder, pushing deeper and higher into me with each jump until the cheering for Unitas becomes the rhythm of our fucking and all around us everyone is on our side, cheering us and the touchdown...it's hard to separate the two now. It's Unitas' last down, everything depends on him; we're racing madly, almost at our own touchdown. My excitement gets wilder, almost out of control as I scream for Unitas to make it as we do, so that we all go over the line together. And as the man behind me roars, clutching me in a spasm of pleasure, Unitas goes over and I...

"Tell me what you are thinking about," the man I was actually fucking said, his words as charged as the action in my mind. As I'd never stopped to think before doing anything to him in bed (we were that sure of our spontaneity and response), I didn't stop to edit my thoughts. I told him what I'd been thinking. He got out of bed, put on his pants and went home.

— from *My Secret Garden: Women's Sexual Fantasies* by Nancy Friday, 1973

best-selling *Thy Neighbor's Wife* was finally published in 1980, a brilliant piece of reporting that, for the first time, revealed the types of people who were behind the scenes of communes, group sex and the pornography industry. More than anyone had previously done, Talese acknowledged the unspoken market of porn — the legions of lonely men in America — and why they turned to X-rated materials for release. Unfortunately, the book took an unnecessary self-indulgent turn toward the very end, as Talese abruptly slipped into a third-person voice, describing his own sexual history and marital tension generated by research for the project. The Doonesbury comic strip mocked him for weeks, and the New York journalism community celebrated his efforts with several nasty magazine articles.

Concurrent with the above theories and movements was the concept of feminism, as American women writers fought to redefine their sexuality and demand an equal playing — and paying — field. The first published work to really focus on women was a survey of 200 of them, conducted by a magazine writer and mother of three named Betty Friedan. Her book, published in 1963 titled *The Feminine Mystique* defined the term as the discrepancy between the reality of women's lives and the image to which they attempted to conform — the post-World War II ideal housewife and mother. Millions of women read this bestseller and their thoughts echoed those of the women interviewed: "Is this all?"

Kate Millett's *Sexual Politics,* appearing in 1970, examined sexual stereotypes and the widening gap between the sexes. Also a bestseller, this book is credited with first establishing the concept of sexism, coining the term "sex object" and ripping to shreds such macho authors as D.H. Lawrence, Henry Miller and Norman Mailer.

The following year saw the debut of *Ms.* magazine. Several female writers, including journalist Gloria Steinem, had proposed the idea of a publication to *New York* magazine editor Clay Felker. He agreed to finance the first issue as an insert in *New York*, and *Ms.* quickly attracted an enormous readership. Feminists now had a monthly voice in the mainstream media.

Other books appearing during this time included *My Secret Garden* by journalist Nancy Friday, a collection of female sexual fantasies that articulated the unspoken thoughts of American women, such as: "While my boyfriend is making love to me I often fantasize about my best friend...Does this mean I'm a latent homosexual?" British writer Germaine Greer, described as a bad girl and "saucy feminist," lived the smart randy life she wrote about in her book *The Female Eunuch*. Occasional model Shere Hite sent out sex-related questions on National Organization of Women letterhead to 3,000 women, asking questions about orgasm, masturbation, clitoral stimulation and the "future of intercourse." Answers were compiled and published as *The Hite Report*, a mid-'70s best-seller that showed that social science research was just as valid — and certainly as popular — as its academic counterpart. "At best, an organ-moving cataclysm: my ovaries, uterus, breasts, and brain become one singing dark pulsating sea of the most exquisite feeling," answered one woman. Another said, "An orgasm cancels out all rage and longing for at least forty-eight hours, and the day an orgasm bores me, I think I'll commit suicide."

Guys were perhaps puzzled by the emerging feminist movement, unsure of how to respond. Eventually they would nod their heads in sensitive understanding, remembering that sex wasn't just about the guy getting off. If they didn't, they weren't going to get laid.

Compounding the confusion were the number of photos circulating of feminists who had posed naked at some point in their lives. Such images were gleefully rushed into print by smirking male publishers. Late-'60s nude modeling shots of Shere Hite appeared in *Hustler* in 1977. When nude shots of Germaine Greer ran in the European sex rag *Suck*, her legs hiked up over her head, Al Goldstein obtained copies and dutifully reprinted them in *Screw*.

But the ultimate battle of the sexes may have manifested on March 31, 1971 — an event billed as the Theater of Ideas, held at Town Hall in Manhattan. On hand to debate the new feminism were Germaine Greer, NOW's Jackie Ceballos, Diane Trilling, Jill Johnson from the *Village Voice* and providing a male perspective, Norman Mailer, author of *The Prisoner of Sex*. Most accounts described the audience as packed to overflowing, and as the clash of the super-egos picked up steam, the evening nearly turned into a riot. When it came her turn to speak, Johnson invited two of her girlfriends onstage to demonstrate lesbian lovemaking. As the three of them rolled around in their dirty jeans, hugging and kissing each other, Mailer reportedly exclaimed, "Jill, get up and act like a lady....You can get as much prick and cunt as

He felt a hate for the legions of the vaginally frigid, out there now with all the pent-up buzzing of a hive of bees, souped-up pent-up voltage of a clitoris ready to spring! yes, if there were women who came as if lightning bolts had flung their bodies across a bed, were there not also women who came with the gentlest squeeze of the deepest walls of the vagina, women who came every way, even women who seemed never to come yet claimed they did, and never seemed to suffer? yes, and women who purred as they came and women who screamed, women who came as if a finger had been tickling them down a mile-long street and women who arrived with the firm frank avowal of a gentleman shaking hands, yes, if women came in every variety — one could hardly reach the age of forty, call it forty-seven, soon to be forty-eight, without knowing something of that, even the most modest men could know something of that — then how to account for the declaration that vaginal orgasm was myth, and friction upon the clitoris was the only way an excitation could discharge? No, he had boobed along like the other men, mind trying to fix a reasonable balance between the dictum that the best of feminine orgasms was vaginal against his experience which seemed to speak of a splurge of orgasms in women which came not so near to being defined, orgasms which spoke back and forth, until Emily Dickinson herself might have cried, "Where the button, who the hole?," orgasms which came from you knew not where. (From Heaven, was the unvoiced hope.) Now the bitter gruel — women came uniquely from the clitoris. That was the word; the rest was lies. Women, went the cry, liberate yourselves from the tyranny of the vagina. It is nothing but a flunky to the men.

— from *Prisoner of Sex* by Norman Mailer, 1971

A full bosom is actually a millstone around a woman's neck; it endears her to the men who want to make their maumet of her, but she is never allowed to think that their popping eyes actually see her. Her breasts are only to be admired for as long as they show no sign of their function: once darkened, stretched or withered they are objects of revulsion. They are not parts of a person but lures slung around her neck, to be kneaded and twisted like magic putty, or mumbled and mouthed like lolly ices. The only way that women can opt out of such gross handling is to refuse to wear undergarments which perpetuate the fantasy of pneumatic boobs, so that men must come to terms with the varieties of the real thing. Recent emphasis on the nipple, which was absent from the breast of popular pornography, is in women's favor, for the nipple is expressive and responsive. The vegetable creep of women's liberation has freed some breasts from the domination of foam and wire. One way to continue progress in the same direction might be to remind men that they have sensitive nipples too.

— from *The Female Eunuch*, Germaine Greer, 1970

A lthough completely physical, the male is unfit even for stud service. Even assuming mechanical proficiency, which few men have, he is, first of all, incapable of zestfully, lustfully, tearing off a piece, but is instead eaten up with guilt, shame, fear, and insecurity, feelings rooted in male nature, which the most enlightened training can only minimize; second, the physical feeling he attains is next to nothing; and, third, he is not empathizing with his partner, but is obsessed with how he's doing, turning in an A performance, doing a good plumbing job. To call a man an animal is to flatter him; he's a machine, a walking dildo. It's often said that men use women. Use them for what? Surely not pleasure.

— from *S.C.U.M. (Society for Cutting Up Men) Manifesto* by Valerie Solanas, 1967

you want around the corner on Forty-Second Street for two dollars and fifty cents. We don't need it here."

The sweaty audience of feminists shouted back at Mailer: "Fascist pig!" "Chauvinist motherfucker!" Drag queen Candy Darling was heard to comment: "I've never seen anything so disgusting in my life. Real ladies don't behave this way."

The Town Hall crowd would pale in comparison to the true heavyweights in the Are Men Necessary? Club, those women who truthfully had little use for the opposite gender. First and foremost would have to be Andrea Dworkin, an obese, bib overall-wearing Bennington grad and battered wife who underwent a transformation after reading Kate Millett's *Sexual Politics*. Dworkin took it upon herself to investigate pornography and publish articles about how evil it all was. Although she became known for her passionate public speaking engagements and her book *Intercourse*, a smoldering indictment of all penises, her anti-porn ravings were coveted among porn aficionados because they were so rife with overt S/M images.

Teaming up with Dworkin on the hardcore feminist lecture circuit was Catharine MacKinnon, a Yale Law graduate who had worked with the Black Panthers. Together the two pushed to enact Canada's Tariff Code 9956, which bans the sale and importation of all materials "which depict or describe sexual acts that appear to degrade or dehumanize." Which must have cut into Canadian sales of Dworkin's own S/M books.

Perhaps the ultimate statement in feminism came from Valerie Solanas, the writer/prostitute who shot Andy Warhol and nearly killed him. While working with Warhol, she wrote the infamous *S.C.U.M. (Society to Cut Up Men) Manifesto*, which although humorously written, begged women to go out and kill all men. Bootleg editions of the *Manifesto* have continued to appear over the years, but Solanas was never able to cash in on her underground reputation, and after years in and out of prison and mental institutions, she died in 1988, turning tricks in a San Francisco welfare hotel.

Which brings us to the more dubious theories of the era — those produced by nutbags and crackpots who proved there was not necessarily a right or wrong to postulating a thesis about sex. What mattered most was how many people paid attention to you.

Gavin Arthur, aka Chester Alan Arthur III, was the son of a millionaire and grandson of president Chester Arthur. Raised in private European boarding schools, Arthur shunned politics to travel the world with the Merchant Marines. He drank with rich and famous people, from family friends to Alan Watts and Havelock Ellis, and hung out with convicts and prostitutes. This was one trust fund that wasn't going to follow in grampa's footsteps. At some point, Arthur realized his immense personal sexual experience was going to waste unless he wrote about it. He moved into a dingy apartment in downtown San Francisco, surrounded himself with autographed photos of celebrities he had befriended and composed his opus. Published in 1966 as *The Circle of Sex*, the World According to Arthur arbitrarily charted human sexual preferences and personality types on a bizarre astrology-based wheel, split into 12 slices.

Another strange survey began as a hoax and ended up a national news story. For six weeks a man who called himself Dr. Harrison T. Rogers drove a mobile home across the United States, drumming up interest for a supposed upcoming International Sex Bowl, an event that would involve couples from various countries competing in rounds of sexual activity. Along this route, the Sex Bowl Committee handed out questionnaires to assess the nation's sexual readiness for such an event. When the survey results had been compiled, it was announced that an embarrassing 92.7% of Americans had failed to pass the "Harrison T. Rogers Sex Test." Sample questions included:

Can a person suffocate from fellatio?

Is it dangerous to have a wet dream under an electric blanket?

What happens to foreskins when they're cut off?

Can you draw the male and female genitals from memory?

Is it true that 43 percent of all male dwarfs die during climax?

Is it possible to wear out the sex organs from too frequent use?

The news story ran in 200 papers, with most of the journalists venting their rage at such immoral depravity. It was then announced that "Dr. Harrison T. Rogers" was in reality prankster Alan Abel, and the entire concept was a giant hoax. Years earlier, Abel had fooled the country with the Society for the Indecency of Naked Animals, an activist group dedicated to clothing animals for the sake of decency. Abel cast a young actor named Buck Henry as the company's spokesman, and the straight-faced Henry went on national television to be interviewed by Walter Cronkite and Johnny Carson.

Do you think your vagina and genital area are ugly or beautiful?

	Q. II	Q. III
Beautiful, I like them	245	71
Fascinating	23	8
Ugly	116	28
Average/Okay	90	24
Neither: neutral	192	30
Part of the whole, natural, functional and utilitarian	53	18
Varies, mixed feelings	17	4
Strange	8	5
	744	188

— from *The Hite Report* by **Shere Hite**, **1976**

WHAT'S YOUR SIGN?:
Gavin Arthur, grandson of a U.S. president, based his personal theories of sex on astrology charts

Free-love communes weren't all populated by knife-wielding Manson hippies. There were thousands who desired an alternative sanctuary more permanent than fern bars and wife-swapping parties, where they could retreat from the world and concentrate on pursuing their own lifestyle. People had been congregating to get naked and fool around for centuries, but the earliest documentation of the American sexual/communal lifestyle might be found in the history of the 19th-century Oneida Community in upstate New York, between Syracuse and Albany. Founded in 1848 by a Yale Divinity School student named John Humphrey Noyes, Oneida was his experiment in religious and social

Fornication Congregation

reorganization, striving for a life of perfection and sinlessness. Reaching an apex of 300 inhabitants, the community practiced Noyes' teachings, among them the concepts of Complex Marriage, where every man was married to every woman, Male Continence, wherein a couple had sex without the man ever ejaculating, and Ascending Fellowship, in which 14-year-old virgins were introduced into adulthood by older, more spiritual members. Of course this went against the very moral fiber of Christianity, but Oneida managed to last 30 years

AMERICA AFTER HOURS:
Bullets fly over a 1960s California nudist colony (left); Strangers get to know each other for the weekend (right)

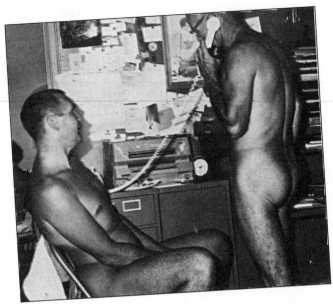

HELLO, IT'S ME:
Nudist powerhouse T.H. Latimer
frequently got on the horn to
round up more recruits

Patience is a virtue we horses have quite a bit of. Maybe nudists like the sun, but this fur coat I have on is hot. I am hoping we can all go rest in the shade....I learned quite a lot myself that day. Being used to riders wearing heavy boots and spurs, riding pants and such, I never knew how good it could be to have a nudist in the saddle. They're lighter in weight and don't ride me too darn fast!

— **from "Bareback Bares," 1960s nudist article written from the point of view of a horse named Paint**

during which time the community built a successful economy in the manufacture of luggage, silk products and other exports.

The demise of Oneida didn't stop religious leaders from taking their flocks to the woods and letting their robes fall to the forest floor. The early 20th-century nudist enclaves were jump-started largely by spiritual seekers, and after World War I they started getting organized. The American Sunbathing Association was founded in 1933 in New Jersey, and membership climbed to 12,000 by 1966. The mid-century increase in nudism is often attributed to T.H. Latimer, a former World War II Navy lieutenant commander who not only was a fixture in the scene for decades — even voted 1958 Nudist Man of the Year — but was also an aggressive public relations dynamo. The ABA executive secretary estimated that in 1967 there were 250,000 American nudists.

Other professional organizations formed, from the National Nudist Council, based in Ohio, to Iowa's Central Sunbathing Association. Nudists flocked to geographically desirable areas of the U.S. throughout the 1950s and 1960s, in particular California and Florida. Nude resorts appeared on former farms and dairy ranches, often no more than a piece of choice sunny real estate, with trailer homes and a volleyball net. Names of popular nudist clubs included the Sul-Tan Club, the Sunshower Club, the Running Bares, the Sundial Club and the Solair Recreation League.

Old-timers acknowledge the heyday for nudism as the 1950s, an era of great technological advances, Cold War paranoia and commie finger-pointing. Many figured it was time to head for the hills, lay out in the sun and escape all the escalating insanity. Nudist calendars, filmstrips and magazines flourished, still years away from being overtaken by *Playboy* and *Penthouse*. Travel packages offered 21 days at nudist resorts in six countries. Most of the nation's sanctioned nudist spots have evolved little since this era. Overt sexual behavior is still frowned upon. Members of most resorts and clubs claim to be participants out of a desire to relax in the nude. Families are welcome, and activities are largely wholesome things people usually do at campgrounds and resorts, such as swimming, reading or volleyball.

As the 1960s unfolded, and nudism grew more popular, other communities started up to catch the wave. One of the most popular and enduring is Elysium Fields, eight acres of landscaped acreage tucked up in Topanga Canyon, 20 minutes from Los Angeles. Named for the blissful, classical mythology abode of the blessed after death, Elysium was founded in the 1960s by Ed Lange, a former *Vogue* fashion photographer and avid nudist. Elysium immediately became such a popular spot among Southern California nudists, Lange opened a publishing division, released books and magazines devoted to the clothing-optional life, and fought concerned neighbors in the courts over the right to host naked people frolicking in the canyon. Elysium continues a strong presence in book publishing as well as the World Wide Web, and after Lange's recent death, his daughter, Dana Mia Lang Newman took over the operation.

With the increase in communities came the desire to take flesh to the beach. The first legitimate nude beach in the world reportedly opened in 1967 at Northern California's San Gregorio Beach, which still attracts 500 nudists on a good day. Santa Barbara's Rincon Beach was considered the world's nude beach capital until 1978, when sheriff's deputies used helicopters and horses to clean the area of all those disgusting naked people. From the late '60s to the mid-'70s, the most popular skinny-dipping scene in Southern California was Venice Beach, where upwards of 10,000 people horsed around nude at one time. Although a swimsuit-optional status was voted out in a 1977 election, it remains a popular clandestine nudist attraction.

All this nudity was obviously going to attract those who wanted something more. In 1960, a run-down Midwest nudist resort called Zoro was purchased by a multiple sclerosis-afflicted high school dropout named Dick Drost, in collaboration with his parents. The paraplegic Drost renamed the resort Naked City, and billed it as the world's largest nudist camp. Located in Roselawn, Indiana, 30 miles south of Gary, Naked City featured a giant statue of a naked female leg coming out of the ground, with the majority of the facilities contained in a gold circular building, doorways modified to accomodate Drost's wheelchair.

Drost excitedly hosted annual Miss and Mr. Nude America Contests, attracting celebrity judges like porn star Harry Reems, who were ushered from the airport in a red fur-lined limo. Each year the newly crowned female winner paraded around the camp in a motorized wheelchair, sitting on Drost's lap, swarmed by photographers . To traditional nudists, the camp had been turned into a crass pornographic sideshow. They hated Drost's guts.

Most of the contestants turned out not to

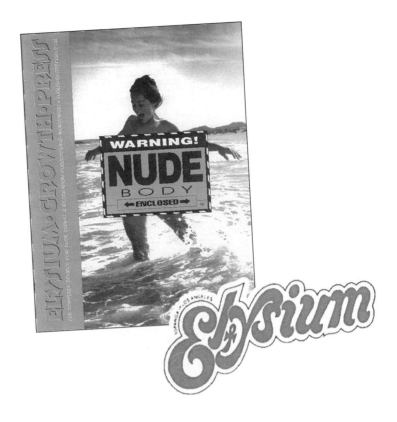

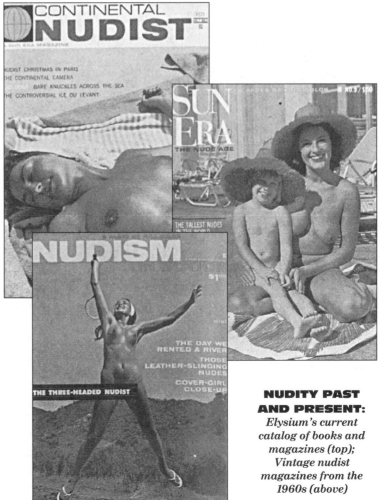

NUDITY PAST AND PRESENT: *Elysium's current catalog of books and magazines (top); Vintage nudist magazines from the 1960s (above)*

Photographed in one of the largest and most beautiful Nudist Camps in Florida!

Hideout in the Sun
IT HAPPENED IN A NUDIST CAMP

"The Best of the Newest Nude Films."
N.Y. Times

Filmed in Gorgeous EASTMAN COLOR *in* NUDERAMA

Once the clothes are off, it takes about ten seconds to get accustomed to being naked in public. You don't for a moment forget you're naked, but you adjust to it and damn if it doesn't feel good. Knowing that your entire body is getting suntanned, you fantasize how great you will look in a dimly lit bedroom back in the city. You find yourself more sensitive to subtle shifts in the wind. There are only three situations in which nakedness feels funny: passing from indoors to outdoors and vice versa; standing in line at a snack bar; and wearing shoes.

— from "Nudist Reverie" by Mike Aron, *Playgirl*, 1973

be nudists at all, but strippers imported solely for their exhibitionist qualities. Drost produced calendars and magazines, hustling his utopian vision of himself as the next Hefner. The reality of Naked City was that the place only made money a few days a year. The rest of the time, Drost hunkered in for the winter with his girlfriend and parents, subsisting on home-cooked meals, while the Indiana snow collected on the giant female femur outside. Drost was eventually kicked out of the state, either because of the increasingly explicit activities, or some say, the mob forced him to pack up and leave. Undaunted, Drost moved Naked City to the desert outside Los Angeles, and since 1981 has continued his version of a nudist retreat, sponsoring events like a "Jack-off and Jill-off Chili Cook-off."

For others, the idea of a clothing-optional community represented a plane of higher purpose, a sanctuary to improve human potential. Formerly a run-down resort on the California coast at Big Sur, the Esalen Institute was founded in 1962 by Harvard dropout Richard Price and Stanford philosophy major Michael Murphy, and rapidly became a focal point in the '60s and early '70s for touchy-feely personal growth. Thousands of enlightenment seekers from all over the world came to find themselves in the famous 110-degree natural hot springs, taking supervised LSD trips and experimenting with sex. Famous names of the era wandered through the lush gardens of the trendy clothing-optional retreat — the Maharishi Mahesh Yogi, Paul Simon, Ravi Shankar, the Beatles and hundreds and hundreds of news reporters. Zen guru Alan Watts could often be found stoned and nude, facing the ocean, chanting over the sound of the waves. The staff of *Rolling Stone* was kicked out of the baths for partying too loudly. Amidst all the groovy drug/orgy stories, one still circulates about the time Gestalt psychologist Fritz Perls publicly spanked the ass of actress Natalie Wood. The sex and acid parties are now supposedly part of the past, and Esalen continues as a therapeutic center in the same location.

Also prominent in the field of nude encounter groups was therapist John Yacenda, a former public health educator and devotee of Ram Dass. Yacenda, a self-described hedonist and showman, wrote books on sexual freedom, and purchased acreage in the Santa Cruz Mountains, where he established a residence he named the GRO Center. Weekend GRO workshops offered classes — nude and clothed —

in human sexuality, sensory reawakening, T'ai Chi, massage and something he termed the GRO Process. Yacenda openly believed in having sex with his clients as part of their therapy, male as well as female, and directed all sessions, accompanying the orgies with his acoustic guitar. Before Yacenda pulled the plug on the project, his hippie sex empire had grown to nine GRO centers throughout California.

But no '70s sex commune could measure up to the notoriety of Sandstone, a human lab experiment that flourished in the Topanga Canyon hills outside L.A. Founded by an electronics engineer named John Williamson, and beginning with nude meetings in his Mulholland Drive living room, Sandstone attempted to articulate Williamson's vision for a new program that would demolish the sexual double standard, liberate women and create a sexually free environment, without jealousy, guilt or lying. The group moved in 1970 to a 15-acre estate in the canyon. Topanga's cliffs and scrubby meadows were popular among fringe groups, from right-wing gun nuts and conciousness-expanding workshops to the Elysium nudist retreat.

All branches of hipster cognoscenti made the pilgrimage to the group sex scene up in the hills — erotica collectors Phyllis and Eberhard Kronhausen, *Joy of Sex* author Alex Comfort, journalist Gay Talese, football players, artists, actors, anthropologists and publishers. One evening, guests came upon a famous Hollywood ventriloquist, continuing to banter with his nonexistent wooden dummy, while simultaneously performing cunnilingus on a schoolmistress. Sandstone was said to be the only place in the nation where women could enjoy recreational sex in an open, non-threatening environment, and was the role model for several other communities around the country. The original version closed in 1973, and a short-lived reincarnation run by therapist Paul Paige offered classes, lectures and massage sessions.

There would also be the mutations of a communal lifestyle. Founded by alcoholic Charles Dederich in the late '50s in a Santa Monica storefront, the Synanon substance abuse program eventually moved to Northern California, where, in 1968 the therapeutic idea ended. It became an alternative lifestyle community, running highly profitable businesses like ADGAP (Advertising Gifts and Premiums), which manufactured logo-emblazoned pens, keychains and other trinkets for major

Sandwich Delight

The group had formed two sandwiches on the floor, in one of which were, starting from the back, Carly, Arty, Sally, Larry, Kay, Baily, Sherry, and Bill. They began the exercise in this order and kept moving the rear person to the front until Carly was again in the rear position. This process usually took anywhere from twenty to sixty minutes depending on what people got into.

I was strumming and picking away at my guitar and looking over occasionally at the sandwich, which at first appeared to be a mass of moving hands and arms. Then I got more interested and saw what was happening.

Carly was reaching over two bodies to hold Sally's hand. Arty was stroking Carly's right breast with his right hand and reaching underneath and around Sally's head and neck to stroke her left breast with his other. Carly and Sally both reached for Arty's erect penis and played with it...

...I hadn't realized that those leg contortions Larry and Kay were involved in were a disguise for rear-entry sex of a fashion I hadn't seen in quite a while. I only realized what they were doing when Larry groaned rather conspicuously as he came.

"There goes another one I missed. Oh, well," I thought to myself. Not that I got a rise out of watching people be sexual together (it was often very boring to me). It was just that I generally felt very lax at this time of the group and was not as concerned with the flow since the sandwich was a concluding exercise...

...With the change in the order of the sandwich's ingredients, a new taste became evident. Bill had been intrigued with Carly from the beginning of the group but had yet to be with her in any exercise. Now there she was in front and up against him. They squeezed tightly, his penis and scrotum protruding enough to slide in between the crease of her buttocks. I was sitting in a chair almost directly over them, still playing my guitar...They lay there, their passion increasing by bounds until they were so quietly consumed with each other that the heat of their union semed to penetrate my legs and feet...I turned away to the other group, having the sense that the other activity I had not been concentrating on too much — among the foursome Sherry, Baily, Larry, and Kay, and between Sally and Arty — was going much in the same direction. I thought to myself, "Impossible. I can't stop them; I don't want to; and I can't join them. How shitty, strum and pick...strum and pick..."

— from chapter entitled "Hedonists' Nude Weekend" in *The Nude Experience* by John Yacenda, Ph.D., 1978

Barbara Williams led me into a huge living room of the main house which over-looked the Pacific. A young man stood naked (and unembarrassed) on the porch. It was 10 a.m. Barbara, who was wearing slacks and an Indian blouse, went off to get me a cup of coffee and I wandered around. Someone in the kitchen said I ought to take a look at the ballroom downstairs. I did. It was a different kind of ballroom.

Waterbeds were scattered all over the place. One room joined to the ballroom by a bathroom without doors at either end was done in wall-to-wall mattresses. I went back upstairs, and Barbara presented me with a cup of coffee. She certainly didn't come on like some lecherous voluptuary. She had short blonde no-nonsense hair, wore granny glasses and her matter-of-fact voice, too, was grandmotherly. "Please don't call Sandstone a fuck club," she said.

At first blush, I said, it was hard to see Sandstone as anything but that. What else did all those people — Sandstone has 275 member couples — come for? Barbara admitted that many of them were drawn precisely beause they'd heard it was the nicest place in town to enjoy group sex. But there was more, she said, much more. "We have a community of a dozen persons here, experimenting with alternate life styles. We're not young. We're in our 30s and 40s, and we are really cutting some new pathways."

— **from "Sandstone — A Love Community" by Robert Blair Kaiser, from** *The Wonderful World of Penthouse Sex***, 1975**

corporations. By 1978 ADGAP's gross sales were nearly $10 million annually. Population of Synanon peaked at between 1,000 and 2,000. Dederich was the subject of major articles in *Time* and *Life*, and his ability to turn a phrase resulted in the immortal slogan, "Today is the first day of the rest of your life."

Things grew more strange at Synanon. All members, male and female, were suddenly required to shave their heads. In 1977, all men who had lived there longer than five years were required to undergo vasectomies — except for Dederich — and all pregnant women received abortions. Virtually all couples, married or not, were required to change partners. Synanon kept extensive statistics and documents on sexual affairs between members. The organization collected guns, and slapped lawsuits on any media that dared to criticize their way of life.

Lawyers for *Time* magazine described one evening at a Synanon facility that turned into an orgy, where participants yelled out the names of those with whom they wanted to spend the night.

"It was a crazy night," remembered one member, "and everybody was going bananas, making phone calls, answering the telephone, running off to bed with a bowl of fruit in hand and a new wife and two sticks of incense in the other."

A woman recalled: "I feel sexually, totally liberated. I thought I would never want to screw or even could screw another man, and now there are at least three of them that I would like to screw, and I know that I will screw every one of them."

Another woman said later, "I was confused. I also felt I was doing something strange, against what I was brought up to believe."

Other communities sprouted up on the East Coast and throughout the Heartland, but California seemed to attract them more than other states. One Los Angeles group called the Guyon Society was made up of 50 or so families, and advocated sex for young children as a way of deterring them from drugs and crime. Their slogan: "Sex by the age of eight or else it's too late." The Morningstar Ranch nude retreat, set in the Northern California Sonoma area, was formed by Lou Gottlieb, a musician and member of the Limelighters acoustic folk group. In its heyday, Morningstar was known for little kids running around naked, and adults fucking out in the open fields. Robert Rimmer's novel *The Harrad Experiment* about a co-ed school inspired a similar house for couples in Berkeley called Harrad West. A few miles from Berkeley, California is the headquarters for Morehouse, a utopian sensuality school of bright purple buildings founded in 1968 by appliance salesman Victor Baranco, which spread to include satellites in Oregon, New Mexico, Pennsylvania, New York and Virginia (see epilogue for more details).

For some adventurers, a sexual community wasn't complete unless you threw some dope into the mix. The Psychedelic Venus Church formed in November 1969 in Berkeley, and by March 1970 had 130 members. Its stated goals — "humanist hedonism and religious pursuit of body pleasure" — were achieved via the sacraments of sex and marijuana. Their newsletter *Intercourse* claimed that "Grass is the commonest sacrament of Shiva worship in India."

"High priests" operated from a wooden house in southwest Berkeley: Church president Reverend Jefferson Fuck Poland (also of the Sexual Freedom League), vice president and secretary Mother Boats; and licensed street evangelist Peter Lawrence Downham. Membership fee was $5, and so many guys turned out for church socials and marijuana communions, restrictions had to be placed on a maximum number of single hetero males. Highlight of the Psychedelic Venus bunch was undoubtedly the Genital Sacrifice, performed four times a year at Witches' Sabbath. In front of a nude congregation, one person from each sex offered themselves to the altar. The genitals of the two volunteers were spread with globs of honey, and one by one, the congregation approached the altar to worship, and licked the honey off the sex organs of each host.

Another drug/sex community that became popular was Kerista, founded by former Air Force pilot John Presmont, who got the idea for the organization while smoking hash and reading the Koran. A voice supposedly spoke to him, and told him to start his own religion. "Why me?" asked the dumbfounded Presmont. "Because you're so gullible," answered the voice.

Presmont changed his name to Jud the Prophet, and summed up his teachings in a statement called the 69 Positions, the first ten of which were: "Legalize prostitution. Legalize adultery. Legalize fornication. Legalize bigamy. Legalize sodomy. Legalize cunnilingus. Legalize group sex. Legalize pornography. Legalize homosexuality. Legalize lesbianism." Chapters formed in major cities around the country. Keristans were devoted to group sex, but drug busts and other societal frownings forced Jud and his major disciples to flee to Central America. They resurfaced in San Francisco in the 1980s, repositioning the organization as a

The ancient rites of Venus — presiding over orgies of fucking, sucking and pot — date back to pre-history. Venus was known as Aphrodite to the Greeks, and as Ishtar to the Babylonians. Herodotus, the father of history, visited Babylon and made note of the following: *Every Babylonian, whether male or female, went to the Holy precinct of the Temple of Venus on his or her sixteenth birthday, and there served as a temple prostitute for a month, the proceeds going to the Goddess for the maintenance of Her Temple.* The ancient faith, along with the worship of Diana, Eros and Adonis (all sex Gods of one sort or another) was outlawed by the Code of Justinian in 528 A.D. The Code provided that persons who were caught performing the sex rites should be punished by *Amputation of the sinful instrument, or the insertion of sharp reeds into the pores and tubes of most exquisite sensibility.* Justinian's wife, Empress Theodora, was called the *Harlot of Constantinople* by Gibbon. She was a whore before she was married. She was known by the street people of the day as the *Champion Cocksucker of the World.* She once took on a bet that she could suck off 200 men in a night — and won! When she got too old for sex, she became a Christian. Historians blame her sexual jealousy of young people and her anger with the loss of her beauty — claiming them as the cause of the Justinian anti-sex laws. Her importance in history can hardly be overestimated, since English common law — and through it American law — are offshoots of the Justinian Code. The Catholic Church canonized her as St. Theodora, for her zeal in outlawing sex fun.

— historic justification of smoking pot and having sex, by a member of Berkeley's Psychedelic Venus Church, quoted in the *L.A. Free Press*, 1970

desktop computer publishing company — no doubt the first with regularly posted sex-partner sleeping schedules.

The modern definition of an alternative sex community would have to include the communes set up by the Bhagwan Shree Rajneesh, a charismatic, giggly Indian swami with a talent for repackaging Eastern teachings to suit his own goals. Rajneesh's emphasis on finding inner peace through excess found an enormous audience among those who enjoyed getting stoned and having group sex.

In the late '70s he purchased 265 acres in central Oregon and renamed the town Antelope to Rajneeshpuram, building up the area to include a shopping mall, disco, casino, luxury hotel, restaurants and private airline. News reporters fixated on his fleet of Rolls Royces, which he was fond of veering off the roads and into ditches. At its height, Rajneeshpuram totalled 3,500 happy sex disciples, part of an international chain of meditation centers that claimed 350,000 members, all coughing up money and property to feed the gaping maw. The dream began to unravel in the early 1980s with rumors of cult brainwashing and exposés published by former members. Fed up with their antics, Oregon locals bombed a Rajneesh hotel in Portland. A security force was established on the commune, followers patrolling the grounds with Uzis. Charged with violating immigration laws, Rajneesh fled back to his ashram in India, and the commune disintegrated. By the end of 1987, Oregon had reclaimed the town of Antelope. Three years later Rajneesh died in India, and was given the posthumous name "Osho."

The novelty and media attention wore off years ago, but many of the communes still exist today, such as the nudist resorts, Esalen, Morehouse and the hundreds of Osho centers still scattered around the world. Sexual escapades, if they remain at all, are toned down and not advertised. If one is diligent, one can still find a room or open field full of naked people — you just have to know where to look.

Tom's old scientific training, so long repressed by politics, had come back in a curious form, and he demonstrated that with normal sexual functioning over a lifetime every man could be linked with (I think) 5,000 women and every woman with 50,000 men and the "amative ties" between any two people in our three-and-a-half billion world population would, by 2000 A.D., be reduced to about four. That is, very concretely, if everybody followed his program, in the year 2000 any man or woman in, say, Peoria, Illinois, would be part of a four-person chain of sex that would include somebody in, say, Canton, China, or Paris, France. The "extended family" found in some communes today would then be virtually planet-wide. There were demographic and sexological tables to prove the mathematical soundness of this, but behind it was the huge unproven assumption that people would not kill other people who had balled with somebody who had balled with somebody who had balled with somebody that they had balled.

— description of an article written by Reverend Tom and his LSD-inspired Church of One Flesh, located in a storefront on Coney Island's boardwalk, from *Sex & Drugs: A Journey Beyond Limits* by Robert Anton Wilson, 1973

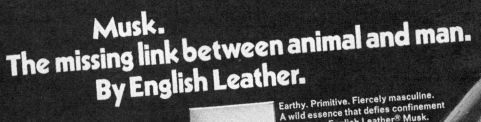

15

Looking at the state of advertising today, sex seems so integral, a necessary and natural ingredient in the megalithic industry of motivating Americans to buy things they don't realize they need. An entire generation has grown up with TV and print ads filled with jiggling breasts and oral fixations, almost to the point of diminishing return. But in the Era of the Hetero, the rules of advertising were still being broken and stretched.

Product slogans teased the unsuspecting magazine reader with single-image innuendos like "Does she or doesn't she?" and "All my men wear English Leather." At the same time,

Buy It & Live It

television's audio/video combination doled out similar messages, hammering home the sex with extreme prejudice. America's living rooms were treated to the Nair hair removal campaign trotted out by girls high-stepping in hot pants, singing, "We wear short shorts!" Viewers were treated to pantyhose pitches of female asses sashaying down the street, with one young temptress bending down into range of the camera to whisper "Makes you look like you're not wearin' nuthin'!" A young woman shilling for Pearl Drops Tooth Polish slowly licked her full lips in extreme close-up, and purred, "Mmm, it's a great feeling!" Actress Susan Anton posed in a slit-to-the-waist dress and breathed, "Hey big

ANIMAL ATTRACTION:
The bait was cast, and a nation was hooked

Dr. Dichter was called upon to explain a fact puzzling marketers of the auto. While most men bought sedans and rarely bought automobiles they evidently were more attracted to convertibles. Dealers had found that they could draw more males into their showrooms by putting convertibles in the window. After exploring the situation Dr. Dichter concluded that men saw the convertible as a possible symbolic mistress. It set them daydreaming of youth, romance, adventure just as they may dream of a mistress. The man knows he is not going to gratify his wish for a mistress, but it is pleasant to daydream. This daydreaming drew the man into the auto salesroom. One there, he finally chose a four-door sedan just as he once married a plain girl who, he knew, would make a fine wife and mother. "Symbolically, he marries the sedan," a spokesman for Dr. Dichter explained. The sedan is useful, practical, down to earth, and safe. Dr. Dichter felt that the company would be putting its best foot backward if it put its main emphasis on sedans simply because that was the car most men ended up buying. Instead, he urged the company to put the hope of mistress-adventure a little closer to males by giving most prominent display to the convertibles. The

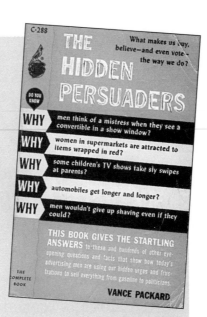

spokesman went on to explain Dr. Dichter's line of thinking: "If we get a union between the wife and mistress — all we sought in a wife plus the romance, youth and adventure we want in a mistress — we would have... lo and behold, the hardtop!" The hardtop was soon to become the most successful new auto style introduced in the American market for several years, and Dr. Dichter's organization takes full credit for inspiring it by its "Mistress versus Wife" study.

— from *The Hidden Persuaders* by Vance Packard, 1957

Thanks to color photography, and then to color TV, the magnetic city has become a single erogenous zone. At every turn there is an immediate encounter with extremely erotic situations which exactly correspond to the media "coverage" of violence. "Bad news" has long been the hard core of the press, indispensable for the moving of the mass of "good news" which is advertising...The close relation between sex and violence, between good news and bad news, helps to explain the compulsion of the admen to dunk all their products in sex by erogenizing every contour of every bottle or cigarette. Having reached this happy state where the good news is fairly popping, the admen say, as it were: "Better add a bit of the bad news now to take the hex off all that bonanza stuff." Let's remind them that LOVE, replayed in reverse, is EVOL — transposing into EVIL and VILE. LIVE spells backward into EVIL, while EROS reverses into SORE. And, we should never forget the SIN in SINCERE or the CON in CONFIDENCE. Let's tighten up the slack sentimentality of this goo with something gutsy and grim.

As Zeus said to Narcissus:

"Watch yourself."

— **Marshall McLuhan, 1973**

spender," on behalf of disgusting little Muriel cigars. A man applied Hai Karate aftershave to his face and was immediately besieged by screaming girls, resorting to martial arts moves to defend himself.

Occasionally, copywriters went too far. One 1970s-era print ad for sheets depicted an Indian maiden lying on a mattress with her dress hiked up. Next to her reclined an exhausted male Indian, with the headline: "A buck well spent on a Springmaid sheet." The ad was pulled from circulation.

It's a wonder we weren't all raping and pillaging in front of our sets. How had we arrived at such a juncture? Warnings of such an assault on the sensibilities could be traced to the essay collection *Generation of Vipers* by *New Yorker* contributor Philip Wylie, a scathing critique of American society written in 1942:

"About seventy-five percent of the unmarried young men of America copulate with girls. Of the adult, single young women, hardly half are virgins. Harlots are ubiquitous everywhere in the U.S....Americans were always a hell-for-women folk; all people are; religion has no longer a strong enough hold on the population to set up sex taboos in more than a fifth of it, at most; an enlightened attitude toward sex morality has, for many, relieved extramarital coitus of social infamy; and — more important — in sleeping even with strangers, people do not need to contract venereal diseases and women do not need to risk impregnation. On the subjective plane, the major media of articulation in the land implicitly admit our sexual gregariousness. Advertisers in those media tend not just to condone it, but to promote it directly and indirectly, in hundreds of ways. The eyes and ears of Americans are incessantly turned upon sex reverie and fetish with the purpose of selling goods. But the real effect, unweighed and largely unrecognized, is to sell mass-produced libido."

The seeds were definitely sown a decade later, according to the 1957 best-seller *The Hidden Persuaders* by Vance Packard, when ad agencies began hiring MR (Motivation Research) analysts to explore merchandising possibilities within our deeper psyches. Many kept resident shrinks on retainer. New York's prestigious McCann-Erickson ad agency secured five psychologists to man a special motivation department. Specialists emerged, some preferring motivation only, others focusing solely on the use of colors. Agencies utilized all sorts of tests, from word association to sentence completion and the Minnesota multiphasic inventory, hunting for hidden shortcuts to increase sales.

America at mid-century was still a few y ears away from a true sexual revolution, but the marketing world was pushing the boundaries as much as the movies or the wife-swappers. Lingerie ads depicted women proudly wearing Maidenform bras while riding the subway. The trend developed for advertising to offer both men and women sexual reassurance, that it was okay to be a male and act like a male, or that it was perfectly reasonable to act female and use your femininity to get what you wanted. Products traditionally associated with one gender were now being marketed to the other gender, such as a can of he-man beer to women, because they were confirmed to be the primary purchaser. Marlboro cigarettes, originally designed as a woman's smoke, were repackaged a more masculine product, with "man-sized flavor." Men identified with the image of the virile guy in the ads, and women also found themselves attracted to the studs with the cigs.

One of the most enduring studies dealing with sexuality in advertising came from the Institute for Motivational Research, directed by Dr. Ernest Dichter, who conducted his empire from a 30-room stone mansion atop a mountain overlooking the Hudson River. With a staff numbering over 25 specialists, and a blue-chip client list including such corporations as General Foods, Lever Brothers and American Airlines, Dichter had earned the nickname of "Mr. Mass Motivations." His groundbreaking study for Chrysler automobiles, called "Mistress Versus Wife," concluded that men looked to the convertible model of car as a symbolic mistress, attracted more to the open top than the practical, boring sedan, and should be pandered to as such.

By the 1960s, it was apparent that much of the country's advertising was produced by horny ad executives out on the three-martini lunch, brainstorming the newest campaign, hoping to weave into the words and images an unmistakable sheen of the sexual revolution. Sex wasn't just for pin-ups and auto calendars anymore. It was a powerful sales tool, and who cared if the product was banal. If you bought this hair coloring, stereo or gear shifter, young naked people would soon be begging at your feet for sexual favors. Categories in particular that pushed a sex-related image were liquor, tobacco, beauty, electronics, clothing and automobiles.

If you wore an After Six tuxedo, a woman would come over to your bachelor pad and take off her clothes. If you bought an Akai

FOOLS FOR FOOTSIES:
Not-so-subliminal action below the knees

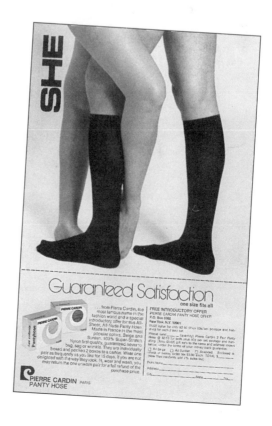

The world's best-fitting jeans.

Jeans never fit like this before. Because now every inch is accounted for!

Your exact waist size? You've got it. Exact leg length? It's yours. And imagine, the seat and thigh are proportioned so everything goes with everything else.

Put these jeans on and you'll know it's no put-on to say they're the best fitting jeans in the world.

Heavy denim and other rugged shape-holding jean fabrics that keep the fit perfect forever.

chic by h.i.s
1411 Broadway, N.Y. 10018

FOR NEAREST RETAILER
CALL TOLL-FREE 800 821 7700 EXT. 317
IN MISSOURI CALL 800 892 7655

DITTOS.
WE WROTE THE BOOK ON FIT.

A curvy lady never had a fit as good or as flattering as the Dittos fit.

Because we spent eight years writing "The Book On Fit."

For Classic Curves, sizes 8-18.

Dittos. You simply can't buy better looking (or better fitting) jeans, pants and tops, not even at twice the price.

ASS ATTACK:
America rediscovers its own butt

THE JORDACHE LOOK

JORDACHE
Designer Jeans by P. Jordache

Showroom 498 7th Ave. N.Y.C. 10018 212-279 7243

"Bend Over Pants have the soft, relaxed fit I love. They're smooth and sleek, and they don't cut or bind anywhere. And the concealed elastic waistband is really flattering."

"I can't imagine a better fit than Bend Over™ Pants."

"It's perfect! My Bend Over stretch gabardine pants from Levi's® Womenswear let me feel extra comfortable while I look extra dressed up."

"Try Bend Over Pants—in stretch gabardine or the new poly/wool blend. And don't miss the great Levi's Womenswear tops they have to go with them. Comfort has never looked so pretty." Ask for Bend Over Pant 25113-38 misses, 29113-98 women's. Skeleton Leaf Blouse 68726-78

Levi's WOMENSWEAR

QUALITY NEVER GOES OUT OF STYLE

DEEP RUMBLINGS:
The formula was simple: hot car equals hot sex

AKAI ? NATURALLY!

4-channel excellence for the sophisticated lover...of music!

Go all the way ... swing with the foremost foursome ... turn on with 4-channel stereo from AKAI — the most provocative breakthrough in sound reproduction. Surrounds you with excitement.

There's nothing like it!

The heart of the system is AKAI's remarkable 280D-SS. true 4/2-channel tape deck. Superbly engineered with 4 heads — 3 motors — 4 pre-amplifiers. Plus stereo Sound-on-Sound. And it's compatible with conventional stereo sound systems. Equipped with 2-channel Automatic Continuous Reverse and 4-channel Automatic Repeat. What's more, for a limited time only, the price of this magnificent unit has been reduced from $649.95 to $499.95.

Sound great? There's more!

Like the AKAI AS-8100S. Innovatively combines a

true 4-channel/2-channel stereo amplifier system... a 2-channel stereo AM/FM multiplex tuner ... and a 4-channel stereo matrix circuit. You can adjust perfect 4-way speaker balance with AKAI's exclusive Stick Shift Balance Control. Designed with 2 sets of tape monitor switches—FET front end for extra sensitivity—automatic FM stereo/mono switching. And a dynamic 100 watts of music power (72W ...

And the final touch ...

Four ST-300 air suspension type speakers. A perfective complement. Provides pure natural sound, flat response that will astound you.

Our 4-channel stereo system will wrap you in sound. A good reason to see your AKAI dealer. Because he'll demonstrate how you can ...

THE S...

AKAI™

AKAI America, Ltd./P. O. Box 55055, Los Angeles, California 90055
For your nearest AKAI dealer call 800-243-6000 Toll Free. In Connecticut, 1-800-882-6500.
In Canada: Pro-Sound Distributors, Ltd., Vancouver, B.C. In Mexico: Mexico International Imports, S.A., Apartado Postal 66-672,

when she's in the mood for beautiful music... play a TDK.

When it's time for peace and serenity, be sure that the music you play comes through pure and beautiful; be sure of exceptional fidelity, flawless reproduction, and a completely trouble-free cassette.

TDK is the ultra-reliable, ultra-high-fidelity cassette that never creates unpleasant, unwanted sounds, and won't screech, hiss, spill or jam. Ever.

Famous for super fidelity, TDK is the music lover's first choice all over the world. Cassettes, cartridges and reel-to-reel in the world's widest choice of lengths and formulations — including cassettes running as long as three hours.

When you want just the right music for the right mood, call on TDK— the mood maker.

Purity in Sound ◆ **TDK** ◉ HIGH FIDELITY
ELECTRONICS CORP.

For those nights you want everything to be just right...

Let the luscious sound of soft music from your superb new stereo system help you set the mood... reveal your taste, your style, your deepest feelings to him. You can create the most romantic atmosphere with this beautiful, contemporary Apollo system from Electrophonic.

You'll let him know, too, that you're involved in the "today" sound. Because Electrophonic gives you 200 Watts of purring power. Air-Suspension speakers that catch every subtle whisper. FET/IC Circuitry for instant "on". An 8-track tape player, an AM/FM/stereo radio and a Garrard Record Changer with cueing control, diamond stylus.

This fabulous Electrophonic stereo system gives you even more. It's equipped with a Speaker Matrix Switch to go all the way to full four-channel sound with the addition of two speakers. And the Apollo series is also available with recording facility so you can create your own professional tape at the push of a button.

You can choose which of the smart decorator colors will blend with your own decor ... pale, pale champagne or very cool blue ... at fine department stores in the U.S. and Canada.

All this glamour and mood-setting can be yours—and his—now, so why wait? Tonight might be one of those nights.

Electrophonic AMERICA'S LARGEST STEREO MANUFACTURER

IN THE MOOD:
Proper audio equipment would put everything within your grasp

four-channel stereo, four chicks in expensive evening gowns would end up in your bed. If you wore the Sirena Lycra bikini, a handsome man with chest hair would materialize behind your shoulders, devoted to pleasing you and only you. If you wore Jovan musk oil, you were experimenting with a scent so powerful, it was unbelievable that it was legal.

Some marketing campaigns defied any logical explanation. If you used Contac cold medicine, a beautiful young woman would take care of you and say, "You belong to me." If you wore Converse Jack Purcell tennis shoes, you'd soon be playing footsies under the table with your friend's girlfriend. And if you were considering purchasing new headers for your car engine, you had a choice of brand names — Hooker or Hedman.

By the 1970s, advertising agencies had surpassed the practice of keeping shrinks on staff to keep abreast of the innate sexual appeal. It was now being taught in classrooms. Advertising textbooks weren't just recognizing the power of sex in ads, they were devoting chapters to explaining it. One book frequently used in schools was titled *Subliminal Seduction* by Wilson Bryan Key, an infamous 1973 analysis of hidden sexual messages in everyday advertising. Key's wild imagination was not completely without merit. Hidden messages and/or pictures had already been discovered in Jan van Eyck paintings, and illustrations by Al Hirschfeld. Perhaps the ad folks were more canny than anyone realized.

Key may have been influenced by a series of experiments conducted in the 1950s by marketing researcher James Vicary, using a slide projector-type machine called a tachisto-scope. Vicary visited a New Jersey movie house and during the feature film flashed subliminal messages to "Drink Coca Cola" and "Eat popcorn," each lasting 1/3000 of a second. Vicary claimed a noticable increase in sales at the concession stand, but was scoffed at by psychologists. Since that time nobody has provided concrete evidence that 1/3000-of-a-second messages can dictate behavior. Just to be sure, the National Association of Broadcasters soon banned subliminal material on all its member stations.

By that time, Key had already published his book. His stern warning to Americans reasonated deeply with a nation torn by JFK/RFK/MLK assassination paranoia and anti-government resentment. Key claimed to expose not just hidden advertising, but the all-out "sexual

**ACCESSING THE
INNER EROS:**
*Odd appeals to clean-shaven women
and gamblers*

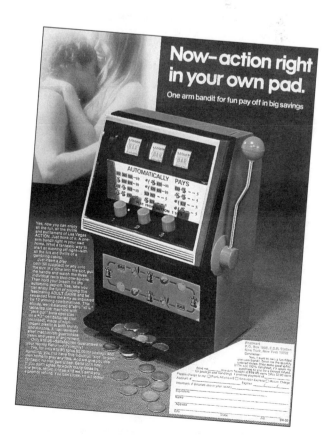

Break out the frosty bottle

GILBEYS

LONDON DRY

GIN

and keep your tonics dry!

The melting ice on the bottle cap could symbolize seminal fluid — the origin of all human life. The green color suggests peace and tranquility after tensions have been released. Therefore, the scene is likely after orgasm, not before. This interpretation is reinforced by the less than fully extended penis. The melting ice on the frosty bottle, of course, could also suggest seminal fluid. Who could ever have guessed Gilbey's had so much to offer these 24.2 million readers?

At this point, if you are curious and broad-minded, you might look between the reflection from the tonic glass and that of the bottle. The vertical opening between the reflection has subtle shadows on each side which could be interpreted as lips — vaginal lips, of course. At the top of the opening is a drop of water which could represent the clitoris.

If the scene were put into a story line, this still-open vagina is where the discharged penis has just been. The seminal frost all over the bottle might suggest to a primitive part of the human brain — the portion some theorists call the unconscious — that *coitus interruptus* had just occurred, or as the copy would suggest: "and keep your tonics dry!"

There appears one additional female genital symbol horizontally drawn into the tonic glass reflection. The vagina is closed, suggesting the owner might be lying down awaiting her turn.

When you add up the number of individuals symbolized subliminally in various parts of the advertisement, there are five — three women and two men, including our Kilroy-like voyeur in the top ice cube. The subliminal promise to anyone buying Gilbey's gin is simply a good old-fashioned sexual orgy which developed after "breaking out the frosty bottle."

— part of several pages of subliminal analysis of 1971 ad for Gilbey's gin

HOW CLEAR DOES IT HAVE TO BE?:
Terse warnings that existed under our noses every day

Coolness, remoteness, aloneness, aloofness, separateness, disengagement. These further resulted in fear, near panic, helplessness, and hopelessness.

Now it is scary! I don't even want to look at it. I want to put this "thing" as far away from me as I can get it.

It is hideous, like a monster. I feel trembling and I can feel perspiration on my hand. My rate of breathing has increased. This is so queer! I enjoyed the coolness of it initially. What has happened to me? I feel such a fear of this thing!...Now I don't even want to look back at the ad to analyze it. Right now I dread the thought of doing so tomorrow night. It is as if by doing so I'll have to face something painful. I would rather look at a nest of wiggling snakes.

— reaction from "Test Subject B," a female high school teacher, 35

— *Subliminal Seduction* by Wilson Bryan Key, 1973

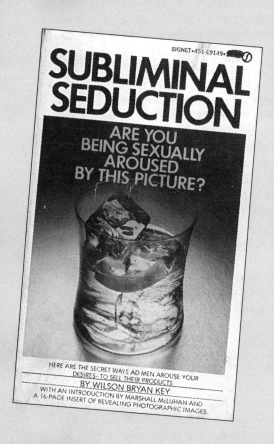

SIGNET•451•E9149•

SUBLIMINAL SEDUCTION

ARE YOU BEING SEXUALLY AROUSED BY THIS PICTURE?

HERE ARE THE SECRET WAYS AD MEN AROUSE YOUR DESIRES—TO SELL THEIR PRODUCTS.
BY WILSON BRYAN KEY
WITH AN INTRODUCTION BY MARSHALL McLUHAN AND A 16-PAGE INSERT OF REVEALING PHOTOGRAPHIC IMAGES.

assault" on individuals, to specifically arouse them and manipulate them for ill-gotten gains. He produced evidence of magazine covers and ads for every type of product imaginable. The naked man with a big erection, hidden in the camel on a pack of Camel cigarettes. The ice cubes that spelled out the letters "S-E-X." Even an ad for Mattel's Baby Tender Love was guilty for "oral, anal and genital touching contacts between the child and the doll."

Key's most famous study was of a *Time* magazine ad for Gilbey's gin. His analytical brain dove into the hidden messages with almost McCarthyist enthusiasm. The melting ice on the bottle cap was seminal fluid, the reflections from the glass and bottle were subtle vaginal lips, a drop of water was meant to represent the clitoris, the bottle and bottle cap reflections were a man's legs and partially erect genitals. Key monitored reactions to the ad from over 1,000 subjects. Although 62% of men and women reported feelings of sexual excitement or stimulation, absolutely none of the respondents said they were consciously aware of the subliminal content "until it was explained to them after their responses were recorded."

According to Key, even the use of certain words in advertising copy teetered on the prurient, possessing incredibly devious, subliminal power. The word "shot" was just one letter away from "shit," for example, as was "whose/whore," "cult/cunt," and "tastes/testes." Key proudly announced that 26 ads in one issue of *Life* magazine used the word "come" in their ad copy.

Despite the Herculean efforts of Key and other researchers, advertising in America still teems with sexual messages. Whether it's subliminal or not, people don't seem to care anymore. Copywriters still resort to the cheap innuendo, and *Life* magazine still has not banned use of the word "come."

Another one of those things your mother just wouldn't understand.

"Stuck? What's stuck? What did you say, Mom? What drawer?...oh...*that* drawer...er...that guy who lived here before me?...well he left that stuff here... yeah...I figured he'd be back for it...three years?...I been there *that* long, eh, Mom?... Well, he may pop in here any day now, y'know? Oh...that magazine is dated *last* month?...wonder how *that* got in there?... dirty?... Really?...Y'know I never really noticed...right...real gangster shoes...sex fiend?...I wouldn't doubt it Mom...whaddya worried?... of course you taught me better...incinerator?...hey that's O.K., Mom...you just relax... I'll take care of it later..."

— copy from a magazine ad for a two-toned platform shoe from Dexter called the "Aquarius," resting on a stack of sex-related books and magazines

READY TO WEAR:
Instant sex appeal below the belt

An ALBERTO GRIMALDI Production

Marlon Brando

Last Tango in Paris

America's #1 Bestseller at $6.00 / Now 50¢

THIS IS THE GROVE PRESS EDITION,
THE ONLY UNEXPURGATED VERSION
EVER PUBLISHED IN AMERICA

LADY CHATTERLEY'S LOVER

BY D. H. LAWRENCE

COMPLETE AND
UNABRIDGED

This and only this is the uncensored edition making today's headlines!

INTRODUCTION BY MARK SCHORER
PREFACE BY ARCHIBALD MACLEISH

I Am Curious (yellow)
The complete scenario of
the film by Vilgot Sjöman
with over 250 illustrations

Our video shops and bookstores are pretty much as depraved as we'd ever want to get. We can now legally purchase newspapers that cater to transvestite nuns, rent enema bondage movies or watch humans and eels get it on. But all this intellectual freedom means somebody else took the fall so that we may revel in our own specific sexual interests. People paid fines, went to jail or appealed their cases up to the Supreme Court, employing hundreds of expert witnesses, for our right to e-mail photos of bare breasts to a friend in Florida.

Three major Supreme Court decisions have allowed Americans to hold their pornography

Can't Do That!

close to their chests and pant quietly.

The Roth decision of 1957 upheld the conviction of New Yorker Samuel Roth, who peddled softcore magazines and pulp books. The court drew a distinction, however, between sexual and obscene material. What was sexual was not necessarily obscene. Its standard became the now-classic: "Whether to the average person, applying contemporary community standards, the dominant theme of the material taken as a whole appeals to prurient interests."

In the *Fanny Hill* decision of 1966, Supreme Court Justice William J. Brennan, Jr.'s majority decision overturned a Massachusetts ban on the 18th-century novel *Memoirs of a Woman of*

OBSCENE AND NOT HEARD:
Censored works we almost never saw

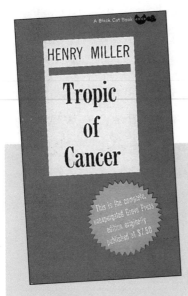

The trouble with Irène is that she has a valise instead of a cunt. She wants fat letters to shove in her valise. Immense, *avec des choses inouïes*. Llona now, she had a cunt. I know because she sent us some hairs from down below. Llona — a wild ass snuffing pleasure out of the wind. On every high hill she played the harlot — and sometimes in telephone booths and toilets....She lay in Tottenham Court Road with her dress pulled up and fingered herself. She used candles, Roman candles, and door knobs. Not a prick in the land big enough for her...*not one.* Men went inside her and curled up. She wanted extension pricks, self-exploding rockets, hot boiling oil made of wax and creosote. She would cut off your prick and keep it inside her forever, if you gave her permission. One cunt out of a million, Llona! A laboratory cunt and no litmus paper that could take her color....She never bought a bed for her King Carol. She crowned him with a whisky bottle and her tongue was full of lice and tomorrows. Poor Carol, he could only curl up inside her and die. She drew a breath and he fell out — like a dead clam.

— from page 6 of *Tropic of Cancer* by Henry Miller, 1934, banned in the U.S. until 1961

And it seemed she was like the sea, nothing but dark waves rising and heaving, heaving, with a great swell, so that slowly her whole darkness was in motion, and she was ocean rolling its dark, dumb mass. Oh, and far down inside her the deeps parted and rolled asunder, in long, far-travelling billows, and ever, at the quick of her, the depths parted and rolled asunder, from the center of soft plunging, as the plunger went deeper and deeper, touching lower, and she was deeper and deeper and deeper disclosed, and heavier the billows of her rolled away to some shore, uncovering her, and closer and closer plunged the palpable unknown, and further and further rolled the waves of herself away from herself, leaving her, till suddenly, in a soft, shuddering convulsion, the quick of all her plasm was touched, she knew herself touched, the consummation was upon her, and she was gone. She was gone, she was not, and she was born: a woman.

Ah, too lovely, too lovely! In the ebbing she realized all the loveliness. Now all her body clung with tender love to the unknown man, and blindly to the wilting penis, as it so tenderly, frailly, unknowingly withdrew, after the fierce thrust of its potency. As it drew out and left her body, the secret, sensitive thing, she gave an unconscious cry of pure loss, and she tried to put it back. It had been so perfect! And she loved it so!

– from *Lady Chatterly's Lover* by D.H Lawrence, 1928, banned in America until 1959

Pleasure, also known as *Fanny Hill*. (Supposedly, those interested in the book previously found it only in the rare book room at the Columbia University library, where it was stored in a locked case.) Under this new standard, a work could be ruled obscene only if it met three requirements: "(a) the dominant theme of the material taken as a whole appeals to prurient interest in sex; (b) the material is patently offensive because it affronts contemporary community standards relating to the description or representation of sexual matters; and (c) the material is utterly without redeeming social value."

Fanny Hill was promptly reissued by American publishers in numerous editions, and a low-budget porn film version was released. This expanded definition opened the floodgates, and obscenity trials were filled with people testifying that they could detect a trace of social value in whatever was on trial.

The Miller ruling of 1973 involved porn pusher Marvin Miller, who was nabbed sending brochures through the mail that advertised nude photo books and X-rated films. The Burger court ruled 5-4 in favor of community standards. Local juries would have to decide what was offensive to the standards of taste, and convict that which they found that "taken as a whole, lacks serious literary, artistic, political or scientific value."

This was the turning point for much censorship, as state after state began applying its own criteria to what exactly its citizens should be subjected to. Noteworthy cases included some of the biggest names of the era.

Ralph Ginzburg started publishing *Eros* magazine in 1962, and began his legal problems that same year with an indictment for obscenity. In 1965, he went before the Supreme Court, charged with obscenity for three of his publications: *The Housewife's Handbook of Selective Promiscuity*, an issue of the biweekly newsletter *Liaison*, and a hard-bound volume of *Eros*. Unlike previous cases that considered the specific inherent obscenity value, the court regarded the appeal to prurient interest based on Ginzburg's advertising campaigns, in which the cocky publisher attempted to obtain second-class mailing privileges in the Pennsylvania towns of Intercourse and Blue Ball, before getting them in Middlesex, New Jersey. He was sentenced to three years for obscenity. Before entering a federal prison in Pennsylvania, he stood in front of the facility, delivering a final sidewalk speech to the press, after which he crumpled a parchment copy of the Bill of Rights and tossed it into a wastebasket.

Ginzburg would eventually launch a new cutting-edge art publication called *Avant-Garde,* defiantly publishing erotic drawings by Pablo Picasso, but his career as highbrow pornographer was coming to an end. In 1972 he went to jail for eight months, later to emerge as a photographer for the *New York Post.*

From 1961 to 1964, comedian Lenny Bruce was busted at least four times for obscenity in U.S. nightclubs, charged with using language that today is the staple of most club comics. He was banned from touring in both England and Australia, and once his mouth was even taped shut at a hospital, for fear of his uttering foul words. Continual hassle from police eventually broke his spirit as well as his wallet, but not before he recycled court documents as comedy material at the few clubs in which he was still allowed to perform. While awaiting yet another trial, he died of a heroin overdose, broke and destitute, in 1966.

National porn kings like Reuben "Doc Johnson" Sturman had been chased for years by authorities, with feds following the trail of bookstores, films and sex products. In 1970 Sturman's main competition, Mike Thevis, finally got nailed. Federal agents said he was worth $100 million, distributing 40 percent of all the porn in the country. To stay out of jail Thevis even donated his $5 million mansion to the city of Atlanta, but it didn't work, and he went to prison in December 1974. He escaped in 1978, was recaptured and died in prison in 1982.

Films often fell victim to community standards, even mainstream Hollywood releases we now find in the dusty sections of video shops. Although the 1971 Mike Nichols film *Carnal Knowledge* played in nearly 5,000 theaters in every state and was seen by 20 million people, it was immediately declared obscene in Albany, Georgia, because of scenes of full nudity for Ann-Margret and Jack Nicholson (rear and side). The Albany theater manager was convicted by a Superior Court jury, the verdict was later reversed by the U.S. Supreme Court and the case of Jenkins v. Georgia remains a leading decision in ruling national First Amendment standards over local community standards.

Although director Bernardo Bertolucci and star Marlon Brando were both nominated for Oscars for *Last Tango in Paris,* the 1973 film was seized by Shreveport, Louisiana police on the

When we had sufficiently graduated our advances towards the main point, by toying, kissing, clipping, feeling my breasts, now round and plump, feeling that part of me I might call a furnace-mouth, from the prodigious intense heat his fiery touches had rekindled there, my young sportsman, embolden'd by every freedom he could wish, wantonly takes my hand, and carries it to that enormous machine of his, that stood with a stiffness! a hardness! an upward bent of erection! and which, together with its bottom dependence, the inestimable bulge of lady's jewels, formed a grand show out of goods indeed! Then its dimensions, mocking either grasp or span, almost renew'd my terrors...

...Slipping then a pillow under me, that I might give him the fairest play, I guided officiously with my hand this furious battering ram, whose ruby head, presenting nearest the resemblance of a heart, I applied to its proper mark, which lay as finely elevated as we could wish; my hips being borne up, and my thighs at their utmost extension, the gleamy warmth that shot from it made him feel that he was at the mouth of the indraught, and driving foreright, the powerfully divided lips of that pleasure-thirsty channel receiv'd him. He hesitated a little; then, settled well in the passage, he makes his way up the straits of it, with a difficulty nothing more than pleasing, widening as he went, so as to distend and smooth each soft furrow: our pleasure increasing deliciously, in proportion as our points of mutual touch increas'd in that so vital part of me in which I had now taken him, all indriven, and completely sheathed; and which, crammed as it was, stretched, splitting ripe, gave it so gratefully strait an accommodation! so strict a fold! a suction so fierce! that gave and took unutterable delight...

...I not only then tighten'd the pleasure-girth round my restless inmate by a secret spring of friction and compression that obeys the will in those parts, but stole my hand softly to that store bag of nature's prime sweets, which is so pleasingly attach'd to its conduit pipe, from which we receive them; there feeling, and most gently indeed, squeezing those tender globular reservoirs; the magic touch took instant effect, quicken'd, and brought on upon the spur the symptoms of that sweet agony, the melting moment of dissolution, when pleasure dies by pleasure, and the mysterious engine of it overcomes the titillation it has rais'd in those parts, by plying them with the stream of a warm liquid that is itself the highest of all titillations, and which they thirstily express and draw in like the hot-natured leach, which to cool itself, tenaciously attracts all the moisture within its sphere of exsuction. Chiming then to me, with exquisite consent, as I melted away, his oily balsamic injection, mixing deliciously with the sluices in flow from me, sheath'd and blunted all the stings of pleasure, it flung us into an extasy that extended us fainting, breathless, entranced.

— from *Fanny Hill (Memoirs of a Woman of Pleasure)* by John Cleland, 1748-49; suppressed in the U.S. until 1963

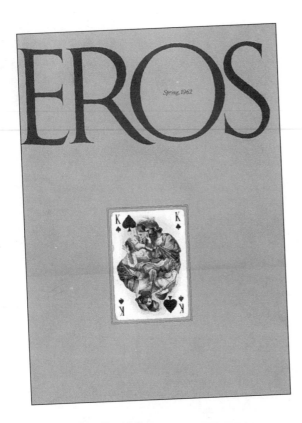

BETTER OFF IN PRISON:
Volume I, Issue I of Eros *magazine, Spring 1962,
that would eventually send its publisher Ralph
Ginzburg to jail (above), and one of its horribly
offensive images, "Adonis Discovers Venus" by
Annibale Carracci (below)*

second day it was shown and the theater
manager arrested. The very next day, the
manager showed another print of the same film,
and again he was arrested and the film seized.
A District Court judge found the film obscene,
a decision which was later reversed by the state
Supreme Court.

In 1969, three Jackson, Mississippi police
officers dressed in plainclothes purchased
tickets to the Paramount Theater's screening
of the film version of the Terry Southern novel
Candy, starring Marlon Brando, Richard
Burton, Walter Matthau, John Huston, Ringo
Starr and James Coburn, with a screenplay
by Buck Henry. After viewing the film, the
officers arrested the theater's manager and
projectionist, and seized the print of the film.
The defendants were found guilty in a criminal
trial of "exhibiting to public view" an obscene
film. The U.S. District Court heard an appeal
and denied it; the film remained obscene until
later vacated by the U.S. Supreme Court.

Many crafty filmmakers who desired big
distribution avoided courts by adding redeeming social value into their storylines. In Russ
Meyer's 1969 softcore hit *Vixen*, a big political
discussion occurs on an airplane in the film's
last 10 minutes, after all the sex scenes. When
word reached Chicago audiences, theaters
began emptying as soon as the characters
boarded the airplane. Nevertheless, the film
would be banned in Duval County, Florida and
in Ohio, where the state Supreme Court would
"pierce the veil of contrived social commentary
totally unrelated to the dominant theme of the
picture," and find it obscene.

The pretentious art film *I Am Curious –
Yellow* premiered in 1967 in Sweden, the story
of a young actress making a film for a director
while at the same time being his lover. Included
amongst the footage of political upheaval were
scenes of full-frontal nudity, maturbation and
oral sex. The film attracted the attention of
Barney Rosset, who was in the business of
importing literature formerly considered
obscene. But when Rosset's Grove Press
attempted to bring a print of the film into the
country, it was seized at the border by U.S.
Customs. A U.S. District Courtroom convened
to decide whether to prosecute for obscenity.
Witnesses appearing on behalf of the film
included novelist Norman Mailer; film critics
from *The New Republic, Newsweek, The New
Leader* and *Saturday Review*; assorted psychiatrists, sociologists and ministers; and flown over
from Sweden, the film's director, Vilgot Sjöman.

The prosecution's only witness, Rev. Dr. Dan M. Potter, was a clergyman involved in many censorship drives. Despite such distinguished defense witnesses, the jury found the film to be obscene. The ruling was overturned on appeal in 1968, and the film went into circulation, but attracted attention from more censors, and an appeal went to the Supreme Court. Liberal America held its breath; this could be the precedent. Conservative Nixon appointees forced a 4-4 split vote, with Justice William O. Douglas dissenting because Rosset's *Evergreen Review* had reprinted a chapter from Douglas's book "Points of Rebellion." In the following three years, the film would be banned in fifteen states. According to a Phoenix Superior Court judge, the film "had no plot, no economic message, and no religious dogma. Its only message is immoral copulation, public fornication, and illicit habits." Despite such harsh criticism, the film eventually grossed $14 million nationwide.

Increased scrutiny of mainstream films left those in the hardcore biz no choice but to retaliate and make the best of it. Porn producers spiced up their advertising by self-rating their films as X, or even XX and XXX.

In Oakland County, Michigan the print of the X-rated film *Naked Came the Stranger*, based on the best-selling novel ghostwritten by the staff of *Newsday*, was seized four separate times by authorities, who remembered on the fourth raid to also jail the theater manager overnight and remove the projection equipment. A federal District Court ordered the prosecutor to refrain from further arrests and seizures, and to please return the projection equipment. The U.S. Supreme Court held that repeated arrests and seizures were appropriate for crimes such as bank robbery, but were inappropriate and unconstitutional when applied to materials presumed to be protected by the First Amendment.

Also in Michigan, *The Devil in Miss Jones, Deep Throat, Little Sisters* and *It Happened In Hollywood* prompted civil action against several Wayne County theaters for being "public nuisances." According to the court, the films were apparently "an example of the trash that a few sick, demented minds are spewing out across our country in search of the easy dollar. Films of this type, no doubt, scar the minds of many people, young and old, who, out of a natural curiosity, view them. These films can greatly weaken, if not destroy, the moral and wholesome fiber which the citizens of this country possess in abundance. To permit this moral sabotage to continue would be to

I was arrested for obscenity in San Francisco for using a ten-letter word which is sort of chic. I'm not going to repeat the word tonight. It starts with a "c." They said it was vernacular for a favorite homosexual practice — which is weird, 'cause I don't relate that word to homosexuals. It relates to any contemporary woman I know or would know or would love or would marry. But they hung up with faggotry. Alright.

Well, the whole scene was that Dirty Lenny, Dirty Lenny said a dirty word. And I got busted for it, and *schlepped* away in a patrol wagon.

Now when I took the bust, I finished the show — I said that word, you know, the ten-letter word — and the heat comes over and says,

"Ah, Lenny, my name is Sgt. Blah-blah-blah. You know that word you said?"

"I said alotta words out there."

"No. *That* word."

"Oh. Yeah?"

"Well, Lenny, that's against the law. I'm gonna hafta take ya down."

"O.K. That's cool."

"It's against the law to say it and to do it."

"But I didn't *do* it, man."

"I know, but uh, I just have to tell you that."

"O.K."...

...Now, get into court, take fingerprints. The judge? A tough outside *verbissener. Tough-o.* Right? He comes in:

"Blah-blah-blah. Siddown."

Swear the heat in.

"What did he say?"

"Your Honor, he said blah-blah-blah."

The judge: "He said *blah-blah-blah?!*"

Then the guy really *yentaed* it up: "That's right. I couldn't believe it. Up on the stage, in front of women and a mixed audience, he said *blah-blah-blah.*"

The judge: "This I never heard, blah-blah-blah. He said *blah-blah-blah?*"

"He said *blah-blah-blah!* I'm not going to lie to ya."

It's in the minutes — "I'm not gonna lie to ya." Alright.

The D.A.:

"The guy said blah-blah-blah. Look at him. He's *smug.* He's not gonna repent. He's *glad* he said blah-blah-blah!"

Then I dug something: they sort of *liked* saying blah-blah-blah. Because they said it a few extra times. They really got *so* involved, saying blah-blah-blah. The bailiff is yelling, "What'd he say?"

"*Shut up,* you blah-blah-blah."

They were *yelling* it in the court.

"He said blah-blah-blah."

"*Blah-blah-blah!*"

"Goddamn! It's *good* to say blah-blah-blah."

"*That blah-blah-blah!*"

....Here's how it ends. One day I'm going to get an order to appear in court: "Oh, shit, what is it this time?" But when I get there the courtroom will be all decorated, dig, with balloons and streamers and confetti, and when I walk in they'll all jump up and yell *"Surprise!"* And there'll be all the cops that busted me, and the judges and DA's who tried me, and they'll say,

"Lenny, this is a surprise party for you. We're giving you a party because even after everything that happened you never lost respect for the law."

— from live routines of Lenny Bruce, transcribed and published as *The Essential Lenny Bruce*, edited by John Cohen, 1967

CURIOSITY KILLED THE MORALITY:
A scene from I Am Curious — Yellow

A U.S. District Courtroom convened on May 20, 1968 to decide the validity of *I Am Curious — Yellow*. Long-winded novelist Norman Mailer was the final witness to take the stand:

Q: Would you please state whether you felt the film *I Am Curious — Yellow* had artistic importance.
A: Well, if I may, could I take my time to get to that point, because the problem was a large one for me before I went to see the picture, and if I might I would like to present a deep reservation I had about the picture before I saw it because I think the question is attached to the answer. In other words, my preliminary remarks are attached very much to the answer about the artistic merit or lack of it in the film....I have thought a lot about the problem of sexuality in movies. I have been obsessed with the problem and concerned with the problem and devoted to the problem in one way or another for twenty years of writing novels...

[several pages pass]

...The main thing about the picture was that it gave me a good feeling finally about men and women, particularly about this woman in this picture. I had a feeling they were all more noble than I thought before I saw the picture. The picture left me with a feeling of — I heard the word sanctity used here yesterday, and though I wouldn't use that word, I would say that I felt slightly shriven, a slightly more moral man, and that is a rare feeling to get from a movie. The moral and social values are to me self-evidenced through the emotions that the picture aroused in me and left me with."

ignore the spreading of a deadly plague...we are not about to permit this disease to spread." The trial court deemed the theaters to be padlocked shut for one year as "public nuisances," meaning "any building, vehicle, boat, aircraft or place" used for the purpose of "lewdness." The state supreme court reversed the closings, holding that the nuisance statute applied only to houses of prostitution.

The granddaddy of porn classics, *Deep Throat* was no stranger to obscenity charges. From 1972 to 1981, it was banned in California, Colorado, Florida, Georgia, Illinois, Iowa, Kentucky, Louisiana, Maryland, Massachusetts, Michigan, Mississippi, Missouri, Nebraska, New Hampshire, New Jersey, New York, North Dakota, Ohio, Pennsylvania, South Dakota, Tennessee and Texas. A print of the film brought into the country from Canada was seized by U.S. Customs in Boston, and during a 1973 trial in the First Circuit Court of Appeals, expert witnesses testified that the movie "puts forth an idea of greater liberation with regard to human sexuality and to the expression of it," and would benefit the "many women [who] have an unreasonable fear of the penis."

Watchdog groups emerged to monitor the nation's growing pornography industry. In 1968, LBJ appointed a Presidential Commission on Obscenity and Pornography, comprised of 18 members who would determine the effects of hardcore material on the republic.

They spent $2.6 million, hired a staff of 22 — measured blood flow in erect penises, interviewed peep show patrons. Dr. Paul Gebhard of the Kinsey Institute remembered commission chairman Bill Lockhart saying to him, "Look, I'm discovering that the commission members don't know what to discuss. Some of them think *Playboy* is hardcore." Lockhart asked the Kinsey group to provide a survey of their erotica collection.

Dr. Morris A. Lipton, a research psychiatrist at the University of Carolina Medical School, devoted over 1,000 hours to the commission. His team tested 23 male undergraduates, who spent 90 minutes a day, five days a week for three weeks, in a room. They could do anything except homework or fall asleep. Dr. Lipton provided each room with a four-drawer filing cabinet containing porn movies, porn still photos, porn books, and copies of popular magazines. Urine tests were run on each subject to measure for an enzyme that indicated sexual arousal. Dr. Lipton told one interviewer, "We found quick satiation. After a day, they were looking at *Popular Mechanics*. The only antisocial effect was that they borrowed the movies to show back in their dorm rooms."

In 1969 Nixon was able to replace one member of the commission with his ringer: Charles H. Keating, whose anti-porn lobbying efforts in Cincinnati earned him the press nickname "Mr. Clean." Keating had founded his own group called Citizens for Decent Literature. They wanted to close down bookshops, and boycott stores and broadcasting advertisers. The CDL grew in the '60s to have 32 chapters in 20 states, and an estimated 350,000 members, many of whom were congressman, clergyman, politicians, and district attorneys. And it didn't hurt that in Cincinnati, Keating's brother Bill ran the most influential newspaper in the city, the *Cincinnati Enquirer*. The CDL encouraged big-city newspapers to refuse ads for X-rated films. Keating would later make headlines in the 1980s for bilking the nation's elderly in the S&L scandal; a subsequent bailout would cost the government $2.6 billion.

In 1970 Nixon's commission concluded that porn was not a national threat, and recommended the abolition of obscenity laws. But Keating warned Nixon that his commission had come to the incorrect conclusion, and filed a suit that stalled publication of the commission's report. Keating attempted to rally people behind him, and convinced Nixon to reject the commission's findings. As the commission report was published, Keating released a separate 175-page report that attacked his own commission's results, citing police records and quotes from Puritan observers like Arnold Toynbee and Alexis de Toqueville.

The president was convinced:

"So long as I am in the White House, there will be no relaxation of the national effort to control and eliminate smut from our national life...The Commission contends that the proliferation of filthy books and plays has no lasting, harmful threat on man's character... Centuries of civilization and ten minutes of common sense tell us otherwise...American morality is not to be trifled with."

A few years later Nixon would resign under threat of impeachment.

There would be other porn fighters, diligent watchdogs who waved the flag of chastity in the face of an increasingly erotically charged America. As a federal prosecutor in Memphis between 1972 and 1976, Larry Parrish indicted 60 people for obscenity, including porn stars

DOWN ON THE FARM:
Star-studded, X-rated adaptation of John Barth's novel

The Killing of Sister George (1968)
Greetings (1968)
Midnight Cowboy (1968, won the Oscar for best picture)
A Clockwork Orange (1970)
Myra Breckenridge (1970)
Futz (1970)
End of the Road (1970)
Quiet Days in Clichy (1970)
Last Tango in Paris (1973)

— big-budget X-rated films that were categorized informally as "quality X's"

During the 1960s obscenity trials, the *Washington Post* published articles by Nina Totenberg which described the Supreme Court justices watching the porn films in question. Most judges were embarrassed or catatonic, except the Hon. Thurgood Marshall, "who had been overheard by clerks to be laughing in the screening room, and occasionally expressing words of encouragement to the actors."

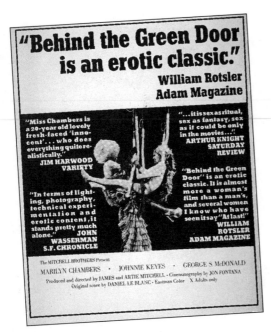

In 1973, a Suffolk County, New York theater owner showed a print of *Behind the Green Door* in his modern 600-seat shopping-center theater, which had opened a few months before with *The Sound of Music*. He was arrested and found guilty of exhibiting a film that "appeals to prurient interest in sex, goes substantially beyond the customary limits of candor, and has utterly no redeeming social value. Despite trial testimony by expert witnesses, who claimed the film contained a "ritual quality reminiscent of Ravel's *Bolero*," the film was found obscene. It would also, between 1974 and 1981, be banned in Texas, Colorado, Georgia and California.

VIVA LA VIXEN:
Despite the inclusion of a big political discussion to add redeeming value, Russ Meyer's 1969 softcore hit was banned in Florida and Ohio

Harry Reems and Georgina Spelvin. New York Jesuit and veteran porn fighter Father Morton Hill declared in 1976, "There should be better control over what children can see or hear, and we should keep porn out of public view." That same year, fellow religious figure Dr. Billy James Hargis should have been listening to his colleague more closely. *Time* magazine revealed he had sodomized both male and female students at his fundamentalist college. But despite the shenanigans of the spokesmen, the religious right continued to pump out the propaganda. A best-selling Biblical love manual by Drs. Ed and Gaye Wheat called *Intended for Pleasure* cautioned married couples that "Oral-genital sex definitely limits the amount of loving verbal communication that husband and wife can have as they make love." And defending pornographers against such crusaders were attorneys who specialized in obscenity. Harold Fahringer, from Buffalo, New York, won many courtrooms over by emphasizing that America's corner newsstand should be considered the "poor man's library or art museum."

One notable anti-filth crusade occurred in the 1980s, but implicated much material from the Golden Age of Hetero. Cartoons from softcore men's mags dating back to the 1960s were the focus of a 1985 study by Dr. Ruth Reisman, costing $734,000, funded by a Justice Department grant. Reisman had no scientific studies, academic experience or previous publishing background to justify her résumé, but she was once a songwriter for the children's program *Captain Kangaroo*. After her research was completed, Reisman showed a slide-show presentation, declaring: "The coders identified 2016 child cartoons and 398 child visuals, of which 681 were pseudo-children, in all issues." Her study was so unscientific it was never released by the Justice Department.

At the same time theaters and newsstands fought their battles, a similar war was waging on the nation's airwaves. One of radio's crowning moments occurred on the evening of November 7, 1971, with the introduction of the word "cock." Initially brought on as a guest of radio DJ Howard Hesseman on San Francisco's KMPX, sex advice columnist Dr. Hip Pocrates was given his own call-in show on the hippie KSAN. On the night in question, he was talking with prostitution activist Margo St. James when she allowed the fateful word to slip out. A listener complained, and many letters of complaint were sent to the FCC. Six months of legal wrangling ensued, with Metromedia attorneys racking up $200,000 in fees to save the station's license. Dr. Hip collected letters of support and documents to prove that the comment was made as part of a professional medical program designed to educate listeners, but the effort was in vain. He was booted off the station. The incident remains on the FCC record books as a hallmark of broadcast obscenity.

Network television was perhaps the most fearful of censorship. If sponsors pulled out of a program, it meant millions of dollars lost in ad revenue. In the 1960s, the big threat to decency was the sight of a woman's navel. Dawn "Mary Ann" Wells' belly button on *Gilligan's Island* was a big problem, not to mention Cher's revealing fashions on the *Sonny & Cher Show*. Network censors refused to let the camera see Barbara Eden's bare navel for the entire run of *I Dream of Jeannie*, from 1965 to 1970, but finally relented for a 1985 reunion special.

Other instances of censorship seem completely banal by today's standards. In 1977, four minutes of the BBC program *I, Claudius* were removed before the show premiered on the American PBS — a bare-breasted tribal dance in Africa, and scenes of Caligula eating his wife/sister's aborted child. The opening sequence of the 1977 premiere episode of *The Richard Pryor Show* showed the host naked from the waist up, saying to the camera he had not lost anything in his battles with the censors. As the camera panned down his body, it revealed Pryor to be completely nude, sans genitals (he was actually wearing a nude body stocking). The segment was killed.

Implied intimacy between races also raised the blood pressure of television executives. On the 1968 TV special *Petula*, a scene had to be reshot quickly before broadcast, because star Petula Clark held guest star Harry Belafonte's arm during a song. The advertiser, ad agency and network all freaked out, believing an interracial touch would suggest sexual attraction and alienate the audience. Television had to wait until 1977 to actually represent a romantic inclination between races, with the TV movie *A Killing Affair*, starring Elizabeth Montgomery and O.J. Simpson as cops in love. And no, she didn't get her throat slit.

Law books became cluttered with all sorts of bizarre sexual cases, some of which remain as classic aberrations of the legal system. After a 27-year-old man was completely paralyzed from the waist down as the result of a 1965 elevator accident, a New York Court of Appeals ruled several years later that his wife was

THE CRAZY BUSINESS WE CALL SHOW:
Linda Lovelace in a pivotal scene from Deep Throat, *another favorite scapegoat of censors*

I have never lost hope that the day will come in this country when pornography will no longer be feared as some sort of witchcraft. I am convinced that obscenity breeds and multiplies in the dark crevices of a frightened society preoccupied with a sense of self-censorship. Once pornography is exposed to the strong sunlight of a completely free and uninhibited people, its appeal will surely diminish. I have an abiding confidence in the American public. I believe an adult can read or see anything without being morally corrupted. Therefore, the control of obscenity must be left to the self-regulating forces of the public's taste. More importantly, the choice of what books people will read or what films they will see for their own amusement must be left to them and not to the government. The right to read and see what we choose must include every book, film, magazine or newspaper — or in the long run it may include none.

— **New York attorney Herald Price Fahringer, whose clients included Al Goldstein, dominatrix Monique Von Cleef and the films *Deep Throat* and *The Devil and Miss Jones***

WHERE'S THE BUTTER?:
*Maria Schneider waiting for
Brando to finish lunch, from* Last
Tango In Paris

entitled to damages for the loss of his sexual
companionship. In the mid-'60s, a former dance
instructor named Gloria Sykes filed suit in U.S.
court — the first such suit ever to seek damages
for increased sexual activity — claiming a San
Francisco cable car accident converted her
from a "proper young lady" into a raging
nymphomaniac. Following the accident, Sykes
reportedly hit the town and had sex with over
100 different men, thoughtfully keeping a
calendar of each affair. The court sympathized
with her plight, and awarded her $500,000 in
damages. (Members of her courtroom might
have taken a break at a local legal saloon
named the Jury Room, whose rest rooms
were labeled "Hung" and "Split.")

In 1966, a Times Square book vendor named
Robert Redrup was arrested for selling obscene
pulp books to plainclothes policemen. The
publisher went to bat for him, and in 1967 the
Supreme Court ruled the books, *Lust Pool* and
Shame Agent, were not legally obscene. Nearly
30 obscenity cases before the Supreme Court in
1967 were overturned with one word — Redrup,
who wasn't even a regular employee of the
newsstand, but who had agreed to fill in for a
friend who took the day off because of illness.

Des Moines businessman Richard Davis
applied for a license for an adult movie house
in Mason City, Iowa in 1970. When the mayor
refused to sign his license, he took the case to
court and won. In 1973, the First District Court
of Appeals turned down Aaron Katz's request
for a personalized California license plate that
would read EZ LAY, saying the DMV's refusal
served a substantial government interest and
was only an incidental restriction of free speech.

One of the more ridiculous cases of
censorship, responsible for the formation of
two anti-porn organizations, occurred in 1975 in
New York City. Rumors were spreading about
the latest perversity called snuff films, where
human life was actually taken on-screen.
Nobody had ever seen such a film, because they
didn't exist, but that didn't stop an enterprising
producer from Monarch Releasing Corporation
named Allen Shackleton, who took advantage
of the rumors the following year. He came into
possession of unused footage shot in South
America wherein a Manson-like band of hippie
girls tortured men by tying them to trees and
whipping them, before eventually killing them.
Shackleton slapped on a hasty ending, and
renamed the film *Snuff*, promoting it with
cryptic tag lines like "From South America...
where life is cheap!"

Following a sudden jump cut to Shackleton's new epilogue, the camera pulls back to reveal a film crew. The director of the crew takes the script girl into a back room, then kills and disembowels her, even taking a pair of scissors to one of her fingers. Despite the obviously faked, no-budget blood-and-guts special effects, completely ridiculous by today's standards, rumors circulated that the girl was killed. Feminists were outraged, and that year two organizations formed — Women Against Violence Against Women, and Women Against Violence and Pornography in the Media — to tour the country holding anti-pornography lectures and screenings. *Snuff* received a wider audience than Shackleton had ever hoped.

Critics of erotica and sexually related materials have focused their efforts to broadcast media in recent years. The much-lauded V-chip technology, for instance, has completely changed the way youngsters sneak their pornography on the television set. And although currently under pressure from anti-porn groups — including the Virginia-based Enough Is Enough, headed by Donna Rice — the internet remains relatively censorship-free. On June 26, 1997, the CDA (Communications Decency Act) was ruled unconstitutional by the U.S. Supreme Court; the transmitting of adult materials over the internet remains legal.

DOCTOR: Well, you say — and I think it's true — that many men say they're not interested in oral sex because they don't like the odor.

STUDIO GUEST: Yeah. But I think if they just got down there and burrowed around for a while, they'd adapt — they'd get used to it. I know people that dig it, that no matter, some guys say the funkier the better, y'know, it's really real. You know, I believe in bathing and I know the hairs collect the smells and all that; you have to wash the hair very well.

DOCTOR: Incidentally, the definitive work on oral sex is called *Oragenitalism* by G. Legman, and it's about 360 pages explaining every conceivable variation, position — it even gets down so to speak, to the kind of lighting you should have in the room, the elevation of the bed and furnishings in the room.

GUEST: How fantastic! And the guy's name is "Legman"?

DOCTOR: Legman — L-e-g-m-a-n. G. Legman believes that the function of pubic hair was to collect the secretions, because when man walked on all fours, of course, the pubic hairs would collect the secretion and act as a sexual stimulant.

GUEST: Right, yeah.

DOCTOR: So, what do you recommend?

GUEST: Women should take a taste test of themselves every once in a while and eat a lot of yogurt.

DOCTOR: Why does that help?

GUEST: Well, I think yogurt has the same bacteria that should be present there in order for it to taste good. I've never tried putting yogurt in directly, but —

DOCTOR: A yogurt — yogurt douche?

GUEST: Yeah, I've never tried that but, you know, it might be something.

DOCTOR: It might be something.

GUEST: But I know that if I take yogurt —

DOCTOR: Plain or —

GUEST: I know I taste very —

DOCTOR: Blueberry?

GUEST: No one's ever complained about my taste. No, straight, plain yogurt, none of that sugared stuff. Lay off that sugar. Healthy yogurt. Unpasteurized, if they can get it.

DOCTOR: What about the many women who are leery about participating in oral sex?

GUEST: Well, I must admit that eating pussy is easier than sucking cock.

DOCTOR: (turning to engineer) Well, that's, let's see — we can't — is that all right? (Background — someone says, "It's all right.")

DOCTOR: You could've said "penis."

GUEST: Oh, penis, well —

YOU COULD'VE SAID "PENIS":
Transcript from November 7, 1971 radio broadcast which cost Dr. Eugene Schoenfeld his job

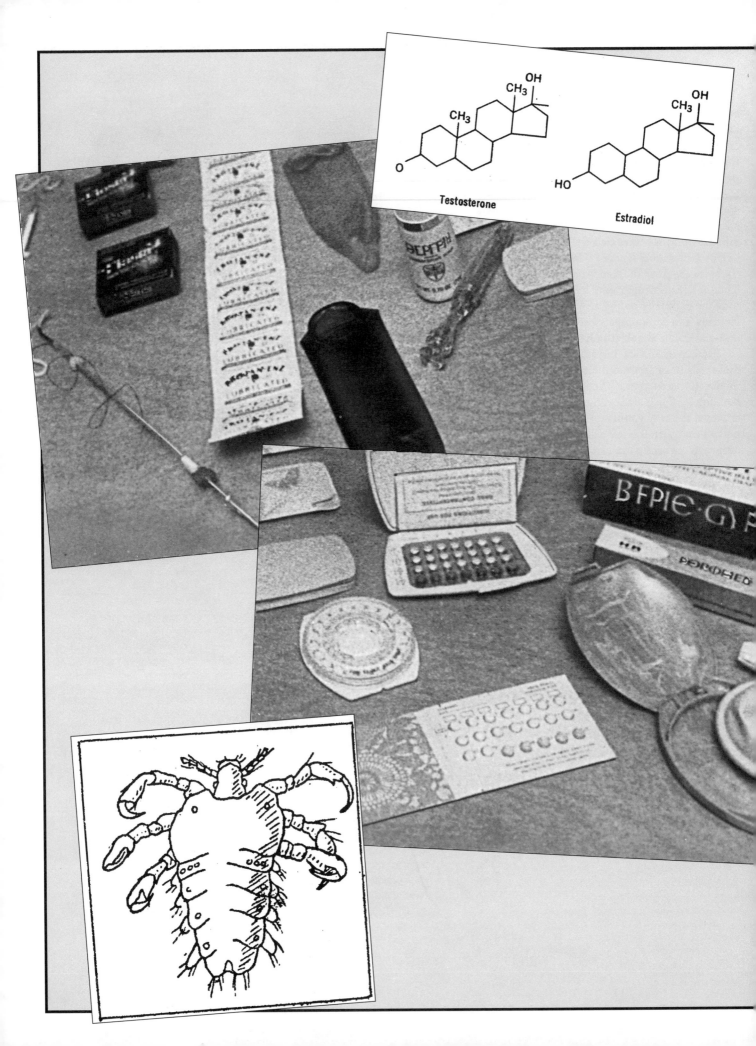

Testosterone

Estradiol

During the pre-AIDS era, hetero sex evolved into a marvelous time-wasting activity that certainly had its health drawbacks, but nothing life-threatening. You could have cheese blasting out of your crotch, piss burning its way out of your shaft or tiny claw-snapping crustaceans falling out of your pubes, and all you needed was a shot of penicillin or a quick trip to the pharmacy ointment shelf, and you were back in the game. With this apparently unlimited recreational resource available to every man and woman with a working set of privates, naturally we weren't satisfied, and insisted on pumping all sorts of chemicals and concoctions into our systems to enhance the orgasm and bring us to

Nice Body

bone-shuddering pinnacles of ecstasy. Not only was sex the darling of pop culture and the media, people grew more curious on an intuitive, personal level. How can I have sex and not get pregnant? How can I cure this bizarre disease I've contracted? Who should I ask about all this stuff? And once all this is taken care of, what should I ingest to increase the orgasms? Strangely enough, all of this hand-wringing began courtesy of American farmers, who helped jump-start the entire mess by purchasing tractors and other agricultural equipment.

In the early 1950s, a Harvard-trained biologist/geneticist named Goody Pincus was introduced by Planned Parenthood's Margaret Sanger to Katherine McCormick, heir to the International

BACK TO THE BASICS:
(clockwise from upper left) The wondrous cornucopia of birth control available during the 70s; Chemical breakdowns of the male and female hormones; Our friend the genital louse, who produces three eggs a day and cements them to our pubic hair

"To the pill I can credit harmony, communication, fulfillment, satisfaction, happiness, stability, understanding, acceptance, relaxation, achievement, compatibility, courage, love, peace, and Christ."

— letter to the editor of *Time* magazine's Latin-American edition, early 1970s

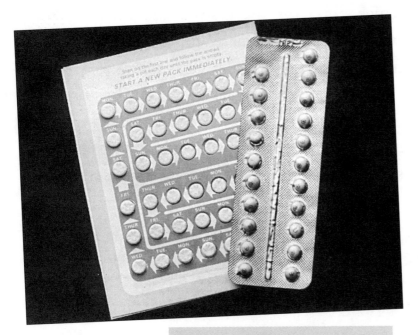

Birth control research occasionally veered into the ludicrous. One Cornell doctor tested prisoner volunteers with a diamine compound. The experiment was successful in making the inmates sterile, appeared not to affect libido, lowered their sperm count to zero, did so with no bad side effects, and when the drug was stopped, the men regained their virility. This was believed to be an incredible breakthrough until after several doctors, who were on the drug, happened to have a few drinks. The docs suddenly became red-eyed and their blood pressures dropped drastically, quickly marking the end of the research.

Female test subjects suffered through experiments with a strange form of IUD called the "Detectron," a magnetized intrauterine coil designed to register on a transistor radio-sized detector if the coil was in place.

Harvester fortune. For whatever reasons, McCormick believed that the sex drive in humans was so strong, it should be separated from reproductive functions, and Pincus's ongoing birth control research convinced her to help finance it, to the tune of $150,000 a year. Convinced a pill was conceivable that would use progesterone to block ovulation in humans, Pincus teamed up with Dr. John Rock, distinguished physician at Harvard Medical School. In 1956 the two conducted mass progesterone tests on childless women in Puerto Rico and Haiti, using a pill called Enovid, made by Searle. The Puerto Rico tests were very successful, and in 1957 the FDA authorized marketing of the Pill for treatment of miscarriages and menstrual disorders.

(Depending on which research you follow, Carl Djerassi may have been the first scientist to synthesize norethindrone, a progestational oral contraceptive, while working for Syntex S.A. in Mexico City in the early 1950s. Now a novelist and chemistry professor at Stanford, Djerassi boasts it was he who was the Father of the Pill, winning the National Medal of Science for his efforts. Unfortunately, his story isn't as good as the tractor-heir financier.)

In May 1960 the FDA approved Enovid as a contraceptive device; by the end of 1961, 408,000 American women were taking it. By the end of 1962 it was over a million, doubling by the following year, and we were off to the races.

People initially got the Pill through free clinics, or through prescriptions from dermatologists. One primary medical risk — thrombophlebitis, or clotting of the blood in the veins — was minor when compared to all that sexual freedom. Six million women were using the Pill by 1967. In 1972 the *New York Times* exclaimed that the Pill "changed the sexual and real estate habits of millions: motel chains were created to serve them."

Condoms had been around for years, but the 1960s marked a new dawn in sex without babies. In addition to the Pill, other methods of birth control emerged. The intrauterine device (IUD) appeared in 1965, and initially was thought to be the answer to the world's overpopulation. You didn't have to remember to take the damn pill every day! It could remain in the uterus for several years! The Dalkon Shield went on the market in 1970, and unfortunately, the handy string it sported was made of a material that allowed pathogens to race upwards right into the uterus and pelvic cavity. Any woman who used it and accidentally became pregnant was at risk for septic abortion and death. Thousands of liability lawsuits were filed against the product's owner, A.H. Robins Co., a Richmond, Virginia-based pharmaceutical company, and Robins eventually paid out millions of dollars in punitive damages.

(With such bad press, IUDs are chosen today by only about 2 percent of American women using birth control. The Pill — now available in a lower dose, and usually in combinations of estrogen and progestins — is used by 8 percent of women worldwide.)

The IUD was soon followed by a slough of other, less effective measures — foams, creams, jellies and suppositories — as well as some experimental methods that bordered on the work of Josef Mengele. Injecting a capsule filled with synthetic male hormone into an arm, leg or inside the groin, which continuously leaked out a dose, was thought to keep a man sterile for his entire life. Injections of liquid silicone were believed to harden and form a plug, blocking the sperm from passing through the vas deferens to the penis. Another procedure, the immunization of a man against his own sperm, hoped to produce enough antibodies to halt sperm production. Less radical methods have found their way into actual use, including the morning-after pill, and Depo Provera injections and implants.

The subject of abortion should be mentioned, if only for the 1973 Roe v. Wade decision to legalize it. Many young women used it as a method of birth control, often traveling across state lines to find a physician willing to perform the procedure. Faced with a boom in teen pregnancies, families of the young mothers often helped shop for abortion doctors, or in some cases, adopted their daughters' babies. While sex education classes increased awareness about getting pregnant, religious groups hustled their side of the debate via fear-mongering literature. By 1980 three out of ten pregnancies in the United States would end in abortion, and in recent years the argument has escalated to the public forefront with demonstrations, bombings of clinics and discussion of the number of weeks a fetus may grow before it is considered a person.

With all this rampant humping in the streets, venereal diseases were more prevalent than ever. In 1969, more than 600,000 cases of gonorrhea were reported, an increase of 130 percent over the reported cases of 1963, and by 1972, VD was thought to be the second most common infectious illness, after the cold. It wasn't just for freaks like Mozart anymore.

WHERE MEN HELD THE DOOR:
An idyllic women's VD clinic setting, where it's all smiles and no tears (top); One of the few appearances by a man in the women's sexuality handbook Our Bodies, Our Selves *(below)*

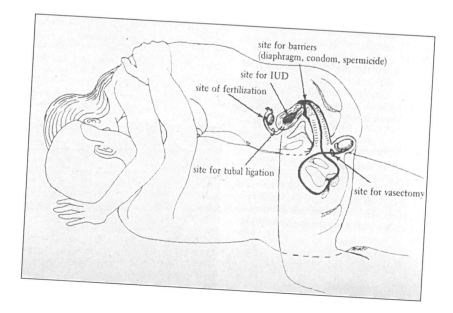

WRITING ON THE WALL:
*Award-winning 1973 VD advertising
campaign (above); Syphilis infection
chart which foreshadowed later AIDS
transmission documentation (below)*

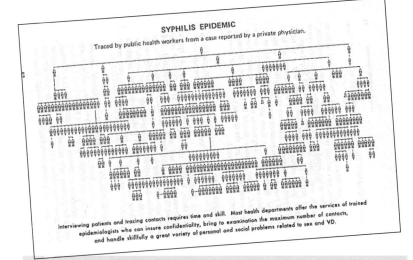

SYPHILIS EPIDEMIC

Traced by public health workers from a case reported by a private physician.

Interviewing patients and tracing contacts requires time and skill. Most health departments offer the services of trained epidemiologists who can insure confidentiality, bring to examination the maximum number of contacts, and handle skillfully a great variety of personal and social problems related to sex and VD.

Candidiasis aka "Thrush" (discharge, itching, odor)
Chancroid (sores)
Chlamydia aka "Swimming Pool Conjunctivitis" (discharge, red eyes)
Condyloma (warts)
Nonspecific Vaginitis (discharge, itching)
Cytomegalovirus (swollen glands)
Gonorrhea aka "The Clap" (discharge)
Granuloma inguinale (genital pimples)
Hepatitis B (general illness, jaundice)
Herpes simplex (sores, blisters)
Lymphogranuloma venereum (pimples, swollen organs)
Molluscum contagiousum (papules)
Mycoplasmal infection (possible discharge)
Pediculosis pubis aka "Crabs" (intense itching)
Scabies aka "Itch" (itching, welts)
Streptococcal "Group B" infection (no particular symptoms)
Syphilis (sores, rashes)
Trichomoniasis (discharge, itching)

— popular venereal diseases and their accompanying symptoms

New words entered our everyday vocabulary, like "Gonococcus," the germ that causes gonorrhea; "Ping-Pong VD," which referred to a disease that bounced back and forth between partners; "Rhagades," the scars left from congenital syphilis; or the dreaded "Pelvic Inflammatory Disease," a painful infection of the female internal sex organs. Syphilis became known as "the great imitator" because symptoms of its second stage were so confusing — sore throats, rashes on palms and falling out of hair in patches might last for up to three years.

The newest addition to the VD family was herpes, the mere mention of which was enough to put people off sex. It had no known cure, and could lie dormant in the body without the host even knowing he had it. Support groups were established to deal with its long-term implications.

But the specter of death from sex was unimaginable in this era — all of these health hazards were treatable. Public service announcements ran in the media, catchy jingles blasted forth from televisions and radios, clinics accelerated their treatments and people went on having sex. Pharmacies loaded up on ointments, and doctors doled out the penicillin. So many rock stars and their groupies were contracting crabs in Los Angeles that stores had to order extra stock of Topicide and the kerosene-based Cuprex. Some people waiting in line at free clinics for penicillin would recognize the people they had sex with the previous weekend. Women with herpes diligently held blowdryers aimed at their snatches, following doctors's orders to keep their pussies dry. For those too shy to visit a clinic, a youth-oriented VD info hotline called Operation Venus began in Philadelphia in 1970 and expanded in the next few years across the country, in affiliation with the United States Alliance for the Eradication of Venereal Disease.

A new breed of media personality emerged — the sex expert. One of the first was Dr. Hip Pocrates, alias San Francisco physician Eugene Schoenfeld. Beginning in 1967, Dr. Hip's weekly column originally appeared in the underground *Berkeley Barb*, offering advice and answering readers's often highly explicit questions on sex and drugs. The column was so popular that in 1969 the long-haired doc syndicated it to a dozen national mainstream newspapers, including the *San Francisco Chronicle*, the *Chicago Sun-Times* and the *Minneapolis Star-Tribune*. A collection of his columns was voted one of the country's ten best nonfiction books of 1969. After writing several books and spending years hosting a radio advice show (mentioned in the censorhip chapter), he now operates a private psychiatry practice in Sausalito, living on a houseboat and tooling around the Bay Area in a convertible Mercedes.

Darling of the late-night chat shows was San Diego psychiatrist David Reuben, author of *Everything You Always Wanted to Know About Sex*. Through his giggly media appearances and a nationally syndicated column, Reuben provided many with their first glimpse of sexual discussion. Unfortunately, his advice was often inaccurate and occasionally ludicrous, i.e. homosexuality was curable with psychiatry. Other advice-givers would follow, including a column aimed at adolescents called Ask Beth that was begun by the wife of a *Boston Globe* editor; a tiny, gruff woman named Dr. Ruth; and the Ask Isadora column by Isadora Alman. Since then, the sex advice field has exploded to take up space in hundreds of newspapers, magazines and Web sites.

Many doctors and anthropologists agree that human beings don't really need aphrodisiacs because our libidos already make us inherently one of the horniest creatures on Earth. Of course, that couldn't possibly be good enough for the smartest animal, and so for centuries we have hunted for the magic potions to unlock what's left of our inhibitions, whether it's bark from trees or chemicals dreamed up in a lab, and enhance our sexual experiences.

One of the more infamous and legendary aphrodisiacs is Spanish Fly, made from dried insects, and commonly sold in pill or powder form to be surreptitiously added to a beverage. Spanish Fly's active ingredient is a poison called cantharidin, extracted from the dried powder of a blister beetle. In small amounts, this causes an irritation of the kidneys and urinary tract, perceived as a sexually tingling sensation, which would seem to virtually guarantee the user an evening of raucous sex. Unfortunately, many have taken too much, and experienced abdominal pain, vomiting, shock and even death, symptoms that do not ordinarily occur in the vicinity of great sex.

This period of history was also a time of extreme pill culture — prescriptions for Valium, Ritalin and Dexadrine were considered a common part of the landscape, and if a pill calmed you down, helped you get to sleep or kept you awake, imagine what it could do for you in the sack. To steer the kids away from all the awful things their parents were up to, school

MICKY: ...All over. Face to feet. I about freaked out over that until, like all of a sudden, it went away, all by itself. So this time I told myself: "Cool it, Mick. Don't get a thing on. It'll pass. Keep this up and you'll get ulcers." But the pain hung in there all through the rest of the class period. Between classes, I made a dash to the restroom. I thought that might help. It didn't. Then just inside Mr. Johnson's general science lab, down I went in a heap on the floor. I blacked out.

MR. JOHNSON: I picked Micky up and put her on one of the lab tables. She was only out a minute, and when she came to, she turned on her side, drew her knees up and hugged herself, groaning and letting out deep sighs, the way you do when you're completely exhausted. I thought I'd better dismiss the rest of the class.

MS. PERISELLI: Something clicked in my mind. Maybe it was the VD posters I'd been putting on the bulletin boards that week. Could this young girl have pelvic inflammatory disease from a gonorrhea infection? This condition often shows up during or just after menstruation. And it was no secret that Micky had been dating many different boys, one after another, for almost a year.

DR. MILLER: Dr. Krouse and I saw Micky in the emergency room. Both of us suspected an inflamed appendix. Then Dr. Laney came in, and we asked his opinion. Maybe we should operate at once. Laney's reaction may have been biased by the fact that he works part-time as a volunteer clinician at a West Side hippie clinic. He thinks clap when nobody else does.

DR. LANEY: I got her on the examining table immediately, and inspected the vaginal vault. The area was red and inflamed, especially the cervix — the opening to the uterus, or womb,

you know. There was also considerable whitish discharge. I took samples with a swab and prepared some cultures.

Then I persuaded my colleagues, Drs. Krouse and Miller, that we did not, after all, have a case of appendicitis, but almost certainly an advanced case of gonorrhea.

BRIAN: I met Mick and we made out on the second date. I only had sex with her once....She told somebody at the health department about me. They didn't tell me it was her that told, but I figured it had to've been. At first I was really mad. But now I'm kind of glad she did, because that way I found out I had syph, too, and I hadn't got rid of the clap, either...It turned out it wasn't such a big thing after all at the clinic. They were OK. I'd go right straight there next time, if there is a next time. But I hope there won't be. I can do without that whole scene.

— anatomy of a teenage venereal disease, "Michelle's Story," *The VD Book* by Joseph A. Chiappa & Joseph J. Forish, 1976 boards stepped up their drug education programs. Junior high students sat in classrooms watching drug scare movies, with a camera weaving about an orgy, dirty hippies swallowing handfuls of pills from bowls and lolling around on beanbag furniture, with Ringo Starr on the soundtrack singing, "Yes, I get high with a little help from my friends."

Drugs gained reputations for their sexual enhancement properties. From pot and LSD to powdered rhino or reindeer horns, ginseng root or yohimbe, America's sex-obsessed were on a divine mission to elongate the orgasm and consider druggy sex as another key to

A Matter of Taste

Is anal-lingue (oh not to the exclusion of other "linguistic doings") not to be enjoyed under any conditions?

There are more bacteria present in the mouth than in any other body orifice. Assuming there are no diseases present such as gonorrhea, syphilis, typhoid, or infectious hepatitis, it just comes down to a matter of taste.

— from the sex advice columns of Dr. Hip Pocrates, *Berkeley Barb*

What's the one exception [to water, as the liquid of choice in a female douche]?

Coca-Cola. Long a favorite soft drink, it is, coincidentally, the best douche available. A Coke contains carbonic acid which kills the sperm and sugar which explodes the sperm cells. The carbonation forces it into the vagina under pressure and helps penetrate every tiny crevice of vaginal lining. It is inexpensive (ten cents per application), universally available, and comes in a disposable applicator.

How is it used?

After intercourse, the woman doesn't even have to get out of bed. She merely reaches over to the table, picks up a bottle of warm Coke, uncaps it, places her thumb over the top, shakes vigorously, and inserts the neck of the bottle into the vagina. A bowl under her hips to catch the overflow helps. Instantly she has an effervescent douche. The six-ounce bottle is just the right size for one application.

— from *Everything You Always Wanted to Know About Sex (But Were Afraid To Ask)* by David Reuben, 1972

Dear Dr. LaVey: I have a compulsion to take my clothes off whenever I have a few drinks. Would the Devil approve? Marge B., Jamaica, NY.

Dear Marge: It depends on what you look like!

— from "Letters from the Devil" newspaper column by Church of Satan high priest Anton LaVey, 1969

Woman is here for man, not man for woman. God speaks through man to woman. So a woman is a reflection of her father unless a stronger man can take over her ego completely...and showing where her strength comes from. Woman with ego is not a woman and will never find peace, and love will be just another word.

— from "Advice to the Lifelorn" by Charles Manson in the *L.A. Free Press*, 1970

enlightenment. 'Ludes were common decor on the floors of dance club restrooms. Cocaine in particular became regarded as a sex drug, the initial high after a few snorts giving one tremendous confidence of one's sexual energy. Coke fiends were finding they could maintain erection even after several orgasms, and many a party culminated the next morning with a roomful of naked, exhausted people picking coke boogers out of their nostrils. People eventually discovered that coke might have been great for guys, but it dried out women's lubrication glands, and an astonishing array of lubricants were distributed on the market, perhaps just for this purpose.

Tonic tea for genital health and strength plus increased sperm production (Afro-Dee-Tee)

Cubeb Leaves	1 oz.
Damiana	2 oz.
Ginseng	1 oz.
Gotu Kola	2 oz.
Fleeceflower Root	1 oz.
Saw Palmetto Berries	2 oz.
Calamus	1 oz.
Sarsaparilla	1 oz.
Buchu Leaves	2 oz.
Serpolet	2 oz.
False Unicorn Root	1 oz.

All ingredients are purchased in powdered form. To blend, combine herbs in a 2-pound coffee can, cap it, and shake vigorously for 5 minutes. 1 or 2 teaspons of this powder are placed in a cup and made into a slurry by moistening with hot water and stirring. More hot water is added to fill the cup. 1 to 3 cups of this tea may be taken daily over a period of 2 to 8 weeks for increasing sexual vigor, sperm production, and genital tone.

— **herbal blend aphrodesiac formula, from *Sex Drugs and Aphrodisiacs* by Adam Gottleib, 1973**

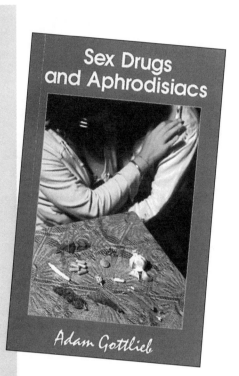

In a 1968 study published in the *American Journal of Psychiatry*, when a group of marijuana users was asked why they continued to smoke pot, 73 percent answered "to increase sexual satisfaction."

Let me put it this way, compared with sex under LSD, the way you've been making love — no matter how ecstatic the pleasure you think you get from it — is like making love to a department-store-window dummy....The three inevitable goals of the LSD session are to discover and make love with God, to discover and make love with yourself, and to discover and make love with a woman.

— **Timothy Leary in *Playboy*, claiming that LSD was the most powerful aphrodisiac ever discovered**

Amphetamines make you very wild and degenerate about sex, they really do...very creative and demented. It's like an eight-hour non-stop stretch of sniffing amyl nitrate. You have no idea. No idea! So wonderful, so inspired, so uninhibited...it's one of the truly inspired sex accessories there ever was. You became a sex addict — it's divine. That's the main reason so many of that crowd took it, beause that's what they all had in their minds ninety percent of the time: sex. Totally sex-oriented. Amphetamine was only fabulous for that. Everything else that it did for you was boring.

— **Bobby Andersen, describing the 1960s New York scene, *Edie***

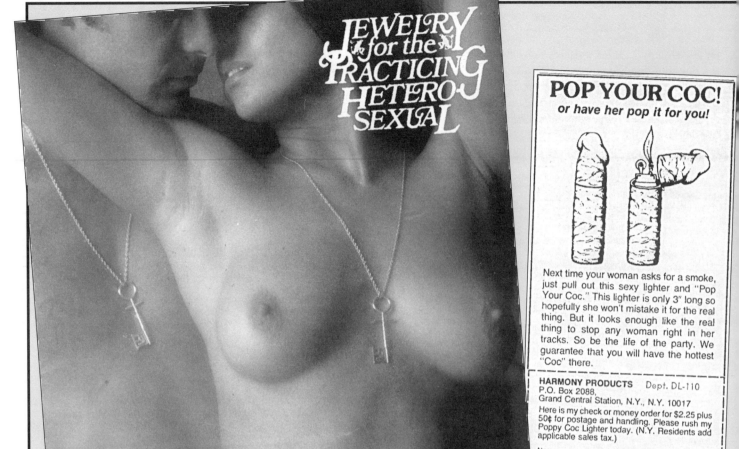
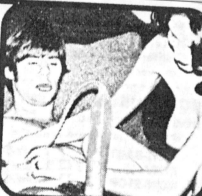

In the 1960s and 1970s, prurient titillation was easily available in movie theaters and massage parlors, but there was an even larger demographic to be served — the American who preferred the discreet pleasure of unpacking a sexual goodie in the privacy of the home. The business of such mail-order devices has been around for decades, but during this time period a torrent of what Frank Zappa has termed "lonely-person products" flooded the postal system, from vibrators and dildos to blow-up dolls, Ben-Wa Balls, Emotion Lotions, Sta-Erect Sheaths, Anal Love Beads, and LED wristwatches that illuminated not-so-subtle messages like "LET'S FUCK." We were obviously

Plain Brown Wrapper

evolving as a species. It was now a question of which direction were we headed, and how much was the public willing to spend.

The initial appeal, as it had been for decades, was marketed as one of innocence. Those tapered, cylindrical, battery-operated, portable vibrators were depicted as ideal for relieving stress in hard-to-reach shoulder areas. Those oils and ointments were said to be perfect for revitalizing the epidermis and increasing circulation. Inflatable dolls and X-rated board games were harmless gag gifts, a big hoot at

CHECK OR MONEY ORDER ONLY:
Examples of mail-order bliss delivered to your door

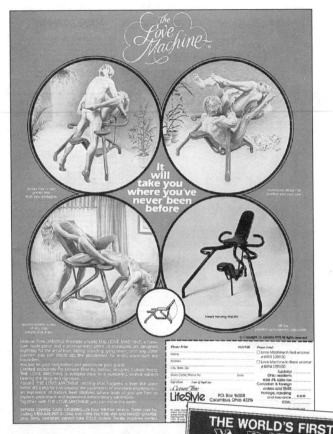

PORN PET ROCKS:

*More junk that would later clutter
up the garage*

office parties and wedding showers. But it would be difficult to disguise the intent of a plastic penis with an evil bulbous head at both ends.

The back pages of magazines grew cluttered with mail-order ads, pitching discreet brown-wrapper delivery of an ever-growing variety of dildos, vibrators and other marital aids. By the 1980s, it was estimated there were at least 5,000 different "sexual enhancers" on the U.S. market. Cargo planes and 18-wheelers crisscrossed the country, unloading crates of genital gizmos at any hamlet large enough to support an adult store. The sexual equivalent of Tupperware parties emerged, and living rooms across the country noisily discussed topics like butt plugs, penis pumps and the pros and cons of a battery-powered vibrating egg.

Those lucky enough to live near one of the hundreds of adult bookstores in suburban areas also had the advantage of being able to examine such contraptions before purchasing them. For the first time people saw what they were getting before mailing off a check. Curiosity seekers wandered the smut shelves, inspecting the often flimsy blow-up dolls, poking the phony pussies, wiggling the dildos. While couples nudged each other in amusement, teenagers were snickering at their private jokes, and lonely men quietly imagined what they would name the rubber vagina.

In tandem with the evolution of adult bookstores, the women's movement was reinventing the notion of sex, with books and magazines steadfastly preaching the advantages of having an orgasm for yourself. If bestsellers like *The Sensuous Woman* and all those issues of *Cosmo* were saying "Go out and get a vibrator," well by golly, it was time to go out and get a vibrator.

While vibrating devices were already marketed for therapeutic massage, dildos required an early '70s landmark case in Texas to be legally sold. According to a law that deals with disabled veterans, the U.S. government is required to replace any missing body part of a veteran with a prosthetic device. For instance, if an arm is missing, Uncle Sam is supposed to provide the veteran with an artificial arm. Attorneys found their star witness, a veteran who had been castrated in the war, and who was willing to testify he really needed his dildo. The court ruled that the devices had a legal reason to exist, and their sales should not be barred. Veterans, and many others, rejoiced.

But few ever stopped to wonder who was responsible for providing the country with such marvelous devices that brought everyone one step closer to sexual nirvana. Somebody had to sit down and determine how to manufacture and distribute these items. Some of these early entrepreneurs lived lavish lifestyles full of Rolls Royces and expensive vacations, others kept as quiet as possible, but in either case, there were many in the business who quickly became millionaires.

In 1965 ventriloquist Ted Marche toured the country — as he had done for years — with a trunk full of dummies, performing his schtick at trade shows and conventions. He wasn't Edgar Bergen, but he did okay. The following year must not have been as profitable. After a conversation with a friend who made prosthetic penises for a medical supply company, Marche saw the light at the end of the tunnel. He opened a small dildo factory in North Hollywood, and started pumping out the phony puds, selling them through mail-order ads and bookstores. At first he specialized only in black dildos, then began offering models in both black and white. Ten years later, as his ventriloquist dummies moldered in their cases, Marche Manufacturing was producing 350 different products, the reliable dildo still being the flagship of the fleet, selling 4,975,000 units annually. When *Time* magazine called Marche Manufacturing, gathering information for a 1976 cover story on porn, Marche's son Steven told the reporter, "These toys have saved more marriages than all the preachers in the world."

Another "Dildo King" began manufacturing sexual devices in the 1960s after firstly, realizing the vast market potential, and secondly, discovering a surplus of leftover rubber from his deep-sea diving company. He told reporters his name was Jim Holland, and boasted he was a former television announcer for the 1950s CBS program *Spacey Places*, starring Rock Darling. Holland's company was named Sinep, Inc. (penis spelled backwards), and by the early 1970s he owned bookstores, film labs and print shops, flying across the country with suitcases of cash to minimize the paper trail. Perhaps in homage to himself, Holland also produced an adult film about a door-to-door dildo salesman.

The largest supplier in the U.S. grew to be the Doc Johnson line of products, begun in the 1960s by Cleveland peep-show entrepeneur Reuben Sturman and his son David, and named so because it sounded both medical and vaguely Swedish. The company grew like an octopus into several brand names, both to make obscenity charges harder to file, and also to build a

BIRTH OF AN EMPIRE:

Original vibrator patent illustration (above); typical ad from Doc Johnson, King of the Vibrators (right)

**WOMAN'S BEST
FRIEND:**

*The first Good Vibrations
catalogue (top); the first
Eve's Garden catalogue
(middle); typical classified
ad for vibrators that
appealed to women
(above); early 20th-century
ad for stress-relieving
vibration device (right)*

labyrinth that would discourage attention from the IRS. By 1986 Doc Johnson reportedly grossed $1 million a day, and was estimated to account for 70 to 75 percent of the market, trucked or shipped by rail to thousands of retail outlets throughout the U.S. A longtime cleanliness freak, Sturman always appeared for court appearances wearing a surgical mask. After years of hiding money in banks from Switzerland to the Cayman Islands, Sturman was finally convicted in 1989 for back taxes totalling over $15 million.

In the 1960s, many women used electric scalp massagers and body massagers as vibrators. It was inevitable that a market of sex products would emerge that catered to a primarily female clientele. One of the earliest sex-toy outlets opened in New York in 1971 called the Pleasure Chest. Begun originally as a waterbed store, the two male founders added sex products to their stock — lotions, cock rings, handcuffs and dildos — and sales immediately took off. Business grew even more brisk when the owners actively pursued female customers by carpeting the store and installing pink lighting. But it was still run by guys.

The first feminist sex store opened in New York City following many conversations between Dell Williams and artist Betty Dodson, both of whom had been active in the women's lib movement, coordinating workshops and sexuality conferences for the National Organization of Women. In 1974 Williams opened Eve's Garden, a combination retail store and mail order-business for women to buy their sex goodies without that embarrassing trip to the sleazy porn shop. Women around the country were soon sending in their orders, or visiting the store in person to try out the latest and greatest off the rack. The company remains based in the same office building on West 57th Street, and continues to be a reliable resource for therapists, counselors and of course, women in the market for a vibrator. And Williams can still be found working behind the counter.

At roughly the same time, on the West Coast, Joani Blank was doing counseling and workshops, and in her spare time collecting vibrators with her husband. She had self-published a few books, including a guide to vibrators titled *Good Vibrations*. Realizing the popularity of Eve's Garden in New York, she opened her own Good Vibrations store in San Francisco in March of 1977, specializing in vibrators and massagers. Besides offering a then-whopping total of 30 different vibrators, the store also featured a Vibrator Museum of odd, antiquated contraptions from the turn of the century. Blank produced a catalog of vibrators that could be ordered by mail, and hand-lettered all the calligraphy herself. The shop has expanded to include books and videos, and Blank has moved on to other projects, but Good Vibrations is still women-owned and -operated.

Dildos and vibrators would seem almost Vatican-approved when compared to the host of other, stranger products that were emerging on the sexual landscape and entering the vocabulary. Inflatable blow-up dolls, also known as "fornicatory dolls," frequently appeared as gag comic props in 1960s films and TV shows like *Love, American Style*. Their stiff arms and legs and silly O-shaped mouth were anything but erotic, and virtually guaranteed a laugh when shown on-camera. In fact, such pneumatic females had been around for centuries. The modern love doll could be attributed to post-war Germany, where ingenuity never sleeps. In the late 40s and early 50s, German manufacturers began exporting an inflatable woman called a *Seemannsbraut* ("Sailor's Bride"), which sold for $80 (vaginal opening only) to $100 (both vagina and anus). The idea was quickly stolen by companies in the U.S. and Hong Kong, and cheap imitations continue to flood the market.

Other sexual knick-knacks appeared, from the aforementioned racy wristwatches to jewelry made from mink or raccoon penises and frisky board games like Get Loose. Mail-order customers could purchase satin sheets, slutty lingerie, a belt buckle shaped like the human buttocks, spearmint-flavored Body Candy or a pot bong shaped as a pair of breasts. T-shirt and poster distributors did booming business, the Roach decal company even claiming it sold "shirts for swingers." The Suck-U-Tron phony vagina was complemented by a pussy tightener called Tighten Up. In 1971, a hairdresser named Kenneth released Cleavage Delineator, Bosom Highlighter and Tip-Blush — make-up for breasts that came packaged together in a bright pink box.

The race for marketing dominance soon found another cash cow, in the form of odor protection.

"The pill is just not enough," proclaimed a 1969 issue of *Women's Wear Daily*, bible of the fashion world. "It might give the American girl sexual freedom, but getting the man is still an art. What could be more artful than a sweet-smelling vagina?"

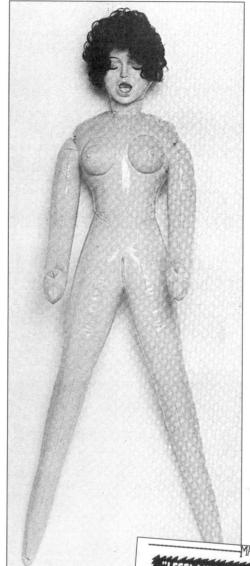

FOLDS FOR EASY TRAVEL:

Variations on a blow-up doll theme

Aunique gift for your bachelor friend or that friend that has everything. A different fun item to dress up your office and become the conversation piece of your clients. Be the talk of the neighborhood with this PLAY-GIRL at poolside (she even floats). Sitting on the seat beside you in your car she makes a delightful traveling companion — no back seat driving. Be the scandal of the season with this other woman in your life — keep the wife on her toes. Set by a window at home she will be the "somebody at home" when burglars are casing the neighborhood. Give your daughter a gift of the biggest doll in town. She'll be delighted. What better status symbol could you find at the price.

NOTICE TO MARRIED MEN: SORRY — NO TRADE-INS

— advertising copy for late-60s mail order blow-up doll named Gretchen ($9.95; $16.95 for deluxe model which included wig, bikini and "interesting" accessories)

CUT TO THE CHASE:

Sometimes it's all about tits and ass

THE SENSUOUS SIGNAL

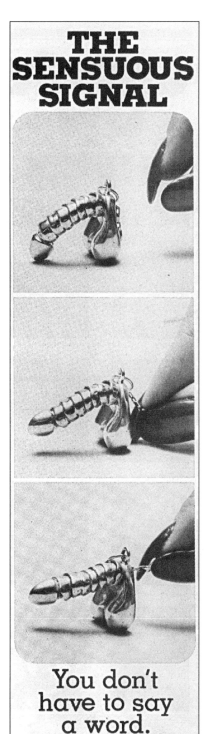

You don't have to say a word.

The most original and striking piece of erotic jewelry ever designed. Pull the tiny chain on the back, and the scalloped shaft stirs slowly to life. In solid gold (GWSG) $125.00. Also available in sterling silver (GWSS) $49.95. Plus $2.00 postage and handling per item. Send check or money order or charge it to your BankAmericard. (Please give charge number, expiration date and your signature.) Mail to: **Evelyn Rainbird, Ltd., Box 548, FDR Station, New York, N.Y. 10022.** New York residents add 8% sales tax.

FOR THE MAN WHO HAS EVERYTHING AND NO PLACE TO PUT IT!

The versatile Banana Warmer. One size fits all. It holds and protects anything from a banana and two plums to the family jewels.

Use it as a pipe and tobacco pouch or use your imagination. Keep it in your drawers and your forbidden fruit can come in from the cold!

Penthouse Products Dept. 8021274PH
909 Third Ave. New York, N.Y. 10022

Sock it to me! Send me _____ Banana Warmer(s) at $4.95 each. I enclose my check □ money order □
for $ _____.

Dicky Raccoon Lucky Charms

DICKY RACCOON ™
ALWAYS READY

Woodsmen have known for ages that the luckiest animal alive is the male raccoon (or the female, depending on one's point of view). Today you can share the raccoon's secret and his good fortune. As he matures, his genital organ turns to bone, making him a round-the-clock lover until the day he dies (and he gets bigger and better with age). We have duplicated his "lucky bone" for you in 5 attractive styles: pendant/charm, key ring, tietac, brooch and the original "lucky bone". While we can only guarantee that these amazing conversation pieces are beautifully handcrafted faithful reproductions of the real article, satisfied customers swear that if you rub the "lucky bone" frequently you (or your partner) may acquire the raccoon's special gift.
Distributor/wholesale info on request. No C.O.D.'s.
C 1974 - S.L. Stapleton

The ultimate conversation piece now can be yours! One of nature's most prolific creations, the mink, is endowed with a perpetual boner enabling him to sustain copulation up to three hours. Hence, the often heard phrase, "Screws like a mink!" We've used the actual penile bone from a mink and fashioned a great looking pendant. Express YOUR unspoken desires to that special someone. The wearing of this fine jewelry will always be a reminder of intimacies shared.

MINK PHALLUS

Shown Actual Size. (Chain NOT included)

BACK TO THE PANTS:
Nothing more entertaining than the penis

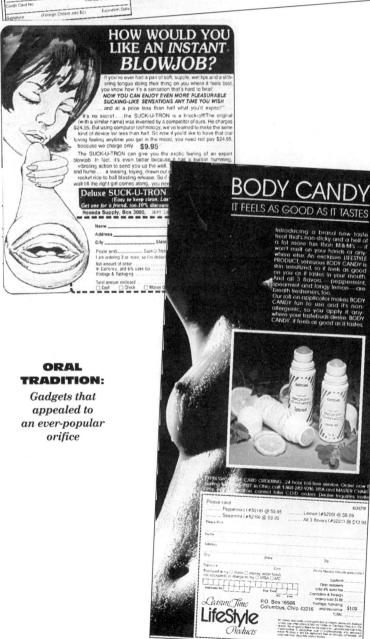

**ORAL
TRADITION:**

*Gadgets that
appealed to
an ever-popular
orifice*

The artful product known as feminine deodorant spray (FDS) debuted in 1966, and tests supposedly proved it reduced vaginal odor up to 78 percent better than soap and water. Within a year there were over 40 competitors, including Pristeen, Vespré, Naturally Feminin, Demure, and Feminique. But if vaginas had odors, so did scrotums. The industry quite naturally led to male genital deodorants, like Pub's Below the Belt, and Man's Other Deodorant from Bill Blass, who admitted, "If there's a part of the human body to exploit, you might as well get into it." Revlon's ad copy for Braggi Genital Deodorant for Men boasted: "This will become your second deodorant. It is the first genital spray." The modern descendants of this sexual mail-order boom have consolidated their resources, and their mail-order ads now primarily ask readers to send away for a catalog of products. Not only is a display ad for a catalog more discreet than artwork depicting the Suck-U-Tron, it allows the company to advertise their entire warehouse at once. Eve's Garden and Good Vibrations continue their mail-order divisions, and newer companies like the San Francisco-based Xandria advertise in many major publications. Also operating from San Francisco is DechTar Direct, a nine-year-old company whose full-page "Intimate Treasures" ads run in over 60 national magazines, including *Cosmopolitan, American Woman, Playboy* and *Penthouse*, pitching sex catalogs from over 300 companies. A recent IPO investment package for DechTar proclaims it the largest adult mail-order advertising company in the business.

Since its boom years of the '60s, the industry of sex devices has progressed to a level some would call exorbitant, where vibrators are now manufactured in electric neon colors, or sculpted in the shapes of sleek porpoises and wiggling woodland creatures. Dildos are available that are carefully molded from plaster casts of porn stars' genitalia. What was said about them twenty years ago still applies today: such apparatus is either still saving marriages, entertaining birthday parties or providing temporary relief for lonely people.

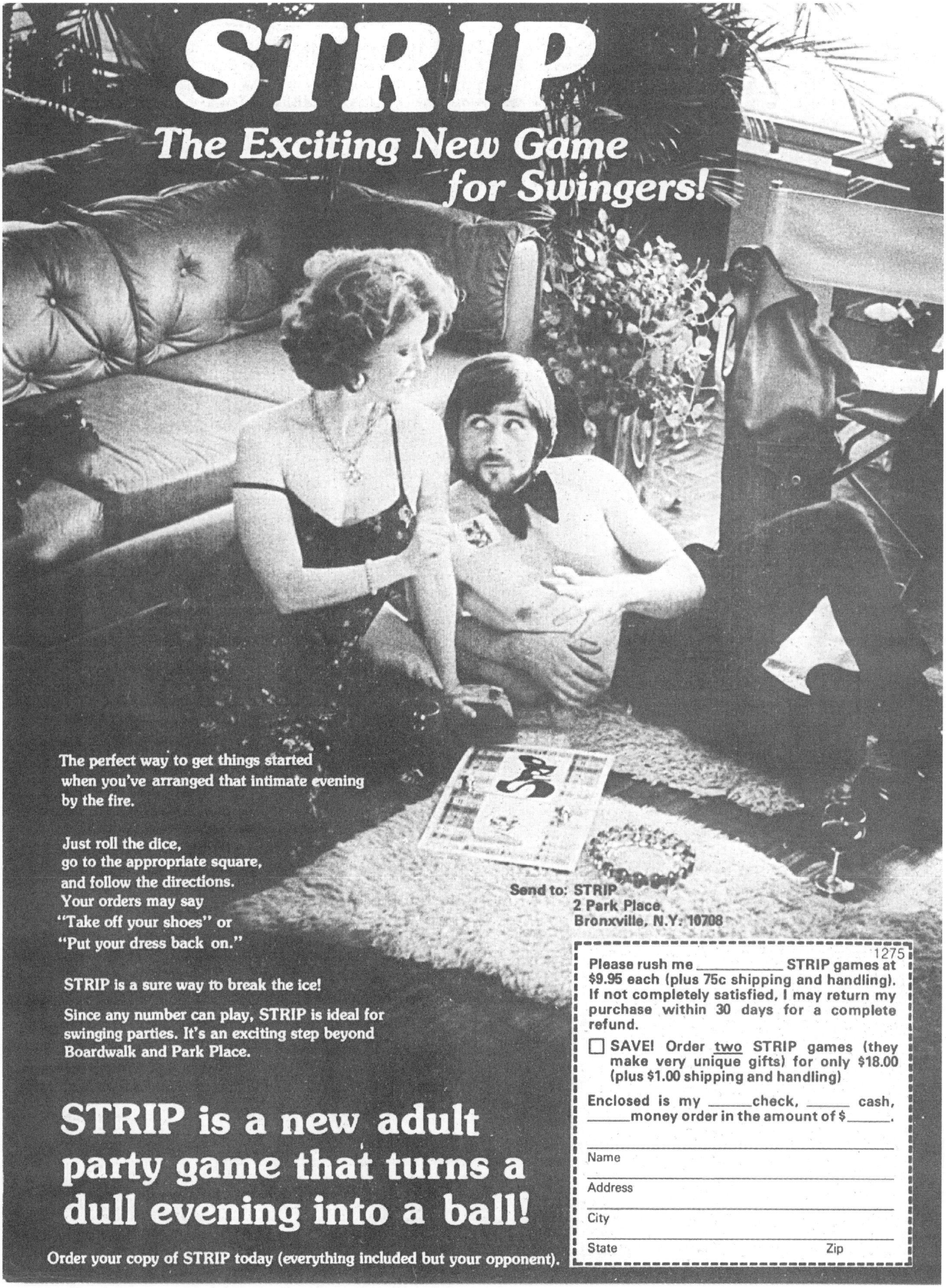
STRIP
The Exciting New Game for Swingers!
The perfect way to get things started when you've arranged that intimate evening by the fire.
Just roll the dice, go to the appropriate square, and follow the directions. Your orders may say "Take off your shoes" or "Put your dress back on."
STRIP is a sure way to break the ice!
Since any number can play, STRIP is ideal for swinging parties. It's an exciting step beyond Boardwalk and Park Place.
STRIP is a new adult party game that turns a dull evening into a ball!
Order your copy of STRIP today (everything included but your opponent).
Send to: STRIP 2 Park Place Bronxville, N.Y. 10708
1275
Please rush me ________ STRIP games at $9.95 each (plus 75c shipping and handling). If not completely satisfied, I may return my purchase within 30 days for a complete refund.
☐ SAVE! Order two STRIP games (they make very unique gifts) for only $18.00 (plus $1.00 shipping and handling)
Enclosed is my _____check, _____ cash, _____money order in the amount of $_____.
Name
Address
City
State
Zip

REMEMBER WHEN AIR WAS
CLEAN AND SEX WAS DIRT

The repressive '50s were behind us, and along with them, any shred of sexual hesitation. Americans just didn't care anymore. We were on a mission to the furthest outposts of sexual excess. Variety and quantity were the goals. If you went to a party or concert, you expected to go home with somebody. Wide lapels jostled for space at fern bars with tube tops, low-cut disco dresses shook their best parts on the dance floors, and at the end of the rainbow was another line of coke and a hot tub. Couples bored with their marriages experimented with swinger parties and orgies. Families walked around the house nude. People did it everywhere, from love hotels to the back of the van and city

Lust for Life

parks — right there in the open, by god! Sex Addicts Anonymous didn't exist, because nobody had yet gone on a binge. Now was the time.

Marriage was seen as a convenience, rather than an obligation. For instance, when political activist Michael Lerner staged his wedding outdoors, in San Francisco's Golden Gate Park, surrounded by the upper echelon of anti-war lefty intellectual society, he arranged for the top of his matrimonial cake to display the words "Smash Monogamy."

While the kids were mocking tradition, the older generation were growing restless at how they missed out on all the fun, and dialed the divorce attorneys. Some statistics cited over half of all marriages were splitting up, the highest percentage

AMERICA CUTS LOOSE:
Revealing new fashions, and the men who enjoyed them (top); Typical bumper sticker from the 60s (middle); Who needed to leave the house to party? (bottom)

Strangely, adulterous triangles instigated by female aggressors are often more apt to burst into violence than those started by men. The reason is that the man is generally only interested in satisfying his desires when he lets his roving eye fall on a woman. All too frequently women who deliberately entice a man into adultery have

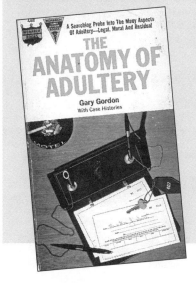

other motives than simple sex. Sometimes these are quite sinister.

One of the most notorious cases of this kind ended in the sensational Snyder-Gray trial, a crime which, in the words of a reporter, "probably made many a peaceful, home-loving Long Islander of the Albert Snyder type shiver in his pajamas as he prepares for bed."

The triangle involved a suburban dweller named Albert Snyder, his pretty blonde wife Ruth, and a corset salesman named Judd Gray.

One morning Snyder was found beaten to death in his bed. His wife and Judd Gray were charged with the murder. What developed afterward caused a wag with a morbid sense of humor to observe that the marriage vow should be changed to read, "Love, honor, cherish — and be wary!"

— *The Anatomy of Adultery* by Gary Gordon, 1964

In many households there are, in fact, few points of friction between partners, outside the bedroom. The couple is mentally and emotionally attuned to one another. Neither partner seeks to dominate or dictate to their spouse. There is mutual trust; life is lived on a down to earth plane and the couple seems able to overcome those problems presented by any marriage. Unfortunately, although there is a considerable spirit of give and take, sympathy for the other's point of view and a general meeting of the minds on most issues, something is lacking and this ingredient is what we refer to as the Tyranny of Sex.

For although in all its other aspects their married life may be exemplary, if it suffers from sexual incompatibility, it is bound to fail. Should its shortcomings be evident in arguments over money, in-laws, the husband's job, or children, these differences may be resolved. No one of them will, by them

selves, cause the marriage to founder. But if the marriage should be sexually incompatible, it hasn't a chance.

— *The Dangerous Sex — Adultery* by L. Reade Kinneman, 1964

in history. Every time you opened a newspaper, another famous person was splitsville — governor Rockefeller, Howard Hughes, Johnny Carson, Richard Burton, Elizabeth Taylor, Frank Sinatra and those perennial Black Widows, the Gabor sisters. The early '60s guilt trip was done and gone. Screw the kids — they're old enough to feed themselves. Time to take a young lover and dance away your best years. Some even swapped entire families, as in the case of New York Yankees pitchers Mike Kekich and Fritz Peterson, in 1973. One wife told reporters it was "the most unique trade in baseball history."

The randy mood of the oldsters could be attributed in part to the growing population of older men who had chucked their first wives, and were either shacking up with their secretaries or roaming the nightlife in new toupees, trying to sow what was left of the wild oats.

The climbing divorce rate made for many single-parent households and unsupervised children, but some people were also making a fortune off it. Driving a Rolls Royce around Beverly Hills in those days was Marvin Mitchelson, the nation's premier divorce attorney. An unabashed publicity hound, Mitchelson flaunted the flashy attorney lifestyle to the hilt — custom suits from Paris, a Jacuzzi in his office and naked ladies on the wallpaper. His clientele was almost exclusively female, the jilted wives and girlfriends of celebrities and other high rollers. His reputation for obtaining large settlements kept them coming at a steady pace, a general-practitioner clinic for doomed relationships, from divorces and palimony to property settlements, paternity actions and child custody. His successful 1976 palimony suit representing Michelle Triola against Lee Marvin established a new precedent for unmarried couples, and snagged worldwide headlines.

Young people were always on top of the latest fashions, and after so many marriages ending up in messy divorces, we now had an entire country of singles wanting to strut their new freedom and look their best. A logical starting point for those on a limited income was the Frederick's mail-order catalog. During World War II, Frederick N. Mellinger served in the Army, and like most G.I.'s found himself daydreaming of beautiful girls. After his discharge, Mellinger vowed to do something about it, to offer lingerie that would help all women feel more beautiful. He launched the Frederick's lingerie mail-order company in 1947, followed in 1952 by his first retail store, located in Hollywood. The company has remained extremely popular throughout the decades, modifying its line of lingerie to reflect the changing tastes. In the '60s, Frederick's offered hippie clothing, and when disco became the rage, his fashions adapted for the dance floor. The low-budget fabrics and prices meant that although a woman might work for minimum wage, she could still sock away a bit of cash to afford some nice crotchless panties.

Sexy fashions really took off in 1964, when designer Rudi Gernreich introduced the topless swimsuit. It didn't quite catch on, but the following year, British Mod designer Mary Quant introduced the mini-skirt in store windows of New York, and the act of a woman bending over a file cabinet at the office took on a new dimension altogether. The ultimate mid-'60s experimental hip clothing shop of the time was Manhattan's Paraphernalia, run by Paul Young. One Paraphernalia designer named Diana Dew made up electric dresses in which the crotch or breasts would suddenly light up with a flash. Young's media savvy found him predicting to reporters that in the future, people would be able to create their own second skins by spraying liquid fiber onto a mannequin of themselves, and then peeling it off to wear.

The mini-skirt led to the micro-skirt, also referred to as a "pussy-pelmet," which led to the supposedly more mature midi-skirt. Eventually the subject of skirt length ended up in an angry showdown in May of 1970, when major U.S. clothing designers presented their fall/winter collections in New York. As the season's midi-skirts were being unveiled in showrooms high above Seventh Avenue, down below on the streets marched members of the organization GAMS (Girls/Guys Against More Skirt), wearing mini-skirts and carrying signs reading "Keep the Mini on the Market." Meanwhile, the group FADD (Fight Against Dictating Designers) threatened to boycott all department stores that stocked only midi-skirts for fall. Tempers ran high, and fashion was forced to compromise between the factions by offering a style of shorts that announced to the world: "Here it is — come and get it!"

Hot pants first appeared as street fashion in London and Paris in 1970, and when a January 1971 issue of *Women's Wear Daily* coined the term "hot pants," America fell in love. Versions appeared in every exotic material imaginable — calfskin, velvet, snakeskin, silk, satin, mink or monkey fur. Others were decorated with the image of a burning can of Sterno on the butt.

VEE-DEEP
He'll never forget you when he sees you in this acetate jersey with French cuffed, long slim sleeves. The neckline topped with a semi-shirt collar above a deep, deep "V"!

JUNGLE TOP
Awakens his primitive instincts in a clingy, curvy leopard print top. V-neck styling, and long sleeves. Wear it with our leopard skirt for greatest effect.

CALL-OF-THE-WILD
Here's leopard...to bring out the tiger in him! Turtle-neck playsuit has a zipper front, so you can wear it open or closed.

FEMALE ANIMAL
Going on a hunt? Wear a leopard print skirt...and maybe he'll track you down first.

JUNGLE JUMPER
G-r-owl, pussycat, and catch yourself a tiger! You'll be fit to pounce in this leopard print bonded acetate jersey that fits like your second pelt.

THE LEAST ONE
Run-around from morning till night! The least is the most in this hug-me tank shift. Sleeveless! Pullover! And-how scoop necked!

— from 1960s Frederick's of Hollywood brochure

Dr. Zog's Sex Wax
Good & Plenty
Available
Community Chest
Foxy Lady
Plumbers Do It With Their Plungers
I Can't Believe I Ate the Whole Thing
Dangerous Curves

— typical slogans from personalized T-shirts in the 1960s and 1970s

Eenie, Meeni, Minie, Mo — That's As Far As You Can Go!

— slogan on young girls' panties in early 1970s, with the letter O represented by a see-through hole

**SHOES AND SHiRTS AT
THE DOOR:**
*A famous poster (photo by
Charles Gatewood) of a
mid-'60s house party in
Manhattan's Lower East Side,
where nudity was required*

One model called "Jane Pants" was made of
raggedy chamois. Italian designer Valentino
debuted an all-sequin version in Rome. Black
tuxedo versions, with satin stripes down the
sides, were popular at gallery openings and for-
mal galas. Although cold in the wintertime, the
so-called "tarty look" proved perfect for dancing,
and models and actresses appeared in paparazzi
shots flashing acres of legs. Marlo Thomas was
a big fan, as was Ursula Andress, who favored
the bronze velvet variety. While Raquel Welch
chose a pair made of white matte jersey, Jackie
O. opted for Halston's version for "yacht wear."
In September 1971, the Miss America pageant
changed its rules and reluctantly allowed hot
pants to be worn in the talent competition.
James Brown was so taken with the trend he
recorded a hit single called "Hot Pants."

The concept of bras took on new meaning, as most women were either burning them or tossing them in the closet, not to be seen again for 15 years. Tight-fitting dresses hung off the shoulder, slit up completely to the waist. See-through chiffon blouses fought for attention with tube tops, which could be worn dressy or to cultivate that white-trash look. If underwear was worn at all, it was either edible and flavored or consisted of vintage slips and dressing gowns from used-clothing shops. A Greenwich Village flower shop owner named Gonzalo Chavez capitalized on the braless rage by making clothing out of beverage pop tops, and many women wore his vests without anything underneath. Chavez even changed his name to Pop-Top Terp, and told one reporter that a topless dancer who had worn a vest onstage managed to snag her right nipple in one of the rings.

Both men and women started wearing ultra-tight hip-hugger jeans and colorful platform shoes with plastic PVC soles. Guys in particular drifted toward the sex-soaked combination of printed polyester shirts and flat-fronted Haggar slacks, which, when accentuated by a Zodiac medallion or gold-plated coke spoon, spelled Mr. Wonderful to many a woman out on the town. Tight-fitting designer jeans debuted in 1977, the brainstorm of two New York garment makers called the Nakash Brothers. They chose the name Jordache because it sounded elegant and French. Rich women immediately fell for the fancy designer label, and in two years, Jordache had over 30 competitors in the designer-jean market.

America was quickly losing control of its fashion industry. All these exposed nipples and tight crotches were taking the country in an unhealthy direction. Elementary, middle and high schools across the country were forced to adopt stricter dress codes to keep up with the increasingly revealing fashions. Many kids were sent home to change clothing into something that wouldn't distract their fellow students, or get them raped in the parking lot.

In conjunction with clothing, an affinity for sensual, tactile materials was growing. Shag carpets were required floor coverings for the sensuously inclined who liked to walk around barefoot. Americans no longer required a bed to complete their amorous adventures, and people proudly displayed their rug burns from recent encounters. A 1967 Sears catalog even gushed about its shag rugs, "The more it's mussed up, the better it looks!" Fake fur fabrics appeared — made from Orlon, Dynel, acrylic and other

Vice Officer Arthur Johnson: It's only natural that Los Angeles is plagued with many more incidents of car sex than most other cities, because Los Angeles is a car society...Many young people are forced to have sex in their cars; they have no other place to experiment. They can't do it at home with their parents around; they can't afford to go to motels every week; and it's too dangerous to have sexual relations at the beach or in deserted parks.

Lieutenant Ted Hastings: Not only do young people get busted for engaging in sexual activities in their cars. Every week, my men arrest several adults for copulating in automobiles. Many of the adults are worse than the kids. They have homes to use for lovemaking purposes, but they get their kicks by doing it in their cars. They all need psychiatric help.

Sexologist James Collins: Just because a man and a woman enjoy being naked and together outside of their houses or apartments doesn't mean that they are sick and in need of medical help. Sex and nudity are beautiful...on a bed, at the beach, in a car...I'm not advocating car sex. All I'm saying is that it's perfectly normal for a man and woman to crave sex while they are together in a car. A kiss on the cheek, a touch of the breasts, a feel of the penis, and then the magic begins. If it takes place in a car, and no one is hurt or offended, then I say that it should be legal.

— from a crime prevention seminar in San Francisco, 1977

BIRTH OF THE BUBBLES:
*Prostitution activist Margo St. James flashing a wedding reception in
Northern California's Muir Woods (above), as the first hot tub in
America percolated in the trees to the right, beyond the spectators;
Standard designs soon emerged (below)*

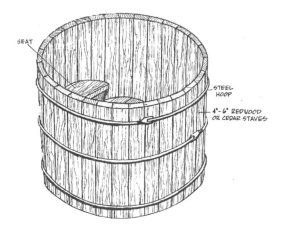

SEAT

STEEL
HOOP

4"- 6" REDWOOD
OR CEDAR STAVES

synthetic fibers — and were available in
simulated white angora, animal-print patterns,
polkadots and Day-Glo colors advertised as
"lustrous" and "iridescent." Such phony fur
found its way onto bedspreads, boudoir walls
and ceilings and the interiors of the nation's
newest bedroom-on-wheels, the customized van.

Originally produced in the mid-'60s as
commercial utility vehicles for delivery,
Americans wasted no time in converting vans
for immoral uses. The inexpensive Volkswagen
Microbus seemed favored by the hippie culture
for its ease of maintenance, and Detroit's finest
from Chevy, Dodge and Ford tended to attract
the California surfers. Highways filled up with
tricked-out vans, sporting custom pinstriped
paint jobs, sun roofs and bubble windows. A
typical chick-magnet model might have included
an airbrushed scene on the outer panels of a
vibrant sunset, or a surfer riding a wave. Inside

could be found a waterbed, or to save on mileage, a foam mattress covered with an Indian blanket purchased at Pier One Imports. Hidden in the fake fur were the requisite Jensen triaxial speakers, wired up to an eight-track stereo playing *Who's Next* or *Led Zeppelin III* in perpetuity. Candles and incense burned on top of the miniature refrigerator, and outside on the bumper, a sticker announced to the world: "If This Van's A-Rockin' Don't Come A-Knockin'." The rush to register a sexually suggestive vanity license plate, such as PUTZ or 4NICK8, drove the state of California to hire specialists who were experts in dirty words in all languages.

While these love lorries ripped up and down the interstate, blasting "Jesus Is Just Alright With Me" by the Doobie Brothers, occasionally a few of them could be found parked at a new type of travelers' accommodations. Although "hot-sheet hotels" had been around for years, offering hourly rates for quickie trysts, the Golden Age of Hetero saw the dawn of the unabashed sex-pad-for-rent. Hotel owners enticed customers with garish room themes, mirrored ceilings and closed-circuit televisions that played pornography. Signs advertised with the silhouette of a young woman putting a finger to her lips in a gesture of secrecy. Beginning in the late '60s, such hotels began featuring waterbeds and hot tubs.

The most believable origin of the hot tub traces back to a San Francisco architect named Roger Somers, who modified a Japanese-style redwood water tub with a heater, pump and filter, and installed it in an open area of Muir Woods, surrounded by trees. Guests were agog at the new device, including Dizzy Gillespie and Zen Buddhist Alan Watts, who was already a big fan of Japanese baths. Watts supposedly had a tub made and installed in his garden, and talked about it to whomever he met. The craze took off from there, and soon California was deafened by the sounds of old-growth redwoods falling to keep up with the demand. And of course, hot tub owners soon realized you had to occasionally clean out the filters, which would become clogged with pubic hair and other human mange.

The waterbed also had its beginnings in the San Francisco area. A student named Charlie Hall needed a final project for a design class at San Francisco State University, and conjured up the idea of a mattress filled with fluid. The first waterbed was born on the kitchen floor of his apartment in 1968, and was filled with cooking starch. His project cost $750, and he received an

The Hot Tub Experience
Enjoy it daily $1499

Already an essential of the good life for Californians, hot tubbing is fast going national. For the simple reason that it exactly fits the spirit of our time. It's healthy, it's natural. It's soothing and sexy. It can be sociable or solitary — however you wish it. And as a practical matter, hot tubs are both ecologically sensible and an excellent investment.

Our brochure will tell you why hot tubbing is becoming the new American experience for all. Anyone can enjoy the benefits, thanks to the low cost of our new do-it-yourself package. You can build one of our tubs into a deck (as shown above), or it may be placed freestanding in the garden or patio. Just one weekend can transform your favorite spot into a sensuous new environment.

We deliver a complete hot tub spa package anywhere in the U.S. for only $1499 plus freight. Comes to your door pre-cut, pre-plumbed, complete. Includes 4' solid redwood tub, pump, filter, heater, hydro-massage spa jets, and accessories. All you need are household tools and a friend — it's that simple!

We offer several tub sizes, solar heaters and other exciting options. Get the entire story from the world's leading hot tub maker.

Call or write today for our free 16-page color brochure, or enclose $1, and we'll also send the photo-story book, *California Hot Tubbing* (Uniplan Publishing, reg. $2.95).

California Cooperage
P.O. Box E San Luis Obispo, CA 93406
(805) 544-9300

☐ Enclosed is $1. Rush me the "California Hot Tubbing" book and your literature, via First Class Mail.
☐ Just send me your free literature, via Third Class Mail.

Name _____
Address _____
City _____
State _____ Zip _____
                                              100

California Cooperage

Definitely it's connected with sex. I don't know any young people who haven't made it in the bath. That's what it's for. You buy a bottle of champagne and you invite a chick to take a bath with you and the result is inevitable. The thing is, it's all so natural. When the heat and the champagne get to you, there aren't any barriers anymore, just being together. Even at parties people you wouldn't expect to have it in them will suddenly get all touchy, and I don't mean nervous. Of course, if you have twelve or fifteen people in a five-foot tub, it's pretty hard not to touch, and so everybody tends to touch everybody else. It's not an orgy, just a lack of inhibitions. You've got to be cool about it. A hot tub isn't the sort of place you can wear a bathing suit. Of course, some of the oldies do if they're using it for their rheumatism, and good luck to them, but I believe the mainstream of the movement is young people finding a new way to swing.

— *Sensual Water: A Celebration of Bathing* by Bernard Barber, 1978

INNERSPACE   the comfort people

The Waterbed and You

You will find the Innerspace waterbed is like nothing you've ever slept on before. It's like drifting off to sleep in the warm waters of the South Pacific. Think about it. We're quite serious... The Innerspace waterbed is better than a conventional bed simply because it conforms exactly to your shape and supports your entire body. There are no pressure points and subsequently you awake refreshed and completely relaxed in the morning. And isn't that what sleep should really be like.

A for his efforts. Hall officially patented his design and water heating system in 1971, after which he opened a company in Sausalito called Innerspace Designs, and expanded it into a chain of waterbed stores up and down the coast of California. Innerspace frames were constructed of redwood, and the high-end price tag attracted celebrity clients like the Smothers Brothers and Jefferson Airplane. A radio interviewer once asked Hall about the sexual benefits of the waterbed. Hall answered that the beds were great for sleeping, but that he felt sex was more comfortable on the floor. One of his retailers called him up, enraged, and begged him never to say that again to the media — sex was the reason most people were buying them.

Cheaper imitations of Hall's design soon appeared, their lower prices appealing to a younger crowd: "Two things are better on a waterbed," boasted ads for Aquarius Products. "One of them is sleep." Other patents were given to motion-deterring designs, which incorporated a baffle inside the mattress. In the '70s, the California legislature was forced to lay down some general rules, because so many beds were leaking and collapsing the ceilings of basement apartments.

With all the accouterments in place, hormones raged unchecked across the national landscape. People hung their bare asses out of car windows, or held up signs demanding "Show us your tits!" The idea of streaking hit its peak with a flasher at the Academy Awards, and a fat hairy guy with a cocktail in his hand, cigar in his mouth, dashing across the stage behind Johnny Carson during his opening monologue. Ray Stevens' hit song "The Streak" brought the idea to the Heartland, and soon high school kids were daring each other to run nude through school assemblies.

Having sex before marriage was not only expected, but seemed oddly mandatory. Young couples got it on wherever and whenever the mood struck them, from public parks to drive-ins, political protests, biker rallies house parties, and concerts. It was common to bring a date to an event and leave with someone else. College campuses offered endless opportunities to continue the nation's mad experiment in sex. Wild parties ensued in fraternities, dormitories, condos — even the lounges of student union buildings were prime rutting locations. One UC Berkeley comparative lit professor was fired for holding classes off-campus that turned into orgies.

But the majority of action fostered in

America's burgeoning singles bars, where everyone it seemed was looking for Mr. or Ms. Goodbar. San Francisco in particular clung tenaciously to its rowdy port town reputation. A frisky bar called Perry's opened in 1969, with one of its main attractions being a photograph of the London skyline, in the corner of which could be seen a couple furiously having sex on a rooftop. A watering hole known as Ripples in the city's Financial District featured magnifying glasses above the urinals, showing movies of dancing go-go girls at eye level. The restaurant Magnolia Thunderpussy, run by the owner of the same name, offered sexually suggestive dishes like the "Montana Banana," a whole skinned banana on a plate, flanked on either side by a scoop of ice cream to look like testicles. Across the bay in Sausalito, Frank Werber took the money he made as manager of the Kingston Trio and opened a waterfront nightclub named the Trident, famous for its beautiful young waitresses clad in regulation see-through blouses.

Down in Los Angeles, a scene revolved around the Factory, where celebrities like Johnny Carson mingled with the likes of Playboy bunnies. The twin apartment towers of Century City gained notoriety for their parties, as did the hipster lofts and warehouses of Hollywood and the sailboat-fronting condos in Marina del Rey.

Chicago horndogs frequented the Near North Side, Old Town and the Prairie Shores highrise complex. Boston's equivalent could be found in Beacon Hill and Back Bay. New York City's singles scene ranged from Maxwell's Plum to P.J. Clarke's and T.G.I. Friday's in the Upper East Side, which supposedly attracted a healthy percentage of women. The legendary Max's Kansas City is remembered as a carnival atmosphere, bathed in red fluorescent lights, where people shot up cocaine right in the club, and flashed each other's bodies for entertainment. It was said that one woman took her shirt off so often people at the tables would say, "Oh, not your tits *again!*"

An unlikely singles scene developed at Anaheim's Magic Kingdom in California, right under the bulbous nose of Mickey Mouse. In the late 1960s and early '70s, all female employees arriving for work at Disneyland underwent a back-pat inspection by supervisors, to make sure each one was wearing a bra. Lust-crazed employees met each other for secret trysts throughout the Magic Kingdom, from the back corners of Inner Space to the basement of the Haunted Mansion, the Sleeping Beauty Castle,

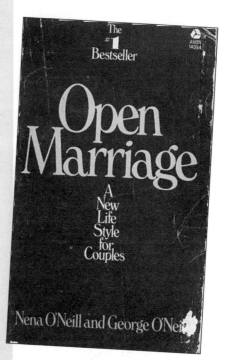

UNREALISTIC EXPECTATIONS, UNREASONABLE IDEALS, AND MYTHOLOGICAL BELIEFS OF CLOSED MARRIAGE
- that it will last forever
- that it means total commitment
- that it will bring happiness, comfort and security
- that your mate belongs to you
- that you will never be lonely again
- that jealousy means you care
- that sex will improve with time if it isn't already the world-shaking experience it is supposed to be
- that the ultimate goal of marriage is having a child
- that having a child is the ultimate expression of your love for each other
- that the person you marry can fulfill all your needs, economic, physical, sexual, intellectual and emotional

— **from the 1973 bestseller** *Open Marriage: A New Life Style for Couples* **by Nena and George O'Neill, who were later divorced**

What to Wear to an Orgy

The most important thing to wear to an orgy is an IUD or vasectomy scar. Let's face it, a diaphragm or condom simply doesn't make the grade. No one likes to end up with a mouthful of spermicidal jelly or rubber while they're trying to drive you to ecstasy...

The best rule of thumb is just to wear what you will be and feel most comfortable in. A simple sweater and skirt, a pantsuit, a sport shirt and golf slacks, or whatever is perfectly suitable. Just make sure it isn't your pretty new taffeta skirt or handsome mohair sport coat which attract stains like magnets. Try to keep in mind that whatever you do wear is probably going to end up in a heap in a corner anyway. Also, more likely than not, there won't be enough closet space for everyone to hang up their jackets and coats, so those will probably end up on the floor somewhere as well....

And oh yes, here's one final must for a man to wear to an orgy: a hard-on!

— **from** *The Beginner's Guide to Group Sex: Who Does What to Whom and How* **by Caroline Gordon, 1973**

I lay back and rested for a while until Roy came in from the orgy room.

Roy: Is there a man in the house with an erection? We have a woman waiting for you

Suddenly the room was quiet. About twenty males were present, each anxiously waiting to see who would accept the challenge. They looked dumbfoundedly at each other and nobody stirred. This last desperate effort to keep a woman warm had failed.

— **description of an evening in 1966, with the East Bay Sexual Freedom League, by Sam Sloan**

SWINGING ONSCREEN: *Producers capitalized on the trend to make films like this one, shot at a "swapping center"*

A tall blond man with the slight good looks of a fraternity president stood at the exit to the cocktail lounge delivering lengthy kisses to every woman who passed by wearing a red plastic apple pin inscribed with her and her husband's first names. "I'm the official greeter for the Happy Apples of Detroit," he told us. "That's our swinger's club. My fifteen-year-old asked what it was and I told him, 'A square-dance group.'"

"You should be in p.r. work, thinking up answers like that," a woman said.

"Yeah," he responded, "I know a lot of Puerto Ricans."

— **from "Weird Harold and the First National Swingers' Convention" by Charles and Bonnie Remsberg, *Esquire*, late 1960s**

the master bedroom of the Swiss Family Robinson's treehouse and the Mark Twain wheelhouse. So many were fornicating in the mountaintop attic of the Matterhorn, they formed their own Top of the Mountain Club. Guests also clocked in their fair share of the horizontal bop, on such locations as the floor of the submarine or Adventure Through Inner Space. On Grad Nites, employees found discarded pantyhose, panties and condoms scattered throughout the Motor Boat ride. One evening on the Pirates of the Caribbean, the dispatcher in the tower of the attraction called to his co-workers to come check out the video security monitors, and all watched a naked couple having sex on the otherwise empty ride. When the couple disembarked the ride fully clothed, the dispatcher exclaimed, "You know, it's really late, and, well, my crew would really like to thank you a lot for making our night," and handed them their tickets back.

Discotheques offered singles on the make an environment in which not to just flirt with words, but to slink around each other's bodies on the dance floor — even if it was merely the lounge adjacent to the Holiday Inn. The first disco in America reportedly was a New York joint called Shepheard's, which opened in 1961. Others soon followed: Whisky-Au-Go-Go in L.A., Tigers-A-Go-Go in San Francisco, the Café-A-Go-Go in Greenwich Village. New York seemed to offer the most variety: the Cheetah, the Peppermint Lounge, the Dom, the Electric Circus, Le Jardin and the Tenth Floor, nicknamed "the Popper Palace." The most notorious would be Studio 54.

Launched by nightclub partners Steve Rubell and Ian Schrager and party promoter Carmen d'Alessio, Studio 54 opened in April 1977 on West 54th Street, in an old CBS studio where "The $64,000 Question" was once taped. Underneath the crystal chandeliers and 85-foot ceilings danced the emerging gay chic and the last vestiges of the Heterosexual Heyday, amongst celebrities like Bianca Jagger, Dolly Parton, Liz Taylor, Liza Minelli, Jackie Bisset, Roger Moore, Aerosmith, the Stones, Bowie and Capote. A "Man in the Moon" prop dropped over the dance floor several times a night, and a giant spoonful of twinkling lights was inserted up its nose, setting off electronic fireworks in its head. Proof of the au courant decadence was captured in a famous series of photos of Margaret Trudeau without underpants.

Also gaining some popularity in the 1970s was the S/M scene. Encouraged by films such as

The Story of O and *The Story of Joanna,* many aficionados circulated around New York's Eulenspiegel Society, named after a masochistic character in German folklore named Till Eulenspiegel, who preferred climbing hills to walking down them. The society ran ads in *Screw,* and attracted members through its publication, *Pro-Me-Thee-Us.* S/M spread to a few cities, San Francisco, L.A. and Chicago, but New York remained the capital, in particular the underground dungeon club Hellfire. Most members in the scene were submissive males, with females split half and half between dominant and submissive. S/M attempted occasional jumps into the mainstream, including a 1975 *Vogue* fashion spread showing a man alternately nuzzling and beating the model, but it would take years before receiving acceptance by the above-ground population.

Despite all the thrills and chills of rendezvous, some segments of the population were concerned primarily with the actual act of sex, and how many folks could get involved at once. It didn't matter where it occurred or what everybody was wearing. Threesomes and wife-swapping were not uncommon, and as the nation grew curious, the swinger culture blossomed.

The late '50s are said to be the initial groundswell of swinging, when publications like *Mr. Magazine* and *La Plume* emerged, and swingers discovered others who shared their interest. The media jumped on the trend, which also increased the ranks, and by the mid-'70s, estimates of swingers ranged from half a million to 14 million couples, with the highest concentrations on the coasts and in the Midwest.

Studies revealed that swinging couples were usually blue-collar, and either married or had been in a relationship long enough to get bored with it. Perhaps their mates had grown overweight, or the romance aspect had become boring and stale. Many built extensive collections of pornography books and films. The next logical step was to cultivate some action on the side, without ending a relationship to do it.

The bestselling book *Open Marriage* by anthropologists George and Nena O'Neill gave credibility to the possibility of changing sexual partners without sacrificing a long-term relationship. The O'Neills described the four phases of swinging as: "1) an initial period of great excitement and frequent participation; 2) a reaction after bad experiences, disillusionment or boredom leading to a substantial drop in the level of activity; 3) a plateau and

Home porn photographers no longer had to worry if the local lab would develop their amateur nudie shots after 1973, when Polaroid announced the release of its revolutionary new SX-70 camera. A photo popped out 1.5 seconds after the shot was taken, and took only five minutes to develop before your eyes. The four-element lens permitted focusing on objects as close up as 10.2 inches, and the 12,000 rpm motor cranked out a new exposure every 1.5 seconds, giving naked girlfriends and wives more freedom to change poses. Now everyone could become Bob Guccione, for a mere list price of $180.

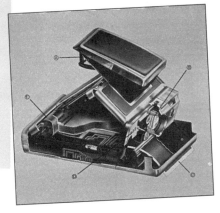

Lights Out for a Change

Now, a game for those who like to "work in the dark." Divide your group into guy-gal teams. Send one team couple at a time into a completely darkened room. The object is to have the couple switch clothing in the dark! The couple that emerges from the room in the shortest amount of time with the most complete switch of clothing, are the winners. A surprise element can be added by "planting" an over (or under) size bra or athletic supporter with one of the participants. For some real extra laughs, try planting a tape recorder in the room where the clothing switch is going on, and then play it back to everyone when the game is finished.

— from *Party Games* (for adults only), Leister Game Co., Inc., 1967

Contract Cohabitation— A Definition:

• Contract Cohabitation is an eating, sleeping, and living arrangement between employer and employee, based on a written or unwritten employment contract.

• The employer-employee relationship can be man-woman or woman-man, depending only on the financial strength and personal goals of the two individuals.

• All contract terms, including salary, are defined by the employer and accepted in advance by the employee.

• Sex is allowed, but can not be demanded or restrained; both parties are free to be together, apart, or with someone else.

• Free hours, annual vacations, and social or work activities outside the relationship are guaranteed by the terms of the contract.

• The employment contract can be canceled at any time by either party without reason or explanation.

A Typical Job Description:

Specific Tasks — Light housekeeping
Meal preparation
Household shopping
Estimated time per day: 2 hours

Companionship — Weekdays: 6:00 to 8:00 P.M.
Saturday: 3:00 p.m. on
Sunday: All day
Bedtime: Normally 11:00 P.M.
Night Off: Wednesday
Vacation Time: One week with pay per year
Client Entertaining: Optional
Social Entertaining: Required

— from **Contract Cohabitation: An Alternative to Marriage** *by* **Edmund L. Van Deusen, 1974**

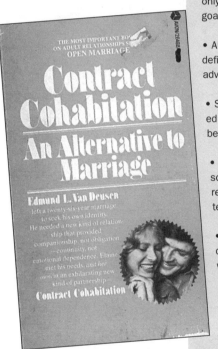

leveling-off; and 4) a total dropping-out or a take-it-or-leave attitude resulting in inter-mittent participation."

Organization was sporadic until the early '60s. In March 1964, Dr. Leo Koch, fired from the faculty of the University of Illinois for favoring premarital sex, formed the American Sexual Freedom Movement in New York. Chapters organized across the country, often near college campuses. At approximately the same time, the Sexual Freedom League formed in New York City, by Jefferson "Fuck" Poland. A few years later, Poland moved to the West Coast, and the Berkeley Sexual Freedom League became the granddaddy of swinger's clubs, sponsoring annual New Year's Eve orgies in San Francisco. The first was reportedly organized by a Bill Cosby lookalike named Richard Thorne, but successive sex orgies were held on a weekly basis by a member of the UC Berkeley chess team named Sam Sloan, attracting over 1,000 people to the events.

To drum up interest, Sloan wrote an article for *Playboy* about the wild SFL activities, and convinced a female friend named Mara Suviks to pose for the magazine in an eight-page spread titled "Mara Loves" in the September 1967 issue. The article attracted a tremendous boost in membership, as swingers joined up hoping to meet Mara, when in reality she had never attended any of the orgies. It's unlikely that she would ever have wanted to. Many avoided the SFL parties because so many of the participants were fat and ugly.

Splinter SFL groups formed in Oakland and San Francisco, the Bay Area humming with the sounds of weekly orgies, which annoyed conservative neighbors. One woman in Oakland filed a lawsuit against the U of C, attempting to open up its student organization records and reveal who the SFL president was, believing the League was part of a Communist plot.

The SFL declined at the end of 1967 when Sloan left Berkeley to play in the U.S. Intercollegiate Chess Championship in Hoboken, New Jersey. The team won the national championship, and Sloan moved to New York, where he got a job and worked on Wall Street in the securities industry for the next 18 years, his co-workers unaware of his previous life as president of the SFL.

Another swinger scene grew around Studio City in Southern California. In April 1966, former movie actor Greg McClure (who played the title role in *The Great John L.*, a film bio of the 1890s boxer John L. Sullivan) and his wife,

Joyce, opened a bar named the Swing, across the street from the Tail o'the Cock restaurant. Their marquee flashed "Luv Thy Neighbor." Opening night was so packed the McClures were forced to throw three consecutive evenings of parties to accommodate the crowds. The Swing's atmosphere was casual personified — strangers necked on the dance floor, and slides of available people flashed on the walls. A mimeographed sheet suggested: "Send a couple a drink via a waitress: don't wait for it to happen, make it happen." In 1971 Greg told *Newsweek*, "In my first marriage I cheated and never felt comfortable about it. Swinging is way ahead of the infidelity scene. I swing so I won't break up my marriage." Joyce added, "We get turned on together. A party may last two hours, but we can talk about it and fantasize about it for weeks before and after." One of the Swing's regulars would be Daniel Ellsberg, who later acquired and leaked the Pentagon Papers to the press.

Swingers remained the subject of much scrutiny and analysis, as major media descended upon the clubs and events, reporters chasing down couples for interviews. America learned that women swingers could be bisexual, but gay male activity was "condemned." Daisy chains were popular, as was oral sex, but there was relatively little anal sex. Major cities had swinging doctors, who offered penicillin shots to the swingers. Last names were never used. Swinging activities were usually hidden from the children. Unique vocabulary words were created, such as "lover's nuts," a physical condition of males after ejaculating too many times. And it wasn't limited to young people. One Northern California group of senior citizen swingers named itself the Den of Antiquity. Most swingers were (and still are) politically conservative. Males wanted a dip in the Fountain of Youth by claiming a harem full of women, and women were more interested in the variety.

It was said that on any given night of the year, upwards of 200 orgies were in progress in the Los Angeles area. In 1967, addressing the Sherman Oaks Chamber of Commerce, Sgt. Norman Draeger of the Van Nuys vice squad warned community leaders about the rampant sex orgies, dirty movies and wife swapping taking place in the hillside homes overlooking the San Fernando Valley. Citizens vowed to organize grassroots vigilante groups to eradicate this sin happening in their own backyards, but nothing ever materialized.

This club runs itself. I'm in the back fuckin' all night. Anyone with half a brain can run a club. I wish they said I was a genius for thinking up Plato's Retreat, but it just happened. No great idea, nothing brilliant, I just happened to be the first one to go public with swinging. Swinging shot through the roof. Now I'm riding the crest. I'm a fat, middle-aged guy....This place could have been started by anybody.

— **Larry Levenson reflecting on the success of Plato's in** *Tales of Times Square* **by Josh Alan Friedman**

KINGDOM OF SWING: *Sample literature from America's most famous swingers' club*

Plato's Retreat
Couples Only

The first on premise Swing Club in N.Y. If you haven't been to Platos', you might as well be living in Kansas. The disco of the 80's. A totally relaxing environment.

Platos' unique no pressure atmosphere features:

● Full length heated swimming pool ● giant communal whirlpool ● waterbeds ● spacious mattress area ● many intimate private areas ● Free bar & buffet ● showers, lockers and steam room.

Come with your mate or favorite date and share the most unique & fulfilling experience of your life.

PLATO'S RETREAT
at the Ansonia Hotel
230 West 74th Street
Telephone: 627-1959   787-3880
Open Wed., Thurs., Fri., Sat., Sun.
9:00 P.M. until early morning

When you're popping your nuts, you can't very well be thinking about whether Mayor Yorty is going to run again. It's a sublimation and a moment of escape that happens in times of stress. And we are living in a stressful society. These are the days in the bunker in Berlin, for Chrissakes. This is the blitz in England. The bombs are dropping. Let's do something. Let's fuck.

— **Leo Gordon, author of 1969 film** *All the Living Couples*

SEEKING SIMILAR:
Personals ads from late-'60s edition of the L.A. Free Press

One magazine theorized this was because off-duty vice-squad officers were themselves involved in the wife-swapping parties.

Southern California's aerospace industry provided the swinger scene with many members. Parties in Malibu were known for getting into kinky things like velvet whips, wet towels, leather and spanking. In 1969, a former engineer named Bob McGinley ditched his job and formed Club Wide World, an Orange County swingers group. By the 1980s it had expanded into a national networking organization, with newsletters and a travel agency specializing in "sexually adventurous" tours.

The rest of the country also got organized. One group of 2,500 Chicago-area mate-swappers wore lapel buttons that said "SWINGERS." Many major U.S. cities had local chapters of the National Key Club (NKC), a swingers association that rented entire floors of hotels for its events. By 1971, swingers were connecting with each other through a network of over 50 different publications. Swinger-friendly bars and clubs opened in major metro areas, where players could meet each other without fear of persecution. In addition to the Swing, there was Captain Kidd in Manhattan, and a San Fernando Valley establishment called Club 101, a hilltop mansion with a uniformed security guard at the gate, that featured a room called "The Cave," furnished with waterbeds, a chamber of mirrors and kaleidoscopic lights. The Red Rooster outside Las Vegas treated its guests to red shag carpet, a sunken living room with circular fireplace and communal hot tubs. The swinger club that would gain the most exposure of all was Plato's Retreat, started by a former soda pop salesman and manager of a McDonald's franchise named Larry Levenson.

In 1977, Manhattan had two swing bars, Percival's, on the Lower East Side, and Plato's, in Gramercy Park on Fifth Avenue. After the New York State Liquor Authority shut down Percival's, Levenson, a high school buddy of Al Goldstein, smelled the heat of anti-swinger oppression and moved Plato's to the Upper West Side. His new site was a 23,000-square-foot space located in the basement of the Ansonia Hotel, the old homosexual Continental Baths, where Bette Midler got her start. Levenson vowed to make the club so big it couldn't be busted. He borrowed $150,000 to renovate the existing disco, pool, Jacuzzi and steam room, and added free beverages and a hot and cold buffet. To avoid hassle from the Liquor Authority, the bar was strictly non-alcohol, a fact played up by the management's signs: "No Booze. No Brew. So What. Let's Screw," announced one. Another boasted: "We may not have booze but we got CLEAN SHEETS!"

Plato's opened its doors five nights a week, and a sexual smorgasbord was legally available, in the heart of America's largest city. On weekends, over 300 couples would stroll through, paying a $30 cover per couple, $5 of which went to a six-week membership. If they returned it was only $25. For $2 you could buy a leather pouch on a string, and wear it around your neck to carry your cigarettes, Quaaludes, etc. Levenson thoughtfully provided complimentary mouthwash in the bathrooms — gallon jugs of the house brand called "Olde Country."

Rooms were designed by theme. An area with mats on the floor was decorated in a black-and-white leopard pattern. Another room was named the "Arabian Tent Fit for a Sheik." The "Jungle Habitat" surrounded a waterless swimming pool filled with shrubbery, and in the rear was Levenson's private swing area, a fully cushioned floor with large pillows lining the sides and a stained-glass mirror on the back wall. To make things hotter, he ordered the air conditioning turned down around 2 a.m.

The New York media couldn't pass up such an opportunity, and the Plato's assignment became a reporter's dream gig. Howard Smith, a *Playboy* contributor and columnist for *The Village Voice*, did a series of stories on the new club. *New York* magazine sent a finance writer to cover the phenomenon. James Peterson, a writer for *Playboy*, admitted: "There were so many writers, TV commentators and such hanging out that a movement was begun to have the club's name changed to the Columbia School of Journalism. Forgive us our press passes."

Other clubs followed the lead of Plato's, but none matched its size or reputation. The King of Swing planned to open franchises around the country, and for a short time a Plato's was open in Los Angeles. Unfortunately Levenson gave the wrong set of books to the IRS, and was busted on tax evasion charges, spending 40 months in prison. In 1985 the NYC Department of Public Health shut down Plato's for good, the last floundering dinosaur of an outdated era America may never see again.

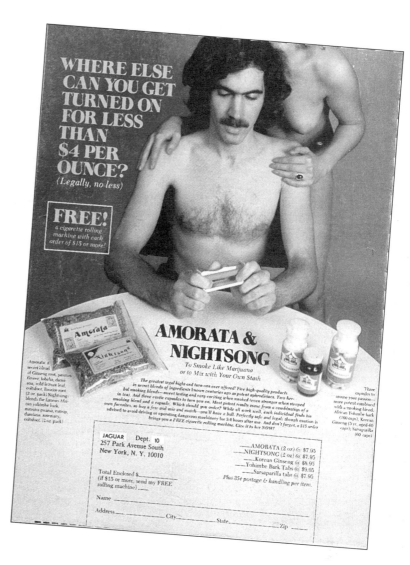

A FRIEND INDEED:
You're never alone with ersatz weed,
according to this mail-order ad

Surrounding this mound of writhing bodies was a circle of fully dressed observers, some of them hunkering, some prone, with hands supporting their heads, eyes transfixed, as they casually passed around joints of grass. Like bleacherites at Yankee Stadium, they often whispered approval of the participants' technique or speculated on the next development.

"How about a little audience participation, you Peeping Toms," suggested a man on one of the mattresses as he climbed off his female companion, "before you have an optical climax." His raillery, as well as his performance, inspired numerous clucks of appreciation — and a couple of takers. They were soon joined by drifters from the living room and several late arrivals. The final vision of two dozen people heaving on the mattresses — beheld by a few fascinated holdouts — resembled a cross between a purple passage from an Olympia Press reader and a goal-line stand between the Colts and the Cowboys.

— description of a '70s swinger party in L.A.'s Benedict Canyon, just above the Beverly Hills Hotel, by John Clellon Holmes

Return to the Flesh District

Poking around the perimeter of America's sexual hot spots — from swinger's hotels to peep shows, nudist resorts, porn movie shoots, strip clubs, sex parties and brothels — brought several points to mind. Like all social phenomena that burst into prominence in the '60s and '70s, the commercial potential of sex drew the blueprints for a booming billion-dollar industry...where the forerunners of pornography and lifestyle frequently had to spend time in court defending some image, word or activity now considered innocuous and almost required, their present-day descendants have had little else to do but make money. Thus, the business has created millionaires both distinguished and sleazy. Sex has advertised products and boosted television ratings. It has built mansions, purchased real estate and luxury cars and customized private jets. It has sponsored the arts and funded political campaigns. It has created its own awards presentations, museums, cable channels and internet firms.

The San Francisco Bay Area seemed a good geographical region in which to begin this blast through the past, and not just because I live there. One glance down the neon lights of Broadway will remind you the city was the birthplace of topless dancing. America's porn film industry also first blossomed there, as well as prostitution activism, and alternative communities like Morehouse and the Sexual Freedom League. It should also be noted that Bay Area used bookstores are among the finest in the country, the sexuality sections often reaching to the ceilings, bursting with all sorts of artifacts from the era. In Manhattan's Strand used bookstore, acknowledged shrine of book publishing in America, the sex department is confined to one measly shelf, but the sociology and psychology sections run for aisles and aisles, proving that New York probably isn't the best barometer of the nation's sex history — people were thinking and worrying too much there to ever have sex. (Either that, or they never sold their books back.) The Bay Area is also ideal for beginning research on this topic because even though its role in the heterosexual pantheon is for the most part over, the region remains in love with its notorious history, and clings to the past with provincial pride.

According to *Playboy*, copulation was first shown on a commercial American screen in San Francisco back in 1969. Those were the days when the *San Francisco Chronicle* ran ads for *I Am Curious – Yellow* the same size as Hollywood blockbusters. As the industry grew, the city boasted nearly 30 adult film theaters, screening hardcore efforts from local directors like the Mitchell Brothers, Alex de Renzy and Bob Chinn, who busily cranked out hundreds of films, supplying the rest of the U.S. with its first glimpses of smut. As to why this city seemed like such a Ground Zero for the fledgling porn film revolution, some have said the town has always embraced intellectual and personal freedoms, and the ever-changing tourist and Navy population gave the area a reputation that whatever you could do or see here, you wouldn't think of doing anywhere else. Journalist Eddie Muller, author of *Grindhouse*, a history of adult films in America, adds, "To tell you the truth, I think it's because a girl would do anything for a free joint."

As the porn industry moved to Los Angeles, and accessibility to video and VCRs increased, small-screen booths became San Francisco's most economical way to exhibit and watch filth-on-film. Projectionists didn't have to change reels, and customers didn't have to sit through tedious storylines. Plus, the Kleenex was usually provided. Coin-op video peeps still operate throughout the city, from Frenchy's and Big Al's to the Regal Show World ("Where every man is king"), and the Nob Hill, whose 120-channel gay video arcade is "maintained at a level Leona Helmsley would find acceptable."

Fans of vintage celluloid will claim victory upon entering the female-owned and -operated Lusty Lady emporium in North Beach. In the rear of the establishment, past the live dancers and video peeps, awaits a solitary 16mm loop projector booth. Just drop your quarters into the sturdy metal coin mechanism and peer through a glass window to an empty black room with a three-foot screen. (Yes, there is room to bring a date.) The unseen 16mm cranks to life, a small nightlight is snuffed for your convenience and history unfolds before you — San Francisco's adult equivalent of the *Birth of a Nation* answer print:

A young man and woman cavort on what appears to be a folded-out sofabed with a quilt spread. The woman wears only saddle shoes, mascara and thick eye shadow, and is in the midst of giving head to a skinny naked guy with Don Johnson-styled hair and a mustache. Their faces are red and shiny. As was characteristic of the era, the cameraman dozes off on a long, long take, then suddenly and inexplicably zooms to a random body part. No annoying wah-wah soundtrack; silence is golden here. The high-resolution photographic warmth of celluloid is apparent even in the detail of her butt hairs, allowing the connoisseur an archival experience not soon forgotten.

The only other adult film theater left in town, the Mini Adult Theatre, is located in a scum-pit Tenderloin building at the intersection of Golden Gate, Jones and Creepy Discomfort. Five dollars ("no in-out privileges") gets you three 16mm X-rated films playing in rotation 24 hours a day here (changing on Tuesdays and Saturdays), in a pitch-black theater holding 30 or 40. The flickering imagery is nicely offset by a muffled sound system that appears to be left over from the FDR Administration. Settling into one of the sticky, uncomfortable wooden seats guarantees an ambiance like no other. A few rows behind me was a woman laughing to her male companion, "Open your pants, muthafucker!" Several men, one at a time, stood up and mysteriously disappeared through a hallway to one side of the screen, before returning a few minutes later. Acting as barker to this backstage activity was a guy in a baseball cap, occasionally lighting a crack pipe, nervously walking up and down the aisle, saying, "Male or female, man, come on!" During all this, the screen showed two hairy hippies having unremarkable sex on a bed underneath an American flag tacked on the wall.

Perhaps the most famous porn house in the country, the Mitchell Brothers' O'Farrell Theatre, still operates at the same location as where the Mitchells' classic *Behind the Green Door* premiered. Several changes have occurred since those days. After Jim Mitchell was convicted of shooting and killing his brother, Artie, in 1993, a lounge on the main floor was converted into a shrine to the brothers's films and philanthropic efforts in the local community, including a glass display case of Marilyn Chambers memorabilia. Another display case in the lobby houses the Mitchell film catalogue that has been converted to videotape, including *Green Door* and its sequel, *Inside Marilyn Chambers*, and *The Grafenberg Spot*. The upstairs lounge, where the brothers once hosted all-night parties around the pool table, is now a computer room, where their web site is generated and updated. The upstairs hallways are lined with framed film posters, press clips and an original Ralph Steadman illustration of Hunter S. Thompson with a cast on his leg. O'Farrell public relations person Rita Benton, who worked on the Mitchell films as a still photographer, tells me the Steadman piece was to be the cover of a book *Playboy* had commissioned Thompson to write about his adventures as night manager of the O'Farrell Theatre, a project for which Thompson reportedly took the advance and never delivered.

The rest of the first floor remains essentially the same as it did in the '70s and 80s, a variety of sex shows, from a traditional burlesque stage to a peep-booth lesbian S/M act, the infamous Copenhagen flashlight show and a room designed as a bathroom. The cover charge is the steepest in the city — $30, with a discount for couples — and girls who dance here have been known to make $1,500 a night. O'Farrell management continues booking specialty acts that range from established porn stars and touring strippers to scripted, choreographed stage shows. In 1995, I attended one such show that featured prostitute Divine Brown, then in the news for getting arrested in Los Angeles with British actor Hugh Grant, and wrote the following magazine article called "The Foreplay's the Thing."

Upwards of a hundred people sit expectantly in the Cine-Stage room of the Mitchell Brothers' O'Farrell Theatre, one soul in a Members Only jacket surreptitiously applying Chapstick. A disembodied voice announces a baritone, Luther Vandross-style introduction so deep, so mellow it barely whispers the vocal chords: "We take you to a nice steamy night on Sunset Boulevard in June...."

The curtains part to whoops from the crowd, revealing a slide projection of a BMW car parked on a city street, a multi-media atmospheric detail that suggests perhaps a direct homage to director George Coates. The bilevel stage is painted as a landscape of asphalt and white dashes. A bench seat sits front and center, providentially padded. San Francisco poises to welcome back another hometown native who left the Bay Area to make it big in Los Angeles — Stella Marie Thompson, aka Divine Brown.

Press materials describe her as the "owner of the lips that busted Hugh Grant," adding that she is far more than a vice squad statistic these days. The AIDS classes, petty fines and community

service are ancient history, clearing the path for a new singing career and an upcoming autobiography. But opening night belongs to the twin muses of comedy and tragedy, as the O'Farrell Theatre marquee blazes to the world, "Hugh got it in the car, and now she's a star..."

Adapted from an original idea by British film actor Hugh Grant, this evening's production essentially is the story of a man, a woman and the harsh realities of civil juris-prudence. The drama finds two people of disparate backgrounds struggling to understand themselves and each other, set amidst a background tapestry of Los Angeles prostitution, British repression and German luxury cars. And as with other bigger-budget productions several blocks closer to Union Square, the Divine Brown script is but a blueprint, a blank canvas in two acts provided for actors to add the brushwork.

Hugh Grant enters, played by a blonde woman in bulging khakis, blue sportshirt and baseball cap that says "Just Do Me." Mr. Grant sits on the bench and mimes driving, to an invigorating disco theme having something to do with neon lights on Sunset. Two slinky meretrixes mince onstage in high heels, each attempting to woo the cuddly English actor, with little success. Mr. Grant adjusts his khakis and waves them off. He is on a mission tonight.

The Luther Vandross narrator suddenly pierces the fourth wall: "Miss Divine Brown...."

And then a blazing crimson vinyl dress struts out, swinging a tiny purse. The crowd gasps. It's her — last year's streetwalker celebrity-by-proximity, the Kato Kaelin of working girls! America embodied, without shame! Ms. Brown commands the stage, controlling her assets with an electrifying presence that leaves each audience member sharing an identical thought: "Wow, she really *has* been a hooker."

Ms. Brown expertly seduces the hapless Brit, who eagerly flashes a fan of U.S. currency. The small amount seems to insult the higher-priced sensibilities of Ms. Brown, *just like it actually happened*, but a deal is eventually struck, and within seconds she has freed Mr. Grant of various clothing restrictions, producing from his trousers an artificial man gland, wrapped in a Union Jack flag. Accompanied by Donna Summer's "Love to Love You Baby," Ms. Brown then gives an enthusiastic and professional demonstration of why she is still in the newspapers, to which someone hollers out from the dark: "You go, girl!"

Suddenly whistles blow, sirens blare, lights flash. Female cops in mirror shades swarm the

stage. Busted in the act! Hugh and Divine! Cuffed, against the wall! Hauled offstage! The curtain closes to a cacophony of pounding hearts.

There is no intermission. The second act unfolds at the hoosegow. While Ms. Brown is fingerprinted and posing for mug shots, Mr. Grant sits dejectedly on a sofa, stage left. He is surprised by girlfriend Elizabeth Hurley, who has chosen a skin-tight white vinyl cocktail dress for her jailhouse visit. His apologetic mewlings are met with a sharp cuff to the head. Simultaneously, up on a second level, the two previously introduced strumpets are cooling their high heels in a jail cell, clearly failing to resist the amorous advances of female officers. Within seconds, it seems, our drama has evolved into a scenario of Paphian proportions. Accompanied by the strains of "Bad Girls," the troupe hurls itself into a vigorous nympho-maniacal frenzy: Mr. Grant and Ms. Hurley, the police and the streetwalkers, Ms. Brown and her arresting officer, etc. This lengthy dramatic high point gives the audience time to note the many communities represented onstage: Latin Americans, African-Americans, Anglo blondes, as well as examples of the home appliance and cosmetic surgery industries. After a final bow from the entire cast, the curtain closes on the still-quivering derriere of Ms. Brown, the stage littered with feather boas, cop hats and condom wrappers — an unforgettable half hour that provides much to discuss on the walk home from the theater.

"I just saw some of the dangest things I ever seen in my life," drawls one young man in thick Coke-bottle glasses.

Like Glenn Close or Sarah Brightman, Ms. Brown graciously makes herself available to fans after the performance, for personal Polaroid photos, autographs and sales of T-shirts. Glittering in a short red sequined dress, she sits on an imitation stone bench underneath a proscenium decorated with a blown-up image of herself in a shiny black biker hat. A small tattoo above her right breast reads in script: "Gangster Brown."

"What are you starin' at?" she asks of a man in a necktie.

"Can't help but look at a good thing, baby," comes his hesitant reply.

A stringer for the *New York Times* asks to pose for a photo, and as she sits down next to Ms. Brown, the actress jokingly yanks open the reporter's blouse to expose her brassiere, just in time for the picture. Laughs all around.

A young woman in blue jeans and hat runs up, exclaiming sarcastically, "Are you Divine Brown? Can I get your autograph?"

"This is my sister," laughs the star. The two sit for a photo, and the sister tugs on Ms. Brown's dress, trying to expose a breast, as the flash goes off and the camera ejects the print.

"I'm givin' it to Mama!" announces the sister, and smacks the arm of Divine Brown, scourge of Hugh Grant and pride of San Leandro, California.

Old-timers later informed me that this show was typical of the Mitchells in their heyday, except that "it would have been black-tie." The theater still pulls out all the stops for its annual invitation-only Christmas party, a perplexing soiree I have experienced on two occasions.

Amidst open bars and tables sagging with the weight of fresh seafood and salads, a strange panoply of politicians, journalists, rock stars, comedians, firemen, fishermen and strippers squeezes through the crowded hallways. A sensation of relaxed liberation is prevalent throughout the party. Folks are smiling and having a good time. Most of life's vices are furnished under one roof. All the sex rooms are cranked up and running. The Ultra Room features live fisting, the New York Stage offers both male and female dancers, accompanied by the wild screams of young stripper girls, who guzzle champagne straight from the bottle. (On one occasion, as the San Francisco rock band the Kinetics was playing, a passel of drunken strippers attacked the lead singer, scratching at his pants and peeling him down to his underwear, rendering him temporarily stunned, unable to choose the next song on the set list.) The famed Shower Room might offer soaking wet lesbians pawing each other like angry kittens, or a circus-themed act of fire-eating and sword-swallowing. The Cine-Stage may host a live show such as *Sexxxtra*, a raunchy S/M show accompanied by strobes, smoke and heavy industrial music. Standing in this room, which is packed elbow to elbow, sipping your second Bloody Mary and watching naked women ravage each other with neon glow-in-the-dark apparati, extracting strings of beads from each other's orifices, it suddenly dawns on you that it's still early afternoon. On both occasions, the party ended at 4 p.m., and I recall distinctly standing outside the theater on the corner of Polk and O'Farrell Streets, full of food and drink, realizing this is one of those rare moments in your life where you have absolutely no fucking idea what to do the rest of your day.

The story of the Mitchell Brothers and their contribution to the sex industry is definitely a colorful tale, having already been the subject of two books and, supposedly, an upcoming movie with Robert De Niro, but all is not as harmlessly nostalgic as it seems. Jim Mitchell sits in a prison cell, monitoring closely an ongoing lawsuit against him by his own dancers. He's beaten the courts before, but this one is the burr under his saddle that hasn't yet gone away.

In 1988, the O'Farrell Theatre reclassified its dancers from employee to independent contractor status. Dancers no longer were paid a wage plus tips, but now had to pay a per-shift stage fee to perform at the theater. It didn't matter that much; even though they were now only working for tips, some girls were still clearing over a grand a night.

In 1993 dancers Jennifer Bryce and Ellen Vickery filed a class-action suit against the theater, with 214 dancers demanding a whopping $5 million in back wages, fees and damages, claiming they were treated as employees without the right of employment. Other Mitchells dancers filed to intervene in Bryce and Vickery's suit.

The rest of the country watched with a keen eye. After all, this was San Francisco, the birthplace of topless dancing, as well as a long history of progressive labor practices. And five million bucks is a lot of lap-dances. Certainly it made sense for some women who worked in some of the city's filthier clubs, and could legitimately use union protection. But was unionization to be the next logical step in an industry where management is accustomed to making exorbitant amounts of cash, and careers of dancers, much like athletes, are largely over by the age of 30? Or was this going to end up another unresolved San Francisco dilemma, such as the legalization of prostitution, in which a schizophrenic city wants both its progressive gender rights image alongside a frisky reputation of the freewheeling Barbary Coast?

In August of 1996, a precedent was set. A majority of the dancers at the female-owned-and-operated Lusty Lady strip club in North Beach signed with the Service Employees International Union, Local 790. The story gained national attention, and other strippers saw it as a sign of progress. While the Mitchell case is still tied up in the courts as of this writing, and dancers in other cities are starting to consider their own union possibilities, the sad truth of the matter is that in strip joints all over the country, businessmen with wallets to burn obliviously grind away in the dark. To these guys, the bread and butter of the entire industry, they could care less whether their lap-dancer is union, independent contractor or extraterrestrial.

As the adult film industry took flight in San Francisco, so did the topless nightclub craze. It may seem difficult to imagine an era without lap-dancing, considering not only the number of outlets across the nation that now offer such services, but also Hollywood's capitalization of sex workers in films like *Striptease, Mighty Aphrodite* and *Leaving Las Vegas*. At one time a dancer simply baring her nipple was the hottest thing going, and on the outer brick wall of the Condor jazz nightclub in North Beach, a bronze plaque stands as a testament to the genesis of it all. Waitress Carol Doda first appeared in a topless swimsuit back in 1964, and began a series of silicone injections that were discussed around the world.

I first paid a visit in the early '80s to discover the Condor was a crumbling wreck — dark, seedy and nearly empty. The only time anybody ever mentioned the club was when a dancer and her big beefy boyfriend, a security guy for the club, decided to have sex after hours on top of the white grand piano, which featured as an elevating prop for the strip shows. Unfortunately the hydraulic mechanism had become jammed, and the piano rose to the ceiling and crushed the guy to death. The girl was pinned beneath him for several hours until the accident was discovered, and local newspapers carefully reconstructed the incident with technical drawings of the malfunction.

The Condor has now been gutted and remodeled as a sports bar, with neon beer signs, TV monitors and pool tables. The killer piano is permanently mounted on the ceiling, and Doda's old dressing room is preserved as some cheesy semblance of the glory days. Framed photos and news clippings line the walls, a quick glimpse for tourists, and fond memories for a diminishing number of old-timers. After gigging with a rock band called Carol Doda and Her Lucky Stiffs, the woman once called San Francisco's "twin peaks" now runs a lingerie store in the yuppie Marina District of the city, and has gained high-society status, hired to make appearances at benefits and galas.

Once a mighty display of flesh unlike no other in the world, most of the remaining nude clubs on the Broadway strip have been taken over by the national franchise Deja Vu Showgirls, whose fast-food-styled clubs come complete with matching carpet patterns, the famous "bottomless" souvenir beverage cup and thick-necked guys running around with clipboards, monitoring each girl to make sure she's dancing exactly one song per fee, and not giving any unauthorized discounts.

North Beach barkers have changed as well. Instead of a shifty little guy in a checkered sportcoat expertly sidling up to the uninitiated, whispering, "Two minutes free," it's a young girl in an ankle-length coat, shivering in the evening chill, smiling gamely at pedestrians. Former '60s attractions like Big Al's speakeasy-themed club — which once featured topless/bottomless gun molls and nightly raids from the cops — have expanded into adult bookstores, selling novelty products and renting video booths to stay alive. Much of the real estate has changed hands to become bars and restaurants, and for clubs like Garden of Eden and the Hungry I that are still open, their once-racy backlit photos of girls are fading into sun-bleached history, the girl's hairstyle hopelessly trapped in the '70s. One blown-up mention from the late *Chronicle* columnist Herb Caen is so old it's actually had its date removed. In the mid-1980s, before the El Cid "He-and-She Love Act" club was renovated into a Chinese restaurant, I asked the doorman how old the woman was in the washed-out photo. He lowered his voice and answered shamefully, "She's sixty-two...it's ridiculous."

Nevertheless, it seemed necessary to plunge into the current tittie bar scene and get up to date. One night I was asked to be a "celebrity judge" at a strip contest in San Francisco's South of Market, and found myself in the midst of a volatile, pre-show argument in the upstairs office of a nightclub:

While the sound system roars below decks and the adjacent VIP lounge fills up with young stripper hopefuls, preening and checking their asses in the mirror, club manager George Lazaneo and a DJ named Matt face off. Their argument is similar to a cocaine conversation: neither listens to the other, but both repeat themselves constantly. As they bicker, Corey, emcee for the evening's event, sits in a chair, going over the announcements he must make. A statuesque blonde named Alexandra crouches on the floor, fastening her shoes.

The conflict continues — Matt wants to choose the order in which the girls will dance. George thinks it's too much trouble. Eventually Matt gets his way. He gathers the strippers around, and holding a clipboard, tells them they each have half a song to dance to by themselves, and if they're the six who are chosen for the next round, they will dance in a group. Matt warns

them that they don't have to show their tits, but the crowd will want it. His suggestion is succinct: "Don't be a prude."

"What's a prude?" asks a young girl with enormous implants, the words tumbling out of a heavily lipsticked mouth that appears to be permanently open, like an infant's.

Tonight's event is billed as the Clash of the Titans, the Mitchell Brothers' theater versus the Gold Club, in a special stripper-of-the-year edition of the Wednesday night Bondage A Go Go, held at the Trocadero, a former gay '70s popper disco turned rock grunge club. Harleys from the San Francisco chapter of the Hell's Angels are lined up out front, and Angels wander the bar in their colors, great big biker beasts, drinking and laughing. One upstairs corner is the bondage S/M scene, which a few years ago would have shocked America, and now is a tourist attraction fast approaching the level of visiting Alcatraz or the wine country. If one could actually see over the heads of the curious, one would see a young man, pants to his ankles, getting spanked with a paddle by a long-haired Renaissance Faire Klingon-type in executioner's outfit and codpiece, various whips and accoutrements hanging from his S/M belt. *Tool Time* with a twist.

But S/M still will never be a spectator sport, no matter how diligently people market it. And so now it has become the domain of suburban kids who drive to the big city to see all the scary stuff. Wednesday night's Happy Hour consists of free drinks for all girls and trannies who willingly handcuff themselves to the bar. Lazaneo proudly calls his club the sleaziest in town.

A co-owner of the Gold Club, an Asian man in a suit, sits in the Trocadero office, making calls on a cell phone. They're three Gold Club girls short, and he's calling the club to make sure the reserves are on their way over, like the owner of a cattle feedlot.

My fellow judges are in their twenties, both with fashionable facial hair. Dave, a filmmaker with white-guy dreadlocks, also works as a DJ/announcer at the Centerfolds strip club. The other is introduced to me as Lucky Bastard, a tattoo artist who sports a tat of a cackling red demon on his neck. We walk out onstage in the dark, illuminated by flashlights from stagehands, and sit in folding chairs. The lights blaze up, the emcee starts his rap, and the audience of sweaty faces extends the depth of the club. It's packed to the rafters. Most of them are out-of-towners — pink, drunk and dumb. They want to see the titties.

And we're off, the girls dancing away. A variety

of females, chubby, svelte, big-boned, anorexic, real tits, fake tits, excited, bored, nervous, all with that golden ring of first prize dancing in their heads — a thousand dollars cash. Judging is not done on poise, style, confirmation, but simply on which ones we prefer. I'm realizing my brain doesn't usually size up women this quickly, and I scramble to keep up with the snap judgments. Selection is ruthless. When we agree that we don't care for the one in the white hot pants, a girl named Rachel walks up, whispers in her ear and she exits the stage, leaving the others still gyrating to the whoops and cheers. We're looking to trim the field to three, and surprise of surprises, it comes down to the butcher-shop basics, which we shout to each other over the music, in quick bursts of pure maleness —

"Her tits are too fake!"

"Too much of a cheerleader!"

"Can't dance!"

One girl actually smokes a cigarette throughout her routine. She does the splits, rolls around a bit, then motions her friend to come over and yanks down the girl's top and begins gnawing on her breasts, cigarette still glowing in her hand. The crowd has a mixed reaction. We judges look at each other, and Lucky Bastard shakes his head. A cheap stunt. Doesn't work.

At last three remain: a Spice Girl-type skinny mulatto; a stocky, implant-heavy girl with a winning smile; and another skinny, hyper-kinetic girl with a perfect body and parabolic movements. They dance another song, and Miss Parabola wins by audience decision.

Backstage, as the girls collect their bikini bras and leopard-print dresses, the other judges ask about my book, and we talk about the sexual revolution.

"Are you gonna write about the one goin' on now?" asks Lucky Bastard. "I fucked three different girls last week."

"I fucked a lot of these girls, before I met my girlfriend," says Dave.

Despite the era of latex and safe sex, they are convinced people are having sex more than ever.

"People are tired of being careful," says Bastard.

"The thing to do is, play the game," advises Dave. "Act like you're not interested. And as soon as you nail one, give it to her good, all the others will come around wanting it....And when they come out with a cure for AIDS..." His voice drifts off, as if he's already imagined the possibilities.

While the Trocadero events and other high-end clubs like the O'Farrell will add up to a pricey nice on the town, other topless fans prefer the lower-rent clubs, those outlets for aficionados on a budget. The Crazy Horse is located on the scummy stretch of Market Street next to the Warfield Theater, a popular music venue. Every topless joint is pretty depressing at 3 p.m., and the Crazy Horse doesn't disappoint. Besides myself, there are perhaps six other guys, one in an Oakland Raiders cap, another white guy in Gap clothing, a black business folder in his lap. All of us observe the code of guys — no talking or looking at each other.

Once a movie theater, the space itself is tall and narrow, painted all black, with black vinyl chairs facing a stage. A DJ patters over music. Behind the red curtain I can hear girls whispering over the songs, deciding who's going on next. One song begins, and for two minutes the stage is empty, until finally a girl in a bikini struts out, chewing gum. Girls circulate, asking "for company." Most are either black, Latina, or Filipino. A dancer named Blaze shows me around the facilities.

In the rear of the club near the door are the "VIP Lounges," where each lap-dance is $20 per song, or $40 if you're in need of a topless configuration. No touching of breasts or genitals are allowed. The "Super VIP Lounge" is an $80 minimum per song, which includes as part of its superness, masturbation and sex toys. We stroll through the little areas, Blaze parting curtains to reveal each, as if she's presenting speedboats on a game show. VIP Lounge #1 features both vinyl wall benches or vinyl pads set into the wall. "Some guys like standing up," explains Blaze. VIP Lounge #2 is a small room with a padded black vinyl chair, in front of which is a round, three-foot carpeted riser. A wall-mounted Kleenex dispenser and plastic bag-lined garbage can appear at the ready.

I agree to a standard lapdance, and soon we're chatting away about the biz. In her late 20s, Blaze has been dancing for four years, and got into it to supplement her meager income as a teacher. It's never occurred to her to do movies, and she doesn't do magazines or photos because she doesn't want her family to find out what she does. They still think she took a break from teaching and is working as a cocktail waitress. In a sense, she still is. She used to dance in Hawaii, but says the laws are much stricter there. The girls can't touch their own breasts onstage, or it's a $500 fine. Undercover cops come into the clubs, put $1 bills in their mouths and try to get the girls to squeeze their breasts together to snatch it away.

Blaze says the main customers are usually either in between girlfriends, bored with their marriage or are sex addicts. Most dancers develop a stable of regulars. One Crazy Horse girl had an older man who brought her home-baked cookies every time he visited. With the rumors floating around about dancers actually turning tricks, I ask her if more explicit acts take place here, like hand jobs or blow jobs. She answers not that she knows of, although it does happen at other clubs, and adds if business keeps dropping off, a few girls might start doing it. She seems happy to talk, rather than just grind away in silence on a guy's lap, and says she enjoys herself at work. Other dancers later told me that the job is grueling, but the money aspect is very addicting, and to quit dancing means a drop from making five grand a month to two grand.

One block from the Crazy Horse is a peep show-style emporium called the Regal Show World. Its slogan: "Where You Are King." They might as well add, "No one will be turned away for lack of funds." Dirty video viewing is just a quarter, and for a mere dollar you can look at a girl dancing buck naked in a booth. One row of peep booths has the doors cut in half, the top half of which is open, with girls dangling out in skimpy bras and bikinis, saying hello to the customers. The effect reminds one of prized thoroughbreds in a barn.

In the first such booth sits a girl with dark eyes and a slight overbite, her dark skin suggesting a Middle Eastern heritage. She gives her name as Parisa, saying, "It's my sister's name." She's been working at the Regal about a year, at the same time holding an office job, and studying classical piano at the Conservatory of Music. Inside her booth, I saw a daily newspaper, a dirty fan mounted on the wall, and a red-walled portion containing a tiny brass bed with sheets and a mini-chandelier.

In a word, elegance.

We chat for several minutes. Most of the Regal's customers are too cheap for the live girls, and go for the quarter peeps. Lunchtime, the place fills up with suits, then there's an afternoon lag, and then an evening crowd. Parisa's booth costs $5 for three minutes, plus a $5 tip for her. What the heck. I go get some change from the counter clerk.

The window raises, and Parisa is now lying on the little bed. The old two-way phone is mounted there on the wall, but we don't talk. Her expression has changed. It's as if we have never met. We're just two strangers caught in the same cubicle under the same arrangement. She undoes

her bra, revealing one nipple with a ring in it, and lies back on the baby-sized bed, stroking herself. Her deep, dark eyes, which three minutes earlier were engrossed in a conversation, are now lidded, staring at my crotch. She plays with herself, pulling the G-string to one side, revealing more piercings. Classical piano by day, pierced sex kitty by night. She turns on her side, rubbing her outer thigh in, I have to admit, a sensual manner. The partition abruptly clicks shut. Our little moment is over.

Parisa opens her horse-stall door, and I give her a small round of applause. She smiles, and our rapport picks up as though the weird little dance had never happened. It is time to try the dollar peep booths.

After several attempts, the mechanism takes my money, the partition slides up and surprises a young topless girl reading a magazine. She sets it down and dashes over to my window. Against one wall of her area are various magazines and books, propped up vertically, as if the dancers have been reading while doing their routines. I could make out an issue of *Black Woman* magazine, and two hardbacks that look like textbooks.

"Tip me so you can see my show!" says the girl in a thick accent, possibly Tagalog. She looks about 19. I slip her a fat $1 bill, and she starts dancing like a child running through a sprinkler, then suddenly turns around and slaps her butt several times. The whole presentation is ludicrous, unintentionally hilarious. I try not to laugh out loud, but she doesn't seem to notice, and is looking over my shoulder at some invisible spot on the wall. She continues hopping around, tugging on her nipples, smiling as if she is the first naked woman I have ever seen. The door clicks shut, and we part ways, me back out into the afternoon sunlight, and she back to her magazines and homework.

Another singular club in the local scene is called Temptations, in the heart of North Beach next to the Condor, reportedly owned by guys who make their money in office supplies. The set-up is similar, with a live DJ, a main dancer stage, and lap-dance booths, but management is all female. Ten bucks gets you inside, to watch girls dance three songs each on the stage, after which a basket is passed for tips. After several girls, they have what's called a "mirror song," where dancers come out with Windex bottles and rags, and shake it while they wipe down the mirrored back wall, which can get a little smudged. In one corner is the newest addition to tittie bars, a live online hook-up. Dancers chat with their fans, fans chat with each other, it's supposedly all very utopian and groovy. I look over someone's shoulder, and see the chat-room conversation deep into the nuances of Frequent Flyer mileage.

Asia has been dancing only a few months. She lives in the East Bay, and started by answering an ad in the paper. She realizes she has to play up her Asian looks, and dances to David Bowie's "China Girl." While we sit at a table and talk, none of the other dancers approach me. When Asia leaves, they all flit over, one at a time: "Hi, I'm Montana, do you want some company?" I explain what I'm doing to another dancer named Ondine, and she immediately starts in about the other clubs, the fact that some girls are blowing guys, even screwing them. "Are you going to mention that in your book?" she asks. Her father hung out in North Beach during the 1960s boom years, and has told her all about it. "I really admire Carol Doda," she says.

Although Carol Doda was "too busy" to talk for this project, some of San Francisco's familiar faces from the randier era are more accessible. Adult film star Richard Pacheco lives across the bay, raising a family and working in commercials and industrial films, and like most in the porn industry, is very low-key about his past. Once a top actor in the biz, John Leslie lives in Mill Valley, and in addition to directing major X-rated features, also has begun singing and playing harp with a kick-ass group called the John Leslie Blues Band. His newspaper ads carry the slogan "Yes...that's him!"

When I visited the home of adult star Annette Haven, one of the first big names of the 1970s, she immediately threatened to kill me if I took notes, recorded our conversation or even hinted at divulging the name of the city where she lives. Once I assured her that I wouldn't endanger her privacy, she put on one of her videos (I think it was by Alex de Renzy), and we sat on her sofa for a very pleasant chat — or rather, she chatted nonstop and I listened, trying to follow her rapid-fire train of thought while sneaking peeks at the on-screen orgy out of the corner of my eye.

Jamie Gillis has appeared in adult films since the early loops, winning all the major awards for best actor over the years, and can often be found in the cafes of North Beach, enjoying a cigar at an outdoor table. Most of his contem-poraries who still work in the business live in L.A., but he prefers the laidback anonymity of the Bay Area, appearing in the occasional feature and video. One sunny afternoon we strolled through the annual Folsom Street Fair together, held on the

streets of the gay S/M district, checking out the latest videos and spanking accessories of the current sexual underground. It was quite interesting to see, in spite of his low-key Northern California lifestyle, how many people recognized his face from his three decades of porn films, and treated him like the rare appearance of royalty.

Prostitution activist Margo St. James, founder of COYOTE and figurehead of the notorious 1970s Hooker's Balls, can now be found working as a guest hostess at an Italian restaurant in North Beach, and moonlighting as a deckhand on a charter boat. Two years ago she revived the Hooker's Ball concept on a smaller scale, providing a catalyst for the various fringe sex industries located in the Bay Area. True to form, Margo's grand entrance to the ball is nothing if not glamorous. At the 1995 event, she was carried in on a sultan's throne by a group of smiling, well-muscled men, and she kicked off the 1996 ball by riding into the club on the back of a burro.

Margo threw a party on election night 1996 for what she hoped would be her entrance into city politics as a supervisor. As the party watched from the pier, the *Ruby* chugged into view, dropped anchor and Margo St. James delicately stepped aboard a rowboat and was oared ashore to the assembled crowd of friends, prostitutes, news photographers and California senator Milton Marks, among others. She began a short speech, during which time her old friend "Dr. Hip" sex advice columnist Eugene Schoenfeld interrupted to yell quite loudly, "SHOW US YOUR TITS!" Without missing a beat, Margo answered back, "They're not real," and continued her press conference. Although her bid for election was narrowly defeated, she has kept busy working as a consultant to sex worker activist groups, and there is talk of selling her story as a live stage production.

San Francisco is also home port for three of the nation's largest sex mail-order firms — Xandria, DechTar, and Good Vibrations. While the first two conduct their business through fulfillment of orders, Good Vibrations also has offered a retail division since its inception in 1977. The newest incarnation of the store continues to be run as a female cooperative, and their selection of vibrators and dildos has expanded to include books, videos and other sex-related products, the sheer volume and variety of which is staggering. Perhaps a dildo in the sleek shape of a dolphin, or maybe a vibrator with a plastic pulsating pink tongue at one end? Sneak a peek into the back room and witness bins of neon butt plugs, stacked to the ceiling. Plaques from local publications hang on the walls, proclaiming Good Vibes the best selection of sex toys in the city, and the store frequently sponsors erotica readings. Good Vibes founder Joanie Blank is no longer involved in the day-to-day operation, but her book company Down There Press, begun simultaneously with the store, still releases titles.

A recent 20th anniversary party for Good Vibrations, held at a South of Market nightclub, provided some insight into the first women-run sex shop on the West Coast. The evening started with video clips of people's memories of what the sexual mood was like in 1977. One woman addressed the camera and said back in those days there was no worry — a shot of penicillin cured everything. The crowd was appreciative and attentive, primarily women, lesbian and hetero couples, with a few older guys lurking around by themselves.

Entertainment was provided by a guy doing acrobatics on a trapeze and a set by comedian Marga Gomez, who got big reactions from her mentions of how chickenshit Ellen DeGeneres was for not coming out of the closet sooner. And then it was time to present the Venus awards.

The awards — little acrylic statues vaguely in the shape of a woman — were being given to local pioneers in the world of sex, presented by local pioneers in the world of sex, which was pretty much everybody in the world of sex who lived in the San Francisco area. Through a miracle of scheduling, nobody was stuck with actually having to present an award to themselves. The statues were not properly affixed to their bases, making each recipient awkwardly clutch the bottom of the award as it was handed him or her. Everyone graciously accepted with profuse thank-yous, from Joanie Blank to writer Susie Bright, photographer Michael Rosen, sex advice columnist Isadora Alman, porn star Nina Hartley (who thanked both her husband and her wife) and authors Pat Califia and Carol Queen, among others. But the pinnacle of the evening was yet to unfold.

Anyone who has heard of Annie Sprinkle, the "Queen of Kink," knows that she sells panties and vials of urine through the mail. We know her live performances culminate with a display of her own cervix to the crowd. We know that you can pose for a post-show Polaroid with your head in between her breasts. I know all of this, and I'd never seen her. Since the 1970s, she has worked in adult films, prostitution and teaching

workshops. Her public relations skills are as honed as her exhibitionism. This night she was on the bill for a special performance.

She danced out very innocently, then coyly shed her bra and began smearing chocolate ice cream on her ample breasts. After pulling on paper doilies, Sprinkle then stuck two candles in the middle of the muck and lit them. Somewhere in the midst of all this, confetti was thrown onto her. The stage had become a sloppy, slippery pig sty. One of the doilies promptly caught on fire, but Sprinkle was too busy smiling and dancing about to notice her own tit was ablaze. Fortunately, her alert assistant discreetly reached over and pinched out the flame.

Sprinkle then got a firm grip on a Hitachi Magic Wand — universally regarded to be the plowhorse of electric vibrators, the standard by which all others are judged, the very mention of the name of which sends women whimpering to their knees — pushed it into her crotch and began a steady wailing, screeching, cater-wauling into a microphone, while at the other end of the stage, the assistant strummed an acoustic guitar and led the crowd in singing "Happy Birthday" to honor the Good Vibrations empire. The spectacle was simultaneously grotesque and charming, the mostly female nightclub floor elbow to elbow, transfixed to the stage, singing along with the words with huge shit-eating smiles, some shouting, others clapping, arms high in the air — the heat and noise melding to create sort of a sensation of being inside a combination giant amniotic sac and an Army/Navy game. It was at once safe and warm and feminine and crackling with zeal — a freedom that could easily snap out of control if provoked. At any moment, banners might have unfurled from the balconies, exposing, instead of swastikas, huge vaginal symbols punctuated by crossed vibrators. A mustachioed babe would be shouting in German at a microphone, pounding the podium for emphasis, a thousand arms would shoot up Sieg Heil-style, as a tank would crash into the facade of the club and clank into the midst of the crowd, barrel covered in papier-mache to resemble a giant latex dildo sculpted in the shape of a porpoise. Women would crawl over the vehicle, stroking and cooing the barrel as ear-splitting polka music blared from the sound system....

Then again, maybe I just needed some air.

San Francisco is also home to the Institute for the Advanced Study of Human Sexuality, a repository of sexual knowledge and

erotica that may well be the largest of its kind in the world. Begun in the mid-'60s by Methodist minister Rev. Ted McIlvenna as the National Sex Forum, the NSF initially was an offshoot of the Glide Memorial Church, set up to protect homosexuals from police harassment, and educate people through sexuality workshops and its own films. In 1970 McIlvenna started the Institute, which has grown into both a graduate-level school, where people may earn an advanced degree in erotology, and the world's largest collection of erotic materials. He has appeared in court hundreds of times to testify as a sexuality expert, and for a time even ran an International Museum of Erotic Art in downtown San Francisco. Throughout the city are scattered entire warehouses of erotic books, videos, publications and 16mm films (some say the films came from porn producers who donated their archives as a tax write-off), all with the barest minimum of cataloging. McIlvenna boasts he has more erotica than the Vatican, the British Museum, and the Kinsey Institute put together.

A phone call finds McIlvenna weary, bitter and pissed-off at the enormous inconvenience of having to explain himself and his organization to yet another college-boy reporter who apparently has no concept or comprehension of the history of sexuality:

"We're a serious academic institution spending $100,000 a year for maintaining the materials," begin McIlvenna in his gruff voice. "We're not interested in publicity."

I mention that I thought the Institute is perfect to be located in San Francisco, which seems to be a focal point for —

"I really couldn't care what you think," he interrupts. "I'm interested in something being accurate, historically. Everybody rewrites history as if it was all discovered by Hefner in the mansion in Chicago. What happens is, we're here. If you wanna come by, you can come by, but it's not gonna be sweetness and light. We're not promoting anything or selling you anything. It's a serious graduate school, where people come and study erotology — which is a systematic study of the graphic depictions of the acts of sex and of love. As far as we know, we try to be historically correct. I was involved in the court cases. I did 680 of them. All these people that are claiming to know about them — they were never there. They weren't involved, they didn't testify. They were scared out of their wits. Now we hear people coming forward, the Playboy Foundation supported the great battles. They were never there. They supported the bits

that made them look good."

McIlvenna seems particularly peeved at the parasitic journalists and amateur researchers — peons like myself — who drop by just to use the materials.

"They don't pay for them," he barks. "We loan it to them, they steal them, and they say, 'It's in the public domain.' The fuck it is. It takes hundreds of thousands of dollars to collect and preserve this stuff. Our attitude about it is, okay, if somebody can prove to us that they seriously want to look at something. We've had 'em — from the people studying the Mitchell brothers to Robert De Niro — come and spend weeks here, doing background stuff for a movie, and then they don't pay us. We can't sue everyone. It's a waste of time for us.

"But guys like you," continues McIlvenna with the tone reserved for discussing rotten garbage. "Nobody checks your sources. That's why people with book contracts — I've written 28 books. So what? I could lie about them. Nobody ever checks the sources. The opinions of some people in the media, who came late — they were never involved in anything."

We talk for a few more minutes about his art collection, and it is made clear to me that Ted McIlvenna is extremely informed about the world of sex, perhaps the most knowledgeable person in the United States, even the Western Hemisphere. And if there were a parallel universe out past the very last glowing heat-ball star of our Milky Way solar system, containing 2 trillion separate sexual artifacts and pieces of information from all known galaxies, the most extensive collection ever assembled in deep space, lorded over by Zorklon-15, an asexual tank of boiling DNA slime capable of making a googol source-checking decisions a second, it wouldn't matter. All of the important stuff is back with Ted McIlvenna in San Francisco.

Sociological studies of the swinging lifestyle in the '60s and '70s point to one of the largest concentrations being located in Northern California. One still-functioning relic of the heyday is the Edgewater West Adult Resort, just a short drive down Hegenberger Road from the Oakland Airport. Behind the high-security gates lies Swinger Central for the East Bay, a semi-circle of 80 hotel suites, whose plate-glass windows all face an enclosed courtyard of swimming pools and hot tubs, punctuated by palm trees and shrubs. Free pornography is piped into each room's TV set, and visitors are advised to avoid the adjoining Chinese restaurant.

Current Edgewater manager Marc Moreno was alerted to his present position by a bodyguard of Hell's Angels figurehead Sonny Barger, and promptly quit unloading trucks at a warehouse to take a job at the hotel. The 35-year-old Moreno presides over the Bay Area's primary alternative to the tedium of 15 years of marriage, and claims it attracts swingers from all over the world. Built in the 1950s, the Edgewater was for years a deluxe convention hotel with banquet facilities, the only one on the strip leading out to the airport. As more and better hotels were built nearby, the Edgewater fell out of favor with companies seeking business accommodations, and by the late '60s had begun attracting clientele who were mostly interested in partying and couple-swapping. The low-key profile meant that the scene remained virtually unknown to residents of the East Bay. Occasionally an unsuspecting family on vacation would check into the hotel, wander through the courtyard with their children and be greeted with the sight of fat hairy bikers smoking pot and carrying on in the hot tub.

The hotel's owners in those days were largely absent, and business guests tapered off in the early '70s, leaving a bunch of frisky swingers who essentially assumed management duties of the facility so it wouldn't close. After an extensive renovation in the early 90s, the Edgewater still boasts an enormous banquet room with picture windows that face the courtyard, but there are few tables or chairs. People don't come here to conduct business. An alcohol-free bar and disco is situated next to the empty room, and behind that is another communal hot tub.

On one visit to the Edgewater, a regular explained the house rules to me. If a room's curtain is open, for instance, it means it's okay to watch any proceedings, and if the door is open, you may enter and participate if invited. Saturdays are couples only, and Moreno claims the place has gotten completely out of hand many times, from lesbian-only weekends to location shoots for porn films. Among the regulars are a salesman in his 50s, married with kids, who has rented the same room every weekend for years, and jerks off to the TV set images, hoping people will peer in the windows and watch him. Other regulars have nicknamed him "The Masturbator." One well-dressed attorney pays $120 for his same room every weekend, and sets up a video camera on a tripod, to film the young woman he has brought with

him. Yet another regular, by day a young computer programmer, prefers to check into a room alone, opens his curtains wide to allow a clear view of himself and lies on the bed, stroking his extraordinarily well-endowed member. He takes great pains to remove all of his body hair with Nair before arriving.

Couples stroll the courtyard, the men fully dressed, the women invariably wearing something flouncy and transparent. Other women wander by themselves, their tanned, wrinkled skin no stranger to nudity. Beefy guys sit alone at tables — lots and lots of guys — drinking from enormous plastic commuter mugs that belong on the dashboard of a Peterbilt. One chubby man sits at the juice bar, smoking a cigarette, wearing a sports cap, green windbreaker and black jockstrap. These are slaves to the sensual, who can experience a three-hour back rub and not get bored, knowing it will culminate in a rambunctious couple-swap with some nice folks from Sacramento. And amidst all of this, black cats scurry across the courtyard at odd intervals, skittish with a sensory overload of so many human beings.

Manager Moreno explains that most people who participate in "the lifestyle" are in their 30s or older, usually folks who have been in a long-term relationship, and want to try something different. Kids in their 20s are too busy running around to nightclubs. The majority are white, conservative and live in the suburbs. Couples new to the scene generally check into a room with another couple, and while remaining monogamous have sex on one bed, while the other couple does the same on the other bed, an activity Moreno calls "same-room sex." Some have been coming to the Edgewater for over 20 years — it's their only form of social interaction. (Serious swingers also will attend the annual lifestyle convention, the largest in the world, which can attract up to 5,000 people.)

The expectation at the Edgewater is staggering, as everybody busies him- or herself with "The Wait" — if we just hang out long enough, something really wild will happen! As their '70s-era brochure says, "perhaps for the first time in your life, truly be who you want to be." But eroticism is always fueled by the imagination, and when nothing is left to the imagination, you've got a roomful of chimps who like to watch. Voyeurs at the Edgewater have a keen sense of action on the horizon, and when a room shows promise of activity, they are drawn to it like moths to a porch light. Rooms on the ground floor are more expensive because they offer an easier view.

On one occasion, several guys are crowded around a room at the end of the courtyard, peering inside a six-inch gap in the curtains. The room is bathed in the glow from a red light bulb, and on the bed is a couple, engaged in a 69 position. The woman is small, barely five feet tall, wearing a nightie, and the man is naked, with a big belly. One guy with a baseball cap turns away from the window, his breath heavy with booze, and slurs into my face, "She ain't even showin' any tit!"

Another evening, I was invited to attend the Edgewater's first-ever Great American Strip-Off dance competition, a Moreno brainstorm that required him to visit strip joints throughout the Bay Area, shopping for contestants. As I entered the courtyard, my first visual was of an older gentleman, leaning nude against the doorway of his ground-level suite, close-up fellatio playing on the TV behind him, hairy belly almost obscuring his flaccid little Elvis. He silently checked out the newcomers. Our eyes met for a creepy moment, and I wondered if he was going to suddenly burst into a crusty British accent:

"Ah, Pemberton, jolly good to see you. Yes, yes, been far too long."

I found later that this was "The Masturbator," surveying his domain from the usual room.

The strip contest was held in the dining room area, on a special stage constructed just for the occasion, and for me best encapsulated the spirit of the Edgewater. Host for the evening was an Edgewater regular, a short balding attorney named Neil, sporting a tuxedo and an emphatic belief that his lascivious wit was charming the pants off the place.

After a young woman named Salacious took the stage and danced two songs. Neil and his celebrity co-host, porn actress Shanna McCullough, joined her for a little chat.

"How did you get your name Salacious?" asked Neil.

The dancer explained that she looked the word up in the dictionary, and it meant "erotic, sexually desirable."

"YES IT DOES!" blurted Neil with an oily chuckle. The audience was silent. A woman selling sexual trinkets at a table behind me let out a groan.

"Oh, Neil, don't be such a pill."

Neil the Pill didn't care, because all eyes were on him, bringing on the flesh with greasy fanfare:

"Her name is Candy, and SHE IS SWEET!"

"Would it be too obvious to say that Venus is a heavenly body?"

A dancer named Angel left the stage, and Neil said with a wink: "She's enough to make you turn to religion!"

After the contest ended and the winners were awarded little acrylic statues, Neil insisted on kissing every contestant on the cheek, whether they were expecting it or not. The master of the one-liner turned to the thinning crowd, thanked them for coming and yelled into the mike:

"It's good to be king!"

Another long-standing alternative community in the Bay Area is the More commune. Situated in an unincorporated area of Lafayette, the 16-acre community has been the subject of local speculation for years, if for no other reason than every single building on the premises, and every car that enters or leaves the property, is painted the identical shade of bright purple. Rumors still fly that the "Purple People" are engaged in rampant child molestation, butchery, blood-drinking and god knows what else, perpetrated by freaky hippies stoned out of their gourds.

Having no prior knowledge of their organization or mission, a preliminary investigation into the inner workings of the Purple People found myself and an associate paying an unannounced visit. After hiking down a hillside and crawling through two barbed wire fences, we stood in a graveled area, flanked by a rotting purple shed, a run-down greenhouse with the plastic roof caved in, cases and cases of empty juice containers and a house with children's toys scattered about. Sort of a Spahn Ranch without the dune buggies.

We knocked on the door of the house, a woman answered and despite our professional demeanor was immediately freaked out and yelled for help. Another man came to the door wearing only shorts and a gold necklace with a peculiar symbol, looking somewhat like an upside-down peace sign with a bar running through it. We explained our presence, he went back inside and made a phone call, then returned to say we had to leave. Strangely, rather than asking us to turn around and walk back up the hill, he wanted to escort us to the main gate.

We began walking down a tree-lined gravel road in the afternoon sun, the man either ignoring our questions entirely, or answering with the barest minimum of words, as in:

"Why is everything purple?"

Five seconds of silence.

"It's the owner's wife's favorite color."

EdgewaterWest
Premier Adult Resort

10 Hegenberger Road
Oakland, California 94621
Phone (510) 632-6262

We soon came upon several futuristic-looking structures that, for lack of a better reference, appeared to be patterned after a combination of the Jetsons cartoons and the old Monsanto home at Disneyland's Tomorrowland. They were roughly mushroom shaped, the lower level a parking area, and the rounded top the living quarters, with windows and chimneys. As with the other buildings, everything was bright purple. Several women were performing routine chores, a few working on top of the mushrooms, while children flitted about. They all stopped and waved at us, and we waved back, but it was clear that Mr. Necklace didn't want to stop and chat.

We continued down the road, passing a bizarre collection of vehicles parked on the grassy shoulder — a Winnebago mobile home, several '70s Cadillac Eldorados and a homemade camper — again, all painted purple. Mr. Necklace stopped us at the front gate to the compound, where inside a wooden hut was a man in a T-shirt and jeans, eating a sandwich, watching a color television. Mr. Sandwich seemed to nominally outrank Mr. Necklace, and also wore the little modified peace-sign emblem. Again we explained the reason for our visit, and like his cohort, Sandwich was oddly silent and not forthcoming with any information other than a general information phone number. (I later discovered this was commune CEO Alexander Van Sinderen, a graduate of both Stanford and Syracuse, and holder of a doctorate in lifestyle from More University, whose dissertation was titled "A Married Couple and a Single Woman as a Social and Sexual Unit.")

Mr. Sandwich pointed us up the road to the highway. We started walking, and looked back to see a sign posted on the guardhouse, reading "Absolutely no trespassing unless you want your feelings hurt."

The commune, also called Morehouse, was started in 1968 by Victor W. Baranco, a Berkeley appliance salesman who, much like others at the time, envisioned his own utopian community and conveniently established himself as the supreme guru, albeit one with a penchant for driving golf carts. In 1971 Baranco moved the commune outside Lafayette, California, and to finance everything, devised a series of classes in "sensuality," using plaster casts of the human genitalia as visual aids to teach students about creating the perfect sexual lifestyle. Jealousy is discouraged, and people can sleep with whomever they want. The idea grew so popular that Baranco opened satellite Morehouse branches in several cities nationwide, including

Atlanta, Boston, Long Island and Hawaii, earning him the nickname the "Colonel Sanders of communes." Students can obtain doctorate degrees from More University, which then qualify them to teach the classes, costing up to $16,000. Typical courses include "Basic Sensuality" and "Mutual Pleasurable Stimulation of the Human Nervous System." From the '60s through the present day, hundreds of people have received their Morehouse education before moving on — some starting up their own utopian sex communes. Baranco's ex-wife Suzanne is responsible for everything being colored purple, and while she still lives there today, acting as dean of the More University sensuality department, Baranco now resides in Hawaii.

In addition to tuition, Morehouse also benefits from its nonprofit groups, Turn On to America and the Private Sector, that take in nearly $1 million a year in charitable donations. Much of the money goes to feed and clothe the 100 or so homeless people who live on the premises in converted ranch-house bedrooms, which one former resident has called "gerbil cages." Other offshoots are Humore Inc., that controls the commune's real estate holdings, and the Institute of Human Abilities, set up to provide communication courses and develop real estate.

Throughout the main Lafayette headquarters, Baranco has designed a network of paths paved with carpet remnants, so that everyone who lives there can also experience the joy of driving a golf cart. Also prominent in the camp's design is a heart-shaped swimming pool and a common-area disco/clubhouse called the Waipuna Lounge. A 1992 undercover investigation by two reporters from the *Contra Costa Times* reported that Morehouse television sets broadcast a nightly closed-circuit news program called KLIT-TV, produced on-site and featuring scenes of parties, safe sex tips, children's music recitals and gossip about who's sleeping with whom. The two young female journalists posed as homeless transients, and although they were allowed access to much of the grounds, they wrote that the atmosphere was so creepy they stayed only 13 hours, and sneaked out the following morning.

As this book was going to press, I had an opportunity to speak briefly with someone from another alternative community — Michael Murphy, founder of the Esalen human potential resort on the coast at Big Sur. In particular I was curious about the often-told story where actress Natalie Wood got her butt spanked at a party. Murphy graciously remembered the scene:

"What happened was that Jennifer Jones started coming to Esalen after David O. Selznick died. We became friends, and she gave a big, big party for Esalen in 1966, at their mansion up in Benedict Canyon. Everybody was there. Rock Hudson, and you know, Terry Southern, and Glenn Ford. They turned out in force. It was Hollywood meets the human potential movement. Everybody was really dressed up. There was plenty of drink. So there was Fritz Perls and Carl Rogers — oh god it was hilarious. At one point, for example, they showed a film — Carl Rogers did — of the first encounter groups. And then he stood and manfully said he was going to conduct one of these groups out around the swimming pool, and anybody who'd like to follow him, follow him. He walked up the center aisle of the showing room. Not a single person followed.

"Later, Perls held forth, out there, instead. Now Perls was very, very dramatic, and forbidding as hell. He looked like something out of the Old Testament. Anyway, he would take on anybody. He did indeed put Natalie across and gave her a big spank on her bottom, at which Roddy McDowell stormed out, and declared to one and all, he was going to take Perls on. Man to man, physically. Roddy McDowell at that point was 35, and Fritz was 75. But I noticed he didn't address that directly to Perls, he was saying that to all of us. So we all egged him on! We'd never seen anyone — so Roddy McDowell versus Fritz Perls. That was all over her getting spanked. She was only spanked once, slapped on the behind, for, as he put it, 'unwilling to open up.' It was a great evening. Not a single cent was raised for the cause!"

Murphy then shrieked with laughter.

Ask any hippie which newspaper covered the West Coast sex scene, and he'll remember the *Berkeley Barb* with fondness. Beginning in 1965, the underground *Barb* provided a vital Bay Area outlet for news and political satire ignored by mainstream media, and in addition to a strange little comic strip called *Zippy the Pinhead* also featured the latest in sexual information and launched the concept of personal ads. Alas, the *Barb* succumbed to the changing political climate and regressed to a few pages of sex ads and classifieds, until Kat Sunlove and Layne Winklebleck purchased it in the mid-80s and relaunched it as a monthly called *The Spectator,* originally the title of the sex-related section that was inserted in the *Barb.*

Ensconced in a small strip mall in Emeryville, California, the *Spectator* offices look pretty much like any publishing enterprise — except for the photocollages of nude dancers adorning the walls of the art department, and the dominatrixes dropping by to place their classified ads. The paper focuses primarily on the sex scene of the Bay Area and occasionally down the peninsula to San Jose, including book reviews, commentaries and photo spreads of strippers and adult film stars. The porn-genre wordsmithing of photojournalist Dave Patrick and David Aaron Clark, formerly managing editor of *Screw,* makes the articles and reviews fun to read, and a regular column by Pat Califia keeps tabs on the latest developments in the world of sex and legality. A recent court decision has forced *The Spectator* to now work overtime producing two versions — one for subscribers and stores, and a toned-down edition for its newsracks. When asked about the predecessor *Barb,* however, the *Spectator* staff is nonplussed. All the archives were tossed some time ago.

Once a month *The Spectator* hosts a luncheon, an informal think tank of the sex industry no doubt more entertaining than an average convening of the Hoover Institute. I was invited to attend one of these luncheons, and marveled at the discussions of Eastern European porn videos and S/M whip techniques as everyone casually nibbled at salads and sandwiches. The crowd was very friendly, from porn star Richard Pacheco to Good Vibrations founder Joanie Blank, erotica writer and historian Michael Perkins and other assorted entities. One man dropped by simply to talk about what it was like working at a porn video shop. Another woman showed up because she was sexually frigid, and was curious as to what path she should pursue. A big scary guy showed up dressed entirely in black leather, and only spoke up when the conversation turned to "single-tailing," i.e., getting whipped with an honest-to-god bullwhip instead of one of those pansy cat o'nine tails whips. Joanie Blank offered up an idea to form an organization to devote time and energy to a specific cause I can't recall now, but *Spectator* publisher Kat Sunlove immediately pledged $1,000 to the effort. At one point Pacheco leaned over to me and whispered, "Bet you never thought you'd be hearing this kind of talk at lunch."

If Northern California has gained a reputation for originality and experimentation, Los Angeles seems to have cornered the market on year-round outdoor communities, ultra-sleazy strip joints and, of course, the megalithic porn video industry. The 1970s Sandstone touchy-feely retreat up in Topanga Canyon no longer exists, but the Elysium nudist community still thrives, both as a clothing-free facility and as a publisher of nudist books and magazines. Founder Ed Lange has passed away, but his daughter Dana Mia Lang Newman has stepped in to carry on the family tradition. Stories have circulated in recent years of young women being dogged by men like a heifer in a bull pasture, but the atmosphere is stressed to be consensual. Visitors to Elysium must first attend an orientation seminar, one supposes to weed out the freaks and voyeurs. Unfortunately, on the weekend I had planned to attend Elysium, my ride for the day developed an outbreak of herpes on her lip, and refused to be seen in public. Not that a herpes sore would be that significant at a nudist colony, but our excursion was nevertheless canceled.

I eventually was able to visit the clothing-optional Lupin Resort, in the hills outside Santa Cruz, as a special guest of Susie Bright, who is not only a big-shot writer, but a Lupin member. The air was quiet, temperature in the '70s, not a cloud in the sky as our group of six stopped at the entrance to fill out paperwork. After entering my name into a computer, a woman handed back my ID with a smile and a thank you. I noticed the guy sitting at the other computer was totally naked, his equipment flaccid, tucked between his thighs. We walked back to the van, shed our clothes and grabbed some suntan lotion. As if on cue, a beautiful young naked woman, wearing only shoes, walked confidently past us down a sloping road. This immediately started a discussion about how ironic it is that when young people's bodies are at their most toned, you're often at your most ignorant, sexually. Satisfied with this insight, we all felt better about ourselves, and set out to explore the grounds.

Lupin is designed in three sections — a residential trailer area; an area of tents and yurts, where people rent spots to camp for the weekend; and an area of houses, some for rent, others with long-term owners. A restaurant/cafe offers sandwiches, juices and beer. Activities suggest a typical resort environment, with various swimming pools, hot tubs, sunning areas and a vicious ongoing game of volleyball — except almost everyone is buck naked.

Total membership runs about 1,000, more male than female. Because women are traditionally more body-conscious, the resort finds it more difficult to attract female members,

and offers body-awareness workshops for those with such concerns. Men don't seem to have much of a problem, judging from all the enormous guts proudly mincing about the pathways on spindly little legs. Out of the hundred or so folks lounging about this weekday afternoon, most were middle-aged couples and little kids, with a noticable absence of teenagers. As kids splashed and played in one end of the pool, and a volleyball game raged on on the adjacent court, adults chatted in lounge chairs, drinking beer. One man stood under a tree, painting at an easel.

Entertainment was on the agenda for later that evening. Bluegrass banjo night had already occurred earlier in the month, but the main lodge was being decorated for the Saturday night dance, themed the "Summer of Love." On one wall of the main dining room were posters of Woodstock, the Beatles and Jim Morrison, the other walls displaying photography prints from members of the "Camera Club," Lupin's informal group of shutterbugs. On dance nights, I was told, people actually have to put clothes on, in order to appear more erotic.

Somebody should do something about the level of eroticism at nudist camps, because there is none. There is nothing sexual about a nudist environment. Everybody's got ample bellies, flabby arms, hairy backs, knobby knees, cottage-cheese butts, saggy breasts and shriveled penises — more weird-looking penises than you could shake a stick at. To compensate for this reality check, you find yourself looking people in the eyes more than usual, paying closer attention to their conversation.

"Was it a lot different than you expected?" smiled Glynn Stout.

Stout has been manager of Lupin since the late 60s, when he left behind a Stanford MBA and a computer industry job to pursue a lifestyle he believed in more. The place was pretty run-down in those days, little improved from the 1930s, when a San Francisco-to-Santa Cruz rail line called the "Sunshine Train" would stop at the resort to drop off nude sunbathers. Over the years, Stout has put up buildings, installed pools and added landscaping to attract an eclectic upscale clientele — up to 35 percent of his members have graduate degrees.

We sat on towels on the lawn, and he talked about the history of nudism in his soft-spoken Texas drawl. According to Stout, the true nudist heyday was the 1950s, a period of experimentation that embraced progress without the '60s rebellion and self-destruction. People were finding work in technology industries, building ranch homes in the suburbs and enjoying the simple pleasures of getting naked in the sun. One Southern California nudist colony occasionally held classes where Hollywood stunt actors instructed others in the fine art of firearms discharge.

Stout is from this earlier era, and seems to have more conservative values at heart than the hippie generation. He remembered that Sandstone "was pretty out there, sexually." Not many people at Lupin try to pick up on anybody, he said, adding that if he sees it, he'll kick them out for harassment.

As we sat on the lawn, a couple walked past who distracted everyone's attention. A blonde man and woman, strikingly attractive, strolling with arms around each other, both with 0.001 percent body fat. They were regulars, and exuded the presence of an Austrian ski champion, relaxing with his Swedish prize after kicking Franz Klemmer's ass on the downhill run. Their narcissism was not overt, but yet amazingly noticeable, a low, audible purr of confidence. Plus, the guy had a noodle like a palomino.

Susie Bright and I hit the tennis court, and although both of us are terrible players, the feeling of athletic activity wearing nothing but tennis shoes was extremely liberating. The positive aspects of nudism were quite evident, especially when the warm Santa Cruz mountain winds began to gently riffle the scrotal hair.

At one time, L.A. was home to a thriving chain of Pink Pussycat strip clubs, but most have closed, and the sole survivor of the dynasty is located on Santa Monica Boulevard in Hollywood. Renamed the Tomkat, the theater today shows exclusively gay porn, but in front of its door is the porn version of the Walk of Fame, where tourists photograph the hand- and footprints of John Holmes, Linda Lovelace, Marilyn Chambers and Harry Reems, as well as a few gay porn studs.

The Tomkat's soulmate in old-school sleaze is Jumbo's Clown Room, a mainstay of the topless scene since 1970. Nestled in an East Hollywood strip mall, Jumbo's has gained some sort of hipster reputation in recent years as a hangout for celebs like David Lynch and Drew Barrymore, and at one time employed Courtney Love as a dancer. The girls don't get completely naked because of state alcohol laws, but there's no cover charge. My first visit there was memorable for first of all, having to step over a very fat guy with an exposed butt crack who was

trying to repair the cigarette machine, with random parts and tools spread out all over the floor. As a girl onstage danced to Rod Stewart's "Do Ya Think I'm Sexy," the mechanic gunned his electric drill, and the sounds of shearing metal added a refreshing industrial sound to the proceedings. The men's room floor was accentuated with freshly vomited Chinese food, and I vividly recall using the urinal and staring at an undigested sprig of broccoli resting on the top of the flushing mechanism. Obviously this was a pretty hip place.

Being in close proximity to film equipment, labs and video dubbing facilities, it's only natural that Los Angeles would become the hub of the modern porn industry. A few years ago I was lucky enough to be invited on the set of a major big-budget adult feature, directed by John Leslie, who starred in many well-known films before moving behind the camera. My experience came with an unexpected bonus — $40 cash for appearing as an extra and delivering a line of dialogue. The following account is adapted from an article written for an Australian magazine, which was censored by the government and spiked in its entirety. While it's not long on analysis, it does provide the reader a glimpse behind the scenes of the present-day world of porn films:

After fitful dreams, I am sitting in a rental car with two acquaintances who are much better connected to such a world, listening to the Howard Stern show in a parking lot of the Refinery bar, in a West Hollywood strip mall next to the Mini Swap Meet Family Gift, Imperial Liquors, Hector's Beauty Center and Rubicon Real Estate. The morning is choked and sunny, a beautiful L.A. smog haze painting the sky as we watch the crew unload equipment. Our only contact is the man who hired us: director Ron Sullivan, aka Andre Pichard, who is functioning as assistant director for the day.

The crew members are industry pros who work on all kinds of films besides porn. The wardrobe girl used to work at the tabloid news show *Hard Copy*. If you were in a car driving past the block, it would appear to be any medium-sized film shoot in Los Angeles — a couple of dressing trailers for the cast, a truck or two for the equipment, a table of food under an umbrella. It could be a soft-drink commercial or fashion shoot — or a top-selling porn video.

We hang out at the catering table, scarfing free food and chatting with the other extras. One old guy looks about 60, wearing a fishing hat. He

could be your perverted grandpa. Another little guy wears a Members Only jacket, and another looks like he should be driving a delivery van for US Courier. There is one woman in her late 30s, wearing lots of jewelry and a B.U.M. jacket with patches, who works in sales for the porn production company Zane. She boasts that she has been an extra in 15 or 20 films. The female stars stay inside the dressing trailer, and the male actors sit out in the sun passing around a bowl of weed. The mood is mellow yet intense — quintessential L.A.

Today's shoot will actually be two scenes, one for the film *Dog Walker* and the other for the *Voyeur* series, both directed by John Leslie, shot on 35mm film stock with a big budget. Crew members tell me with some amount of pride that they've been shooting one film for *over a week*. Featured adult stars on the set are Kristi Lynn, Christina Angel, Tom Byron, Isis Nile and Steven St. Croix. Veteran adult star Jamie Gillis is also some kind of an assistant. Leslie is wound up, a happy, sex-driven guy, yet capable of extreme intensity, sort of like Al Pacino with a constant boner. He walks by the food table, where I'm scarfing M&M's, then suddenly stops and points at me:

"You. Act like somebody's messing with your girl. Say, 'Hey, leave her alone.'"

Hey, leave her alone.

Leslie turns away, still pointing at me. "Great, this guy's gonna do it."

In the first scene to be shot, a fully clothed St. Croix and a slinky Christina Angel get into an argument. I am to sit at the end of the bar behind them, listening to their squabbling, then turn around and interrupt them by saying, "Hey, pal, leave the lady alone!" St. Croix will then grab the collar of my jacket and snarl, "Leave...now." We do at least nine takes. Nothing against St Croix, but just for the record, I nailed my line every time.

Next up is a hand-job scene with Isis and St. Croix. A special light with a blue gel is positioned for the "wood shot." The dialogue is steamy and full of innuendo. Leslie gives specific instructions: "Okay, take his cock out. Twirl your thumb around it." The movies are magic.

The crew relights the bar for a "gangbang," which will be four guys and one woman. In a rare departure from the norm, Leslie will allow all the extras to watch — hence the concept of the *Voyeur* series. Leslie wanders the bar, checking camera angles and positions. He steps over some cables and announces to nobody in particular: "Over in Germany, they can shit on people but they can't

pull the hair." The crew laughs, but they are visibly jealous they won't be allowed to watch.

The shoot resumes, and Kristi Lynn, who can't be more than 19, walks into the bar, Leslie playing the character of her boyfriend. She is wearing a ridiculously tight one-piece leotard-type outfit with built-in garters and high heels, making her butt stick up and out like a bitch in heat. They order drinks from the bartender, and when Leslie orders a soft drink, she chastises him for not having real booze. He doesn't want to stay in the place, but she begs him to. Suddenly, four guys wander over from the pool table and begin rubbing her body. The storyline disintegrates in favor of an extended 45-minute orgy. Lynn's clothes are peeled off and she soon finds herself spread-eagled on bar stools, four dicks waggling at her from every angle. She begins sucking all of them in turn, with one eating her out. The extras sit on bar stools nearby, speechless, watching with saucer eyes. Leslie grabs a handheld Hi-8 camera and maneuvers around the action, a grip tagging along behind him with a portable light.

Leslie stops to reload tape and orders, "Keep the edge, guys."

One of the men slaps his dick to keep it hard; the others idly pull on their puds like spider monkeys. "You don't have to direct me," veteran actor Tom Byron reminds Leslie. "I know exactly what you're going to shoot."

The action resumes, and as Byron slobbers kisses on her mouth, Lynn abruptly pulls back, announces, "Man, you smell like wine," and sticks her gum in his mouth.

We later discover that she will be paid $200 for her work today.

One actor named Paul begins having sex with her from behind, loudly spanking her ass. Leslie hollers, "Don't beat the shit out of her!" Everyone, including Kristi Lynn, cracks up.

At the far end of the bar near the door, an elderly fire inspector casually eats his lunch throughout. Jamie Gillis sits at the bar, yawning and scratching his stomach.

The guys trade positions and keep pumping away, Kristi requesting more lube and at one point asking, "Did my sponge come out?"

"We'll do the anal," announces Leslie with some authority, "then turn her over for the cum shot."

Right on cue, Lynn screams, "Fuck me, fuck me in the ass!" Leslie reiterates: "Put it in her ass, Tom."

Byron obliges, sinking his shaft into her, humping her butt like a crazed collie as three other insistent penises find their way into her hands and mouth. Leslie orders, "I can't see her ass," so Byron holds one leg out of the way, Leslie on his knees, positioning his lens for the all-important angle as Byron stands on the ball of one foot like a Jethro Tull forest nymph. Byron pulls out of her asshole and a concerned Lynn exclaims, "Is it dirty?" All four guys say, "Heavens, no."

(Later someone tells me that many porn starlets take enemas eight hours before, just to keep looking their best.)

The requisite cum shot commences, with four guys ejaculating all over Lynn's face and chest as she screams, rather phonily, in delight.

A guy comes over with a camera to take static shots as if they're continuing having sex. Still photos can't show penetration, but there's a huge market for them, so when the film is distributed, it will be accompanied by action color slides, for reprint in the porn press. The guys are going limp, she's soaked with cum, but the posing goes well.

Someone brings the actors towels, we extras retrieve our eyeballs and pop them back into the sockets. The front door of the Refinery blows open like a submarine's door under extreme pressure, and the rest of the crew, wardrobe and catering people all descend on us: "What was it like? Did you see the gangbang?"

Yeah, we saw it. It was okay.

Being the only state in the Union to legalize prostitution, Nevada has carved out its own garish niche in the sexual landscape of the late 20th century. Although now promoted by tourist bureaus as a family-friendly vacation destination, Las Vegas has not shaken its reputation as a town of players. A closer look, via a package deal from San Francisco's Atrocity Tours (also responsible for the porn shoot experience), belies the city's inherent seediness.

About ten miles outside of town, Greyhound Lane winds through the desolate landscape and passes by a large two-story home, surrounded by a high metal fence. Three or four cars are parked in the gravel lot out front. Since the '70s this has been the location of the Red Rooster, a combination swinger's club and greyhound racing dog kennel, run by a couple named Mike and Chris. During the day they feed and provide a warm bed for *caninus*, and after nightfall the same apparently applies to *Homo sapien*. There are no signs to tell what type of business it is; if you don't know, you don't belong here.

Chris greets you at the door and lets you

inside with a smile. She is now about 50 or so, heavyset but not plump, and fully clothed. Her speech is memorized: the cover charge is $40 apiece, coat check is to your right. Here are the house rules — no entering into a situation without being asked, if a door is shut don't open it, if you want to drink alcohol leave your bottle with the bartender and she'll pour the cocktails. Towels are provided. Other than that, thanks for coming, have a great time, etc.

What hits you instantly upon entering the 12,000-square-foot Red Rooster is the redness — every square inch of the floor and walls is red. But not just red — red shag carpet, a Hefner-vintage sensuality explosion beneath the feet that nevertheless makes you want to keep your shoes on. The walls are decorated with Leroy Neiman Jazz Festival poster prints and other 1970s-era artifacts, as well as a blown-up photo of porn actor Ron Jeremy. Classic '70s rock plays at low volume.

A common living room area features a pool table, sofas, big-screen TV and the bar. Other rooms off to the sides and up on the second floor are simple bedrooms, with beds, lamps and cigarette-burned nightstands. Another sunken living room sports one of those ski chalet-style round gas-burning fireplaces that makes you feel like you're in an advertisement for Swedish tobacco, and behind that is an outdoor jacuzzi courtyard and a large room with round beds on multiple levels, which reminds you of the "Monkey Island" at the zoo.

One lone couple sits together at a table. The man is fully clothed in cap, snap-button shirt and jeans, and the woman sports big-lensed glasses and some type of lingerie which hangs open to reveal her breasts and ample belly. She smokes a cigarette, Neither of them speak, as if they're in a pancake house booth, waiting for a waitress.

There are no single women, of course, but a smattering of creepy guys pad around wearing nothing but white towels wrapped around their waists. As Shirley the bartender informs us, "You have to let the women see your top half first." A naked guy about 45 sits on the sofa, watching porn videos on the big-screen monitor. His wire-framed glasses give him the appearance of a junior high school vice-principal. Occasionally he gets up and abruptly leaves the room, then returns five minutes later, sits back down on the sofa and resumes playing with himself. Just watching him makes you nervous.

At the ski chalet fireplace sits a fully clothed guy, who says he's from Pittsburgh. He gestures across the room to his female companion, who is sitting on a bar stool getting a back rub from three Towel Boys. Apparently they've already had sex upstairs, and he has now placed her at the bar for all the Towel Boys to swarm around, touching her shoulders and stroking her knee. "In a minute I'll go over there and rescue her," he says, and then he does so and they walk back up the stairs. They come here several times a year.

The Monkey Island room suddenly comes alive, and Vice Principal and the Towel Boys all smell it like bloodhounds, crowding into the doorway, touching themselves through their towels. On one of the round beds is a couple having sex without condoms, a squat, mesomorphic woman and a rail-skinny guy. The woman grabs the sheets with her fists and lets out loud moans, not caring who hears or watches, the sure sign of a seasoned hedonist. It is soon over, and the Towel Boys and Vice Principal wander off, either in search of further voyeuristic activity, or perhaps to reflect on what they've just witnessed. The woman looks around the room and asks who's next? She finds a taker and they begin fooling around in a sling suspended from the ceiling, her partner opting to keep on his white sweat socks.

The skinny guy is now clothed, and he sits on a shag-carpet bench and leans against the shag-carpet wall. He's from Los Angeles, and travels frequently to Las Vegas on business, selling palm trees to the casinos that will be replanted and grow into the lush, displaced tropical foliage that decorates the city. Tree Boy says he used to come here more often a few years ago. There used to be a lot more women. On the weekend there would be a crowd of a hundred, people fucking in every room. One of his female friends, who also was a stripper at the local Crazy Horse, once did 12 guys at one time.

Tree Boy's sex partner is named Charlotte. She's in her mid-30s or -40s and lives in the area. Her husband works evenings, so she takes advantage of the nearby Red Rooster on average three times a week. She uses suppositories as birth control, and says, "It's really safe here." In addition to Tree Boy, two other guys will ejaculate inside her tonight.

Once our vehicle leaves the gravel road and hits the paved portion, we come upon a nondescript American sedan, signaling for a left turn onto a darkened frontage road. Behind the wheel, the bench seat moved up as far as possible, can be glimpsed the face of Charlotte, bluish-green in the glow of the dashboard lights, headed home after another fruitful evening at the Red Rooster.

"I later traveled back to Vegas on assignment to cover the annual AVN Awards, the Oscars of the porn industry. Awards for adult film achievement have been presented since the Blue Oscars were first organized by *Adam Film World* in 1975, and are now sponsored by *Adult Video News*, the *Vogue* magazine of the porn industry. Although the majority of pornography is produced in the San Fernando Valley, it makes perfect sense to celebrate its achievements in Las Vegas. An adult bookstore/video emporium called Pistol Pete's Las Vegas Showgirls is the site of the adult film Hall of Fame. Each year breasts of major porn starlets are imprinted in cement a la Grauman's Chinese Theater, and the concave concrete slabs are displayed on the walls of the store. The year I attended, adult film journalists were chatting about one star who, instead of placing her breasts into the fresh concrete, chose to make an impression of her open mouth. The following is adapted from an article that ran in the *HotWired* web publication, caused IBM to temporarily pull all of its advertising on the site:

I got my dildo right here — never leave home without it!" giggles porn star Alicia Rio to a friend, patting her purse as she strolls through the VIP reception for January's AVN Awards, the Oscars of smut. Sponsored by the slick monthly *Adult Video News*, the 13th annual gala is choking the lobby of the Aladdin Theatre for the Performing Arts in Las Vegas. Thick-necked men in tuxedos jostle for drinks; photographers elbow for candid shots; rail-skinny starlets parade ridiculous ballooned breasts stuffed into diaphanous gowns; and "suitcase pimp" boyfriends/husbands ride their women's coattails to sup from the trough of the billion-dollar adult entertainment industry. It may be glamour, but with an odor of thick perfume.

After sifting through the 5,500 adult films released in 1995, *AVN*'s editors selected the winners in some 97 categories, from best actress and director to best original CD-ROM concept, best group scene, and two separate awards for best anal sex scene. Last year John Wayne Bobbitt won for best new talent.

Anxious to hear this year's results, feverish fans have paid up to $150 apiece for tickets. Comedian Bobby Slayton faces a difficult task as master of ceremonies, competing not only with celebrity guests such as Ice-T and *Screw* publisher Al Goldstein (wearing a Los Angeles Coroner's Office sweatshirt that barely covers his stomach), but also with a toilet-mouthed ventriloquist puppet act called Otto and George, which, believe it or not, steals the show, with lines such as: "Some of the kids who sucked his cock had to be burped later!" and "Suck my cock like you're drowning and my balls contain oxygen!"

As with any awards event, recipients are often overcome with emotion upon being recognized for their artistry. *Where the Boys Aren't* star Jenna Jameson bursts into tears at the podium. Actor Rocco Siffredi brings his pregnant wife to the stage, and dedicates his award for cocksmanship to their unborn child. A French director, receiving the award for most outrageous sex scene, shot under the Eiffel Tower, explains, "This scene was verrah verrah special. It take almost four hours. I want to tank the actors."

Despite the sobs, the glitz, the puppet, even the efforts of drag performer Chi Chi LaRue, a gripping show it is definitely not. By the end of three hours, perhaps a quarter of the audience remains. The rest of the onlookers are back chatting at the bars in the lounge, same as every year.

The AVN Awards are the climax of the adult entertainment convention, which is held annually in conjunction with the Winter CES (Consumer Electronics Show), reportedly the country's second-largest Meeting of the Nerds. For this event, the Las Vegas Convention Center crawls with more than 90,000 totebag-clutching geeks, many of whom will also stick their pimpled noses into the adjacent adult portion, discreetly located further up the Vegas Strip at the Sahara Hotel. One of them enters the lobby and announces loudly to a friend, "Let me see if I recognize anyone from the Internet."

Rows of booths tout videos, lubes, leather gear, choose-your-own-color dildos, even a "virtual reality" display, with a volunteer donning goggles and finger mouse, ready to grope an on-screen vixen. At another booth, a video producer hawks his tape of amputations, executions and other violence: "You can get tits and ass every day, but you can't get death!"

Jar-head jocks wedge through the aisles alongside chubby balding guys, their lonely faces radiant with happiness. These "lookie-loos" have traveled hundreds of miles to this mecca and now patiently wait in line to receive a porn star's autograph that will say, "To Scott – Keep me wet! Love, Anna Malle." Surgically exaggerated nymphs in skimpy outfits – such as Tiffany Million, Catalina Lamour, Jenteal and Sid Deuce – are swarmed for photos.

Male stars like Joey Silvera and Tom Byron circulate quietly, the unsung and underpaid heroes who have worked for years in an industry where women are the attraction. Sprinkled throughout the crowd, and schmoozing with friends, are directors such as John "Buttman" Stagliano and John Leslie. Veteran Bruce Seven, suffering from a recent stroke, sits silently in a wheelchair at his Exquisite Pleasures booth, pillow in his lap, his shaky hands holding a box of Kleenex.

The industry is rife with tragedy. At least three adult stars died in 1995, two by suicide, yet only a passing mention is made during the awards show. If this were the Oscars, you can bet there would be a heartfelt film-clip retrospective of the deceased. But in the world of porn, everything's a party. Let the good times roll, and if you can't keep up the pace and blow your brains out, well, that's just too bad. It's not for everybody.

One astute conventioneer sums it up best when he enters the CES adult section and remarks, "This is where the money is."

Another long-standing sexual icon in the state of Nevada is the Mustang Ranch brothel, nine miles outside of Reno. Founder Joe Conforte no longer owns the business, but through his tenacity and willingness to fight the courts for legalized prostitution, it has survived decades of court battles and remains the most famous and notorious cathouse in the country.

As might be expected from its location on the interstate highway system, the parking lot is a prodigious chunk of pavement, built to accommodate dozens of big-rig 18-wheelers, as well as your horse trailers and stretch limousines. Smaller brothels next door, the Old Bridge Ranch and the Triangle River Ranch, handle overflow traffic on busier days. The morning I visited, the lot was nearly empty, but then again, it was only 10:30 or so.

The main Mustang building is painted bright pink, with a big pink sign overhead. To gain entrance, one must be buzzed in through a tall iron gate and stroll through a miniature front garden to the main door. As you reach for the knob, the door magically opens and a smiling woman ushers you inside with a hearty:

"Good morning, gentlemen. These are the ladies we have for you today."

Your first view is of a row of young women lined up like a hometown wrestling team – that is, if the wrestlers were scantily clad, hair sprayed up big, wearing red lipstick and teetering on high heels. All appear very young and most are fairly thin and attractive, except for a short chubby one at the very end of the line. Your role as customer is to select your preference, then disappear into one of the many side rooms with the girl and do your business. As of 1994, the Mustang Ranch price list was as follows:

$80—hand job
$100—blow job
$120—straight sex
$160—50-50 (oral sex and intercourse)
$500—anal sex

Having neither the inclination, energy nor finances necessary to fully explore the commercial possibilities of the facilities, my traveling companions and I made quick use of the luxurious grey sofas ringing the perimeter of the large central room, again painted bright pink. On opposite walls hung color portraits of Conforte and his wife, Sally. The rear of the room was furnished as a chrome and glass full-service bar, selling souvenir T-shirts in addition to stiffly-priced drinks. The girls quickly realized our intentions as strictly observational, and relaxed to chat. Some of them were from the local area, a few of them were going to school and one enterprising woman flew from Oregon to turn tricks at the Mustang one day a week, helping finance her law school education. Apparently members of my party came across as overly inquisitive, for one girl cut us off and asked:

"Are you guys from CNN?"

The door suddenly buzzed, the girls excused themselves from our conversations and dashed back just in time to again comprise the hometown wrestling team Row of Amorous Potential. As the front door opened, we heard the identical "these are the ladies we have for you today" speech, and two young bucks waltzed in, their gait indicating they were no strangers to the premises. They immediately made their selections and walked off, hand in hand with their maiden of the moment, headed for that familiar little room with the bed and sink, to contribute their part to the state's economy.

While the corporate headquarters of *Playboy* has remained in Chicago since its inception in the 1950s, the magazine's Manhattan offices on bustling Fifth Avenue are home to a large portion of the advertising and editorial staff. On a visit a few years ago for a lunch appointment, I marveled at the polished brass elevators that opened onto an expansive, airy lobby with polished floor, minimalist

furniture and pieces of art, a tweaked and distended sculpture of John Lennon's head standing out in particular. Turning a corner to the editorial department, one hoped to discover a room bustling with the excitement of a photo shoot. Perhaps one of those old photographer swingers like Arny Freytag or Pompeo Posar would be standing on a ladder, squinting through a lens at a young, overly endowed naked woman from Fort Collins, Colorado, standing on tiptoe looking into a mirror, pondering why she likes stormy beaches and can't stand pushy people, and all the while an unmistakable sexual electrical charge would fill the air and mingle with the various perfumes and colognes, an anticipatory pheromonal buzz that would attack all five senses at once, reminding everyone in the building, as it has done for over 40 years, of that sacred primal urge to fornicate for fun with the girl-next-door, and the photo shoot would disintegrate into nude wrestling on a white angora bedspread, bodies smelling like fresh diapers from the baby oil, participants yowling like jungle cats over the jazz on the hi-fi —

Instead, there were a bunch of offices with empty desks.

Editors are based in Chicago and Los Angeles, with Hefner forever ensconced in his L.A. mansion, but some of the key higher-ups work here in New York. Film critic Bruce Williamson works from this floor, and since the 1960s he has been *Playboy*'s adult and mainstream cinema reviewer. The offices of fiction editor Alice Turner and fashion editor Hollis Wayne line a wall of windows, as does the chamber of senior editor Bruce Kluger, who is responsible for assembling the Playboy Interview each issue. On a shelf in his office sat a CD-ROM compilation of Playboy Interviews — including the memorable Jimmy Carter admission of committing lust in his heart — indicating an increased interest in new media, as well as a good way to recycle material. There seemed to be little, if any, nudity in sight, apart from the occasional *Playboy* calendar posted above a desk, and the floor was almost disturbingly quiet.

Associate editor Chris Napolitano escorted me into the magazine's archives room, and handed me a xerox of Hefner's very first issue, which hit newsstands in October 1953, a beaming Marilyn Monroe waving America hello from the cover. Thumbing through the reprints of Sir Arthur Conan Doyle and Ambrose Bierce fiction, cartoons and the famous calendar shot of Monroe sprawled on the red backdrop, I realized that the guts of the publication is exactly the same as when it began — the typefaces, the page numbers, the table of contents, all identical to the current issue of *Playboy*. Unlike every other magazine on the newsstand, it has never been redesigned, except for modern photography and illustrations.

Subsequent issues from the '60s and '70s that I examined chronicled not only America's hetero heyday, but the boom times of *Playboy* as well: the humor pieces by Woody Allen and Dan Greenberg, the short stories of Isaac Asimov and Bruce Jay Friedman, the images of smiling Bunnies leaning over the craps table at a *Playboy* casino, the shots of a lithe Playmate shaking it on the disco floor of a Playboy Club, the behind-the-scenes peeks at celebrities jostling for drinks at Mansion parties and jazz festivals, the demure photo essay of what exactly should constitute a with-it bachelor pad (coincidentally mirroring the apartment of the magazine's editor) and of course, the pantheon of nude girls whose names were etched into the collective male consciousness — Marilyn Cole, Liv Lindeland, Claudia Jennings, Patti McGuire, Debra Jo Fondren, the Collinson twins — all now middle-aged women with families and B-movie credits.

In recent years American males have expressed interest in nude magazines that more accurately reflect their age group, and not that of Hefner and his original circle of contributors. Readership is still high among college fraternities, and the *Playboy* web site is among the most popular in cyberspace, but to boost circulation these days, *Playboy* has amplified its role as the bearer of celebrity breasts. Successful nude layouts of the past ten years like Jessica Hahn, Patti Reagan, Latoya Jackson and Pamela Anderson are now one of the magazine's main attractions. One of the editors mentioned to me that their next issue was to feature a photo spread of O.J. Simpson girlfriend Paula Barbieri, so we examined an untrimmed copy of a preview issue. As I thumbed through the meticulously airbrushed full-nude shots of this woman's fleeting fame by association, I admired, apart from the fact that she was obviously not an ugly-looking person, the timeliness of *Playboy* — O.J.'s first criminal trial hadn't yet begun.

In stark contrast were the offices of *Screw*, situated above a children's toy warehouse on West 24th Street, just down the block from Billy's Topless tittie bar on 7th Street. They have been on these premises only a few years, having moved from a skanky hovel on West 14th, where they were based for over 20 years, sharing a

building with a massage parlor. The lobby of Milky Way Productions is gained by exiting a rattling metal elevator, and walking into a sparse foyer whose walls were lined with yellowing press clips about Al Goldstein, framed under glass. A receptionist sits behind thick plexiglass, reminding the visitor of a high-security bank, or even a fast-food chicken joint in the ghetto. Managing editor Eric Danville greeted me and showed me around the operation. Al Goldstein still runs the magazine he founded in 1968, but no longer lives in New York, preferring to communicate with his staff via dictaphone several times a day from his home in Florida. His secretary's first task in the morning is to transcribe all the memos and distribute them to the staff, bitching about everything from cover type to purchasing gourmet coffee for the office rather than the standard, less expensive brand.

Screw might make Goldstein a lot of money, but you wouldn't know it from browsing the current issues, where he continually rails against his ex-wives for taking him to the cleaners. If he is still in the chips, he certainly isn't throwing it at his offices, which are lined with dirty-grey industrial carpeting, and boast the unmistakable odor of stale cigarette smoke. His co-founder, Jim Buckley, has long since departed to run a bookstore. Besides *Screw*, Goldstein also keeps busy contributing film reviews to *Penthouse*, and his Manhattan cable program *Midnight Blue* is still on the air Mondays and Fridays at midnight on Channel 35, offering rising porn starlets opportunities for publicity interviews and the chance to fend off humorous pleading from Goldstein to have sex with him, even though he's fat and old and has a small penis.

After introducing me to the art staff and a few others, Danville showed me into his office, which was evidently the source of most of the cigarette smoke. On the shelves, the floor, a desk, were stacked boxes and boxes and boxes of porn videos, some piles approaching three feet high, their bright colors and abundant photos of slutty women advertising the latest releases of the jizz biz. If someone was going to be screening these films for review purposes, they hadn't made much headway on the stock at hand. One bookshelf was devoted to reference books and bound volumes of the *Screw* archives, with the first year or two completely missing. Danville had no idea what happened to them.

We chatted for a while about the changing face of the sex scene. Although staff has rotated over the years, *Screw*'s editorial formula has changed very little. It's still printed black and white on newsprint, with a cover color illustration from a well-known (or even unknown) cartoonist. They still make fun of celebrities in the news by running photos of people having raunchy sex, with celebrity heads crudely grafted onto the shoulders. And the back pages are still devoted to the myriad ads for East Coast massage and outcall possibilities — every conceivable preference and fetish represented. As a public service to its readers, *Screw* thoughtfully also runs comprehensive listings of strip clubs, massage parlors, S/M dungeons and other current sexual hangouts, all described in a witty blurb of each business, retaining Goldstein's trademark bargain-basement sense of humor.

Danville lit another cigarette and said he had to get back to work, finishing transcribing a recent interview he had conducted with porn star Kaitlyn Ashley. As I sat down on the dirty carpet, paging through the formative years of *Screw* and taking notes, a boom box played back portions of the interview, which echoed throughout the office, exemplifying in a nutshell the common-denominator level of sexual journalism that resonates with loyal readers, the information the *Screw*-craving public will continue to pay for. The publication's editorial mission, as near as I could tell, could be absorbed and understood from the following exchange, which I heard rewound and played over and over:

SCREW: So, when you do anal, you really like it, right? I mean, like, you *really* like anal, right?

ASHLEY: [*with exaggerated sultriness*] Ohhhh, yeeaahhh!!!

In the early 1970s, the adult-oriented share of Manhattan's Times Square grew to over 150 porn theaters, shops and massage parlors, offering every imaginable type of perversion and depravity, from traditional burlesque dancers to bookstores, full-service massage and grimy loops of women having sex with eels. A local effort at gentrification, combined with a national wave of conservatism and a 1976 Supreme Court ruling that gave zoning power to city governments, has made a significant difference in the neighborhood. According to the *New York Times*, by 1997 the district's porn population had shrunk to just 13 businesses, and is increasingly overshadowed by mega-shopping centers like Disney and Virgin.

Among the stalwart remaining sleaze outlets are peep-booth survivalists like Peepland and Show World, which cater to foot traffic with pockets of quarters and 15 minutes to spare. New York peep shows are still the nation's pinnacle of the genre — glitzy, noisy multi-level shopping malls of smut, quick-fix emporiums where drunks, townies and tourists wander the floors of possibilities, cooed at by girls leaning over the top of the live dancing booths. Other young scantily clad women stand in tiny glass-walled rooms, giving the appearance of a lewd Macy's window display. The energy of the joints is like the consumer excitement on the first day of a holiday shopping season, as guys elbow and jostle each other for the privilege of pumping quarters into a slot, staring at a naked girl from Jersey dance around in big hair and pink fingernails, and depositing their seed into tissues. And just like the holidays, the thrill is soon over.

Stepping back outside, re-entering a world without loud music or rows of blinking lights, New York seems strangely calm, the frenetic traffic, garish billboards and odious franchise restaurants almost soothing in comparison to the sensory overload of the peeps.

As the clean-up of Times Square continues, there is an unmistakable tone of nostalgia when New Yorkers discuss the district. Most who grew up there associate the strip with fond memories of nocturnal misadventures, scurrying through one of the most densely pornographic pieces of real estate in the country. Obvious problems of crime and drugs notwithstanding, they see the gentrification as they would the closing of a favorite restaurant or cafe. This reverence through introspection is typical of not just Times Square, but the bulk of the sexual revolution and the heyday of the heterosexual. Of those who lived through it, a few wince at the memories, but most break into a smile as the thoughts and details of 20 and 30 years ago trickle back to their brains.

While walking through Times Square recently, a friend and I stopped and gazed at a three-story image of Dr. Seuss's Cat in the Hat character, which decorated the facade of yet another building under reconstruction. Jonathan pointed down the street to the rows of boarded-up buildings, soon to be more bloated shopping centers, and wistfully if unknowingly summed up the period when he sighed, "All this used to be porn."

Acknowledgements

Compiling all the material to put this book together would never have been possible without help from the sexual pioneers and archivists who opened up their collections of historical artifacts: Marsha Garland from the North Beach Chamber of Commerce, Ivan from The Magazine, Andy from Red House Books, Rita Benton, Jeff Armstrong and Vince Stannich from the Mitchell Brothers' O'Farrell Theatre, Joanie Blank and Leigh Davidson from Down There Press, Dell Williams from Eve's Garden, Margo St. James and Carol Leigh from COYOTE, Paul Krassner from *The Realist*, Therese Wilson from Planned Parenthood, David Steinberg, Charles Gatewood, Betty Dodson, Trina Robbins, Jay Kinney, Dr. Eugene Schoenfeld, John Marr, Frank Kozik, Bill Wyman, Larry Wessel, Tim Cridland, J. Raoul Brody, Randi Merzon, Naked Eye News & Video, The Cinema Shop, Le Video, Paramount studio archives, Manhattan's Museum of Broadcasting, and all the used bookstores across this great land.

For their insights into the philosophy and business of sex, more thanks due to Jamie Gillis, John Leslie, Annette Haven, Richard Pacheco, Rev. Ted McIlvenna, Marc Moreno of the Edgewater West, David Aaron Clark and the staff of *The Spectator*, Eric Danville at *Screw*, Chip Rowe and Chris Napolitano at *Playboy*, Ron Turner from Last Gasp, Susie Bright, Eddie Muller, Glynn Stout, Dirk Ludigs, Simon LeVay, Chuck Farnham, Shannon René, Jessica Applestone, Becky Wilson, Isis Rodriguez, Britta, Alex and Marisa from Independent Dancers Association, Johanna Breyer from Exotic Dancers' Alliance and George Lazaneo.

For their memories and personal stories, thanks also to Cynthia Roth, Racquel Scherr, Charlie Hall, Captain Clearlight, Laura Hazelett and Candi Strecker. Photographic kudos to Alain McLaughlin, John Caperton, Pamela Gentile, and even though we didn't use the shot of his crotch, Eric Slomanson. Thanks to those who suggested organizational ideas, especially Michael Perkins, Alice Joanou, Patrick Hughes and Barnaby Conrad III.

Finally, extra thanks is due to those who provided support, rides and patience: The editors and staff of *SF Weekly*, especially demon copy editor Deborah Lewis, Jim Mauro, Marc Maron, the staff of *This Is Not a Test*, Tom McNichol, Kim Teevan, George Cothran, Mary Beth Barber, Frank Kuznik, Tom Pitts, Johnny Steele, Jeff Krulik, Greg Bishop, Ralph Coon, Scott Sawyer, Melani Guinn, R.U. Sirius, Troy Dixon aka the Crack Emcee, Kevin Campbell, Jonathan Daniel, Rëzzin, Colin Johnston for designing the whole mess, Adam Parfrey for the opportunity and anyone else I forgot.

Selected Bibliography

BOOKS

Adult Movies. Pocket Books, 1982

Baker, Mark. *Sex Lives: A Sexual Self-Portrait of America*. Pocket Books, 1994

Bartell, Gilbert D., Ph.D. *Group Sex: An Eyewitness Report on the American Way of Swinging*. Signet, 1971

Brecher, Edward M. *The Sex Researchers*. Little, Brown and Company, 1969

Bright, Susie. *Susie Bright's Sexual State of the Union*. Simon & Schuster, 1997

Burks, John and Hopkins, Jerry. *Groupies and Other Girls: A Rolling Stone Special Report*. Bantam, 1970

Chapple, Steve and Talbot, David. *Burning Desires: Sex in America*. Doubleday, 1989

Colacello, Bob. *Holy Terror: Andy Warhol Close Up*. HarperCollins, 1990

De Grazia, Edward and Newman, Roger K. *Banned Films: Movies, Censors & the First Amendment*. R.R. Bowker Company, 1982

Des Barres, Pamela. *I'm With the Band: Confessions of a Groupie*. Jove, 1988

Dodson, Betty. *Sex for One: The Joy of Selfloving*. Crown, 1996

Ehrenreich, Barbara, Hess, Elizabeth, Jacobs, Gloria. *Re-Making Love: The Feminization of Sex*. Doubleday, 1986

Ellis, Albert, Ph.D. *Sex Without Guilt*. Lyle Stuart, 1958

Final Report of the Attorney General's Commission on Pornography. Rutledge Hill Press, 1986

Flynt, Larry. *An Unseemly Man: My Life as Pornographer, Pundit, and Social Outcast*. Dove, 1996

Frank, Sam. *Sex in the Movies*. Citadel, 1986

Friedman, Josh Alan. *Tales of Times Square*. Feral House, 1993

Gagnon, John H. and Simon, William, eds. *The Sexual Scene*. Aldine, 1970

Girodias, Maurice, ed. *The Olympia Reader*. North Star Line, 1991

Heidenry, John. *What Wild Ecstasy: The Rise and Fall of the Sexual Revolution*. Simon & Schuster, 1997

Holliday, Jim. *Only the Best*. Cal Vista, 1986

Hosoda, Craig. *The Bare Facts Video Guide*. The Bare Facts, 1992

Hubner, John. *Bottom Feeders: From Free Love to Hard Core — The Rise and Fall of Counterculture Heroes Jim and Artie Mitchell*. Dell, 1992

James, Darius. *That's Blaxploitation!: Roots of the Baadasssss 'Tude*. St. Martin's Griffin, 1995

Kennedy, Eugene C. *The New Sexuality: Myths, Fables & Hang-Ups*. Doubleday, 1972

Koenig, David. *Mouse Tales: A Behind-the-Ears Look at Disneyland*. Bonaventure Press, 1994

Krassner, Paul. *Confessions of a Raving, Unconfined Nut: Misadventures in the Counterculture*. Simon & Schuster, 1993

Kronhausen, Phyllis and Eberhard. *The Sex People: The Erotic Performers and Their Bold New Worlds*. Playboy Press, 1975

Leigh, Wendy. *What Makes a Woman G.I.B.* (*Good In Bed)*. Penthouse Press, 1977

Lenne, Gerard. *Sex on the Screen: Eroticism in Film*. St. Martin's Press, 1978

Lovett, Anthony R. and Maranian, Matt. *L.A. Bizarro: The Insider's Guide to the Obscure, the Absurd, and the Perverse in Los Angeles*. St. Martin's Press, 1997

McCumber, David. *X-Rated: The Mitchell Brothers — A True Story of Sex, Money, and Death*. Simon & Schuster, 1992

Miller, Frank. *Censored Hollywood: Sex, in & Violence on Screen*. Turner Publishing, Inc., 1994

Miller, Russell. *Bunny: The Real Story of Playboy*. Holt, Rinehard and Winston, 1984

Muller, Eddie and Faris, Daniel. *Grindhouse: The Forbidden World of "Adults Only" Cinema*. St. Martin's Press, 1997

Nelson, Craig. *Bad TV: The Very Best of the Very Worst*. Dell, 1995

Nobile, Philip and Nadler, Eric. *United States of America Vs. Sex: How the Meese Commission Lied About Pornography*. Minotaur Press, 1986

Nobile, Philip, ed. *The New Eroticism: Theories, Vogues and Canons*. Random House, 1970

Parfrey, Adam. *Cult Rapture*. Feral House, 1995

Patrick, Dave. *California's Nude Beaches*. Bold Type, 1988

Perkins, Michael. *The Secret Record: Modern Erotic Literature*. Masquerade Books, 1992

Poland, Jefferson and Sloan, Sam. *Sex Marchers*. Elysium Inc. Publishers, 1968

Poundstone, William. *Big Secrets: The Uncensored Truth About All Sorts of Stuff You Are Never Supposed to Know*. Quill, 1983

Poundstone, William. *Biggest Secrets: More Uncensored Truth About All Sorts of Stuff You Are Never Supposed to Know*. William Morrow, 1993

Reed, Rex. *Do You Sleep in the Nude?* Signet, 1968

Reich, Wilhelm. *The Sexual Revolution*. Farrar Straus Giroux, 1974

Rimmer, Robert H. *The X-Rated Videotape Guide (Vol. 1, 1970-1985)*. Prometheus Books, 1993

Robinson, Frank and Lehrman, Nat, eds. *Sex American Style*. Playboy Press, 1971

Schneider, Charles, ed. *CAD: A Handbook for Heels*. Feral House, 1992

See, Carolyn. *Blue Money: Pornography and the Pornographers — An Intimate Look at the Two-Billion Dollar Fantasy Industry*. David McKay Company, 1974

Sherman, Allan. *The RAPE of the A*P*E*: The Official History of the Sexual Revolution*. Playboy Press, 1973

Southern, Terry. *Blue Movie*. New American Library, 1970

Stallings, Penny. *Forbidden Channels: The Truth They Hide From TV Guide*. Harper Perennial, 1991

Stanford, Sally. *The Lady of the House*. G.P. Putnam's Sons, 1966

Stein, Jean with Plimpton, George. *Edie: An American Biography*. Delta, 1982

Stern, Jane and Michael. *The Encyclopedia of Bad Taste*. HarperCollins, 1990

Stubbs, Kenneth Ray, Ph.D., ed. *Women of the Light: The New Sacred Prostitute*. Secret Garden, 1994

Talese, Gay. *Thy Neighbor's Wife*. Doubleday, 1980

A Tradition of Choice: Planned Parenthood at 75. Planned Parenthood Federation of America, 1991

Vadim, Roger. *Bardot Deneuve Fonda*. Warner, 1986

Vassi, Marco, ed. *The Wonderful World of Penthouse Sex: Radical Sex in the Establishment*. Penthouse Press, 1975

The Visual Dictionary of Sex. A & W, 1977

Vogliotti, Gabriel R. *The Girls of Nevada*. Citadel Press, 1975

Wasserman, Abby. *Praise, Vilification & Sexual Innuendo: The Selected Writings of John L. Wasserman (1964-1979)*. Chronicle Books, 1993

Wilson, Earl. *Show Business Laid Bare*. G.P. Putnam's Sons, 1974

Wilson, Robert Anton. *Sex & Drugs: A Journey Beyond Limits*. New Falcon, 1993

Wolfe, Tom. *The Pumphouse Gang*. Farrar Straus Giroux, 1968

PUBLICATIONS

Assorted back issues of *Adam, Adult Video News, Berkeley Barb, Cavalier, Cosmopolitan, Duke, Esquire, Evergreen, Hustler, Jaguar, Knave, L.A. Free Press, Life, National Informer, National Insider, National Lampoon, Newsweek, The Nose, Penthouse, Playboy, Playgirl, The Realist, Rolling Stone, San Francisco Chronicle, Screw, The Spectator, Time, Viva*, among many others.

IMAGES

Images are credited when appropriate or possible. All artifacts are from the author's collection unless otherwise noted.

Cover photo by Alain McLaughlin, styling by Becky Wilson
Superfly album courtesy Bill Wyman
Cat-related porn movie artwork courtesy Frank Kozik
Condor sign photo by Pamela Gentile
MC5 album courtesy Bill Wyman
back issues of *Rolling Stone* courtesy Bill Wyman
Blind Faith album courtesy Colin Johnston
The Cars album courtesy Bill Wyman
Stewardess porn image courtesy Frank Kozik
Hugh Hefner photo by John Dominis, *Cosmopolitan*, May 1974
Snatch comics cover courtesy Jay Kinney
Wrestlers illustrations courtesy Betty Dodson
woman masturbating courtesy Charles Gatewood
covers of *Felch, Snatch* and *Young Lust* courtesy Jay Kinney
Tits & Clits and *Wet Satin* courtesy Trina Robbins
Tricks comic cover courtesy Margo St. James
photo of SFPD chief Frank Gaines courtesy Margo St. James
Hookers' Ball poster courtesy Margo St. James
The Realist cover courtesy Paul Krassner
Plaster Caster images courtesy Paul Krassner
How to Pick Up Girls books courtesy John Marr
Playbook for Women courtesy Joanie Blank
Tropic of Cancer first edition courtesy Colin Johnston
Radio transcript courtesy Dr. Eugene Schoenfeld
Dildo artwork 1966 patent illustration by Jon H. Tavel, from *American Sex Machines* by Hoag Levins
Eve's Garden catalog courtesy Dell Williams
all other female vibrator images courtesy Joanie Blank
nude party photo courtesy Charles Gatewood
hot tub party photo courtesy Margo St. James
CES adult convention photo by Alice Joanou
author photo by Pamela Gentile, legs courtesy of Mistress Izabella

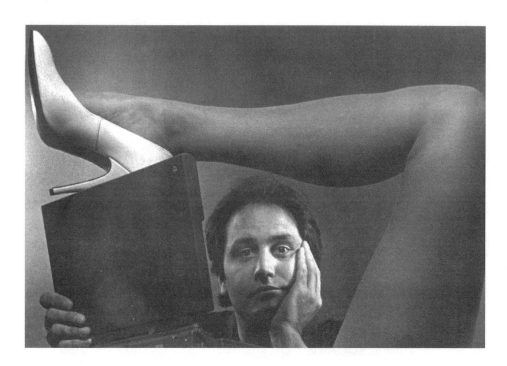

Jack Boulware was founding editor of the satirical investigative *Nose* magazine, and has written for many publications including *Playboy, British Esquire,* and *New York Times Magazine.* He lives in San Francisco, and is a columnist for *SF Weekly.* (photo by Pamela Gentile)

Also From Feral House

CAD: A HANDBOOK FOR HEELS
Edited by Charles Schneider
Salty stories, scrumptious photo spreads, beastly beatniks. *CAD* revives an era, circa 1957, in which a total environment of tease and prurient mystery evoked devilish bachelorhood. Feral House apologizes for the creepy lounge culture fad *CAD* may be partially responsible for inspiring.
8 x 11 • 148 pages • illustrated • $14.95 • ISBN: 0-922915-09-1

CULT RAPTURE
Adam Parfrey
"From cults and conspiracies to isolated loons, from fakes and grifters to the painfully sincere and the seriously terrifying, Parfrey lucidly explores the nation's rarely acknowledged subcultures." —Katherine Dunn. "Compulsive, electric." —*Headpress.* "Mind-blowing." —*Flatland.* "Plumb loco from start to finish and wonderfully entertaining, *Cult Rapture* is some kind of instant classic." —*Loaded*
6 x 9 • 371 pages • illustrated • $14.95 • ISBN: 0-922915-22-9

TALES OF TIMES SQUARE
Josh Alan Friedman
This insanely sordid, memorable account of the once grotesque 42nd Street covers the strippers, porn brokers, hookers, cops and colorful weirdos in a way that is difficult to forget.
5 1/2 x 8 1/2 • 201 pages • illustrated • $12.95 • ISBN: 0-922915-17-2

The titles above may be ordered from Feral House for check or money order plus $3 first book and 50 cents each additional book ordered for shipping. For a free catalogue of publications, send an SASE.

Feral House • 2532 Lincoln Blvd., Suite 359 • Venice, CA • 90291
Visit our new website: www.FeralHouse.com